Manual of Voice Therapy

Second Edition

Jodelle F. Dee
and
Lynda Miller

An International Publisher

8700 Shoal Creek Boulevard
Austin, Texas 78757-6897
800/897-3202   Fax 800/397-7633
Order online at http://www.proedinc.com

An International Publisher

© 2000, 1984 by PRO-ED, Inc.
8700 Shoal Creek Boulevard
Austin, Texas 78757-6897
800/897-3202   Fax 800/397-7633
Order online at http://www.proedinc.com

All rights reserved. No part of the material protected by this
copyright notice may be reproduced or used in any form or by
any means, electronic or mechanical, including photocopying,
recording, or by any information storage and retrieval system,
without prior written permission of the copyright owner.

Notice: PRO-ED grants permission to the user of this book to make unlimited copies of
Appendix B for teaching or clinical purposes. Duplication of this material for commercial
use is prohibited.

Library of Congress Cataloging-in-Publication Data

Prater, Rex J.
    Manual of voice therapy / Rex J. Prater, Roger W. Swift.—2nd
  ed. / Jodelle F. Deem, Lynda Miller.
        p.   cm.
    Includes bibliographical references and index.
    ISBN 0-89079-825-7 (softcover : alk. paper)
    1. Voice disorders—Treatment Handbooks, manuals, etc.   I. Swift,
  Roger W.   II. Deem, Jodelle F.   III. Miller, Lynda.   IV. Title.
RF510.P73   1999
616.85'506—dc21   99-31323
                                                                      CIP

This book is designed in Frutiger and New Century Schoolbook.

Printed in the United States of America

    3   4   5   6   7   8   9   10   03

Contents

◆ ◆

Preface

◆　◆　◆　◆　◆　◆　◆　◆　◆　◆　◆　◆　◆　◆　◆　◆　◆　◆

Prater and Swift's *Manual of Voice Therapy* has long been a favorite reference for clinicians of voice disorders. Among its attractions were that it was comprehensive, well organized, easy to read, and included material (e.g., the chapter on neurological disorders) not often found in books on the voice. Revising Prater and Swift's original book has been both a privilege and a daunting assignment. The privilege has come from viewing the field of voice disorders through their lens, whereas the challenge has lain in retaining the outline format and in trying to improve on an already stellar guide.

Just as the original *Manual of Voice Therapy* was intended as a single-source therapy manual for clinicians, so we intend for this second edition to contain in one volume the most pertinent information the voice clinician will need. We have revised and updated the original chapters from Prater and Swift, while at the same time retaining the material still pertinent to today's clinical needs. In those chapters in which material remained relatively unchanged, we have retained Prater and Swift's descriptions, as they continue to be easy to read and well organized.

As already stated, we have kept the outline format, as it is clearly organized and easy to follow. In addition, when figures and tables show information or material still in current use, we have retained some of the originals, whereas others have been revised to show more recent information or data. In most instances, any new figures are depicted using the same simple line drawings used by Prater and Swift.

Readers will notice that we have rearranged the order of chapters and we have added an introductory chapter, in which we give a bit of history for the voice. Also, we have included three appendices: Appendix A contains five standard reading passages commonly used in the evaluation of the voice; Appendix B contains a set of reproducible informational handouts for the various disorders that the clinician can give to clients, family members, and the client's friends; and Appendix C contains a list of resources for voice therapy.

In choosing to keep many of the original citations and references used by Prater and Swift, we encountered a stylistic difference in reporting original sources. The reference citation style in 1984, when *Manual of Voice Therapy* was published, did not include page numbers for chapters in larger volumes, and included only the starting page of articles from journals. In deciding to include the original citations, we took two approaches. For journal articles, we kept the 1984 style, in which only the starting page number of the relevant article is listed. For chapters, however, we tried to trace as many as we could easily find. Sharp-eyed readers will discover that some of these chapters show page numbers, whereas others do not. Those without page numbers simply reflect our inability to track down the original citation. For all citations added to the original book, we have used the conventional APA style.

Chapter 2 introduces the anatomic components of the several systems used in voice production. Chapter 3 provides detailed procedures to be used in evaluating clients with voice disorders, including a step-by-step motor speech evaluation of the cranial nerves involved in speech production. Chapters 4 and 5 are companion chapters that describe phonotrauma and the adverse effects on voice production. We have included descriptions of vocal rest programs for children and adults, a program of vocal hygiene, and techniques to facilitate the reduction of laryngeal hyperfunction. Chapter 6 deals with the functional and spasmodic dysphonias, disorders which occur as a result of stress, anxiety, or psychological difficulties, and disorders resulting from focal dystonias. Chapter 7 describes congenital and organic laryngeal anomalies. In Chapter 8 we provide an extensive presentation of the neurogenic dysphonias. Chapter 9 describes disorders of vocal resonance, and Chapter 10 contains a comprehensive discussion of the approaches to voice therapy intervention with patients with laryngeal cancer.

We both wish to express special thanks to people who helped us get this revision to print.

From Lynda Miller: I extend particular gratitude and appreciation to Lynn, who graciously shared her computer and printer during several extended periods when I was operating from deep within the labyrinths of Murphy's Law. Travis and Alex both contributed significantly—each in their own unique and charming way—to whatever success I can claim for my part of this project. To my coauthor, Jody, who takes collaboration—and humor—to a higher plane. Thanks to her, I have had an opportunity to revisit the field of voice and voice disorders and to discover to my pleasure that the graduate voice class I took with Dr. Paul Moore has stuck with me after all these years. I have rarely enjoyed a joint project as much. And, finally, to Jim Patton at PRO-ED, for his thoughtfulness and guidance throughout.

From Jody Deem: My most important debt of gratitude is to Nancy, who patiently cared for our 11 "children" and waited for this project to be finished. To my coauthor, Lynda, who writes like I wish I could, I owe my thanks for inviting me into this wonderful experience. Her depth of interest and understanding of voice disorders was a delightful surprise in a friend I had pigeonholed as a language and learning expert. My sincere thanks to Ellen Hagerman and Brian Owens, each of whom knows voice disorders at least as well as I, for their willingness to share their expertise and to listen to countless hours of "what do you think of this?" as the book developed. I also owe a debt of thanks to the faculty and staff of the Clinic in Otolaryngology, Head and Neck Surgery at the University of Kentucky, especially to Dr. Sanford Archer. Through the clinic I met the patients whose life experiences provided us with the "real world" perspective. Thanks to Jim Patton and PRO-ED for trusting us with this project. Finally, thanks to Leon, who helped me write this book but who had to leave before it was finished.

Chapter 1
Prelude

♦ ♦ ♦ ♦ ♦ ♦ ♦ ♦ ♦ ♦ ♦ ♦ ♦ ♦ ♦ ♦ ♦ ♦ ♦

I. **The Nature of the Voice.** The voice was regarded in ancient times as being both magical and mysterious. Although it is often said that someone has a "beautiful voice," rarely are those words used to describe articulation or resonance. When several graduate students were asked to think of someone who would personify the "voice of God," they quickly came up with the names James Earl Jones, Barbara Jordan, Maya Angelou, Charlton Heston, and Gregory Peck, just to name a few. Those well-known personalities came to mind because of their beautiful, resonant, distinctive voices.

The word *voice* is used to paint pictures in our literature, for example, "the voices of the cloud forest," "the voice of the wildcats" (a University of Kentucky tradition), "in a different voice," and "finding your voice." No other part of the speech mechanism can paint a literary picture like the image of the voice. The voice gives melody and feeling to messages and tells the world if the speaker is tired, happy, sad, or discouraged.

This book is about the human voice and its problems. We invite the reader to take time while reading this book to appreciate the magic and mystery of the voice.

II. **A Brief History of Voice Disorders and Their Management.** Stemple, Glaze, and Gerdeman (1995) and von Leden (1997) have particularly outstanding and interesting summaries of the history of voice disorders and their management. In summary, some of the most interesting and important points from their discussion include the following:

A. There were written descriptions of voice disorders as early as 1600 B.C.

B. Early accounts of management of voice disorders from the 7th century B.C. included many strategies rooted in religion and spiritualism, including Hindu "gargles" of oils, juices, vinegar, honey, and the urine of sacred cows.

C. By the 5th century B.C., Hippocrates had described diseases of the throat and voice and noted that observing voice quality contributed to the diagnosis of disease.

D. In the 4th century B.C., Aristotle referred to the larynx as the organ that creates voice, and in the 2nd century B.C., Galen proved that the larynx was the anatomic site of the voice.

E. Very little progress was made in science and medicine through the Dark Ages until the 1500s, when Leonardo Da Vinci made his detailed anatomical sketches.

F. Through the 15th, 16th and 17th centuries, numerous scientists described structures and the function of the larynx, including writings about the function of the epiglottis, the laryngeal ventricles, and the laryngeal cartilages. In the mid-1500s, Bartolomeus Eustachias (after whom the eustachian tube is named) made detailed descriptions and carvings of the larynx. By the mid-1800s, Muller had advanced the myoelastic–aerodynamic theory of voicing and Ryland had written an extensive work describing diseases of the larynx.

G. In 1854, Garcia developed the laryngoscope, which was followed in 1861 with the addition of artificial illumination to the laryngoscope. Laryngoscopy and stroboscopy were developed in the late 1800s.

H. According to Stemple et al. (1995), voice management remained in the arena of medicine until the 1930s, when Charles Van Riper and others began writing about remediation techniques in voice disorders and about classification systems in voice disorders. There have been many methods of classifying voice disorders since Van Riper first suggested classification by acoustic characteristics in 1939. Classification systems are used to organize writing and research about a subject, and in the case of voice disorders, to develop a systematic approach to management. Although there is considerable overlap among some of the approaches that have been used, the student of voice can benefit by understanding the evolution of approaches to voice management. **A voice disorder (dysphonia) is said to exist when a person's pitch, loudness, or quality differs from those of similar age, sex, cultural background, or geographic location** (Boone, 1977; Stemple et al., 1995). Voice disorders have been discussed and classified in the following ways:

1. **Acoustic characteristics.** Voice disorders have been described by their acoustic characteristics—that is, pitch, loudness, quality, and so on.

2. **Symptoms.** This approach includes acoustic characteristics as well as respiration, resonance, phonation—that is, what symptoms present in the voice need to be modified?

3. **Severity.** Is the voice problem mild, moderate, or severe? This strategy is usually used after the voice pathology is already known. Because there is no reliable relationship between the perception of dysphonia and the severity of the pathology, this method of classification is limited.

4. **Mass-size and approximation.** Does the voice problem cause an alteration in the mass or size of the vocal folds or change the ability of the vocal folds to approximate (Boone, 1977)? The problem with describing voice disorders in this fashion is that a nodule that alters the mass of the vocal folds may also alter the ability of the vocal folds to approximate.

5. **Functional** (or psychogenic, or behavioral) **versus organic.** This approach has similar problems to the mass-size/approximation approach (Boone & McFarlane, 1994). A vocal nodule may be due to a functional or behavioral cause (muscle tension and phonotrauma), but regardless of origin it results in an organic change on the vocal fold.

6. **Etiology.** Some voice therapists have simply referred to disorders by the actual cause that explains the disorder's signs and symptoms.

7. **Multidimensional.** This system extends the functional versus organic dichotomy to a more multidimensional system. In this approach, classifica-

tion headings might include trauma-related voice disorders, neurogenic voice disorders, congenital dysphonias, geriatric voice disorders, and so forth. This approach is descriptive in nature, and it may better characterize the complex differences that exist among the many voice disorders.

III. **Challenges in the Management of Voice Disorders.** Investigating and treating the voice are both challenging and rewarding. However, despite amazing technological advances, there are still some problems in the quest to provide good voice care:

A. **There is no direct relationship between the perception of a voice disorder and the presence of pathology.** The speech–language pathologist and otolaryngologist will see patients whose voice qualities vary significantly. Although perception is always an important part of the speech–language pathologist's diagnostic tools, the perceptual severity of a voice disorder is not directly related to the size or type of pathology. A patient with laryngeal cancer may be only mildly hoarse, whereas a patient with benign vocal nodules may sound severely dysphonic. The speech–language pathologist's ear is important in diagnosing the dysphonia (the voice disorder), but the actual problem or pathology must be diagnosed by a physician using appropriate imaging instrumentation.

Researchers are constantly working to uncover a perceptual or acoustic (noninvasive) method of accurately detecting and diagnosing vocal pathology. Acoustic measures—such as jitter, shimmer, harmonics-to-noise ratio—have all been studied for their success in detecting pathology. Although perceptual, acoustic, and physiologic data are important in describing the dysphonia and in creating a picture of the problem, they do not replace the physician visit and an actual look at the larynx.

B. **Social acceptance of voice problems creates a significant challenge for the voice therapist.** Everyone experiences voice problems from time to time, and such problems often are brushed off as nothing or being related to a cold or an allergy. Most people are so accepting of voice disorders that vocal symptoms are typically ignored in those around us. On the other hand, articulation or fluency problems are not as acceptable as a problem with the voice. An individual who reaches adulthood with an articulation problem or a significant fluency problem pays a higher price for her or his communicative problem than someone who has a dysphonia.

One of the reasons for this is that most listeners are more likely to be uncomfortable talking with someone who has an articulation or fluency problem than talking with someone who has a dysphonia. Everyone knows someone who has a voice problem, and might think "everyone knows that's just the way he talks . . . it's okay." This problem of social acceptance is partially the reason why so many laryngectomee patients are sent to total laryngectomy surgery immediately after their first visit to the otolaryngologist (commonly referred to as an ENT). Voice symptoms were simply ignored for too long.

Because of this problem of social acceptance, patients with voice disorders may be less motivated to faithfully follow through with a voice therapy program. Some patients may return to therapy several times over the course of several years. They will return to voice therapy, promise to follow the therapy plan, and then drop out after a few sessions. The patient may not follow through faithfully until the voice problem causes significant economic or occupational hardship, or until a physician tells the patient that she or he is facing serious medical or surgical consequences.

C. **The patient's level of motivation to restore vocal health will be related to the importance of the voice in his or her profession.** Koufman (1998b) describes a four-level scale of vocal usage that may be beneficial to the speech–language pathologist in estimating the patient's perception of the importance of his or her voice. Level I is the elite vocal performer (singers, actors, etc.); Level II, the professional voice user (clergy, teachers); Level III, the nonvocal professional (physicians, lawyers); and Level IV, the nonvocal nonprofessional (laborers, clerks, etc.). A patient at any level may experience a significant functional or emotional impact because of a voice problem (Stemple et al., 1995). However, a Level I patient may be more likely to come to the voice clinic with an acute problem, while the Level IV patient may be more likely to come with a chronic, long-standing problem. It is a challenge for the speech–language pathologist to motivate each patient to discover and maintain her or his "best possible voice" (Boone & McFarlane, 1994).

D. **Terms used to describe voice disorders are often misunderstood among professionals.** Outstanding technological advances have improved the ability to accurately describe the acoustic, aerodynamic, and physiologic parameters of a patient's voice. Despite these advances, it is common to receive a referral in the voice clinic for a patient who is described as "hoarse" or "harsh," but for whom there are little accompanying objective voice data. A patient who has been seen by several professionals may be described as "hoarse" by one professional, and "harsh" or "rough" by another. As early as 1960, Fairbanks discussed *harshness, breathiness,* and *hoarseness* as the primary types of quality disorders.

1. **Harshness** was described by Fairbanks (1960) as irregular, aperiodic noise commonly caused by laryngeal tension. Hard glottal attack was reportedly prevalent in harsh voices, as was low fundamental frequency.

2. **Breathiness** was described as vocal fold vibration with insufficient glottal closure, continuous airflow, and limited vocal intensity.

3. Finally, **hoarseness** was described by Fairbanks (1960) as a combination of the features of harshness and breathiness, with the features of harshness prevailing in some hoarse voices and the feature of breathiness prevailing in others. In a study of perception of synthesized pathological voices, Huang (1998) confirmed Fairbanks' finding that hoarseness is some combination of harshness and breathiness. Colton and Casper (1996) indicated that the terms *hoarse* and *rough* are sometimes used interchangeably and are often associated with other descriptors, such as breathiness, tension, or strain.

4. Colton and Casper (1996) reported that, in their experience, voice patients commonly report symptoms that are a combination of voice quality symptoms, such as hoarseness, pain, and other symptoms. The authors listed nine symptoms that are commonly reported by voice patients: hoarseness, vocal fatigue, breathiness, reduced range of phonation, total loss of voice or aphonia, pitch breaks or pitch that is inappropriately high, strain or struggle in

the voice, tremor or shakiness in the voice, and pain or other sensations of discomfort.

IV. **The Voice Care Team.** The voice is a complex mechanism requiring a multidisciplinary team to restore optimal vocal health. Ideally, the following professionals are members of a comprehensive voice care team:

- The **patient.** The patient should play the primary role in his or her own voice rehabilitation. Only the patient can decide if he or she is willing or able to follow through with a particular therapy regimen or surgical alternative. The patient should work with the other members of the team in deciding goals for voice care. Colton and Casper (1996) present a model of voice care in which the patient is in the center of a circle of professionals, with all other team members interacting with the patient from the periphery.

- The **family physician.** Whether a pediatrician, internist, or family practitioner, the family physician is often the first contact for the patient with a voice disorder. The family physician needs to be able to recognize the signs and symptoms of a voice disorder and be informed about the voice care specialties available (Colton & Casper, 1996).

- The **otolaryngologist.** The otolaryngologist is the appropriate medical professional to diagnose and medically or surgically manage disorders of voice. Some otolaryngologists specialize in problems of the voice and have unique abilities in the area of restoration of vocal health.

- The **speech–language pathologist.** The speech–language pathologist is the professional who is called upon to diagnose and manage the dysphonia or voice disorder that results from a particular vocal problem (e.g., nodules). As with otolaryngologists, there are speech–language pathologists who specialize in care and treatment of the voice. Recently the term *vocologist*—from *vocology* or study of the voice—has been used to refer to any appropriate professional (e.g., speech–language pathologist, otolaryngologist, voice teacher) who specializes in care of the voice (Verdolini, 1998b)

- The **voice teacher or voice coach.** A professional voice teacher or coach can be invaluable in helping a patient restore and maintain vocal health, especially when the patient is a professional voice user. Many hospitals and universities routinely include vocal coaches as members of the medical voice care team. The voice teacher or coach may be a professional singer, speaker, or actor, depending on the needs of the patient.

- **Other members.** It is not unusual for several other professionals to be called upon to assist in voice management or diagnosis. Some of these might include a radiologist, an allergist, a neurologist, a nutritionist, a speech scientist, and a psychologist or psychiatrist.

V. **Voice Care Guidelines for Patients and Professionals.** These guidelines serve as general rules for patients and professionals. It is important to recognize that they are just that—general rules—and not without exception.

A. If a voice change persists for approximately 2 to 3 weeks, the individual should see an otolaryngologist (S. Archer & G. Abbas, personal communication, 1999).

B. Before voice therapy is initiated with a patient, the patient's vocal folds should be viewed by an otolaryngologist (S. Archer & G. Abbas, personal communication, 1999). The speech–language pathologist does not diagnose organic lesion or structural change of the vocal folds. The role of speech–language pathology is to diagnose and treat the dysphonia that results from the vocal pathology.

C. In the United States, most voice therapy involves about one or two therapy sessions per week for approximately 6 to 8 weeks (Stemple, 1997; Verdolini, 1998b).

VI. Counseling Functions of the Voice Care Professional. Masterson and Apel (1997) and Webster (1977) offer guidelines for the speech–language pathologist, who also often also serves in a counseling role while working with a patient with a voice disorder.

 A. The professional should **view the patient as a specialist in their own care** and should use strategies that will facilitate open dialogue with the patient. Strategies that might facilitate openness include the following:

  1. Adopting a nonjudgmental attitude. When a counselor (speech–language pathologist, otolaryngologist, etc.) listens nonjudgmentally, he or she has little need to question whether or not a topic is appropriate for discussion with the patient. If it is important to the patient, it will likely prove to be valuable in the patient's voice care. It is then left up to the patient to make the judgment about the appropriateness of a topic to her or his voice care. Verdolini (1998a) makes an excellent point in this regard in discussing the commonly used terms *vocal abuse*. In her discussion, Verdolini urges adoption of the term *phonotrauma* because the word *abuse* is culturally and morally troublesome, judgmental, and potentially harmful.

  2. Actively listening. Webster (1977) described active listening as **listening for the real meaning** in the patient's message. The counselor listens with an attitude of inquiry, wishing to understand as fully as possible what the world of the other person is like. The counselor listens without planning what to say next, but simply to try to understand the patient's real message. The counselor then restates in his or her own words what the patient has said. Patients will generally stay connected to a counselor who genuinely listens for the meaning in their message, even if the counselor guesses wrong in restating it.

  3. Allowing periods of silence between the patient and professional. Webster (1977) believed that periods of silence often make the professional feel uncomfortable, but they can be used to formulate hypotheses or hunches about the patient's intended message, to formulate questions for the patient, or to serve as a coping method for moments of emotion.

 B. Boone (1998) stated that speech–language pathologists are now better equipped to make objective, instrumental assessment of the voice than they were 30 years ago, but are less equipped to really know voice patients as people. Boone encouraged voice therapists to **offer a more supportive, counseling role** in therapy, and he indicates that there are basic counselor functions that speech–language pathologists should use in professional interactions. (For an excellent resource for the speech–language pathologist who wishes to better understand the counseling role in patient care, see Crowe, 1997). During the patient–counselor interaction, it is appropriate to use any or all of the following in a continuous and dynamic way:

1. **Receiving information.** The speech–language pathologist, using the strategies discussed earlier, receives—nonjudgmentally—information, opinions, feelings, and questions from the client, any or all of which may have an impact on the patient's voice care.

2. **Giving information.** Patients seek services from speech–language pathologists because they need information. Giving information is possibly the easiest of the four counselor functions because of the expertise of the speech–language pathologist in relation to the needs of the patient. However, patients can only process a certain amount of information at any one time. The counselor's role in giving information is to listen and provide information based on the patient's need.

3. **Clarifying.** Webster (1977) argued that one of the counselor's major functions is to help patients perceive more clearly and to deal more constructively with issues impacting their voice problem. The counselor's (speech–language pathologist's) ability to listen to understand will be the most critical factor in helping the patient clarify effectively.

4. **Helping to change behavior.** For the patient to successfully change behavior, the speech–language pathologist must continue to exercise all three of the other counselor functions as learning takes place. The first step in changing patterns is to explain clearly the target behavior and its potential benefit (e.g., increased water intake to create healthier vocal folds). If certain behaviors are contributing to the patient's problem, the counselor must clearly state what those behaviors are and how they must change. Changing behaviors (learning) will involve discussion, practice, observation, and role-playing, among other things.

C. Buber (1970) introduced the concept of I–Thou relationships. According to Buber, when an individual regards another as Thou, that person is then regarded as someone to be respected and revered. In the I–Thou construct, the other person is a whole being who cannot be dissected into (in this case) a collection of fundamental frequencies, airflows, and stroboscopic data. Each human and each patient is more than that. Webster (1977) urged professionals to be aware that counselors and patients are more alike than different, and that they share a desire for growth and a desire to become better than they are now.

The nature of voice therapy is such that it is dependent upon compassion, understanding, and empathy at least as much as it is dependent upon an acoustic measure or airflow data. Stemple (1993) argued that the voice therapist must do the following:

1. **Consider the whole person.**

2. **Understand that to examine a voice is to examine an individual.**

3. **Understand that the way the person feels physically and emotionally is reflected in the voice.**

      4. Know that voice therapy requires counseling and motivational skills and that a person's voice truly is the mirror of her or his soul.

  D. Boone (1998) urged voice therapists to remind themselves when working with a voice patient that "among the good and bad things happening in the life of that person, there is **also** a voice problem" (p. 5).

Chapter 2
Anatomy and Physiology of Voice Production

◆　◆　◆　◆　◆　◆　◆　◆　◆　◆　◆　◆　◆　◆　◆　◆　◆　◆　◆

T he anatomic components of the systems that are used in voice production are
uniquely related to each other. Although the primary biologic purpose of many of
these systems is to assist in life support, they have also been adapted to function
in the process of voice production. A basic understanding of the primary and adaptive
functions of the anatomic components of these systems, as well as the complexities of
the systems themselves, is essential to the understanding of normal and disordered
voice. This chapter focuses on three anatomic systems that serve special functions in
voice production: the phonatory system, the respiratory system, and the resonatory
system.

I. **The Phonatory System.** The production of voice is dependent upon three primary systems, but the system that actually produces the sound that we call the
voice is the phonatory system. This system consists of a cartilaginous structure
called the larynx, all of the muscles and ligaments that bind the larynx together
and move its various parts, and the hyoid bone, a structure to which several extrinsic laryngeal muscles are attached.

A. **Laryngeal cartilages.** The human larynx is composed of nine individual cartilages onto which various ligaments and muscles make their attachments. The
three largest cartilages (thyroid cartilage, cricoid cartilage, epiglottis) are
unpaired, and the three smaller cartilages (arytenoid cartilages, corniculate
cartilages, cuneiform cartilages) are paired (see Figure 2.1).

1. The **thyroid cartilage,** the largest of the laryngeal cartilages, is shaped
like a shield and consists of two plates, called lamina, that are joined at an
angle at their anteromedial margins. This angle, which forms the most anterior portion of the thyroid cartilage (the laryngeal prominence), is usually
quite noticeable in adult males and is commonly referred to as the Adam's
apple. The angle of this prominence is more acute in males, forming an angle
of about 80°, and more rounded in females, forming an angle of about 90°
(Dickson & Maue-Dickson, 1982; Passavant, 1869).

Two inferior extensions of the thyroid cartilage (inferior horns) articulate
via the cricothyroid joints with another laryngeal cartilage, the cricoid cartilage, which forms the base of the larynx. The principal movement associated with the cricothyroid joint is rotation through a horizontal axis that
extends through the center of the joint.

2. The **cricoid cartilage,** the name of which is derived from its signet-ring
shape, is located directly on top of the trachea and forms the base of the

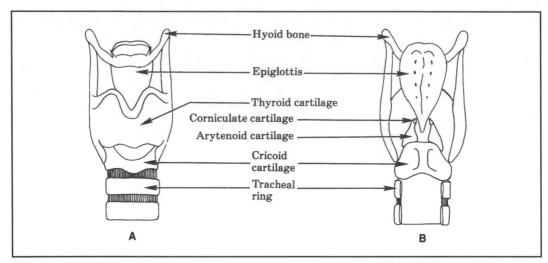

Figure 2.1. Laryngeal cartilages and the hyoid bone. **A.** Anterior view. **B.** Posterior view. *Note.* Adapted from *Illustrated Speech Anatomy* (2nd ed.), by W. M. Shearer, 1968, Springfield, IL: Thomas.

larynx. There are two articular facets on the lateral margins of the cricoid cartilage into the inferior horns of the thyroid cartilage fit, thus forming the cricothyroid joint. The posterosuperior surface of the cricoid cartilage also provides articulation surfaces (the cricoarytenoid joint) for the arytenoid cartilages.

3. The **epiglottis** is a broad, leaf-shaped, laryngeal cartilage that is attached to the medial surface of the thyroid cartilage and projects upward toward the tongue. The uppermost, free margin of the epiglottis lies just posterior to the root of the tongue. The upper tip of the epiglottis may be observed in children during an examination of oral structures. The function of the epiglottis is to prevent food from entering the larynx during deglutition (swallowing). The epiglottis does not function in the production of voice.

4. The **arytenoid cartilages** are paired, pyramid-shaped, laryngeal cartilages that articulate with the posterosuperior surface of the cricoid cartilage via the cricoarytenoid joints. These specialized joints allow the arytenoids to articulate with the cricoid cartilage through rocking and sliding movements. Although authors of modern anatomy textbooks suggest that the arytenoids are capable of rotary movements, there is sufficient physiologic information to indicate that rotation about a vertical axis through the cricoarytenoid joint is untenable because of the functional morphology of the arytenoid cartilages (Kahane, 1982).

The apex of each arytenoid cartilage is flat, and both arytenoid cartilages articulate with a separate corniculate cartilage. The base of each arytenoid cartilage is characterized by two prominent extensions, one extending anteriorly (called the vocal process) and the other extending posterolaterally (called the muscular process).

Attached to the vocal process of each arytenoid is the vocal ligament, which is a white cord that extends to the posteromedial surface of the thyroid cartilage where it converges (anterior commissure) with the vocal ligament from the other side. The vocal ligament forms the medial margin of each vocal fold. Muscle attachments to the muscular process of the arytenoids and to the cricoid cartilage permit the specialized movements of the arytenoids, which are primary to laryngeal function.

5. The **corniculate cartilages (cartilages of Santorini)** are paired, and each articulates with the apex of its associated arytenoid. The corniculate cartilages play no significant role in laryngeal function; however, they may have played a role in protecting the airway at an earlier stage of laryngeal evolution.

6. The **cuneiform cartilages (cartilages of Wrisberg)** are embedded within folds of muscle and ligaments (aryepiglottic folds) that extend from the sides of the epiglottis to the apexes of the arytenoid cartilages. The cuneiform cartilages are not present in all larynges, but when present they function to assist the aryepiglottic folds in maintaining an open airway into the larynx.

B. The **hyoid bone** is shaped like a horseshoe, is superior to the thyroid cartilage of the larynx, and does not articulate with any other bone. The hyoid bone is connected superiorly to the skull by various muscles, muscle slings, and ligaments. It serves as a superior attachment for many of the extrinsic muscles of the larynx, which is suspended just inferior to the hyoid bone.

C. The **muscles of the larynx** can be divided into two groups on the basis of functional and anatomic differences. One group of muscles, the **extrinsic muscles,** has one point of attachment on the larynx and the other attachment to structures that are external to the larynx. The extrinsic muscles function to fixate, elevate, and lower the position of the larynx within the neck. The **intrinsic laryngeal muscles** have all points of attachment within the larynx. These muscles function to give the larynx phonatory as well as closure capabilities for purposes of trapping air below the level of the larynx or for preventing foreign substances from entering the lungs.

Names of most of the laryngeal muscles are derived from each muscle's two points of attachment. Table 2.1 summarizes the functions of the extrinsic and intrinsic laryngeal muscles.

1. The **extrinsic laryngeal muscles** can be subdivided into two groups: the suprahyoid group and the infrahyoid group. The suprahyoid muscles, which, as the name suggests, lie above the level of the hyoid bone, act principally to elevate the larynx, while the infrahyoid group (located below the hyoid bone) act as laryngeal depressors (see Figure 2.2).

   a. The **suprahyoid muscles** are extrinsic laryngeal elevators, which function to lift the larynx within the neck. Elevation of the larynx occurs when high vocal pitches are sung (laryngeal elevation improves vocal tract resonance for higher tones by shortening the overall length of the vocal tract) and during swallowing. The muscle pairs that constitute the suprahyoid group are the following:

      (1) Digastric

      (2) Geniohyoid

Table 2.1. Summary of the Functions of the Extrinsic and Instrinsic Muscles of the Larynx

Muscle	Function
Extrinsic muscles	
Suprahyoid muscles	
Digastric, geniohyoid, hyoglossus, mylohyoid, stylohyoid	Raise the hyoid bone and, indirectly, raise the larynx via its attachment to the hyoid bone
Infrahyoid muscles	
Omohyoid, sternohyoid	Lower the hyoid bone and, indirectly, lower the larynx via its attachment to the hyoid bone
Sternothyroid	Lowers the thyroid cartilage and lowers the larynx
Thyrohyoid	Raises the thyroid cartilage and raises the larynx or, with the larynx fixed, lowers the hyoid bone
Intrinsic muscles	
Cricothyroid	Lengthens and tenses the vocal folds
Lateral cricoarytenoid	Adducts the vocal folds
Oblique arytenoid	Adducts and assists in medial compression of the vocal folds
Posterior cricoarytenoid	Abducts the vocal folds
Thyroarytenoid	
Thyromuscularis portion	Adducts the vocal folds and reduces vocal fold tension
Thyrovocalis portion	Tenses the vocal folds, shortens the vocal folds, and increases vocal fold mass
Transverse arytenoid	Adducts and assists in medial compression of the vocal folds

      (3) Hyoglossus

      (4) Mylohyoid

      (5) Stylohyoid

   b. The **infrahyoid muscles** are extrinsic laryngeal depressors, which function as antagonists to the suprahyoid group and act to lower the larynx in the neck after it has been elevated by the suprahyoid muscles. The infrahyoid muscles also lower the larynx during the production of low vocal pitches (laryngeal descension improves vocal tract resonance for lower tones by increasing the overall length of the vocal tract). The muscle pairs that constitute the infrahyoid group are the following:

      (1) Omohyoid

      (2) Sternohyoid

      (3) Sternothyroid

      (4) Thyrohyoid

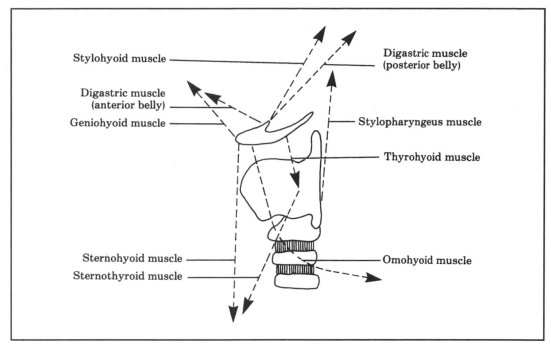

Figure 2.2. Extrinsic muscles of the larynx.

2. The **intrinsic laryngeal muscles** are each capable of making fine, discrete movements. However, although each intrinsic laryngeal muscle is capable of functioning independently of the others, these muscles frequently operate synergistically in the performance of various laryngeal functions.

   a. **Functions associated with the intrinsic laryngeal muscles**

      (1) **Assistance in respiration.** The primary and most important function of the intrinsic laryngeal muscles is to assist in the process of respiration. During inhalation, the entire larynx descends in the neck and increases in its transverse dimension, thus facilitating the subsequent inward flow of air into the lungs. During quiet, at-rest inhalation, the vocal folds abduct only very slightly (intermediate position). Forced inhalation, however, will naturally cause the vocal folds to abduct to a wider position (lateral position) and thus increase the airway capacity even further. During quiet exhalation, the entire larynx moves upward.

      (2) **Phonation.** In addition to assisting in respiration, the intrinsic laryngeal muscles also serve an adaptive function that permits the production of voice (phonation). Phonation is accomplished by the actions of the intrinsic laryngeal muscles as they move the various laryngeal cartilages and thus change the positions of the cartilages relative to each other. These movements of the laryngeal cartilages cause the vocal folds to either approximate each other (adduction) or to separate from each other in a wide open position (abduction). Cartilage movement resulting from contraction of the intrinsic laryngeal

muscles also causes the mass, length, and tension characteristics of the vocal folds to be altered.

The production of voice is dependent upon the finely balanced relationship between the forces exerted by the intrinsic muscles of the larynx and the force exerted by air (air pressure) as it is exhaled from the lungs. The smallest deviations from this precarious balance result in a noticeable alteration in the pitch, loudness, or quality of the voice produced.

The **aerodynamic–myoelastic theory,** as the name implies, is a description of how phonation is made possible by the interplay of the physical forces of aerodynamics and the elastic tissue force of the muscles of the larynx. During inhalation, the vocal folds are abducted to either the intermediate or lateral position. As exhalation begins, the intrinsic adductor muscles cause the vocal folds to approximate each other. These muscles must quickly balance their force of contraction against the force of the exhaled airstream. The outflowing air accelerates as it moves through the increasingly narrow glottis.

Because the velocity of the air between the folds increases, there is a concomitant decrease in the air pressure between the folds due to a phenomenon known as the **Bernoulli effect.** Because there is a partial vacuum created between the vocal folds, the Bernoulli effect causes the vocal folds to be drawn together. Once the folds are pulled together to completely occlude the airway, air pressure below the vocal folds (subglottic pressure) increases until the pressure is sufficient to blow the folds open. As the subglottically impounded air is allowed to escape between the folds, subglottic air pressure decreases and the tissue elasticity of the vocal folds as well as the Bernoulli effect cause the folds to once again approximate each other. This sequence of events repeats very rapidly, with the number of repetitions per second corresponding to the fundamental frequency (vocal pitch) of an individual's voice. The faster this cycle repeats itself, the higher the vocal pitch, and the slower the cycle becomes, the lower the vocal pitch. The range of average fundamental frequencies is approximately 124 Hz for young adult males (Hollein & Jackson, 1973; Hollein & Shipp, 1972) and around 227 Hz for young adult females (A. Kelley, 1977).

Another important component in the understanding of phonation is the **Body-Cover Model** by Hirano (1981). The model states that the vocal folds are multilayered vibrators 17 to 20 mm long in adult males and 12 to 17 mm long in adult females. The layers of the vocal fold excluding the muscle are 1.3 mm thick. These layers have different vibratory properties that help to explain individual voice production. The layers of the folds are listed in (a) through (d) in the following passages and are illustrated in Figure 2.3, as described by Stemple et al. (1995) and Kahane and Folkins (1984).

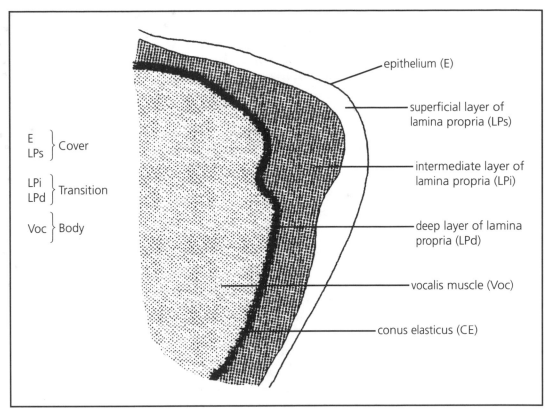

Figure 2.3. Layered structure of the vocal fold.

THE COVER (also called **the mucosal layer**):

(a) The cover is made up of an outside layer of **stratified squamous epithelium (E),** which is only approximately eight cell layers thick.

(b) The cover is also made up of the superficial layer of the **lamina propria (LPs),** consisting of loosely woven elastic fibers and a few collagenous fibers. The LPs is very loose, pliable, and gelatin like. The LPs is also called **Reinke's space.** Laryngitis attacks in Reinke's space (or LPs) with fluid and swelling. Some cancers also start in Reinke's space. The greatest activity in voicing occurs in the cover of the vocal folds.

THE TRANSITION

(c) The **transition** includes the intermediate layer of the lamina propria **(LPi),** which has a lot of densely packed elastic fibers and an increased number of collagenous fibers that are often described as being like soft rubber bands. It also includes the deep layer of the lamina propria **(LPd),** which is mostly collagenous (collagen fibers are stiff) with only a few elastic fibers interwoven, often described as like stiff cotton thread. These two layers (LPi and LPd) are called the vocal ligament. This layer is somewhat unique in human anatomy because it is unusual for a ligament to have both resiliency and elasticity. These layers, along with the layers of the cover, are also referred to as the vocal fold mucosa.

THE BODY

(d) The **body of the vocal fold** is made up of the vocalis muscle (or the thyrovocalis), which attaches to the vocal portion of the arytenoid cartilage. The more lateral fibers are called the thyroarytenoid, whereas the more medial fibers are called the thyrovocalis. The fibers of the body are often described as being like stiff rubber bands. The least activity in voicing occurs here in the thyrovocalis and thyroarytenoids.

Structurally, all of the layers of the vocal fold are different, so mechanically they vibrate differently from one another. In general, this layered structure of the larynx gives it its unique vibratory characteristics. Also, when discussing voice disorders, we can discriminate which layer or layers of the folds are affected by pathology. For the ENT physician, the location of the pathology might help in making a differential diagnosis and may have implications for treatment (Kahane, 1982; Hirano, 1981).

Much of the ability of the human voice to signal emphasis, stress, or emotion occurs as the result of small pitch variations **(vocal inflections)** that occur during speech. Vocal inflections are simply minor pitch variations that are centered around the fundamental frequency of a person's speaking voice. These variations in the fundamental frequency of the voice result when the intrinsic muscles of the larynx effect mass, length, and tension changes in the vocal folds.

The **compliance, length, elasticity, and mass** characteristics of the vocal folds determine the rate at which they vibrate. Increased mass causes vocal fold vibration to be slowed, resulting in a lowered vocal pitch, whereas decreased vocal fold mass results in higher pitches. Higher vocal pitches are also related to increased vocal fold length (which reduces the effective mass of the folds) and to increased tension of the folds. As can be seen, any change in vocal pitch results from the combined influences of vocal fold compliance, length, elasticity, and mass.

Vocal variety, often called **vocal registers,** is influenced by the interplay of forces of compliance, length, elasticity, and mass, as well as changes in subglottal pressure (Psub), airflow, and so on.

(3) Protection during swallowing. A third function of the intrinsic laryngeal muscles is a biologically protective one whereby the larynx protects the lungs from the ingestion of foods or liquids during swallowing. When swallowing occurs, the epiglottis moves posteriorly and forms a tight seal over the top of the larynx to prevent aspiration of foreign substances.

(4) **Assistance in increasing muscular mechanical advantage.** The fourth function of the intrinsic laryngeal muscles is called the **glottal effort closure reflex.** The glottal effort closure reflex is characterized by a tight, uniform adduction of the entire larynx, including both the true and false vocal folds, which occurs when heavy physical effort is exerted. With air trapped in the lungs and with the consequent chest expansion, thoracic and upper arm muscles are given a mechanical advantage that permits a person to lift, push, pull, and otherwise expend more physical force than would be possible if the airway were to remain open. In addition, when the thoracic cavity is expanded, the abdominal viscera can be compressed, which assists in coughing, defecation, and urination.

b. **Descriptions of the intrinsic laryngeal muscles**

(1) The **thyroarytenoid muscles** are paired muscles that constitute the muscular portion of the true vocal folds (**the body**) and extend from the arytenoid cartilages to the inner surface of the thyroid cartilage. The thyroarytenoid muscles are actually composed of two groups of muscle tissue. The more medial group is called the thyrovocalis portion and the more lateral group is called the thyromuscularis portion.

The **thyrovocalis muscle** is bound on the medial margin by the vocal ligament, which stretches from the anterior commissure to the tip of the vocal process of each arytenoid. The thyrovocalis muscle courses parallel to the vocal ligament and attaches to the vocal process of the arytenoids. The **thyromuscularis muscle** also extends from the inner surface of the thyroid cartilage, is lateral to the thyrovocalis muscle, and extends to the lateral surface of each arytenoid.

Upon contraction, the thyrovocalis portion shortens the vocal folds, increases vocal fold tension, and increases vocal fold mass for the production of lower vocal pitches. The thyromuscularis portion, when contracted, assists in vocal fold adduction while simultaneously reducing vocal fold tension.

(2) The **cricothyroid muscles** are paired, fan-shaped muscles that extend from the anterolateral margins of the cricoid cartilage to the thyroid cartilage above (see Figure 2.4A). The cricothyroid muscle is actually divided into two parts. The lower of the two parts, called the pars oblique, courses upward and backward to insert into the anterior margin of the inferior horn of the thyroid cartilage. The upper part, called the pars recta, extends almost directly upward into the lower margin of the thyroid cartilage. Upon contraction, these important muscles decrease the space between the cricoid cartilage and the thyroid cartilage. This movement causes an increase in the distance between the thyroid cartilage and the vocal process of the arytenoids; thus, the length and tension of the vocal folds are increased for the purpose of changing vocal pitch (see Figure 2.4B, C).

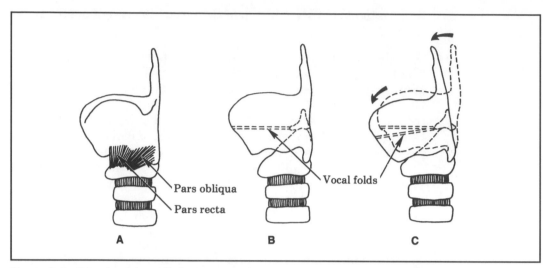

Pars obliqua

Pars recta

Vocal folds

A   B   C

Figure 2.4. Cricothyroid muscle function. **A.** The cricothyroid muscles (pars recta and pars obliqua). **B, C.** As the cricothyroid muscle contracts, the thyroid cartilage tilts forward, thus increasing the length of the vocal folds.

(3) The **lateral cricoarytenoid muscles** are paired muscles that course from the lateral margins of the cricoid cartilage to the muscular process of the arytenoids (see Figure 2.5). These muscles function as adductors of the vocal folds. Upon contraction, these muscles cause the arytenoids to rock and glide in an anteromediocaudal direction, thus causing the vocal folds to approximate each other.

(4) The **posterior cricoarytenoid muscles** are paired, fan-shaped, intrinsic laryngeal muscles that course from the posterior surface of the cricoid cartilage to the vocal process of the arytenoids (see Figure 2.5). These muscles are direct antagonists to the lateral cricoarytenoids. Contraction of the posterior cricoarytenoids causes the arytenoids to rock and glide in a posterolaterocranial direction (see Figure 2.6A). The posterior cricoarytenoid muscles are the only laryngeal muscles that abduct the vocal folds.

(5) The **transverse arytenoid muscle** extends from the lateral and posterior margins of one arytenoid to the lateral and posterior margins of the other arytenoid (the transverse arytenoid muscle and the oblique arytenoid muscles are sometimes called the interarytenoid muscles because they course between the two arytenoid cartilages) (see Figure 2.5). Upon contraction, this muscle causes the arytenoids to approximate each other. Its most important function, however, is to cause the vocal folds to be compressed medially (see Figure 2.6B).

(6) The **oblique arytenoid muscles** are also paired and course from the muscle process of one arytenoid to the apex of the other arytenoid and then upward to the lateral margin of the epiglottis. Upon contraction, these muscles cause the vocal folds to adduct (see Figure 2.6C).

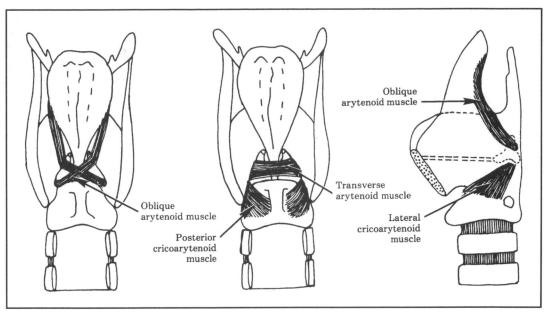

Figure 2.5. Intrinsic muscles of the larynx. *Note.* Adapted from *Illustrated Speech Anatomy* (2nd ed.), by W. M. Shearer, 1968, Springfield, IL: Thomas.

D. **Spaces or cavities of the laryngeal area.** The **glottis** (sometimes also called the **true glottis** or **rima glottidis**) is the space between the folds. It may be separated into the **cartilaginous glottis** and the **membranous glottis,** depending on the corresponding place along the vocal fold. The **ventricle** is the space immediately superior to the true vocal folds, but below the ventricular (or false) vocal folds. The **vestibule** or **supraglottic area** is the area above the ventricular folds and behind the epiglottis. The **subglottic area** is the area below the true vocal folds.

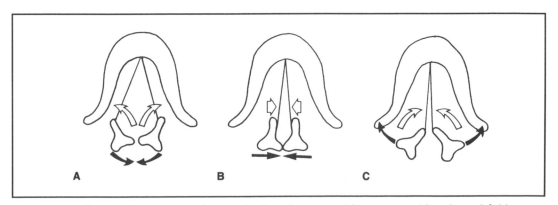

Figure 2.6. Effect of laryngeal muscles attached to the arytenoids on arytenoid and vocal fold movement. **A.** Abduction of the vocal folds caused by contraction of the posterior cricoarytenoid muscles. **B.** Medial compression of the vocal folds caused by contraction of the transverse and oblique arytenoid muscles. **C.** Adduction of the vocal folds caused by contraction of the lateral cricoarytenoid muscles.

E. **Innervation of the phonatory system.** The muscles of the phonatory system are innervated by the following cranial nerves (CN): vagus (CN X), trigeminal (CN V), facial (CN VII), and hypoglossal (CN XII). The vagus nerve is entirely responsible for innervating the intrinsic muscles of the larynx, and the other cranial nerves (CN V, VII, and XII) innervate the extrinsic laryngeal muscles. Table 2.2 summarizes the motor nerve supply to the muscles of the phonatory system.

1. The **vagus nerve** arises from the nucleus ambiguus in the medulla. As this cranial nerve exits from the skull, it divides into three branches—the pharyngeal nerve branch, the superior laryngeal nerve branch, and the recurrent laryngeal nerve branch (see Figure 2.7).

   a. The **pharyngeal nerve branch** supplies motor nerve fibers to the pharynx and to all the muscles of the soft palate except the tensor veli palatini.

   b. The **superior laryngeal nerve branch** subdivides into two additional parts—the internal laryngeal nerve and the external laryngeal nerve.

      (1) The primary purpose of the **internal laryngeal nerve branch** is to carry sensory information from the mucous membranes of the epiglottis and the interior of the larynx.

      (2) The **external laryngeal nerve branch** is a motor nerve to the cricothyroid muscle and the inferior pharyngeal constrictor muscle.

   c. The **recurrent laryngeal nerve branch** receives its name from the fact that this nerve courses past the larynx and descends into the neck

Table 2.2. Summary of the Motor Nerve Supply for the Phonatory System Musculature

Muscle	Innervation
Intrinsic muscles	
Cricothyroid	Vagus (superior laryngeal nerve branch)
Lateral cricoarytenoid, oblique arytenoid, posterior cricoarytenoid, thryoarytenoid, transverse arytenoid	Vagus (recurrent laryngeal nerve branch)
Extrinsic muscles	
Suprahyoid muscles	
Digastricus (anterior belly)	Trigeminal (mylohyoid branch)
Digastricus (posterior belly)	Facial (digastric branch)
Geniohyoid	Hypoglossal (geniohyoid branch)
Hyoglossus	Hypoglossal (hyoglossus branch)
Mylohyoid	Trigeminal (mylohyoid branch)
Stylohyoid	Facial (stylohyoid branch)
Infrahyoid muscles	
Omohyoid, sternohyoid, sternothyroid	Hypoglossal and ansa cervicalis
Thyrohyoid	Hypoglossal

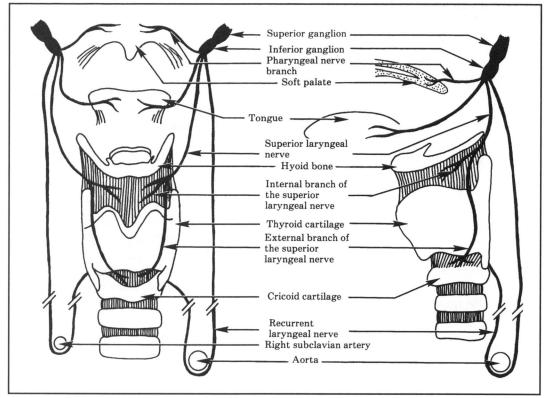

Figure 2.7. The vagus nerve. *Note.* Adapted from Neuroanatomic Bases of Hearing and Speech, by C. R. Larson and B. E. Pfingst. In *Speech, Language, and Hearing. Vol. I. Normal Processes,* by N. J. Lass, L. V. McReynolds, J. L. Northern, and D. E. Yoder (Eds.), 1982, Philadelphia: Saunders.

and upper chest before it returns to the larynx to innervate all intrinsic muscles of the larynx except the cricothyroid muscle.

2. The **trigeminal nerve** provides a motor nerve supply via its mylohyoid branch to the mylohyoid muscle and the anterior belly of the digastricus.

3. The **facial nerve** activates the posterior belly of the digastricus muscle and the stylohyoid muscle.

4. The **hypoglossal nerve** provides a motor nerve supply to the following extrinsic laryngeal muscles:

   a. Geniohyoid

   b. Sternohyoid

   c. Omohyoid

   d. Thyrohyoid

   e. Sternothyroid

II. The **respiratory system** is composed of many different organs (respiratory tract) through which air must flow, and the system relies upon a musculoskeletal framework that plays a central role in the process of breathing. The respiratory tract begins rostrally at the nose and mouth and terminates caudally with the alveoli in the lungs (see Figure 2.8).

The respiratory tract can be divided into two parts that are distinguishable by both structure and function. One part of the total tract, the **upper respiratory tract,** is composed of the nasal cavity, oral cavity, pharynx, and larynx. In addition to playing an important role in the process of respiration, this portion of the respiratory tract also functions in the processes of mastication (chewing), deglutition (swallowing), articulation (producing individual speech sounds), resonation (modifying the spectral characteristics of voice), and phonation (producing voice).

The **lower respiratory tract** (tracheobronchial tree) is composed of the trachea, the two bronchi, and the lungs, which contain the bronchioles and the alveoli. The lower respiratory tract functions exclusively for the processes of respiration for life support and respiration for speech production.

A. **Course of the respiratory tract.** The respiratory tract is F-shaped. There are two parallel entrances into the tract (which are analogous to the two arms of the letter *F*) that merge into a single, common tract (analogous to the upright portion of the *F*). The uppermost entrance into the respiratory tract is through the **nose.** The nose is the only entrance into the nasal cavity, and it is within this cavity that incoming air is warmed and moistened. The posterior section of the nasal cavity is called the nasopharynx and is separated from the oropharynx below it by a muscular valve referred to as the velopharyngeal port (see section **III.C**).

The second entrance into the respiratory tract is through the **mouth.** Air entering the respiratory tract in this way passes through the oral cavity and then posteriorly into the oropharynx. Beginning at the oropharynx, the respiratory

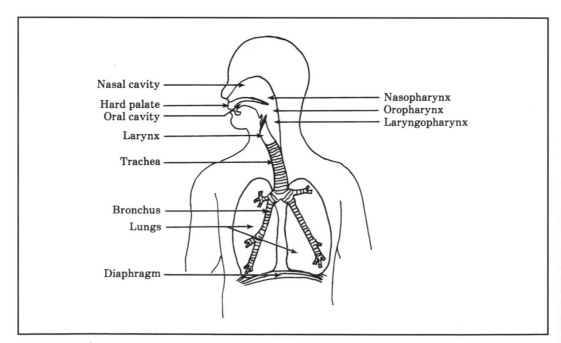

Figure 2.8. The respiratory tract.

tract begins its downward descent through the laryngopharyngeal region to the larynx. The tract continues through the larynx, passing between the ventricular folds (false vocal folds), through the laryngeal ventricle, through the open space (rima glottides) between the abducted (open) vocal folds, and then downward into the trachea. The trachea bifurcates (divides into two branches) into two bronchi that enter the lungs and that further divide into bronchioles that terminate into smaller sacs called alveoli.

B. **Function of the respiratory tract.** Although some of the organs in the respiratory tract contain muscles and are capable of independent movement, the respiratory tract as a whole is incapable of effecting any exchange of air between the lungs and the external environment. Respiration is accomplished by the actions of external, musculoskeletal forces that act upon the various organs of the respiratory tract.

The lungs are housed in a bony cage (thoracic cavity) consisting of 12 rib pairs that are supported by the vertebral column and joined anteriorly at the sternum. Because of a membranous connection (the pleura) between the lungs and the thorax, they expand and contract as a single unit.

Dimensions of the thoracic cavity can be increased along three different planes of expansion. Because of the particular manner by which the ribs are attached to the vertebral column, elevation of the rib cage by various muscles results in an increase in the transverse dimensions (see Figure 2.9A) and the anteroposterior dimensions (see Figure 2.9B) of the thoracic cavity. The longitudinal dimension is increased by descension of the diaphragm.

Musculoskeletal forces that act to increase and decrease the volume of the thoracic cavity will cause a concomitant volumetric change in the lungs. As lung volume is altered, there are proportional increases and decreases in the

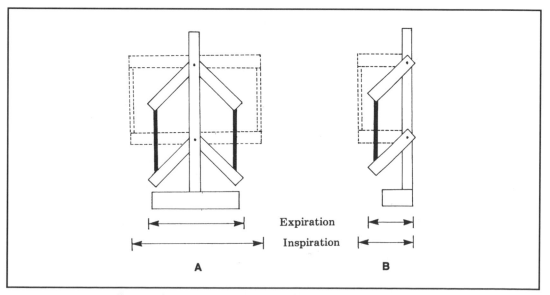

Figure 2.9. Schematic view of the planes of expansion of the thoracic cavity. The dashed lines indicate the position of the rib cage at the peak of inhalation. **A.** Transverse increase. **B.** Anteroposterior increase.

pressure of the air contained within the lungs. These pressure differences within the lungs (which are created by external forces acting upon them) are responsible for the exchange of air during respiration.

The inward and outward flow of air that is commonly associated with the process of respiration results from a particular physical property of gases. This property of gases is explained by a law of physics, discussed as follows: When a gas-filled chamber increases in volume, there is a proportional decrease in the pressure of the gas contained within that chamber (relative to external air pressure); conversely, a decrease in the volume of the same chamber will result in a proportional increase in the pressure of the contained gas. Similarly, as lung volume is increased, there is an associated decrease in the pressure of the air contained within the lungs, at least with regard to normal atmospheric air pressure. When lung volume is increased, air that is external to the lungs has a higher pressure relative to the air contained within the lungs. This air pressure differential causes an inward rush of air through the respiratory tract **(inspiration)** and into the lungs so as to equalize air pressure within and outside the lungs. Conversely, a decrease in lung volume results in an increase in air pressure in the lungs, causing air to flow in the opposite, or outward, direction **(expiration)**.

C. The **respiratory muscles,** with the exception of the diaphragm, are all attached externally to the rib cage. Upon contraction, these muscles either elevate the rib cage and increase the thoracic volume, or they depress the ribs and decrease the dimensions of the thorax. Table 2.3 summarizes the functions of the respiratory musculature.

The muscles of respiration can be conveniently divided into two groups: the muscles of inspiration and the muscles of expiration.

1. Although all of the **muscles of inspiration** are active during forced inspiration, only a few are required for quiet, at-rest inspiration. The muscles of inspiration and their relative contribution to quiet versus forced breathing are as follows:

   a. The **diaphragm** is the principal muscle of inspiration. Upon contraction, the dome-shaped diaphragm pulls downward on the central tendon and thus increases the vertical dimensions of the lungs and thoracic cavity.

   b. The **external intercostals** are situated between each of the ribs. Upon contraction, the external intercostals elevate the rib cage and thus increase the transverse and anteroposterior dimensions of the thoracic cavity.

   c. The **sternocleidomastoid** muscle, which is active only during deep breathing, is a major accessory muscle of inspiration. It is attached at its upper end to the mastoid process of the skull and to the sternum and clavicle at its lower end. The sternocleidomastoid elevates the rib cage via its attachment to the sternum and clavicle when the position of the head is fixed. A secondary function of the sternocleidomastoid muscle is to assist in turning the head by drawing the head toward one or the other shoulder.

Table 2.3. Summary of the Functions of the Respiratory Musculature

Muscle	Function
Inspiration muscles	
Diaphragm	Acts as the primary muscle of inspiration and increases the vertical dimension of the thoracic cavity
External intercostals	Raise the rib cage when the first ribs are fixed
Sternocleidomastoid	Raises the sternum and, indirectly, raises the ribs when the head is fixed
Scaleni	Raise first and second ribs and act as accessory muscles of inspiration
Pectoralis major	Raises the sternum and upper six ribs when the shoulder is fixed and acts as an accessory muscle of inspiration
Pectoralis minor	Raises ribs three through five and acts as an accessory muscle of inspiration
Expiration muscles	
External and internal obliques	Depress the lower ribs and compress abdominal viscera
Internal intercostals	Lower the ribs
Rectus abdominis, transverse abdominis	Compress abdominal viscera

    d. The **scaleni** are three muscle pairs that attach to the cervical vertebrae and to the first and second ribs. During forced inspiration, contraction of these muscles assists in elevation of the rib cage.

    e. The **pectoralis major** and **pectoralis minor** are two accessory muscles of inspiration capable of pulling the upper ribs upward and outward when the upper arm and shoulder are fixed. These muscles are active in respiration only during the final phase of maximal inspiration.

  2. Unlike the muscles of inspiration, the **muscles of expiration** work in concert with the passive forces of torque, tissue elasticity, and gravity. At the end of a normal, unforced, inspiratory cycle, the muscles of inspiration gradually relax and the passive forces cause the dimensions of the thoracic cavity to decrease: (1) **gravity** pulls downward on the rib cage; (2) **tissue elasticity** pulls the rib cage downward and inward and causes the diaphragm to move upward into its normal, relaxed position; and (3) **torque** of the twisted ribs causes them to descend. As respiratory demands increase during speech or during forced respiration, some or all of the following muscles of expiration may be required to assist the passive forces of expiration:

    a. Several **abdominal muscles** aid in expiration by compressing the abdominal viscera, which forces the diaphragm upward, thereby decreasing the size of the thoracic cavity. Other abdominal muscles that have attachments to the rib cage are able to decrease thoracic dimensions by depressing the lower ribs. The abdominal muscles of expiration are the following:

(1) Rectus abdominis (compresses abdomen)

(2) Transverse abdominis (compresses abdomen)

(3) Internal oblique (depresses lower ribs)

(4) External oblique (depresses lower ribs)

b. The **internal intercostal muscles,** which are located between the ribs, depress the ribs during expiration.

D. **Innervation of the respiratory system.** The muscles of the respiratory system are under both involuntary and voluntary control. Vegetative breathing is primarily under involuntary neurologic control, whereas breathing for speech or other nonspeech activities results from a blending of involuntary as well as voluntary influences.

1. **Inspiration for vegetative breathing** is most likely triggered when the carbon dioxide level in the bloodstream reaches a critical level. Chemoreceptors that are capable of sensing the level of carbon dioxide send sensory impulses to the respiratory control center located in the reticular formation. Upon receiving this feedback information, the control center sends motor impulses via the phrenic nerve, which innervates the diaphragm, and via other cranial nerves and various spinal nerves to the other muscles of inspiration. As the lungs inflate, special stretch receptors located in the lungs send inhibitory impulses to the nuclei of the inspiratory nerves and thus terminate inspiration. With the termination of inspiration, the pressure forces of expiration cause the lungs to deflate. Table 2.4 summarizes the motor nerve supply for the muscles of the respiratory system.

2. **Inspiration for speech** and some nonspeech activities involves the same nerve network used for involuntary control, but there is voluntary control of additional muscles of inspiration, and voluntary control of accessory muscles of expiration.

III. **The Resonatory System.** Although the larynx is the primary contributor to the production of voice, the human voice would sound very thin and weak if it were not for the acoustic influence of the resonatory structures situated above the larynx. Most of the quality and loudness characteristics that are commonly associated with the human voice can be attributed primarily to the unique arrangement of the supraglottic resonators found in humankind.

A. **Acoustic features of resonance.** Resonance is the acoustic phenomenon by which a vibrating structure (sound source) excites the air in an air-filled chamber, which in turn causes the chamber walls to vibrate similarly. Vibrations from the source may be transmitted to the chamber in one of two ways. First, the source can excite the surrounding air and those vibrations will, in turn, cause the air in the chamber to also vibrate. Or, the sound source can cause the chamber to vibrate by transmitting its vibrations to the chamber via a direct attachment.

Acoustic resonance is probably best exemplified in a description of how a stringed musical instrument functions. On most stringed instruments, each of

Table 2.4. Summary of the Motor Nerve Supply for the Respiratory System Musculature

Muscle	Innervation
Inspiration muscles	
Diaphragm	Phrenic plexus
External intercostals	Intercostal nerves
Sternocleidomastoid	Spinal accessory
Scaleni	C-2 and C-3 (anterior rami)
Pectoralis major	Medial and lateral anterior thoracic nerve
Pectoralis minor	Brachial plexus
Expiration muscles	
External and internal obliques, rectus abdominis	T-6 through T-12 (anterior rami)
Transverse abdominis	T-7 through T-12 (anterior rami)
Internal intercostals	T-2 through T-12 (anterior rami)

several strings is stretched over and attached at both ends to an air-filled chamber that forms the main body of the instrument. If one of the strings were to be removed from the instrument, stretched between two points in the air, and then plucked, little if any audible sound would be produced. However, when the same string is attached to and stretched over the opening of the large, air-filled body of a musical instrument, it produces a fully resonant, audible, musical tone when it is made to vibrate by plucking. What causes the production of an audible tone in the second situation and not in the first is the fact that in the second situation the string is associated with an acoustic resonator (the instrument body) that serves to amplify the tiny vibrations of the individual strings.

Because the strings of the instrument are in proximity to the resonating chamber (resonator) of the instrument, the small vibrations that occur when the string is plucked are transmitted through the air and directly to the resonator, causing it to vibrate similarly. Because the resonator has a much larger surface area than any individual string, it is capable of causing more air to vibrate and consequently produce an audible tone. On the other hand, a vibrating string that is not attached to a resonator has such a small surface area that it can produce only very small, inaudible vibrations in the air.

In much the same way that the weak vibrations of the strings of a musical instrument are amplified by the resonating body of the instrument, the weak, thin tone that is produced at the level of the vocal folds can be resonated to a more full and audible level by the large, air-filled chambers located above the larynx. The human voice would sound much like a weak, fluttering noise if it were not for the acoustic contribution of resonance.

The degree to which a particular resonator can be excited by the weaker vibrations of the sound source is dependent upon the degree to which the size, shape, and resiliency of that resonator are acoustically tuned to that specific source. Fortunately, the supraglottic resonatory system in humans is capable of being altered in size, configuration, and tautness by the muscles and organs that comprise the resonatory portion of the vocal tract.

In general, contractions of the pharyngeal and extrinsic laryngeal muscles are responsible for altering the size of the resonatory portion of the vocal tract. As a result of the contraction of these muscles, the vocal tract can be lengthened and shortened for the purpose of improving resonance at lower and higher vocal pitches, respectively. Alterations in the configuration of the vocal tract that result from various tongue postures or from coupling of the nasal resonator (nasal cavity) to the rest of the vocal tract result in remarkable acoustic changes. Females, for example, have slightly different vocal tract configurations than males. Consequently, male or female speakers are often easily identifiable even if pitch differences are ignored. Characteristics such as length, cross-sectional area, and ratio of oral to pharyngeal cavity size help to determine individual voice qualities.

B. **Anatomic structures of resonance.** The structures responsible for shaping the resonatory characteristics of speech are all superior to the larynx. The resonatory system occupies the uppermost portion of the F-shaped vocal tract and consists of the pharynx, oral cavity, nasal cavity, and the valve-like soft palate.

  1. The **pharynx,** which is shaped like an inverted cone, consists of two layers of muscle and several different membranous layers. The pharynx is widest in its uppermost portion and tapers caudally as it descends from the base of the skull to the top of the larynx.

     The two muscular layers of the pharynx are innervated by a group of nerve fibers, collectively termed the pharyngeal plexus, which is derived from cranial nerves IX, X, and XI. The outer muscular layer, which forms the major portion of the pharynx, is made up of the three pharyngeal constrictor muscles—the superior, medial, and inferior pharyngeal constrictors (see Figure 2.10). These muscles function to constrict the pharynx during swallowing or gagging. The pharyngeal constrictor muscles form the posterior and lateral walls of the pharynx. Each pharyngeal constrictor muscle courses anterolaterally from the midline (pharyngeal raphe) and inserts into various structures anteriorly, thus leaving the pharynx open along its anterior portion.

     The inner layer of muscles forming the pharyngeal tube—the stylopharyngeus, salpingopharyngeus, and palatopharyngeus—contract to elevate the pharynx during swallowing (see Figure 2.10). Contraction of the palatopharyngeus also results in a narrowing of the faucial pillars, whereas contraction of the stylopharyngeus assists in moving the lateral walls of the pharynx medially. Table 2.5 summarizes the functions of the resonatory system musculature.

     The pharynx can be anatomically divided into three sections based upon connections to various resonators via openings in the anterior wall of the pharyngeal tube (see Figure 2.10). The most superior opening is continuous with the nasal cavity, and this portion of the pharynx, which lies above the

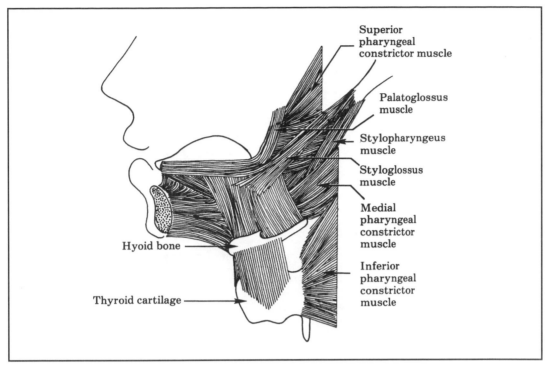

Figure 2.10. The pharyngeal muscles.

level of the soft palate (velum), is called the **nasopharynx** (epipharynx). The section of the pharyngeal tube that opens into the oral cavity and extends from the velum to the tip of the epiglottis is called the **oropharynx** (mesopharynx). The remainder of the pharyngeal tube, from the tip of the epiglottis to the larynx, is frequently referred to as the **laryngopharynx** (hypopharynx).

2. The **oral cavity** is continuous with the pharynx and cannot be separated from it. Postural adjustments of the tongue, jaw, and lips are responsible for changes in the size and shape of the cavity, as well as the dimensions of the external opening (mouth) to the oral cavity. Each of these changes directly affects the resonance characteristics of the voice.

3. The **nasal cavity** is superior to the oral cavity, from which it is separated by the hard and soft palates. Coordinated movements of the soft palate and pharyngeal muscles can cause the nasal cavity to be completely cut off from the remainder of the vocal tract. During respiration, the soft palate is relaxed, thus leaving the nasal cavity contiguous with the other sections of the vocal tract. During speech production, however, the nasal cavity is connected to the vocal tract only momentarily for the production of the English nasal consonants /m/, /n/, and /ŋ/.

4. The **soft palate,** or velum, is a muscular structure that extends posteriorly from the posterior border of the hard, or bony, palate. The major portion of the soft palate consists of five muscle pairs: tensor palati, levator palati, uvulus, palatoglossus, and palatopharyngeus. All of the muscles of the soft

Table 2.5. Summary of the Functions of the Resonatory System Musculature

Muscle	Function
Pharyngeal muscles	
Inferior, medial, and superior constrictors	Constrict the pharynx
Palatopharyngeus	Raises the pharynx, narrows the faucial pillars, and lowers the soft palate
Salpingopharyngeus	Raises the pharynx
Stylopharyngeus	Raises the pharynx and assists in medial movement of the lateral pharyngeal walls
Soft palate muscles	
Levator palati	Raises the soft palate superiorly and posteriorly
Palatoglossus	Lowers the soft palate
Palatopharyngeus	Lowers the soft palate, narrows the faucial pillars, and raises the pharynx
Tensor palati	Tenses the soft palate
Uvulus	Shortens the soft palate

palate except the tensor palati are innervated by the pharyngeal plexus. The tensor palati is innervated by the trigeminal nerve (CN V).

Each major muscle pair of the soft palate acts to pull the velum in different directions (see Figure 2.11). Velar movement occurs as a result of the combination of all the vector forces contributed by each of the muscle pairs. The levator palati elevates the velum both superiorly and posteriorly. The tensor palati tenses the anterior portion of the velum. The palatoglossus and palatopharyngeus are both velar depressors; however, the palatoglossus pulls the velum both inferiorly and anteriorly, while the palatopharyngeus is capable of moving the velum only in an inferior direction. Although the uvula was once thought to be a vestigial organ, studies by Azzan and Kuehn (1977) and Langdon and Kuebler (1978) have shown that the uvula may assist in velopharyngeal closure by adding a muscular bulge to the dorsal surface of the velum.

C. **Mechanism of velopharyngeal closure.** The velopharyngeal mechanism consists of the velum and that portion of the pharynx that approximates the velum. Precisely coordinated movements of both the velar and pharyngeal muscles are responsible for the velopharyngeal closure that occurs during speech and nonspeech activities.

The velopharyngeal port functions to separate the nasal cavity from the remainder of the vocal tract. This separation is necessary during the speech tasks of producing vowels and nonnasal consonants and during nonspeech

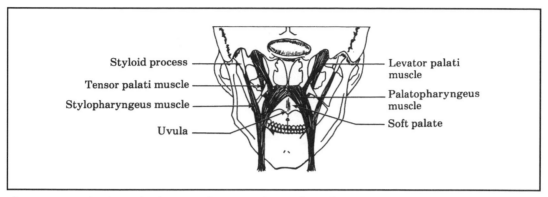

Figure 2.11. Palatal muscles (rear view). *Note.* Adapted from *Illustrated Speech Anatomy* (2nd ed.), by W. M. Shearer, 1968, Springfield, IL: Thomas.

activities such as swallowing in order to prevent the escape of food or liquids through the nose.

Velopharyngeal closure occurs as the velum is elevated in a posterosuperior direction to the posterior pharyngeal wall by the synchronous actions of the levator palati and tensor palati muscles while, at the same time, the lateral walls of the pharynx move medially to approximate the lateral margins of the velum. Obturation of the nasopharyngeal airway is dependent upon adequate and coordinated movement by all of the muscles involved in velopharyngeal closure.

Some authors erroneously have reported that the posterior pharyngeal wall moves anteriorly during velopharyngeal closure. This confusion, no doubt, has arisen from the research of Passavant (1869), who was the first author to report anterior movement of the posterior pharyngeal wall during speech production. Modern cinefluorographic and nasoendoscopic methods have shown that anterior displacement of the posterior pharyngeal wall rarely accompanies velopharyngeal closure for speech (Graber, Bzoch, & Aoba, 1959; Hagerty & Hill, 1960).

D. **Innervation of the resonatory system.** The muscles of the resonatory system are innervated by branches of several different cranial nerves. Table 2.6 summarizes the motor nerve supply for the muscles of the resonatory system.

The motor supply for the pharyngeal constrictor muscles comes from the pharyngeal plexus. The pharyngeal plexus is a large bundle of nerves that arises from the glossopharyngeal, vagus, and spinal accessory nerves (CN IX, X, XI). Sensory information from the pharynx, as well as from the faucial pillars and soft palate, is sent to the brain via the sensory branch of the glossopharyngeal nerve (CN IX).

Motor innervation for the soft palate arises from the trigeminal nerve (CN V) and from the spinal accessory nerve (CN XI). All of the muscles of the soft palate except the tensor palati are served by the spinal accessory nerve. The tensor palati is innervated by the mandibular branch of the trigeminal nerve. Sensory feedback from the soft palate is relayed to the brain via the glossopalatine branch of the facial nerve (CN VII).

Table 2.6. Summary of the Motor Nerve Supply for the Resonatory System Musculature

Muscle	Innervation
Pharyngeal muscles	
Inferior constrictor	Spinal accessory nerve and laryngeal branches of the vagus
Medial and superior constrictors, palatopharyngeus, salpingopharyngeus	Spinal accessory
Stylopharyngeus	Glossopharyngeal
Soft palate muscles	
Levator palati, palatoglossus, palatopharyngeus, uvulus	Spinal accessory
Tensor palati	Trigeminal

IV. **The Aging Voice.** There are lifelong changes in the structures of the laryngeal mechanism with aging. The functional effects of those lifelong changes are not universally agreed upon.

A. **Changes in respiratory support as a result of aging.**

1. **Vital capacity** as a result of aging has been reported to **decrease** by approximately one liter for both males and females. This loss of useable vital capacity results in an increase in residual volume (Pierce & Ebert, 1965). In contrast, total lung volumes remain stable across the lifespan (J. Kahane, personal communication, 1986). Hoit and Hixon (1987) reported that older speakers exhibited no differences from younger speakers in their use of respiration for nonspeech tasks. In speech, however, older speakers inhaled more frequently, more deeply, and faster than their younger counterparts.

2. There may be a **loss of efficiency** in the respiratory system in advanced aging as a result of impaired pulmonary performance resulting from (Kahane, 1990):

   a. decreased vital capacity

   b. loss of elasticity in the thoracic skeleton

   c. muscular weakness

3. As loudness is a function of respiration, there is the potential effect of **reduction of loudness** from reduced vital capacity and pulmonary efficiency. Benjamin (1986) reported that older female voices were perceived as less loud than younger voices. It is possible, however, that this effect may be due to cultural influences rather than physiologic change (Kahane, 1990). Generally, objective data supporting the notion of reduced loudness in older voices have been equivocal (Kahane, 1990), and the presence of reduced vocal intensity in aged male and female speakers has not been objectively quantified in a consistent manner.

B. **Changes in the laryngeal mechanism as a result of aging.**

1. **Laryngeal cartilages** (hyaline) tend to calcify and ossify with advancing age; the only elastic cartilage that appears to escape those changes is the epiglottis. Ossification occurs earlier in males, in some cases as early as the third decade of life. In general, these changes are more extensive in males (Kahane, 1990). In addition, there are changes in the cricoarytenoid joints that may limit the amount of approximation of the vocal folds (Kahane & Hammons, 1987).

2. **The intrinsic laryngeal muscles** themselves undergo some degeneration with advancing age. Specifically, the subepithelial connective tissue of the vocal folds, or lamina propria, show structural changes with advancing age:

   a. **The connective tissue of the superficial layer of the lamina propria** has been shown to thicken and become swollen (Hirano, Kurita, & Nakashima, 1983).

   b. **The intermediate layer of the lamina propria** thins after age 40 (Hirano et al., 1983). Linville (1992) observed a greater incidence of anterior glottic gap, perhaps related to thinning or bowing of the vocal folds, in older females.

   c. **The deep layer of the lamina propria** appears to change more significantly with age in males than in females. The deep layer of connective tissue becomes more dense and there is a breakdown in fiber organization. Changes and breakdown in the lamina propria may contribute to bowing of the vocal folds—often referred to as presbylaryngeus or aging larynx (Kahane, 1990; Stemple et al., 1995).

3. **The functional effects of these changes** in laryngeal cartilages and laryngeal connective tissue are equivocal, although some general comments can be made:

   a. After approximately the fifth decade of life, there appears to be an increase in male fundamental frequency (Hollein & Shipp, 1972), whereas for females there appears to be a tendency toward decreasing pitch (Honjo & Isshiki, 1980).

   b. Increases in cycle-to-cycle variation (pitch perturbation) in fundamental frequency appear to be related to biological health rather than chronological age (Ramig & Ringle, 1983).

   c. There is less pitch control and reduced pitch range with advanced age (Kahane, 1990; Linville & Fisher, 1985).

   d. Vocal quality symptoms of vocal roughness, aperiodicity, and breathiness are reported more frequently in elderly speakers (Case, 1996).

Chapter 3
The Voice Evaluation

◆ ◆

Evaluation of the characteristics of a voice disorder and the effect that disorder has on a patient's ability to communicate is a crucial first step in designing an appropriate program of management. The evaluation process involves the gathering of pertinent information (case history) from the patient and significant others, as well as collecting data on the patient's performance of various tasks. This information enables the speech–language pathologist to assess the voice disorder, determine the relative efficacy of various treatment approaches, and formulate a prognosis. This chapter details procedures that can be followed and questions that can be asked while obtaining a case history from a patient (see Table 3.1). Also included in this chapter are descriptions of numerous procedures that may be used when assessing a patient's respiratory, phonatory, and resonatory systems. A summary of those procedures is given in Table 3.2.

THE CASE HISTORY

The case history is a collection of information that is critical to the evaluation and treatment of a voice disorder. While much of this information can be provided by the patient, certain portions of the case history may be contributed by a parent, spouse, teacher, physician, or other persons who are familiar with various aspects of the patient's life. Not all of the case history information has to be given verbally. The patient can complete written questionnaires before his or her initial visit to the clinic, and letters or reports from physicians and other professionals may be included.

I. **Informal familiarization period.** Preceding the actual period of information gathering, clinicians should familiarize themselves with their patients by engaging them in casual conversation. This familiarization period provides patients with an opportunity to relax and become comfortable with both the situation and the examiner.

   A. **Evaluation of general aspects of communication.** The informal familiarization period provides the clinician with an excellent opportunity to evaluate the more general aspects of a patient's communication skills. Because a voice disorder may be a symptom of other underlying problems, it is important to spend time in informal conversation with the patient.

      1. **Expected patient behavior.** The patient should be able to function in a reasonably comfortable manner in a conversational setting. Conversation should flow smoothly, with only limited signs of discomfort appearing in the patient.

Table 3.1. Summary of the Information Required for a Case History of a Patient with a Voice Disorder

---

Obtain

Basic biographical information
Health history

Have the patient describe

The voice disorder in his or her own words
Other people's reactions to the voice disorder
The effects of the voice disorder on his or her life
What he or she believes caused the voice disorder
The onset and course of the voice disorder

> 2. **Inappropriate patient behavior.** Patients who struggle with the social aspects of communication may exhibit the following symptoms:
>
>   a. **Failure to maintain normal eye contact.** Some patients may find that conversation during the informal familiarization period is very difficult. One of the first signs of this discomfort may be the patient's inability to maintain eye contact. During normal conversational situations, the speaker glances, at least occasionally, into the eyes of the listener. In these normal situations, eye contact consists of a relaxed, friendly exchange of gazes. Looks should not develop into discourteous and disquieting stares. When engaged in conversation with patients, be sure to notice whether they are able to maintain normal eye contact with you or whether they avert their eyes to other parts of the testing room.
>
>   b. **Frequent postural adjustments.** Another symptom of conversational anxiety is inability to maintain a comfortable posture while seated. While engaged in conversation during the informal familiarization period, note

Table 3.2. Summary of the Procedures Used in the Voice Evaluation Process

---

Obtain

An audiocasette- or videotape-recorded sample of the patient's voice (using standard reading passage)
A description of the patient's vocal fold structure and function from a laryngologist

Evaluate

Respiratory capabilities
Strength of glottal closure
Pitch range, optimal pitch, and habitual pitch
Vocal loudness level
Voice quality
Endurance for speech production
Sites of vocal hyperfunction
Oral–peripheral, motor, and sensory aspects of the patient's speech musculature

---

whether the patient is able to sit comfortably in the chair or whether there are constant postural adjustments.

   c. **Rigidity of facial expression.** Conversational anxiety may be indicated in patients who maintain a rigid and unchanging facial expression. Facial expression should be constantly changing during a conversation, with the patient smiling during light, relaxing topics of discussion, and showing a more sober countenance when more serious subjects are being discussed.

B. **Initial impression of voice characteristics.** During this familiarization period the clinician should also record his or her initial impressions of the patient's voice pitch, loudness, and quality. Since this is done before the formal voice testing, it serves as a comparison to later clinical impressions.

II. **Basic background information** should be obtained from every patient. This information should be obtained by having the patient complete a written questionnaire or by asking the patient questions during the initial segment of the interview.

A. **Biographical information.** Basic biographical information about a patient should consist of the following:

1. Name

2. Date of birth

3. Address

4. Telephone number

5. Name of parent, guardian, or contact person

6. Names, ages, and sex of siblings

7. Occupation

8. Education

9. Name of referring agency

10. Family physician

11. Otolaryngologist

12. Medical record or patient number

B. **Health history.** The patient's health history may provide information related to the nature of the voice disorder. This information is generally obtained from the patient or from a parent if the patient is a child. Information should be obtained regarding each of the following:

1. Birth and neonatal period

2. Illnesses (including allergies)

3. Accidents

4. Hospitalizations

5. Medications

    6. Previous contacts with an otolaryngologist or speech–language pathologist

    7. Previous contacts with a psychologist or psychiatrist

III. Patient's description of the voice disorder. One of the most important and revealing sections of the case history involves the patient's description of the voice disorder and what has caused it. This description allows the clinician to better understand the disorder as the patient sees it. Frequently, the patient's description of the voice disorder does not agree with the description of a referring speech–language pathologist or physician. This discrepancy may be due in part to the patient's misunderstanding of the problem.

It is best if the patient has recognized that he or she has a voice disorder and has sought help to remedy it. This is especially important from the standpoint of motivation. Patients who fail to acknowledge they have a voice disorder or who have families that do not consider the patient's voice to be a problem are often poorly motivated to change their voice production.

Probably the best way to understand the impact that a voice disorder has on a patient's life is to listen carefully to the description of the voice disorder as given by the patient. Of special importance are any social or emotional factors that the patient believes may cause the voice to vary. Note particularly the vocabulary that the patient chooses in describing the characteristics of the disorder and its impact on his or her personal and professional life. If subtle signs of concern are evidenced during the description of the voice, be sure to note them. Many times these concerns need to be addressed regardless of whatever else the voice evaluation reveals.

A. Other people's reactions to the voice disorder. Ask the patient to describe how others react to the voice disorder. Some patients report that no one has commented about their voice. It is important not to stop your line of questioning if your patient says that no one has commented about the voice disorder. Some patients do not relate information about others' reactions to their voices unless they are gently prodded to do so. The most important issue, nonetheless, is not other people's reactions to the voice disorder, but how the patient feels about those reactions.

B. Patient's rating of the severity of the voice disorder: The following are methods for obtaining a patient's rating of the severity of the voice disorder:

    1. Method 1 simply involves asking the patient to rate his or her voice on a 1 to 5 scale, where 1 represents *normal* and 5 represents *severe*.

    2. Method 2 is a much better method of obtaining a severity rating. Ask the patient to compare his or her voice with a clinician-made audiotape of several voices, with each voice representing an increasing degree of severity. This type of comparison is often fairly easy for the patient to make. Voice tapes also give the clinician an opportunity to ask the patient which prerecorded voice is most like the voice that the patient desires or expects after voice therapy is completed (some patients may choose a voice that is slightly less than "perfect"). This choice, even if it represents a less than perfect voice, nonetheless gives both the patient and the clinician a target voice at which to aim.

C. Patient's description of the effects of the voice disorder. Ask the patient to describe how much the voice disorder affects his or her daily life.

1. Have the patient rate the effect that the voice disorder has on his or her daily life on a 1 to 5 scale, where 1 represents *no effect* and 5 represents a voice disorder that is *totally disabling*.

2. Compare the patient's severity rating of the voice disorder (see **III.B**) to the degree that the disorder is disruptive to the patient's life. Most of the time, a dysphonia that receives a high severity rating is also noted as being more disruptive to the patient's lifestyle.

D. Patient's description of what caused the voice disorder. Ask the patient to explain what caused the voice disorder. It is interesting to compare the patient's description of what caused the voice disorder with the etiologies hypothesized by a referring physician or speech–language pathologist. Often, any differences between the patient's perception of what caused the voice disorder and suspected or confirmed etiologies must be bridged before voice therapy can be completed successfully. The patient's misconceptions should be eliminated early in the therapy process, and the patient should repeatedly be given a clear explanation of what caused the disorder until he or she demonstrates signs of understanding.

Patients who have poor vocal habits that have resulted in vocal abuse and who report causes that they believe are external to themselves may have difficulty believing that changes in their vocal behaviors will improve their voice. Patients who cannot understand that their behaviors may have contributed to their voice disorders must be made to understand that the prognosis for voice improvement is very poor.

E. Patient's description of the onset of the voice disorder. Often, the patient's description of the onset of the voice disorder can be extremely important in the formulation of both a diagnosis and prognosis.

1. **Patients with voice disorders that have developed and continued over a long period of time** may find it quite difficult to recall much, if any, detail about the onset. This is because the vocal symptoms of some voice disorders emerge gradually over a long period of time, and, as a result, it may be a long time before the patient is aware of the subtle changes that are occurring in his or her voice. For this reason, patients may find it difficult to recall the month and year that the voice disorder began. Nevertheless, these patients should be encouraged to try to recall the **date of onset** as closely as possible.

   For the same reason that pinpointing the date of onset is difficult, getting the patient to provide an accurate **description of the onset** of the voice disorder is also difficult. Nevertheless, gentle prompting and careful questioning can occasionally elicit vital information regarding the onset from a patient who initially responded with an "I can't remember."

   On the other hand, do not question the patient so intently that he or she feels compelled to provide information even if it has to be fabricated. As an examiner, it is better to err on the side of not prompting the patient enough than to put a patient in a position where the patient feels coerced to provide information, even if it is untrue.

2. **Patients with voice disorders that had a sudden onset** are usually more disturbed about the disorder and are often able to describe the onset with much detail.

3. **Speed of onset as an indicator of etiology.** The speed with which a voice disorder appears is usually a clue to the general etiology of the dysphonia.

   a. **Voice disorders with abrupt onset.** Dysphonias that develop abruptly over a period of 1 to 2 days (or perhaps even a few hours or minutes) may be caused by conversion disorders.

   Although dysphonias with other causes (e.g., paralysis of cranial nerve X caused by a cerebrovascular accident [CVA], severe head cold accompanied by laryngitis, or trauma to the larynx) can also have an abrupt onset, there are usually other accompanying symptoms that enable the clinician to differentiate these dysphonias from conversion dysphonia.

   b. **Voice disorders with slow onset.** In making a diagnosis, the clinician must remember that both organic and functional dysphonias can have a slow, insidious onset. Many organic dysphonias, such as those that are neurologically based or the result of growths affecting vocal fold vibration, tend to develop over periods ranging from several weeks to months or years. Similarly, many functional dysphonias (especially those due to excessive musculoskeletal tension) also develop over a period of weeks, months, and possibly years. Consequently, other information besides speed of onset must be obtained and carefully considered before an accurate diagnosis can be made.

4. **Patients with other symptoms associated with voice disorder onset.** Patients may report events that were associated with the onset of the voice disorder. If not, patients must be asked direct questions so that this important diagnostic information can be obtained. Of particular importance to the clinician are neurologic, emotional, and stress-related symptoms that are reported by the patient to have been associated with the onset.

   a. It is important to further investigate any **neurologic symptoms** reported by the patient. The following are symptoms associated with the onset of voice disorder due to a neurologic disorder:

      (1) Difficulty swallowing

      (2) Nasal regurgitation of liquids

      (3) Nasal regurgitation of solids

      Patients who experience a sudden onset of dysphonia as a result of paralysis of the laryngeal musculature caused by a **CVA** usually experience paralysis in other body muscles as well and demonstrate related neurologic symptoms (e.g., aphasia, apraxia). It is unlikely that the laryngeal musculature would be the only muscles involved in a patient who has experienced a stroke.

    b. It is important to note any **emotional or stress-related symptoms** that the patient reports as being associated with the onset of the voice disorder. Of particular interest should be the following symptoms:

        (1) Stress and anxiety related to **other medical problems** that the patient suffers from.

        (2) Stress related to **personal problems** or **problems of adjustment.**

        (3) Job-related stress, which may be caused by:

            (a) Occupational settings that are naturally stressful and require employees to do a great deal of talking under considerable tension

            (b) Dissatisfaction with vocation resulting in emotional strain

F. **The patient's description of the course of the voice disorder since onset.** The patient should be asked to describe any fluctuation in severity of the voice disorder since its onset (i.e., has the dysphonia been episodic or continuous?).

    1. Voices that periodically return to normal. Reports of episodic dysphonia, with the voice returning to normal for periods of hours or days, are common in patients with voice disorders due to musculoskeletal tension or functional dysphonia. It is important to question the patient closely about any episodes of voice improvement in order to ascertain whether the voice did indeed return to normal and, if so, under what conditions.

    2. Voices that never improve. As a general rule, voice disorders due to neurologic involvement or mass lesions of the vocal folds do not improve spontaneously. Although there may be time periods when the severity of the dysphonia remains unchanged, the major trend is for the voice to steadily deteriorate.

    3. Voices that worsen during periods of emotional stress. The clinician must be aware that emotional stress can cause a dysphonia to worsen regardless of whether it is organically caused. Reports of worsened voice production during periods of emotional stress must be carefully considered against the background of the patient's total picture of voice variation since onset of the dysphonia.

THE VOICE EVALUATION PROCESS

The voice evaluation process should begin after completion of the case history. Procedures used in the evaluation process are summarized in Table 3.2. Generally, the entire voice evaluation should be recorded on either audiocasette or videotape. For most purposes, an audiocasette recording is sufficient; however, when there are visual elements that accompany the voice disorder, videotape recordings can also be extremely useful aids to voice therapy. Although patients are frequently distracted by the sight of themselves upon initially viewing a videotape recording, this reaction to their physical appearance tends to decrease with repeated exposure. Consequently, these patients are able to become much more objective in their evaluations of their own vocal productions when they can see as well as hear themselves.

I. **Purposes of the voice evaluation.** The voice evaluation process is implemented to allow the clinician to make several determinations regarding the patient's voice. The three most important elements of the evaluation are (1) a detailed description of the patient's voice characteristics and how those characteristics vary over time, (2) a determination of how severe the patient's voice disorder is, and (3) a determination as to whether the patient would benefit from a program of voice therapy.

   A. One outcome of the evaluation process should be a **complete description of the patient's voice.** It is better to use descriptive statements about the patient's voice, if possible, than to use labels. Describe what the patient does well, what the patient does poorly, and what the patient is unable to do. The description of the patient's voice should include a hypothesis regarding the possible etiology of the vocal pathology or dysfunction.

   B. **Severity rating.** The speech–language pathologist will be able to make a judgment regarding the severity of the patient's voice disorder based on the voice evaluation. Numerical rating scales are useful and may provide the best method for making judgments about severity. The number of units in the rating scale and an indication of which end of the scale represents "normal" voice should be specified. Subjective descriptions of severity (e.g., mild, moderate, severe) are also potentially useful, although they tend to be more general and, therefore, less meaningful than a numerical rating scale.

   In addition to personally constructed severity rating scales, the speech–language pathologist may choose to use one of two widely used severity rating systems that have been developed for the purpose of providing a descriptive profile of a patient's voice. The Voice Profile, developed by F. B. Wilson and Rice (1977) and still often used today, contains one section in which the patient's voice severity is rated on a 7-point scale. Other sections of the profile have scales that are used to describe the patient's degree of laryngeal opening during phonation, pitch, and degree of nasality. Similarly, the Buffalo Voice Profile, designed by D. K. Wilson (1979), and the *Boone Voice Program for Children* rating scale (Boone, 1993) consist of a series of scales that the clinician can use in evaluating various parameters of the patient's voice. The advantage of using either of these two voice profiles is that they provide the clinician with the opportunity to make several simultaneous severity evaluations concerning various aspects of the patient's voice rather than trying to describe the patient's voice with a single index of severity.

   C. **Determining candidacy for voice therapy.** After completion of the evaluation process the speech–language pathologist should not only be able to make an accurate diagnosis of the patient's dysphonia, but should also be able to formulate a statement regarding the patient's potential to benefit appreciably from voice therapy.

      1. **Statement of prognosis.** The prognosis for improved vocal function in the patient is related to and dependent on the following:

         a. Degree of organic involvement and structural and functional integrity of the laryngeal mechanism.

         b. Degree of patient motivation and willingness to change vocal behaviors.

    c. Patient's ability to objectively discern changes in his or her own vocal behavior.

The prognosis for voice improvement is best for patients who report a sudden onset. Because a dysphonia with a sudden onset frequently has immediate impact on the patient's daily activities, the patient is generally well-motivated and usually quite anxious to be rid of the restrictions caused by the dysphonia.

The prognosis for voice improvement is poorer for patients who report a long-term chronic dysphonia. Often, patients with dysphonias of long standing have had the time to adapt to the gradual changes in their voices and are relatively undisturbed by the presence of the dysphonia. These patients may not seek the assistance of a speech–language pathologist on their own but more often do so at the insistence of their physician, spouse, or friends.

    2. **Uncertain prognosis.** If the prognosis for improvement of the voice is uncertain and the possible benefits of voice therapy are unclear at the end of the evaluation, a statement recommending a trial period of therapy is acceptable. Such a recommendation for trial voice therapy should *always* include a statement regarding the length of time that the trial therapy should continue.

II. **Standard reading paragraph.** One of the first steps in the voice evaluation involves asking the patient to read aloud a standard paragraph such as "The Rainbow Passage" (Fairbanks, 1960; see Appendix A for examples of the most commonly used standard paragraphs).

    A. The clinician should **listen** as carefully and objectively as possible to the patient, not forgetting to retain an analytical attitude.

        1. Remember: **the ear is the best instrument** available for evaluating the voice. Critical listening to the patient is essential.

        2. **Learn to trust what you hear.** Do not allow your objectivity to be swayed by your knowledge of the patient's case history, medical history, or diagnosis from another professional. This is not to say that this information is not important to your final diagnosis, but do not "hear" characteristics in the voice that are not present and do not ignore critical elements in the voice that have been previously unreported.

    B. Evaluate. Make judgments about the patient's voice while listening to the patient read the standard paragraph aloud. Judgments should be made regarding the following:

        1. Overall **severity** of the dysphonia

        2. General **aesthetic quality** of the voice

        3. **Intelligibility**

III. **A description of the structure and function** of the patient's vocal folds is essential in making an accurate diagnosis of the voice disorder. Not only is knowledge of vocal fold structure and function important during the initial evaluation of a patient, but periodic reports describing any changes in the condition of the vocal folds during the course of voice therapy are invaluable in many cases.

Examination of the vocal folds is a task that is usually performed by a medical specialist called an otolaryngologist. The otolaryngologist is trained to use several methods to view the vocal folds, but a procedure called **indirect laryngoscopy** or a procedure known as **stroboscopy** are the most frequently used. Indirect laryngoscopy is performed by placing a laryngeal mirror into the pharynx and observing the vocal folds at rest and during sustained phonation, usually of the vowel /i/. Additionally, the otolaryngologist examines other features of the larynx and structures related to it.

Stroboscopy is a procedure that allows inspection of the vibratory movement of the vocal folds during phonation. The human eye can only visualize approximately 5 images per second, whereas the vocal folds can vibrate several hundred times per second. When the strobe light illuminates the larynx at a pulse rate faster than 5 images per second, the eye perceives the images as continuous motion. Thus, stroboscopy permits a visual–perceptual composite of vocal fold motion (Hirano & Bless, 1993). Additionally, the stroboscopic camera can be connected to a video recording device that allows recording and playback. This capability allows the speech–language pathologist to maintain video baseline information for later comparison following voice management. Stroboscopy is not a substitute for the otolaryngologist's expertise using indirect laryngoscopy, but it is a valuable tool for observing vocal fold movement.

Indirect laryngoscopy and stroboscopy are not difficult procedures to learn and many speech–language pathologists have been trained in their use. The use of indirect laryngoscopy or stroboscopy by speech–language pathologists, however, should be limited to viewing the vocal folds to evaluate the progress of voice therapy. The speech–language pathologist should never use the procedure for diagnosis of laryngeal conditions. Diagnosis of laryngeal conditions is clearly the responsibility of the otolaryngologist, who is trained in the identification and treatment of laryngeal pathologies.

IV. **Evaluation of respiration** involves assessment of the patient's ability to control the respiratory mechanism for speaking as well as for vegetative purposes. The general diagnostic question that needs to be addressed is, "Does this patient have sufficient air supply and neuromuscular control of the respiratory mechanism to communicate effectively?"

   A. **Initial observation of the patient's use of the respiratory system.** An in-depth respiratory diagnosis is not required for the majority of patients with voice disorders. Many times, the question of whether the patient is using the respiratory system efficiently enough to effect functional communication can be answered through careful observation of the patient while he or she performs the following four tasks:

   1. **Read aloud the standard paragraph** such as "The Rainbow Passage." (Fairbanks, 1960; see Appendix A).

      a. In people with **normal voices,** termination of phrases or sentences coincides with the termination of exhalation.

      b. Some patients with **voice disorders** attempt to continue speaking past the point where there is sufficient airflow to effect efficient phonation, thus resulting in an increase in laryngeal tension. This behavior may occur in patients who have adequate lung capacity for sustaining speech but nonetheless run out of air because of:

> **(1)** An inability to adequately monitor the amount of air remaining in the lungs for speaking purposes.

> **(2)** A pattern of exhaling much of the air in the lungs before phonation is initiated. This pattern may be due to poor neurologic control of the muscles of exhalation or due to a faulty learned pattern of phonation.

2. Perform a task of **sustained vowel production** (see **B.5.a** later in the chapter).

3. Perform a task of **sustained /s/ and /z/ productions** (see **B.5.b** later in the chapter).

4. Perform a task of **endurance for sustained speech production** (see **IX.A** later in the chapter).

B. Complete respiratory evaluation

1. **Indications.** If a patient has audible speech, a complete respiratory evaluation is not generally warranted. The respiratory system normally provides considerably more flow, volume, and pressure than what is required for speech and singing. Therefore, it is probably not necessary to spend inordinate amounts of time gathering respiratory data for most voice patients (Colton & Casper, 1996). Careful observation of the patient during the evaluation process usually is sufficient for allowing judgments to be made regarding the patient's control of the respiratory mechanism. There are, however, some patients who may require a complete respiratory evaluation. A complete evaluation of the respiratory system may necessitate referral to a respiratory physiologist or other respiratory specialist. The complete respiratory evaluation is generally indicated for the following:

    a. Patients who exhibit **respiratory difficulties,** such as struggling to get enough air or shortness of breath while reading the standard paragraph, or who perform poorly on tasks of sustained vowel production and endurance for sustained speech production

    b. Patients who are affected by any of the following:

    > **(1) Emphysema or other chronic pulmonary disease**

    > **(2)** The later stages of **Parkinson's disease**

    > **(3) Cerebral palsy** (particularly if the patient is a child)

2. **Special instrumentation required.** A respiratory evaluation frequently requires specialized instruments that are generally unavailable to many speech–language pathologists. These instruments might include the following:

    a. Spirometers. Spirometers permit measurement of respiratory volumes.

    b. Strain gauges

    c. Magnetometers

d. Strain gauges, magnetometers, and plethysmographs are noninvasive devices that measure respiratory movements. All of these devices are commercially available, and all require some degree of expertise in their use (Colton & Casper, 1996).

3. **Information regarding lung volumes.** If a complete respiratory evaluation is performed, the following data about lung volumes may be obtained (Landau, 1980):

   a. Vital capacity (the amount of air that can be exhaled following maximal inspiration). Vital capacity measures average 4,800 ml for males and 3,200 ml for females.

   b. Tidal volume (the amount of air that is inspired and expired during a normal, relaxed cycle of breathing) averages about 500 ml for both men and women.

   c. Inspiratory reserve volume (the maximum amount of air that can be inspired following a tidal inspiration). This averages about 3,200 ml in males and 2,000 ml in females.

   d. Expiratory reserve volume (the maximum amount of air that can be expired following a tidal expiration) averages about 1,100 ml in males and 700 ml in females.

4. **Type of respiration pattern.** An occasional patient demonstrates the type of breathing pattern that is often referred to as **clavicular breathing.**

   a. Clavicular breathing is characterized by elevation of the shoulders and expansion of only the upper chest as the patient inhales. This method of respiration may require that the neck muscles be used for inspiration, which tends to result in increased laryngeal tension. This particular type of breathing may affect voice production because of insufficient air intake as well.

   b. Thoracic breathing is characterized by expansion of the midthoracic region during inspiration (Boone & McFarlane, 1994). Although this type of breathing is frequently used by the general population, it is not sufficient to support heavy vocal demands, such as those of an actor or singer.

   c. Diaphragmatic–abdominal breathing is characterized by expansion of the lower thoracic and abdominal cavities during inspiration. This is the most efficient method of respiration because it allows for the greatest exchange of air in and out of the lungs and is mechanically one of the easiest ways to breathe. This method, however, should not be dictated for all voice patients, but rather should be taught to individuals who make heavy demands on their respiratory systems.

5. **Evaluation of phonatory and respiratory efficiency.** The patient's glottal efficiency during phonation and the patient's ability to effectively control the forces of expiration (elastic muscle force, rib recoil, lung tissue pressure, gravity) should be assessed by use of one of the following methods:

   a. Sustained vowel production task for measurement of maximum phonation time. Patients should be able to produce an adequate amount of air and be able to sustain phonation long enough to communicate efficiently. A sustained vowel production task is one method of obtaining a measure called **maximum phonation time** (MPT), or the maximum length of time that a patient can sustain phonation on a single breath. Many parameters of phonation can be examined simultaneously by asking the patient to sustain front, back, high, middle, and low vowels at various loudness levels for as long and as steadily as possible. Use a stopwatch to time three sustained productions. Timing starts at the initiation of phonation and ends when voicing ceases. For evaluation purposes, use the longest sustained phonation time as a measure of the patient's MPT.

(1) Use of MPT for evaluation of **respiratory and glottal closure efficiency.** Probably the most important use of the sustained vowel production task (MPT) is as a measure of the efficiency of glottal closure and efficiency of the respiratory system. The patient's MPT for a task of sustained vowel production should be measured in seconds and recorded. Although most normal adults can sustain vowel production for 15 to 20 seconds, a minimum sustained time of 14.3 seconds for adult females and 15.0 seconds for adult males is acceptable (Hirano, Koike, & von Leden, 1968). Children in early elementary school should typically be able to sustain vowels for approximately 10 seconds (D. K. Wilson, 1979). Shortened duration of the patient's MPT may be due to insufficient respiratory functioning.

(2) **Inadequate respiratory support for sustained phonation** may be related to the following:

(a) the use of inefficient patterns of respiration that result in reduced vital capacity,

(b) neurologic involvement of the respiratory system, which can result in reduced vital capacity because of muscular incoordination or paresis, and lack of coordination between the onset of phonation and expiration, and

(c) a faulty learned pattern of speaking that is characterized by poor coordination of the onset of phonation with expiration.

(3) The clinician can use the sustained vowel production task to make a tentative evaluation of the appropriateness of pitch, loudness, and quality that can later be compared to more extensive diagnostic information (see **VI, VII, VIII** later in the chapter).

b. **Sustained s/z production task for measurement of phonatory and respiratory efficiency.** Another task for assessment of the patient's efficiency in controlling exhalation and phonation is one that requires the patient to make sustained productions of the unvoiced phoneme /s/ and the voiced phoneme /z/ (Boone & McFarlane, 1994). This task makes it possible to estimate to what degree a dysphonia is related to poor expiratory and laryngeal control by examining the ratio between the maximum length of time that a patient can sustain the /s/ and the maximum time she or he can sustain the /z/. Deviations from the normative standards for this ratio may be indicative of respiratory and phonatory inefficiency. The steps of the sustained s/z production task are as follows:

(1) Ask the patient to take a breath and to **sustain the production** of an /s/ for as long as possible. Record this time in seconds. The average sustained production of /s/ has been found to be:

    (a) Approximately 10 seconds in prepubertal **children** (Tait, Michel, & Carpenter, 1980).

    (b) Approximately 20 to 25 seconds in **adults** (Ptacek & Sander, 1963).

(2) After recording the patient's time for sustaining the /s/, ask the patient to take another breath and to **sustain the production** of a /z/ for as long as possible. Record this time in seconds.

    (a) Patients with no vocal fold pathology and no respiratory difficulties should be able to sustain the /z/ for about the same length of time as the /s/, resulting in an /s/ to /z/ ratio of approximately 1.0.

    (b) Patients who have no vocal fold pathology but who have either decreased control of the expiratory forces or reduced vital capacity demonstrate reduced average times for sustaining of both the /s/ and /z/ phonemes. Although the time for the sustained productions is reduced for these patients, the s/z ratio is still approximately 1.0.

    (c) Patients with problems of laryngeal valving are usually able to sustain the nonphonated /s/ for the normal length of time, but may demonstrate shortened duration of the /z/ phoneme, a voiced consonant that requires phonation for production. When a patient demonstrates large time differences (approximately a 2:1 ratio) for the two tasks, it is indicative of poor laryngeal control rather than poor control of expiratory forces. Eckel and Boone (1981) found that 95% of their patients with laryngeal pathologies had s/z ratios that were greater than 1.40. To ensure that nearly all patients with laryngeal pathologies are identified, it has been recommended that an s/z ratio greater than or equal to 1.20 be used as the cutoff value (Boone, 1980).

6. **Evaluation of extraneous respiratory noises.** As the patient performs various speech and nonspeech tasks, the clinician should listen carefully and determine whether the patient's inspirations and expirations are audible or not. Normal vegetative breathing should be relatively silent. Excessive noise (stridor) during inspiration or expiration should be investigated medically. **Stridor** may be due to any of the following:

    a. Asthma

    b. Nasal blockage

    c. Laryngeal neoplasms

      d. Laryngeal webs

      e. Abductor weakness or paralysis of the vocal folds

V. Evaluation of strength of glottal closure. It is important to attempt to make an assessment of the strength of the patient's vocal fold adduction. To do this, instruct the patient to cough sharply, clear the throat, or produce a vowel with a hard glottal attack (an abrupt release of the vocal folds associated with vowel production). Neuromuscular weakness is indicated by a "mushy" cough, weak throat clearing, or a soft glottal attack.

VI. Evaluation of the various measures of pitch—pitch range, optimal pitch, and habitual pitch—can be accomplished using some relatively simple techniques and a tape recorder. Also, the speech–language pathologist can choose to assess these measures using instrumentation such as Kay Elemetrics' Computerized Speech Lab (CSL) Program, which includes several options, such as the MultiDimensional Voice Profile (MDVP) and Visi-Pitch II (also called CSL Pitch). See Appendix C for more information on these programs. Pitch and amplitude perturbations (or cycle-to-cycle variation in fundamental frequency and amplitude) can also be measured with this instrumentation.

    A. Evaluation of pitch range

        1. Use the following procedure to **obtain a voice sample** that can be used to evaluate the patient's pitch range.

            a. Procedure for obtaining sample of lowest pitch. Using an audiocasette or videotape recorder, have the patient begin in the middle of his or her pitch range, and sing down the scale one tone at a time to the lowest pitch that can be phonated. (Some patients may be reluctant to "sing" the tones. A reasonable substitute would be to have the patient count from 1 to 25 while simultaneously dropping the pitch of each spoken number until the lowest vocal pitch is reached.) Each tone should be phonated for approximately 1 to 2 seconds. The quality of phonation at the lowest pitch is unimportant—the primary concern should be that the patient is phonating the lowest pitch possible without the voice going into the range of vocal fry. This procedure should be repeated three times, and the lowest pitch that is obtained should be recorded.

            b. Procedure for obtaining sample of highest pitch. Once the patient's lowest possible pitch has been determined, the patient should start again at a comfortable midrange, then sing up the scale one tone at a time to the highest pitch that can be reached (including falsetto). Again, the quality of phonation is unimportant. Have the patient repeat this procedure at least three times. The patient should be cautioned not to hurry through this procedure but to concentrate on phonating each tone separately until the highest and lowest possible pitches are produced.

        2. Determine pitch range by finding the most extreme pitches that the patient is able to produce.

            a. Procedure for determining pitches. Once the patient's voice sample has been obtained, replay the audiocasette- or tape-recorded sample and identify the most frequent pitches (or the mean frequencies) that the patient produces at each end of the pitch range. These pitches can be measured by matching the recorded tones to a pitch pipe, musical instrument, or other instrument that can be used for pitch analysis, such as Visi-Pitch II (see Appendix C for more information).

   b. **Procedure for determining pitch range.** The patient's complete range of pitch can be determined by recording the highest and lowest notes the patient can phonate and then counting the number of tones present in the patient's complete range. Pitch range can be described either in reference to a range of musical notes (e.g., E_3-C_5) or as a frequency range (e.g., 165–523 Hz). Use Table 3.3 to convert your obtained values from musical notes to pitch frequencies, or vice versa, or play the signals into an instrument such as CSL Pitch and the values will be determined automatically.

B. **Evaluation of optimal pitch.** There is considerable controversy surrounding the concept of optimum pitch. In fact, Colton and Casper (1996, p. 312) refer to the "myth of optimum pitch." Theoretically, optimal pitch has been defined as the pitch level at which the voice is produced most efficiently, with the least

Table 3.3. Musical Notes and Approximate Equivalent Frequencies for the Tempered Musical Scale

| | | | | | | | | | Musical Note: | A_0 | $A_0^\sharp$ | B_0 |
									Frequency (Hz):	28	29	31
C_1	$C_1^\sharp$	D_1	$D_1^\sharp$	E_1	F_1	$F_1^\sharp$	G_1	$G_1^\sharp$	A_1	$A_1^\sharp$	B_1	
33	35	37	39	41	44	46	49	52	55	58	62	
C_2	$C_2^\sharp$	D_2	$D_2^\sharp$	E_2	F_2	$F_2^\sharp$	G_2	$G_2^\sharp$	A_2	$A_2^\sharp$	B_2	
65	69	73	78	82	87	92	98	104	110	117	123	
C_3	$C_3^\sharp$	D_3	$D_3^\sharp$	E_3	F_3	$F_3^\sharp$	G_3	$G_3^\sharp$	A_3	$A_3^\sharp$	B_3	
131	139	147	156	165	175	185	196	208	220	233	247	
C_4	$C_4^\sharp$	D_4	$D_4^\sharp$	E_4	F_4	$F_4^\sharp$	G_4	$G_4^\sharp$	A_4	$A_4^\sharp$	B_4	
262	277	294	311	330	349	370	392	415	440	466	494	
C_5	$C_5^\sharp$	D_5	$D_5^\sharp$	E_5	F_5	$F_5^\sharp$	G_5	$G_5^\sharp$	A_5	$A_5^\sharp$	B_5	
523	554	587	622	659	698	740	784	831	880	932	988	
C_6	$C_6^\sharp$	D_6	$D_6^\sharp$	E_6	F_6	$F_6^\sharp$	G_6	$G_6^\sharp$	A_6	$A_6^\sharp$	B_6	
1,047	1,109	1,175	1,245	1,319	1,397	1,480	1,568	1,661	1,760	1,865	1,976	
C_7	$C_7^\sharp$	D_7	$D_7^\sharp$	E_7	F_7	$F_7^\sharp$	G_7	$G_7^\sharp$	A_7	$A_7^\sharp$	B_7	
2,093	2,218	2,349	2,489	2,637	2,794	2,960	3,136	3,322	3,520	3,729	3,951	
C_8												
4,186												

amount of laryngeal tension, and with the greatest ease of physical effort. Optimal pitch may be determined by the anatomic and physiologic characteristics of individual larynges, and as a result it is the biologically determined "ideal" pitch for a particular patient. Although the concept of optimal pitch remains controversial, some speech–language pathologists use the following methods to obtain a general estimate of the patient's optimum pitch:

1. **Method 1.** Fairbanks (1960) has suggested a standard method whereby optimal pitch can be calculated from a measure of the patient's pitch range (including falsetto). Following this method, simply count the number of full-step musical notes present in the patient's complete pitch range. Optimal pitch for adult males is one-fourth of the way up from the bottom of the total pitch range. Optimal pitch for females is generally several notes lower than this one-fourth measure of their total pitch range.

2. **Method 2.** A simpler method of determining the optimum speaking pitch is to have the patient say "uh-huh" as if responding in agreement to a relaxed, conversational yes/no question. It is important to monitor the patient to ensure that both syllables are phonated at the same pitch level. The pitch at which "uh-huh" is phonated is generally the patient's optimal pitch.

3. **Method 3.** A third method of obtaining optimal pitch involves asking the patient to yawn and then to sigh. The pitch of the relaxed sigh is often the patient's optimal pitch.

C. **Evaluation of habitual pitch.** Habitual pitch (modal frequency level), or the pitch that the patient uses most often in everyday speech, should be determined so that it can be compared to the pitch that has been determined to be optimal for that particular patient's laryngeal mechanism. If the obtained habitual and optimal pitch levels differ by several tones, voice therapy may be indicated. Habitual pitch varies slightly in different settings, but the general habitual pitch level can be determined easily for most patients by using one or both of the following methods:

1. **Method 1.** A measure of habitual pitch can be obtained from an audiocasette or videotape recording of the patient while he or she is engaged in conversation and while reading a selected passage (see **II.B** earlier in the chapter). The tape recorder should be stopped at eight to ten different places in the sample so that the pitch of the patient's voice can be matched to a pitch pipe or a musical instrument. It is important that several such measures be taken, since it is the patient's most frequently used pitch (modal pitch level) that is to be determined. It is much easier to match vocal pitch with a pitch pipe or musical instrument when you can start with a close approximation of the pitch you are trying to determine. As a general rule, you should start with the pitch that has been found to be the average for people of the patient's age and sex. Normal frequency value guidelines are given in Table 3.4.

2. **Method 2.** A second method of determining a patient's habitual pitch is through the use of an instrument that has been specifically designed for pitch analysis. There are instruments (e.g., CSL Pitch Program or Video-Voice Speech Training System; see Appendix C) available commercially that can extract the fundamental frequency and display it digitally as a patient

Table 3.4. Suggested Starting Points for Determining Habitual Vocal Pitches

Age of Patient	Males		Females	
	Nearest Musical Note	F_o	Nearest Musical Note	F_o
3	G_4	400	$F\sharp_4$	380
4	$F\sharp_4$	375	F_4	355
5	F_4	350	E_4	335
6	E_4	325	D_4	295
7	D_4	295	$C\sharp_4$	280
8	D_4	295	$C\sharp_4$	275
9	C_4	260	$C\sharp_4$	275
10	B_3	245	C_4	265
11	A_3	225	C_4	265
12	$G\sharp_3$	210	C_4	260
13	G_3	195	B_3	245
14	F_3	180	$A\sharp_3$	235
15	E_3	165	A_3	220
16	D_3	150	A_3	215
17	$C\sharp_3$	135	$G\sharp_3$	210
Adult	B_2	124	$A\sharp_3$	227

Note. Adapted from *Voice Problems of Children* (2nd ed.), by D. K. Wilson, 1979, Baltimore: William & Wilkins.
F_o = fundamental frequency.

speaks into a microphone that is connected to the instrument. These pitch analysis instruments can be extremely useful for determining not only the patient's habitual pitch level, but also for determining the total pitch range and degree of pitch inflection.

Recent advances in technology will now permit clinicians to take advantage of speech analysis programs that had previously been prohibitively expensive because expensive hardware and software systems were necessary. Kay Elemetrics now offers a lower cost program called Multi-Speech, which is a Windows-based speech analysis software program using standard PC computer hardware to capture, analyze, and play speech samples (see Appendix C). It is designed for those clinics, universities, or individuals with limited budgets or for those who wish to outfit multiple computers with sophisticated speech analysis software. Multi-Speech contains virtually all of the powerful analysis and editing features of the core CSL Program software. However, like all programs based on multimedia hardware, Multi-Speech is limited by the performance of the host computer. Software-only speech analysis programs are now available from several vendors.

Tiger Electronics offers a Windows-based speech and voice analysis software system called Dr. Speech. As with Multi-Speech, Dr. Speech performs sophisticated speech analyses using a standard PC computer without the cost of additional hardware. Another similar software-only system that performs voice analyses is the EZ Voice Program. These software-only speech and voice analysis systems represent a significant improvement in the transition from research to the clinic. With the rapidly increasing processing speed and memory of desktop computers, speech and voice analyses that were limited to the laboratory are becoming more accessible to the clinician. See Appendix C for more information about these programs.

D. **Evaluation of pitch perturbations.** One quantitative way of evaluating whether a patient's vocal folds are vibrating normally or abnormally is to measure the cycle-to-cycle changes that occur in fundamental frequency. The degree of pitch perturbation is a possible indicator of vocal fold pathology (Deem, Manning, Knack, & Matesich, 1991; Iwata & von Leden, 1970). Normal speakers with no vocal fold pathology usually show only minor pitch perturbations, while patients with vocal fold pathology show more frequent and irregular changes in fundamental frequency.

Pitch pertubations (**jitter**) and amplitude perturbations (**shimmer**) can be extracted from the voice through use of a number of commercially available computer-based instruments, such as CSL Pitch Program and CSL with the MDVP option (see Appendix C). The MDVP option provides quantitative assessment of voice quality, calculating over 20 parameters on a single sustained vocalization, including perturbations.

It is important for the clinical voice pathologist to realize that there is an abundance of perturbation measures that use different formulae for calculating cycle-to-cycle variations in the voice. Because an agreement has not been reached about which formula is most appropriate for clinical voice analysis, it is difficult to apply normative data. However, a common method of reporting **jitter** is to establish a percentage figure. Jitter in percent is expected to be below 1% in speakers with normal voices. A common method for reporting **shimmer** (amplitude perturbation) is in decibels. Normative values for shimmer in decibels (dB) are usually in the range of 0.5 to 1.0 dB (or less). It would be wise for voice clinicians to read the user's manual for the clinical acoustic program they use to determine how the program extracts perturbation from the voice. By doing so, the clinician can refer to the literature to apply the appropriate normative data.

It is also important that the clinician not use perturbations as a single, decisive measure of vocal fold pathology. Pitch and amplitude perturbations provide little information unless combined with other voice parameters. Research in the professional literature reveals that one or two voice parameters are not sufficient in profiling a patient's voice. For example, jitter (pitch perturbation) values may fall within normal limits in a patient with breathy voice quality or tremor. By using a multidimensional approach, the clinician can more comprehensively assess the voice disorder and track changes over time.

E. **Evaluation of special pitch problems.** There are several voice problems related to pitch that cannot be easily evaluated using standard methods of pitch assessment. These special pitch problems and the techniques for evaluating them are as follows:

1. **Persistent falsetto.** Occasionally, postpubescent males exhibit a high-pitched, falsetto voice that is inappropriate. This falsetto voice emanates

from a structurally normal larynx that is capable of producing a normally pitched or low-pitched voice. Persistent use of falsetto beyond puberty probably originates from functional causes. Still, the best approach to confirm a diagnosis of persistent falsetto is the Gutzmann technique as described by Brodnitz (1958) and D. K. Wilson (1979). This technique is as follows:

a. Ask the patient to sustain a hum.

b. Place your fingers on the patient's thyroid cartilage and press gently downward. Ordinarily, this maneuver should produce a sudden lowering of the patient's pitch, because digital pressure causes a shortening of vocal fold length and a decrease in vocal fold tension. In patients who demonstrate functional persistent falsetto, however, this maneuver will usually cause the pitch to rise suddenly and then return to the original pitch. Before touching the patient, be sure to explain that you are going to touch her or his neck.

2. **Diplophonia** is a type of dysphonia characterized by the audible production of two distinct pitches during phonation. One pitch is generally normal, with the second pitch being lower than normal. Diplophonia is the result of two structures in the vocal tract vibrating at different rates. Opinions vary as to which structures are involved.

   a. Etiologies of diplophonia

   (1) **Unilateral paralysis of the true vocal folds,** which causes the folds to vibrate at unequal rates during phonation

   (2) **Vibration of the ventricular folds,** which may vibrate at a different rate than the true vocal folds

   (3) **Hyperfunctioning of the vocal mechanism**

   (4) **Vocal fold mass lesion** (e.g., nodule, polyp), which may cause one fold to vibrate at a different frequency than the other

   b. Evaluation of diplophonia. Before initiation of any voice therapy, the source of the second-site vibration must be established. If a second-site vibratory source is confirmed and medicosurgical intervention is indicated, this should be accomplished before the initiation of voice therapy. The source of second-site vibration can best be identified through the use of:

   (1) **Indirect laryngosocopy**

   (2) **Videolaryngoscopy** with or without videostroboscopy

VII. **Evaluation of the various measures of loudness.** The communicative adequacy of the patient's vocal loudness level should be assessed as part of any evaluation of vocal functioning.

   A. Audiometric evaluation should be conducted to determine whether and to what degree the patient has a hearing loss that would contribute to the production of too loud or too soft phonation.

   B. Evaluation of vocal loudness is generally done subjectively. There is no one particular loudness level that is optimal for a particular patient. The patient's voice should be loud enough to be heard over environmental background noise but not so loud as to be uncomfortable for the listener to attend to.

1. **Procedure for evaluation of vocal loudness level.** It is important to evaluate the patient's ability to control his or her overall vocal loudness. Observe whether changes in the loudness of the patient's voice are produced with undue tension. Note any changes in the patient's vocal pitch or quality that occur concomitantly with a change in loudness. Finally, it is necessary to evaluate the patient's ability to alter loudness under each of several conditions:

   a. In settings with differing levels of background noise (e.g., have the patient speak in the presence of music or a tape-recorded conversation).

   b. While performing differing levels of physical activity (e.g., have the patient sit, walk up stairs).

   c. In a large lecture room or auditorium where there is a need to project the voice.

   d. While standing close to the examiner and then moving 10 to 15 feet away. This will allow evaluation of the patient's ability to vary loudness as a function of physical proximity to other individuals.

2. **Etiologies of vocal loudness levels that are too low**

   a. Vocal fold paralysis

   b. Neurologic disorders (e.g., parkinsonism, bulbar paralysis)

   c. Mass lesions of the vocal folds

   d. Personality disturbance that is manifested in the voice

   e. Cultural attitudes in which a reduced vocal loudness level is used according to specific social conversational rules

3. **Etiologies of vocal loudness levels that are too high.** An increase in vocal loudness level may be related to the following:

   a. A **neurologic disorder** that results in respiratory and vocal fold hyperfunction

   b. **Hearing loss**

   c. A **personality disturbance** that is manifested in the habitual loudness characteristics of the voice

C. **Evaluation of the patient's ability to vary loudness.** Not only should the patient's overall loudness level be considered, but the patient's ability to vary the loudness level (suprasegmentally) to convey different meanings should be given attention. This can best be accomplished by asking the patient to read aloud short sentences or phrases with exaggerated feeling or by using contrastive stress drills (see Chap. 8, **VII.B.1 and 2**). Some patients read aloud and speak with little or no fluctuation in loudness and often with little fluctuation in pitch. This boring, colorless voice is called **monotone.** Monotone may be caused by the following:

   a. **Deafness**

   b. **Depression**

   c. **Neurologic disease**

VIII. **Evaluation of voice quality.** Voice quality is a multidimensional vocal attribute that is related to the distribution of acoustic energy in the vocal spectrum. Voice quality does not exist on a single continuum, as do vocal pitch and vocal loudness. Instead, vocal quality probably exists as a series of continua rather than just one. Voice quality is the most difficult parameter of the voice to evaluate, partly because of the vocabulary that is used to describe quality disorders of voice and partly because of the endless variations of voice quality that are possible. Nevertheless, the quality of the patient's voice must be evaluated and the voice quality must be described as a part of the routine voice evaluation.

   A. **General procedures for evaluation of voice quality.** To formulate an accurate assessment of a patient's voice quality, it is necessary to first obtain audiocasette-recorded samples of the patient's voice elicited under a variety of conditions. After making a determination regarding the type of voice quality that is heard, rate the various samples of voice quality on a numerical rating scale of severity. These various ratings can be compared to determine whether the patient's voice quality and the severity of voice quality are consistent from one situation to another or whether the difficulty is specific to a situation.

   B. **Obtaining the sample for evaluation of voice quality.** While the patient is engaged in informal conversation during the interview and while reading the standard paragraph (see **II.B** earlier in the chapter), the speech–language pathologist should make an initial judgment regarding the patient's voice quality. Confirmation of this judgment can be made by noting whether the voice quality remains similar when the patient is engaged in the sustained vowel task (see **IV.B.5.a** earlier in the chapter). It is not unusual for the quality of the voice to vary slightly with the particular vowel that is being phonated and with the particular pitch level at which that vowel is being phonated.

   C. **Determination of the general type of quality disorder.** Disorders of vocal quality can occur because faulty acoustic signals are being generated at the level of the larynx (**quality disorders of phonation**) or because of faulty acoustic coupling of the vocal tract (**quality disorders of resonation**). A determination of which type of quality disorder is being heard and a severity rating of the disorder must be made before further testing can be completed.

   Although it is impossible to find complete consensus among speech–language pathologists regarding the words used to describe voice quality, the following terms are those that are commonly found in the literature.

   1. **Quality disorders of phonation**

      a. **Breathiness** is the term that is used to describe audible airflow during phonation. Breathiness is due to rapid, nonphonated airflow through the glottis.

         (1) **Etiologies of breathiness**

            (a) **Asynchronous vibration of the vocal folds,** which prevents the folds from consistently meeting at the midline even though the folds are capable of complete adduction. As a result, much of the air that flows through the larynx is not converted into phonatory vibration.

(b) **Paralysis of one of the vocal folds in the abducted position.**

(c) **Vocal folds that are bowed** and consequently meet anteriorly and posteriorly but not in the middle portion of the folds.

(2) **Evaluation of breathiness.** The electroglottograph (EGG) can be used to demonstrate breathiness or, the opposite, hard glottal attack (Boone & McFarlane, 1994). The noninvasive device provides a waveform representation of vocal fold dynamics and relative contact patterns during phonation. The EGG signal is unaffected by other activity such as vocal resonance or environmental noise. This feature allows an analysis of phonation "styles" (e.g., normal, pressed, breathy) or vocal quality as revealed in the EGG waveform, and how those styles vary with changes in fundamental frequency. Kay Elemetrics' Laryngograph is an easily transportable electroglottograph that can interface with their CSL to offer a number of voice analysis options (see Appendix C).

The EGG consists of two simple surface electrodes that are placed on each side of the patient's thyroid cartilage and are held in place with a simple elastic strap with velcro attachments. A high frequency electrical current that is imperceptible to the subject passes back and forth through the area of the vocal folds. The EGG provides information about vocal fold contact area by creating an EGG trace or waveform as the subject phonates (Orlikoff, 1998).

To determine whether the breathiness in a patient's voice can be reduced, ask the patient to sustain a vowel while performing an activity that involves the glottal effort closure reflex (see Chap. 8, **VII.E.4.a**), which helps produce firmer glottal approximation. The amount of reduction in breathiness that is achieved through the use of one of these activities represents the best improvement in breathiness that can be attained.

Because the degree of physical effort required for this degree of improvement is probably more than a patient can sustain over an extended period of time, improvement in breathiness, even after voice therapy, will generally be less than that produced during the activities that effect firmer glottal approximation. Nevertheless, an indication of whether the breathiness can be improved through voice therapy designed to obtain firmer glottal closure can be obtained by evaluating the degree of breathiness that is present in vowels produced while the patient is engaged in one of the following activities:

(a) Phonating different vowels while attempting to lift the chair in which he or she is seated

(b) Phonating different vowels while linking the fingers of both hands together and pulling in opposite directions

       (c) Phonating different vowels while pushing against a wall or attempting to move heavy objects

b. **Harshness** is one of the terms used to describe vocal roughness. The term is also used to describe the tension that can be heard when phonation is produced with forcefully adducted vocal folds or through a constricted glottis. When the vocal folds are tightly tensed in the adducted position during phonation, there often will be visible tension in the muscles of the patient's neck, and an accompanying hard glottal attack is not uncommon (see **X** later in the chapter).

Acoustically, harshness is characterized by aperiodicity of the laryngeal tone. It is this aperiodicity across the frequency spectrum that causes listeners to describe the harsh voice as unpleasant or annoying.

   (1) **Etiologies of harshness**

      (a) **Neurologic disease** that adversely affects vocal fold function

      (b) **Structural alterations of the larynx** that affect the mass, compliance, and elasticity of the vocal folds

      (c) **A poor vocal habit** that is characterized by:

         (i) Hard glottal attack

         (ii) Hypertension of the pharynx

   (2) **Evaluation of harshness.** Although there are no special techniques for evaluating harshness, a severity rating of the harsh voice quality should be made. Descriptive statements regarding the specific nature of the harsh voice quality are also helpful and should be included in any diagnostic report.

c. **Hoarseness,** like harshness, is generally used to describe a rough, coarse, husky quality of the voice. Although it is very difficult to acoustically define the noise component that contributes to the perception of hoarseness, it appears that a combination of breathiness and harshness constitutes this vocal descriptor. Because hoarseness is a combination of these two vocal attributes, the exact characteristics of the hoarse voice can vary depending upon the relative contributions of the breathy and harsh components.

   (1) **Etiologies of hoarseness**

      (a) **Neurologic disease** that adversely affects vocal fold function

      (b) **Structural alterations of the larynx** that affect the mass, compliance, and elasticity of the vocal folds

      (c) **Laryngeal edema** resulting from poor vocal habits

   (2) **Evaluation of hoarseness.** Hoarseness can be produced by vocal folds that are too tightly or too loosely adducted. Consequently, the terms *harsh* (too tightly adducted) or *breathy* (too loosely adducted) may be used as modifiers to describe the particular type of hoarseness found in a patient's voice. Although there are no special tech-

niques for evaluating hoarseness, a subjective judgment regarding the degree and type of hoarseness should be made.

d. **Vocal fry (glottal fry)** is a term that is used to describe a crackling or frying sound that is heard when a patient is phonating near the bottom of the pitch range. Vocal fry may be heard in normal voices as intonation drops at the end of phrases or sentences. It is only when vocal fry is used excessively or exclusively that it should be considered a disorder.

(1) **Etiology of vocal fry.** Vocal fry results from a series of discrete laryngeal pulses of low frequency generated when there is a minimum of subglottal air pressure and when the patient's pitch level approaches the bottom of his or her total pitch range.

(2) **Evaluation of vocal fry.** The following areas should be evaluated if vocal fry appears excessively in a patient's voice (Erickson, 1974):

(a) **Frequency** of occurrence of the vocal fry during reading and during conversational speech

(b) **Average duration** of the occurrences of vocal fry in seconds

(c) **Where** in the patient's speech does the vocal fry occur? Is it at the end of a word, a phrase, or a sentence?

(d) Whether vocal fry occurs more frequently on **upward** or **downward vocal inflections**

(e) The effect on vocal fry of elevating the patient's **pitch level.** Use the following procedures to evaluate how easily vocal fry can be eliminated from a patient's voice:

(i) Have the patient **read a passage at a slightly elevated pitch level.** Note whether and to what degree the vocal fry disappears.

(ii) Have the patient **read a passage at a slightly louder level.** Note whether and to what degree the vocal fry disappears.

2. **Quality disorders of resonation** (see Chap. 9 for a more complete discussion of this subject).

a. **Hypernasality** is the term that is used to describe excess nasal resonance. Hypernasality is caused by faulty coupling of the nasal cavity to the vocal tract during the production of vowels. Faulty coupling of the nasal cavity to the vocal tract can also cause a related problem of air escaping through the nasal cavity when high pressure consonants (i.e., fricatives, affricatives, and plosives) are articulated. This nasal escape of air is called **nasal emission.** Although nasal emission is actually a problem of articulation rather than voice quality, it should nevertheless be carefully evaluated along with hypernasality since the two features are related to inadequate velopharyngeal closure.

The variability of hypernasality as it relates to phonetic context should be evaluated carefully. The patient should also be asked to try speaking

with an exaggerated mouth opening, and the speech–language pathologist should then note whether this increased oral opening results in an
improvement in resonance.

(1) **Etiologies of hypernasality.** Hypernasality can result from any
condition that would prevent effective velopharyngeal closure. Some
of these conditions include the following:

   (a) Clefts of the hard or soft palates

   (b) Submucous clefts

   (c) Inadequate velar length

   (d) Paralysis or paresis of the velum

   (e) Paralysis or paresis of the pharyngeal constrictor muscles

(2) **Evaluation of hypernasality.** The following procedures can be
used to evaluate a patient's ability to achieve velopharyngeal closure
and to evaluate the patient's degree of hypernasality:

   (a) While the patient is reading the **standard paragraph** (see
   Appendix A), rate the severity of the hypernasality on a numerical rating scale. It is best to use a sample of the patient's connected speech because some patients are able to effect velopharyngeal closure on single words but not during connected speech.
   Note any nasal emission that occurs.

   (b) In addition to evaluations of connected speech, **single-word
   articulation tests** can also provide useful information, especially in situations in which multiview speech videofluoroscopy
   or nasometry are not available. Because nasal emission is most
   likely to appear with consonants that require the greatest degree
   of intraoral air pressure, an articulation test that assesses these
   specific consonants should be administered. One of the most
   widely used of these is the **Iowa Pressure Articulation Test
   of the *Templin-Darley Tests of Articulation*** (Templin & Darley, 1969). This is designed to differentiate speakers who have
   adequate velopharyngeal closure from those who do not. The other
   is the **Bzoch Error Pattern Articulation Test** (Bzoch, 1979),
   which is designed to assess specific patterns of error production
   in speakers with inadequate velopharyngeal closure. Scores
   from these tests can be used to more objectively evaluate the
   severity of a patient's velopharyngeal incompetence.

   (c) As the patient sustains **phonation of the vowels /i/ and /u/,**
   alternately compress and release the patient's nostrils. If velopharyngeal closure is adequate, there should be no noticeable
   alteration in vowel quality as the nostrils are pinched. If there is
   velopharyngeal incompetence, a flutter-like sound is heard.

   (d) Ask the patient to count from 60 to 100 and evaluate the degree
   of hypernasality that is present. Mason and Grandstaff (1971)
   have suggested the following assessment guidelines for **serial
   counting**:

    (i)   The **60 series** contains the high-pressure front consonant /s/, which is very difficult for patients with velopharyngeal incompetence to articulate well.

    (ii)   The **70 series** contains an embedded nasal consonant (/n/), which allows assessment of the degree of assimilative nasality present in the patient's voice (see Chap. 9, **III**).

    (iii)   The **80 series** should be articulated with few errors since this series contains relatively few high-pressure plosive or fricative consonants.

    (iv)   The **90 series** should sound relatively normal when produced by the hypernasal patient since it is heavily loaded with nasal consonants.

(3) Instrumental evaluation of hypernasality

    (a) Some of the instruments that are used for aerodynamic assessment of the patient's respiratory abilities can also be used in the evaluation of hypernasality. Because oral/nasal air pressures and the rate at which air flows from the oral and nasal cavities are related to hypernasality, **pressure transducers** and **pneumotachographs** can be used to assess the hypernasal patient. The normal patient will typically have no nasal air pressure or airflow during speech except during the production of the English nasal consonants. Hypernasal patients will exhibit increased nasal air pressure and nasal flow rate during the production of both nasal and nonnasal consonants and vowels.

        Kay Elemetrics' Nasometer is a PC-based, hardware/software system designed for quantitative measurement of nasality (see Appendix C). Normative data for the Nasometer have been published on standardized passages (i.e., with and without nasal phonemes) in English and many other languages (Kay Elemetrics, 1995). These findings can be used by the clinician in the evaluation of the patient's ability to attain velopharyngeal closure.

    (b) The adequacy and specific patterns of velopharyngeal closure can be assessed through the **combined use of fiberoptic nasopharyngoscopy and videofluoroscopic techniques.** A fiberoptic nasopharyngoscope is an instrument that has a flexible fiberoptic probe for viewing and a self-contained light source. Flexible nasopharyngoscopes permit a superiorly based view of velopharyngeal closure via a transnasal insertion of the instrument. This superior view of the velopharyngeal port allows for a more accurate assessment of the relative contributions of velar elevation and lateral pharyngeal wall movement to velopharyngeal closure than can be accomplished when these structures are viewed intraorally. Lateral–posterior and anterior–posterior view videofluoroscopic techniques should also be used in conjunction with the fiberoptic nasopharyngoscopy to provide a total visual assessment of velopharyngeal closure.

b. **Hyponasality and denasality** are terms that are used interchange-ably to describe a lack of nasal resonance when the nasal consonants /m/, /n/, and /ŋ/ are phonated. Hyponasality is caused by failure of the nasal cavity to be coupled to the remainder of the vocal tract.

(1) **Etiologies of hyponasality.** Hyponasality can be caused by any obstruction of the nasal cavity. Nasal obstruction is most frequently related to one of the following:

(a) **Deviated septum**

(b) **Nasal polyps**

(c) **Enlarged adenoids**

(d) **Improper velar timing**

(2) **Evaluation of hyponasality.** To evaluate a patient for hyponasal voice quality, use the following procedures:

(a) Ask the patient to read a word list or a reading passage that con-tains many nasal consonants. Hyponasal voice quality can be confirmed if the patient produces articulatory substitutions of b/m, d/n, and g/ŋ.

(b) Another positive indicator of hyponasality is the patient's inabil-ity to hum or to hum clearly.

(c) Ask the patient to read a list of words that begin with /m/ as the nostrils are alternately compressed and released. No change in voice quality as the nostrils are pinched is indicative of inade-quate nasal resonance (i.e., hyponasal voice quality).

c. **Cul-de-sac resonance** is a term used to describe a voice quality that is usually perceived as hollow and affected.

(1) **Etiology.** Cul-de-sac resonance is generally considered to be a dis-order of muscle hyperfunction. This type of resonance is produced when the tongue is retracted into a ball in the back of the mouth, causing the locus of the resonance to be situated too posteriorly in the oral cavity.

(2) **Evaluation**

(a) Ask the patient to phonate the vowel /a/. Note whether the tongue is obviously retracted posteriorly.

(b) If the patient's tongue is retracted, have the patient read sen-tences or word lists containing tongue-tip sounds such as /t/, /d/, /s/, and /z/; the front vowels /i/, /ɪ/, and /e/; and the front conso-nants /w/, /hw/, /p/, /b/, /f/, /v/, /ɸ/, and /l/ (Boone, 1983). Note whether there is an improvement in overall vocal resonance.

d. **Thin voice quality** is a term used to describe a voice quality that is gen-erally considered to be lacking in resonance with an accompanying ante-rior tongue carriage. Often, an elevated pitch level accompanies the thin voice quality.

    (1) Etiologies. Thin voice quality is related to the excessively anterior tongue carriage that eliminates most oral resonance for vowels. Thin voice quality is generally a functional voice disorder and is rarely related to organic vocal dysfunction, although it is sometimes heard in individuals with hearing loss.

    (2) Evaluation

        (a) Determine whether the patient is using an appropriate pitch level. Elevated pitch often accompanies thin voice quality.

        (b) Have the patient read sentences or word lists containing many back vowels and the back consonants /k/ and /g/. Note whether there is an improvement in vocal resonance.

IX. Endurance. Assess the patient's ability to maintain sufficient muscular effort over a time period long enough to permit effective communication.

    A. Procedure. Endurance for speech can be evaluated by asking the patient to count rapidly to 200. Note any decrement in the following:

      1. Phonation

      2. Velopharyngeal closure

      3. Articulation

    B. Patients with **myasthenia gravis** (see Chap. 8, **I.B**) can rarely count beyond 40 without signs of the following:

      1. Increased breathiness

      2. Increased hypernasality

      3. Imprecise articulation

    C. Patients with advanced **parkinsonism** experience decreased vocal intensity before reaching a count of 10 (see Chap. 8, **IV.A**).

X. Identification of the sites of vocal hyperfunction. Sites of muscular hyperfunction that may be associated with a patient's dysphonia should be identified. The extrinsic and intrinsic laryngeal musculature is particularly susceptible to stress and stress-related tension. Excessive tension in these muscles may be the primary or secondary etiology of the voice disorder and almost always plays a significant role in psychogenic dysphonia or aphonia.

    A. Effects of laryngeal tension

      1. Elevation of the larynx

      2. Elevation of the hyoid bone

      3. Occasional elevation of the tongue

    B. Positive indicators of laryngeal tension

      1 . Observing **excessive tension in the muscles of the neck and face.** Many times, the muscles appear to stand out from the neck. The loci of excessive muscular tension can be determined by feeling the neck area of the patient with the hand.

2. Listening for auditory cues such as a **strained vocal quality** and **hard glottal attacks.**

3. Listening to patient **complaints of laryngeal pain or discomfort** in the presence of structurally normal vocal folds or patient identification of the degree and locus of muscular tension related to voice production.

C. **The degree of laryngeal tension is directly proportional to:**

1. The **amount of elevation of the laryngeal structures**

2. The **amount of pain** reported by the patient

MOTOR/SENSORY EVALUATION OF THE SPEECH MUSCULATURE

In addition to the procedures required for a general voice evaluation, a noninstrumental, motor and sensory, speech and nonspeech evaluation of the entire speech musculature should be performed to identify dysphonia that may be present in a patient as a symptom of **dysarthria** or **apraxia** (see Chap. 8 for a more complete discussion of this topic).

There are six cranial nerves that provide both motor and sensory innervation to the muscles of the vocal tract. To evaluate the function of each of these cranial nerves, it is necessary to examine the specific muscles that a particular cranial nerve innervates while those muscles are (1) at rest, (2) involved in a nonspeech task, and (3) participating in various speech-related activities. Additionally, for those cranial nerves that have sensory as well as motor functions, it is important to evaluate the integrity of these sensory feedback channels. The following are descriptions of the functions of the cranial nerves involved in speech production and instructions for evaluating the motor and sensory aspects of each nerve.

I. **General positioning.** The patient should be seated, with his or her head in a natural upright position. The speech–language pathologist should be seated directly in front of the patient at the same eye level as the patient. The examination room should be well lit, with a penlight being all that is necessary to provide additional illumination.

II. **Evaluation of the facial nerve.** The speech–language pathologist should first evaluate the integrity of the facial nerve (cranial nerve VII), which is mainly a motor nerve to muscles of the face and a sensory nerve from the soft palate and the anterior portion of the tongue. A summary of the procedures used for evaluation of the facial nerve is given in Table 3.5.

A. **Evaluation of the facial nerve with its associated muscles at rest.** The patient should be instructed to look straight ahead. His or her face should be relaxed as completely as possible and the mouth should be closed. As the patient sits facing the examiner, the following assessments should be made:

1. The patient's face should be examined to see if it is **symmetrical.** The normal face is fairly symmetrical (perfect symmetry is rare). The clinician should carefully examine the patient's forehead, eyes, and corners of the mouth.

Table 3.5. Procedures for Motor/Sensory Evaluation of the Facial Nerve (CN VII)

Evaluation with the muscles at rest

Ask the patient to look straight ahead with the face relaxed and the mouth closed.

Evaluation using nonspeech tests

Ask the patient to perform the following:
  Gaze upward and then downward with a frown
  Smile and show the teeth
  Protrude the lips into a pucker
  Alternately pucker the lips and smile
  Puff out the cheeks by sealing air in the mouth

Evaluation with speech-related tasks

Ask the patient to perform the following tasks:
  Take a deep breath and repeat the syllable /pʌ/ as rapidly as possible for 10 to 20 seconds
  Take a deep breath and repeat the syllable sequence /u/ - /i/ - /u/ - /i/ as rapidly as possible for 10 to
    20 seconds

Evaluation of sensory function

Ask the patient to discriminate between the tastes of sugar, salt, and something sour placed on the
  anterior two-thirds of the tongue.

Absence of forehead wrinkles on one side is indicative of unilateral, upper-face weakness. Muscular weakness may also be indicated by unilateral or bilateral **ptosis (drooping) of the eyelids.** If one corner of the mouth is lower than the other, it is an indication of unilateral weakness. **Excessive parting of the lips** indicates bilateral neuromuscular involvement.

2. The clinician should carefully observe whether there is a **rigid or masked appearance** of the face, especially if the patient does not blink the eyelids. Rigid facial features are generally indicative of hypokinesia (see Chap. 8, **IV**).

3. Carefully observe the patient's face for the presence of **tremors, grimaces,** or **tics** (involuntary, rapid, irregular, muscular contractions). These extraneous facial movements should be noted, since they may be related to neurologic or psychologic abnormalities.

B. **Evaluation of the facial nerve using nonspeech tasks.** Nonspeech evaluation of cranial nerve VII generally involves instructing the patient to assume several different facial postures. As the patient attempts these postures, the clinician should carefully observe (1) whether the movements are asymmetrical (i.e., does one side of the face move and not the other?), (2) whether the movements are reduced in range (i.e., do the muscles make an excursion through the total range of possible movement?), and (3) whether the movements are performed slowly. The procedures for a nonspeech evaluation of cranial nerve VII are as follows:

1. Because the nonspeech evaluation immediately follows the at-rest evaluation, the patient can be instructed to remain facing forward and to **gaze**

upward as if looking at an airplane flying overhead. Then the patient should be instructed to **gaze downward** at the ground while frowning. The clinician should note any unilateral or bilateral absence of forehead wrinkling, which would indicate neuromuscular weakness.

2. The patient should be asked to **smile** and show the teeth. Both corners of the mouth should elevate symmetrically.

3. Next, the patient should be instructed to **protrude the lips in a pucker.** Note whether the lip protrusion is symmetrical. Deviation to either side indicates unilateral neuromuscular involvement. The lips deviate to the weak side.

4. The patient should be instructed to **alternately pucker the lips and smile.** The clinician should note the presence of any groping movements required to perform the pucker–smile task. Note whether the pucker–smile movements are performed symmetrically.

5. Finally, the patient should be instructed to **puff out the cheeks** by sealing air in the mouth. To ensure that there is no air escape through the nose due to velopharyngeal incompetence, the clinician should occlude the patient's nose with the thumb and index finger. Lip strength can be evaluated by gently pushing on one cheek and then the other. If the patient has unilateral or bilateral weakness, it is indicated by reduced ability to maintain a sufficiently strong lip seal to maintain the intraoral air pressure as the cheeks are pushed.

C. **Evaluation of the facial nerve using speech-related tasks.** Speech evaluation of cranial nerve VII involves the assessment of **diadochokinetic rates** (the patient's ability to rapidly move the articulators between two alternate points). These rapid movements of the articulators are sometimes referred to as **alternate motion rates (AMR).** The procedures for an evaluation of CN VII using speech-related tasks are as follows:

1. The patient should then be instructed to take a deep breath and **repeat the syllable** /pʌ/ for 10 seconds using a steady, even pace. At least three trials should be elicited and the average number of repetitions of /pʌ/ for the three trials should be computed. The patient's productions of /pʌ/ should be equally spaced and should average 3.0 to 5.5 repetitions per second (Bloomquist, 1950). Watch carefully to see if the patient uses mandibular assistance (CN V) in producing the lip repetitions (CN VII).

2. Finally, the patient should be instructed to take a **deep breath and repeat /u/-/i/-/u/-/i/ for 15 seconds.** At least three trials should be elicited and the average number of repetitions for the three trials should be computed.

   a. The patient should average 10 repetitions of /u/-/i/ in less than 5 seconds (Hutchinson, Hanson, & Mecham, 1979).

   b. The clinician should observe the patient's mouth during this speech task and note any asymmetry of lip movement.

III. **Evaluation of the trigeminal nerve** (CN V) involves examination of the muscles of mastication. Cranial nerve V carries motor signals to the masseter and temporal muscles and conducts sensory information away from the face and mouth. A summary of the procedures used for evaluation of the trigeminal nerve is given in Table 3.6.

A. **Evaluation of the trigeminal nerve with its associated muscles at rest.** Since instructions to the patient for the at-rest evaluation of the trigeminal nerve are identical to the instructions given for the at-rest evaluation of the facial nerve (see **II.A** earlier in the chapter), both of the cranial nerves can be evaluated simultaneously. The clinician should carefully observe the patient's mandible to determine if one side rests lower than the other.

B. **Evaluation of the trigeminal nerve using nonspeech tasks** involves the following four basic procedures:

1. The patient should be instructed to bite down hard and clench the teeth tightly. The clinician should palpate the masseter and temporal muscles. Any muscle weakness or atrophy (unilateral or bilateral) should be noted. While the patient's teeth are still clenched, the clinician should put force on the mandible by pulling downward on the patient's chin. Any reduction in the patient's resistance to jaw opening would indicate weakened function of the masseter and temporalis.

2. Next, the patient should be instructed to lower the jaw against examiner resistance. Weakness can be estimated by the degree of difficulty that the patient has in overcoming the examiner's resistance. Be aware that, due to their role in mastication, the muscles that hold the jaw closed are normally stronger than the muscles that open the jaw.

3. Instruct the patient to slowly lower and then slowly elevate the mandible. The clinician should note whether there is any shift of the mandible to either side of midline or whether any groping movement occurs. With unilateral weakness, the mandible deviates to the neuromuscularly intact side.

Table 3.6. Procedures for Motor-Sensory Evaluation of the Trigeminal Nerve (CN V)

Evaluation with the muscles at rest

Ask the patient to look straight ahead with the face relaxed and the mouth closed.

Evaluation using nonspeech tasks

Ask the patient to perform the following movements:
  Bite down hard and clench the teeth tightly
  Lower the jaw against examiner-applied resistance
  Slowly lower and then raise the jaw
  Open the mouth widely and resist the examiner's attempts to push the jaw left and then right

Evaluation using speech-related tasks

Ask the patient to take a deep breath and repeat the syllable /ja/ as rapidly as possible for 10 to 20 seconds.

Evaluation of sensory function

Ask the patient if she or he is experiencing any numbness of the face.
Test the face for touch, pain, and temperature sensations.

4. Finally, the patient should be told to open the mouth widely and resist the clinician's attempts to push the mandible to the left and then to the right. With unilateral weakness, the mandible can be pushed away from the neuromuscularly weak side.

C. **Evaluation of the trigeminal nerve using speech-related tasks** involves instructions to the patient to take a deep breath and then repeatedly produce the syllable /ja/ for 10 seconds using a steady, rapid, even pace. At least three trials should be elicited and the average AMR for these three trials should be calculated. The patient should be able to produce 10 repetitions of /ja/ in less than 3 seconds. The syllables should be equally spaced and any restriction of mandibular movement should be noted.

D. **Sensory evaluation of the trigeminal nerve** involves the following procedures:

1. The clinician should ask the patient if he or she has ever experienced any **numbness of the face.** If so, note the duration of the numbness and whether it was unilateral or bilateral.

2. In addition, the clinician should test the skin of the face **for touch, pain, and temperature sensations.** Any decrease in sensitivity to these stimuli indicates impaired sensory function of the trigeminal nerve.

IV. **Evaluation of the glossopharyngeal, vagus, and spinal accessory nerves** can be done by examining the movements of the palatopharyngeal and laryngeal musculature. The glossopharyngeal nerve (CN IX) is both motor and sensory, with motor signals traveling to the pharyngeal musculature and sensory signals traveling away from the pharynx and posterior portion of the tongue. The vagus nerve (CN X) supplies both motor and sensory fibers to the larynx, pharynx, and soft palate. The spinal accessory nerve (CN XI) is a motor nerve that serves several muscles of the soft palate, neck, and chest. A summary of the procedures used for evaluation of the glossopharyngeal, vagus, and spinal accessory nerves is given in Table 3.7.

A. **Evaluation of the glossopharyngeal, vagus, and spinal accessory nerves with their associated muscles at rest** involves giving instructions to the patient to open the mouth as widely as possible while relaxing the tongue on the floor of the mouth. The procedures for the at-rest evaluation of cranial nerves IX, X, and XI are as follows:

1. While using a penlight for illumination, observe whether the patient's **uvula** hangs symmetrically in the midline while at rest. Unilateral muscular weakness is indicated if the uvula deviates to either side. The uvula generally deviates toward the neuromuscularly intact side. If the uvula is bifid, it may indicate the presence of a submucous cleft.

2. Next, the tongue should be depressed using a wooden tongue depressor, and the clinician should observe the **soft palate** region in its at-rest position. Unilateral muscular weakness may cause one side of the soft palate to rest at a lower level than the other. The clinician should be aware that many normal soft palates appear asymmetrical due to contracture of posttonsillectomy scar tissue. The presence of any scarring in the region should be noted.

Table 3.7. Procedures for Motor/Sensory Evaluation of the Glossopharyngeal (CN IX), Vagus (CN X), and Spinal Accessory (CN XI) Nerves

Evaluation with the muscles at rest

Ask the patient to open the mouth as widely as possible while relaxing the tongue on the floor of the mouth.

Evaluation using nonspeech tasks

Ask the patient to perform the following movements:
   While the tongue is held out of the mouth, inflate the cheeks with air and keep the cheeks inflated as long as possible
   Shrug the shoulders upward against examiner-applied resistance

Evaluation using speech-related tasks

Ask the patient to perform the following tasks:
   Produce a sustained and then an interrupted production of the syllable /a/
   Sustain the vowel /u/ while alternately occluding and releasing the nose
   Cough sharply, clear the throat, or produce a vowel using a hard glottal attack
   Vary vocal pitch by imitating high and low pitch models

Evaluation of sensory function

Ask the patient to relax and breathe gently through the nose while the posterior wall of the pharynx is stroked with a tongue depressor.

Bilateral weakness of the soft palate is indicated if both sides of the velum are positioned at a low level, approximating the surface of the tongue.

3. The only way to directly observe movement of the **muscles innervated by the vagus nerve** is through an indirect-mirror laryngoscopic examination or fiberoptic laryngoscopy. These examinations are usually performed by a laryngologist, with whom the clinician should consult. If the laryngologist reports that there is a visible paresis or paralysis of the patient's vocal folds, it is usually indicative of a lower motor neuron lesion. Upper motor neuron lesions rarely result in visible asymmetries of the vocal folds.

B. **Evaluation of the glossopharyngeal, vagus, and spinal accessory nerves using nonspeech tasks** involves assessment of the patient's ability to impound intraoral air, to shrug the shoulders, and to turn the head against resistance. The procedures for the nonspeech evaluation of cranial nerves IX, X, and XI are as follows:

1. Take a small gauze pad between the thumb and index finger and use the gauze pad to gently pull the patient's tongue forward. While the patient's tongue is being held by the examiner, the patient should purse his lips around his tongue, blow up the cheeks with air, and keep the cheeks inflated as long as possible. By holding the patient's tongue out of the mouth, the examiner prevents the posterior portion of the tongue from providing compensatory assistance to soft palate elevation, which would tend to mask the presence of velopharyngeal incompetence. If circumoral weakness was

detected during evaluation of cranial nerve VII (see **II.B.5** earlier in the chapter), this procedure is contraindicated due to the patient's inability to form an adequately airtight lip seal around the tongue.

2. **Cranial nerve XI** innervates the trapezium and sternocleidomastoid muscles. To assess the integrity of the innervation, the patient should be instructed to shrug the shoulders upward against downward resistance applied by the examiner. The examiner should next place a hand against one side of the patient's jaw and instruct him or her to forcefully turn the head against the resisting hand. The procedure should be repeated on the opposite side. During these tasks, the examiner should note any weakness, asymmetrical movement, reduced range of movement, or reduced speed of movement.

C. **Evaluation of the glossopharyngeal, vagus, and spinal accessory nerves using speech-related tasks** involves assessment of the degree of velopharyngeal competency and the adequacy of phonatory production. The examiner should be aware that, because of restricted visual access, only limited information about velopharyngeal closure can be obtained during a visual inspection of the size, shape, and function of the palatopharyngeal structures. Measures of airflow, as well as fiberoptic nasopharyngoscopy combined with videofluoroscopic techniques (see **The Voice Evaluation Process, VIII.C.2. a.(3)(b) and (c)** in this chapter), may be required to further evaluate velopharyngeal function. The procedures for a motor speech evaluation of cranial nerves IX, X, and XI are as follows:

1. **Evaluation of palatopharyngeal musculature**

   a. One method of evaluating the palatopharyngeal musculature involves instructing the patient to open the mouth as widely as possible while relaxing the tongue on the floor of the mouth and sustaining the vowel /a/ for as long as possible. The patient should then produce an interrupted /a/. If one side of the soft palate elevates higher than the other, it is indicative of unilateral weakness. As mentioned previously, in such cases the uvula generally deviates toward the neuromuscularly intact side. Bilateral weakness is indicated if both sides of the soft palate fail to elevate during sustained production of the vowel. The examiner should note the presence or absence of hypernasality and nasal air emission (see **The Voice Evaluation Process, VIII.C.2.a** earlier in this chapter).

   b. A second method of evaluating the adequacy of the palatopharyngeal musculature for speech production involves giving instructions to the patient to sustain the vowel /u/ while alternately occluding and releasing the nose with a thumb and index finger as described earlier in this chapter (see **VIII.C.2.a.(2)(c)**). The presence of a "fluttering" quality indicates velopharyngeal incompetence.

2. **Evaluation of the laryngeal musculature**

   a. A speech evaluation of the laryngeal musculature involves instructing the patient to cough sharply, clear the throat, or produce a vowel using a hard glottal attack for the purpose of evaluating the strength of vocal fold adduction. Neuromuscular weakness is indicated by a soft glottal attack or a "mushy" cough.

b. To further evaluate the laryngeal musculature, instruct the patient to take a deep breath and sustain the vowel /a/ for as long, steadily, and clearly as possible (see **The Voice Evaluation Process, IV.B.3.e.(i)**). The following assessments should be made of the patient's **sustained-vowel production:**

(1) The clinician should note the **patient's vocal quality during the production of the sustained vowel.**

(a) A **breathy voice quality** generally indicates incomplete closure of the vocal folds, which may be due to unilateral or bilateral vocal fold weakness or paralysis. Breathiness is not, however, always related only to neurologic dysfunction. A breathy voice quality may also result from the following:

(i) **Asynchronous vibration of the vocal folds** (due to increased loading by a vocal fold lesion) that prevents the folds from consistently meeting at the midline even though the folds are capable of complete adduction

(ii) **Interarytenoid lesions** that limit the approximation of the arytenoids and consequently limit vocal fold adduction

(iii) **Glottal lesions** on the margin of the vocal folds that are of sufficient size to prevent complete vocal fold closure

(b) A **strained–strangled voice quality** generally indicates limited excursion of the vocal folds, which may be due to spasticity or hypertension.

(c) Harshness is often due to asynchronous vibration of the vocal folds, which may result from neuromuscular incoordination or hypertension.

(d) A **gurgling voice quality** due to the pooling of saliva in the pyriform sinuses may occur occasionally.

(2) The examiner should also evaluate the patient's **vocal pitch level** during production of the sustained vowel. Neuromuscular involvement is generally indicated by an excessively low pitch, monopitch, or reduced ability to rapidly change pitch upon command.

(3) It is important for the clinician to assess the **steadiness of production of the sustained vowel.** There should be little variation in pitch. The clinician should note any rhythmic or arrhythmic voice tremors. Intermittent voice arrests should also be noted.

(4) The normal adult patient should be able to sustain the vowel for at least 15 to 20 seconds. **Sustained vowel durations** of less than 14.3 seconds for females and less than 15 seconds for males (see **The Voice Evaluation Process, IV.B.3.e.(I)(a)** in this chapter) may indicate the following:

(a) **Excessive air wastage** during phonation, which is caused by weakened vocal folds that are incapable of achieving complete closure (unilateral or bilateral inadequate adduction).

    (b) Increased respiratory effort, which may be required during strained-strangled phonation. Increased effort causes the patient to tire and quickly give up attempts to phonate.

    (c) Decreased vital capacity resulting from neuromuscular weakness or incoordination of the respiratory musculature can also contribute to shortened duration of sustained vowel productions.

    (d) Shortened duration of sustained vowels may also result from **nonneuromuscular etiologies** such as the following:

        (i) Glottal lesions

        (ii) Interarytenoid lesions

        (iii) The use of **inefficient patterns of respiration** that result in reduced vital capacity

        (iv) A **faulty learned pattern of speaking** that is characterized by lack of coordination between the onset of phonation and expiration

  c. The laryngeal musculature can also be evaluated by assessing the patient's **ability to alter vocal pitch.** The following procedures may be used for this evaluation:

    (1) The patient should be instructed to take a deep breath and then sustain the vowel /a/, using an alternating high and low pitch level. The examiner should note whether the patient is able to rapidly change vocal pitch or whether changes in pitch are difficult, if not impossible, for the patient to effect.

    (2) The patient's ability to vary pitch can also be evaluated by instructing the patient to imitate different pitch patterns that have been modeled by the clinician. If the patient is unable to vary vocal pitch and speaks in a monotone, the clinician should not on the basis of this single item of information conclude that the patient's inability is related to a neuromuscular etiology. Monopitch phonation must be considered with other items of diagnostic information since many normal individuals exhibit varying degrees of monotonous voice production.

D. Sensory evaluation of the glossopharyngeal, vagus, and spinal accessory nerves. Evaluation of cranial nerves IX, X, and XI involves eliciting the **palatopharyngeal gag reflex.** The clinician should ask the patient to open the mouth as widely as possible, relax, and breathe gently through the nose. The clinician should then proceed to stroke the posterior wall of the pharynx with a tongue depressor. The soft palate should reflexively elevate symmetrically in a posterosuperior direction and the lateral walls of the pharynx and the faucial pillars should move medially. Asymmetrical movement is generally indicative of unilateral neuromuscular weakness. Bilateral involvement is manifested as reduced bilateral movement.

Reduced or excessive bilateral movement of the soft palate is not solely indicative of neuromuscular weakness. Relatively insensitive or hyperactive gag reflexes may be found in neuromuscularly normal subjects.

Even though palatopharyngeal movement can be observed visually when the palatopharyngeal gag reflex is elicited, the degree of movement and the degree of velopharyngeal closure do not necessarily correlate. **Multiview videofluoroscopy,** a radiographic technique that produces pictures of velopharyngeal movement, can be used to more accurately evaluate the adequacy of palatal movement. Through use of frontal, lateral, and basal views, palatal movement can be seen easily on videofluoroscopic recordings. Devices that allow direct visualization of pharyngeal movement (fiberoptic **nasopharyngoscopes**) are often used for an additional evaluation of the contribution of pharyngeal wall movement to velopharyngeal closure. Other techniques that can be used to assess a patient's velopharyngeal competence include the use of instrumentation such as the **Nasometer** (see **The Voice Evaluation Process, VIII.C.2. a.(3)(b)** earlier in this chapter).

V. **Evaluation of the hypoglossal nerve.** The last cranial nerve that the clinician should evaluate is the hypoglossal nerve (CN XII), which carries motor signals to the strap muscles of the neck and to the intrinsic muscles of the tongue. A summary of the procedures used for evaluation of the hypoglossal nerve is given in Table 3.8.

A. **Evaluation of the hypoglossal nerve with its associated muscles at rest** involves instructing the patient to open the mouth as widely as possible and to relax the tongue on the floor of the mouth so that the following intraoral examination can be accomplished:

Table 3.8. Procedures for Motor Evaluation of the Hypoglossal Nerve (CN XII)

Evaluation with the muscles at rest

Ask the patient to open the mouth as widely as possible and then relax the tongue on the floor of the mouth.

Evaluation using nonspeech tasks

Ask the patient to perform the following movements:
Protrude the tongue
Lick the upper and lower lips from left to right and then from right to left
Move the tongue back and forth from one corner of the mouth to the other
Elevate the tongue tip to the upper central incisors and then slowly lower the tongue back to the floor of the mouth
Push with the tongue against a tongue depressor held outside of the mouth in front of the lips
Push with the tongue against the inside of the left and then right cheek while outside resistance is being applied by the examiner

Evaluation using speech-related tasks

Ask the patient to take a deep breath and perform the following tasks:
Repeat the syllable /tʌ/ as rapidly as possible for 10 to 20 seconds
Repeat the syllable /kʌ/ as rapidly as possible for 10 to 20 seconds
Repeat the syllable sequence /pʌ-tʌ-kʌ/ as rapidly as possible for 10 to 20 seconds

Evaluation of sensory function

Because the hypoglossal nerve has motor functions only, no evaluation of sensory function is required.

1. The tongue should lie relaxed on the floor of the mouth with the tip just below the edge of the mandibular incisors and the surface just above the other teeth. The clinician should note the **general size of the tongue,** especially in relation to the size of the dental arches. Unilateral or bilateral atrophy is usually indicative of neuromuscular weakness or paralysis.

2. Next, the clinician should carefully observe the **surface of the tongue** for fasciculations (repetitive wrinkling or dimpling movements). These movements can most easily be seen around the edge of the tongue following several minutes of careful observation. Fasciculations are generally indicative of denervation.

3. Finally, the clinician should also note any **tendency for the tongue to remain in motion** rather than to lie on the floor of the mouth. These movements may be indicative of a neuromuscular movement disorder.

B. **Evaluation of the hypoglossal nerve using nonspeech tasks** involves instructions to the patient to perform various tongue movements. The procedures for the nonspeech evaluation of cranial nerve XII are as follows:

1. Instruct the patient to protrude the tongue. The extension movement should be performed symmetrically, without any marked deviation to either side. Normal **tongue protrusion** in adults is 1 to 2 inches beyond the central incisors and ¾ to 1½ inches in children. The examining clinician should note any reduced range or reduced speed of movement.

2. Next, the patient should be instructed to lick the upper lip from left to right and then to lick the lower lip right to left. This movement should be repeated several times and any asymmetrical movement, reduced range, or reduced speed of movement should be noted.

3. Now the patient should be instructed to open the mouth slightly and to move the tongue back and forth from one corner of the mouth to the other. Again, the movement should be repeated several times and the examiner should note any asymmetrical movement, reduced range, or reduced speed of movement during execution of the task.

4. The clinician should place both of his or her thumbs on the patient's chin and place the fingers under the mandible in order to resist the patient's efforts to elevate the mandible during the next procedure. While the clinician gently applies a downward pressure on the mandible to keep the mouth open wide, the patient should be instructed to elevate the tongue tip to the edge of the upper central incisors and then to slowly lower the tongue. This procedure should be repeated several times. Note any asymmetrical movement, reduced range, or reduced speed of movement while the patient is performing this task.

5. To test the **strength of tongue movement,** the examiner should apply resistance that the patient tries to overcome with the tongue.

   a. To evaluate the **strength of tongue protrusion,** the patient should be instructed to protrude the tongue as forcefully as possible against the flat surface of a tongue depressor that the clinician uses to provide resistance. The clinician should note whether the tongue yields to resistance and whether the tongue force appears to be steady.

    b. To evaluate **lateral tongue strength,** the patient should be instructed to push with the tongue against the left cheek first, and then against the right cheek while the examiner is applying resistance to the outside of the cheek with his or her fingers. The examining clinician should note whether the tongue yields to resistance and whether the tongue force appears to be steady.

C. Evaluation of the hypoglossal nerve using speech-related tasks involves AMR and sequenced motion rate (SMR) tasks under different conditions. SMR tasks are designed to evaluate the patient's ability to rapidly and accurately move the articulators repeatedly through a sequence of three or more different articulatory postures. The procedures for the motor speech evaluation of cranial nerve XII are as follows:

    1. The patient should be instructed to take a deep breath and repeat the syllable /tʌ/ for 10 seconds at a steady, even pace. At least three trials should be elicited and the average number of repetitions for the three trials should be calculated. Repetitions of /tʌ/ should exceed 25 in 10 seconds; the syllables should be equally spaced (Nation & Aram, 1977). Watch carefully to see if the patient uses mandibular assistance (CN V) in producing the tongue /t/ repetitions (CN XII).

    2. The clinician should instruct the patient to repeat the steps described earlier in the chapter (see **V.C.1**), only this time using the syllable /kʌ/. The patient should be able to exceed repetitions of /kʌ/ in 10 seconds (Bloomquist, 1950).

    3. To assess the patient's ability to move the tongue to perform a series of rapid articulatory adjustments (SMR), the patient should take a deep breath and repeat the syllable sequence /pʌ-tʌ-kʌ/ for 10 seconds. The patient should be able to exceed eight repetitions of the syllable sequence in 10 seconds (Hutchinson, Hanson, & Mecham, 1979).

Chapter 4

Phonotrauma and
Trauma-Related Dysphonias

◆ ◆ ◆ ◆ ◆ ◆ ◆ ◆ ◆ ◆ ◆ ◆ ◆ ◆ ◆ ◆ ◆ ◆ ◆

Traumatic injuries to the larynx produce distinctive signs and symptoms, one of which is dysphonia. The dysphonia results from mass, elasticity, and tension alterations of the true vocal folds. Causes of trauma to the larynx can be grouped into the following three categories: (1) behavioral traumas, such as vocal hyperfunction (phonotrauma); (2) mechanical trauma; and (3) trauma due to burns (see Table 4.1).

Because of the nature of the submucosal tissue of the supraglottic larynx, fluid or blood can rapidly accumulate following laryngeal trauma and result in edema (swelling caused by a collection of fluid) or hematoma (localized swelling caused by a collection of blood, usually clotted, which is released through a break in the wall of a blood vessel). Laryngeal edema or hematoma may be the sole laryngeal condition and usually resolves spontaneously. Healing of many traumatic laryngeal injuries, however, is frequently characterized by the deposition of granulated material and eventual fibrosis.

The primary treatment for soft and newly formed laryngeal lesions secondary to trauma is removal of the source of trauma to allow for spontaneous healing. Recurrence of the lesion can be expected, however, if the original or other sources of laryngeal trauma are not eliminated. The primary method of treatment for a granulated or a fibrosed lesion is typically surgical removal. Again, traumatic laryngeal lesions can be expected to

Table 4.1. Sources of Trauma to the Larynx

---

1. Behavioral trauma (phonotrauma)
   A. Vocal abuse
   B. Vocal misuse

2. Mechanical trauma (phonotrauma)
   A. External sources
      • Automobile accidents
      • Forceful assault from blunt objects
      • Penetrating injuries to the larynx
      • Complications of a too-high tracheostomy
   B. Internal sources
      • Improper endoscopic examination procedures
      • Endotracheal intubation
      • Indwelling nasogastric tubes

3. Trauma due to burns
   A. Thermal burns
   B. Chemical burns

---

return even after surgical removal unless the source of laryngeal trauma is identified and eliminated.

The speech–language pathologist is most frequently consulted regarding voice therapy for patients with dysphonias caused by lesions that developed consequent to hyperfunction (phonotrauma) of the voice-producing mechanism (Verdolini, 1998a). In certain cases of dysphonia due to laryngeal trauma, voice therapy is the treatment of choice, while in other cases voice therapy is ineffective. Generally, dysphonias that result from phonotrauma can best be corrected through a program that instructs the patient in establishing habits of good vocal hygiene through the identification and elimination of factors related to the individual patient's vocal use, and a voice therapy program that has as its goal the establishment of efficient, effective, healthy voice production. In some cases, an optional program of vocal rest designed to limit laryngeal irritation and to allow the larynx to recover from the effects of hyperfunction may be used (see Chap. 5).

The advantages of using voice therapy instead of surgery to remove lesions induced by phonotrauma are that voice therapy involves less time lost from work, is an effective and nontraumatic treatment approach, is more cost effective, and serves to permanently eliminate the hyperfunctional patterns that caused the lesion to occur. The results of using surgical removal as an initial treatment for newly formed vocal lesions of hyperfunctional origin have been disappointing because these lesions frequently recur following surgery unless the patient's vocal habits have been changed.

Patients with lesions resulting from phonotrauma are best managed by a team consisting of a laryngologist and a speech–language pathologist (i.e., voice therapist). The laryngologist is responsible for the initial diagnosis. The voice therapist is responsible for performing the diagnostic evaluation of the patient's voice and instituting a trial program of voice therapy. The decision of whether to continue voice therapy or perform surgery should be made jointly by members of the management team.

The voice therapist's role is usually more secondary in the treatment of laryngeal injury resulting from mechanical or burn trauma. The primary method of treatment for these types of laryngeal trauma is medicosurgical, and the procedures are usually performed by laryngologists. Laryngologists frequently seek the assistance of the voice therapist on the management team regarding patients with dysphonias that persist following medicosurgical intervention.

I. **Dysphonias Caused by Phonotrauma.** The primary characteristic of phonotrauma is a condition of hyperadduction of the intrinsic and extrinsic laryngeal musculature, which is frequently accompanied by excessive vocal fold vibration. Phonation under conditions of excessive laryngeal tension frequently results in changes in laryngeal tissue. Because these tissue changes can cause mass, elasticity, and tension alterations of the vocal folds, vocal fold vibration is adversely affected. The dysphonia that results from these vocal fold changes is often characterized as hoarse, breathy, or low pitched.

   A. **Phonotrauma** is defined as any vocal behavior that can have a traumatic effect on the vocal folds. The following are common examples of phonotrauma:

   1. **Yelling, screaming, and cheering** are all vocalizations that are produced by hyperadduction and violent vibration of the vocal folds. These vocal activities cause varying degrees of laryngeal irritation, ranging from vascular engorgement to hematoma. Pathologic changes in the vocal folds usually fol-

low extended use of these behaviors; however, in some cases, even a single episode of abuse can be sufficiently violent to cause vocal fold injury. Cheerleaders and children who play sports are particularly prone to laryngeal trauma due to yelling, screaming, and cheering.

2. **Strained vocalizations,** a form of phonotrauma, are typically produced by children who attempt to mimic the sounds made by machinery, such as automobiles, monster trucks, airplanes, rockets, and laser guns. These vocalizations are usually produced with increased loudness, with an elevated pitch, and with the larynx in a state of hyperadduction.

   Strained vocalizations are also produced by adults. For example, when a person is carrying a heavy object, the glottal effort closure reflex is elicited and the vocal folds are tightly adducted to help trap air in the thoracic cavity (air trapped in the thoracic cavity keeps the rib cage expanded, which increases muscular efficiency for lifting or pushing). Any attempts to phonate while carrying or pushing heavy objects must be forceful enough to overcome the hyperadduction of the vocal folds associated with the reflex. However, because the vocal folds are so tightly adducted during such activities, any vocalization will sound strained, as if it were produced against considerable laryngeal resistance. If there are continued attempts at forcefully phonating against this glottal resistance, vocal fold irritation may soon develop.

3. **Excessive talking.** The amount of vocal production that can be extracted without undue strain from the larynx varies from person to person. Although the larynx can be used intermittently all day long everyday, there is a physiologic limit to every larynx.

   People who must use their voices professionally or who talk a lot during their day are the individuals most likely to develop laryngeal pathologies secondary to excessive use of the larynx. Clergypeople, teachers, and singers are very likely candidates because of the amount of professional vocal usage that is required of their vocal mechanisms on a day-to-day basis. Frequently, these patients are unaware of how much they actually use their voices during the course of a day. However, just whose larynx will be affected by heavy vocal use and the degree of impairment that will result cannot be predicted. Constitutional differences probably best account for the differences in the degree of impairment found in various larynges.

4. **Frequent use of hard glottal attack.** A hard glottal attack is produced by adducting the vocal folds prior to the initiation of expiration and then building up subglottic air pressure until it is released as an abrupt explosion that initiates vowel production. Use of a stopped, hard glottal attack for initiating phonation can irritate the vocal folds, which in turn results in a hoarse or harsh voice. Prolonged use of a hard glottal attack may result in more serious lesions, including chronic laryngitis, vocal nodules, or laryngeal polyps (see **I.C**).

5. **Throat clearing and coughing.** Throat clearing and coughing are both nonspeaking activities that can be harmful to the larynx. Excessive use of these behaviors, which cause the vocal folds to vibrate explosively, can result in traumatic injury to the folds. Some patients have developed the habit of

frequent coughing and throat clearing, despite the fact that they have no organic need to do so. Such patients may not be aware that they have developed these habits.

Other patients have a frequent need to cough and clear their throats because of food or other allergies. Poor lubrication of the larynx can also induce a habitual cough. Excessive dryness of the interior of the larynx may result from the use of antihistamines for allergy management, smoking, birth control pills, and chronic alcohol abuse (alcohol has a drying effect on the laryngeal mucosa). Whatever the cause, the end result of excessive coughing and throat clearing is usually a hoarse dysphonia.

6. **Inhalation of dust, cigarette smoke, and noxious gases** can harm the vocal mechanism. Cigarette smoke and environmental pollution are especially harmful to the vocal folds. Extensive tissue changes in the larynx often result from the combined effects of smoking, airborne irritants, and chronic alcohol abuse.

7. **Singing with poor vocal technique or under difficult environmental conditions.** One of the most demanding uses of the voice is singing. The demand on the professional singer's larynx, whether while performing in a recording studio, on a large stage, or in a small nightclub, is substantial. In addition, if a singer uses a potentially harmful vocal style while speaking, the deleterious effects on the voice are compounded.

   Singing at an excessively loud level, at an inappropriate pitch level, while using a hard glottal attack, and while the vocal folds are swollen and reddened by allergy or upper respiratory tract infection are behaviors frequently used by the untrained pop singer. Many pop singers perform in environments and under conditions that are very conducive to vocal harm. Typically, these singers are required to perform for approximately 4 hours nightly in smoke-filled rooms and must project their voices (even if amplified) over the sound of highly amplified musical instruments. Pop singers are also encouraged by nightclub management to mingle with customers during breaks, where they further stress their vocal mechanisms by talking over the noisy nightclub background (e.g., chatter, jukebox music, clinking glasses) (Mowrer & Case, 1982).

8. **Excessive speaking while the vocal folds are in a weakened condition.**

   a. When the vocal folds are reddened and swollen due to the effect of an **allergy** or an **upper respiratory tract infection,** they are extremely sensitive and can be easily damaged when used for a long period of time, even if the voice is used normally. Moreover, they are particularly vulnerable to damage from abusive vocal habits. Medical management should be used to minimize the effects of allergy and upper respiratory tract infections upon the folds. In addition, during periods of inflammation, the patient should limit all vocal use.

   b. The vocal folds can also be affected by the **menstrual cycle** in women (Damste, 1967; Flach, Schwickardi, & Simon, 1969; Frable, 1962; Greene, 1980). Although this effect is not particularly noticeable in all women, it may provide problems for professional voice users (Colton & Casper,

1996). There is hoarseness and a lowering of pitch premenstrually due to a decrease in estrogen and progesterone levels. The effect of menstruation upon the voice of any one particular female patient must be evaluated carefully. If observation of the patient's vocal characteristics suggests the possibility of premenstrual vocal fold swelling, the patient may need to be counseled regarding the vulnerability of the vocal folds during this period.

    c. The vocal folds are also susceptible to damage from excessive use during periods when the mucosal lining of the larynx is excessively dry. Most typically, this dryness results from the use of **antihistamines** for allergy management and occasionally from the use of **birth control pills.** Patients using these medications may need to be counseled to use decreased vocal effort while speaking.

B. Vocal harm may also result from **incorrect use** of the pitch or loudness aspects of voice production. If a person speaks too loudly or at too high a habitual pitch on a constant or intermittent but frequent basis, damage to the vocal mechanism can result.

    1. One cause of **elevated vocal loudness** is talking in situations with high background noise levels. In these situations, people must raise the loudness of their voices in order to be heard. Because the process of elevating vocal loudness is frequently accompanied by an increase in laryngeal tension, the opportunity for vocal hyperfunction exists. If a person is required to constantly or frequently communicate in a noisy environment (e.g., in occupational settings), vocal fold irritation will usually result, with vocal hoarseness following soon thereafter. The following are some other examples of situations in which problems of vocal loudness frequently occur:

        a. Talking while riding in moving **automobiles** that have high background noise levels

        b. Talking while operating or being in the vicinity of **heavy machinery,** such as earth-moving equipment, factory equipment, and farm machinery

        c. Talking while using motorized sports equipment, such as motorcycles, snowmobiles, jet skis, and all-terrain vehicles

        d. Talking while listening to live **rock music** or while listening to very loud rock music through stereo headphones

    2. Elevated pitch levels tend to occur as a consequence of elevated loudness levels. Black (1961) has demonstrated that (1) when an adult male speaks with a raised voice (80 dB) in the presence of background noise, his vocal pitch rises 13 to 17 Hz; (2) when he speaks with a very loud voice (90 dB), his vocal pitch rises 14 to 38 Hz; and (3) when he uses a shouting voice (100 dB), his vocal pitch rises 21 to 74 Hz. These findings demonstrate that increased vocal loudness is usually accompanied by an increase in vocal pitch and that increased pitch alone or loudness alone rarely occurs.

    3. Elevated vocal loudness and pitch can occur for various reasons. Frequently, pitch and loudness increase simultaneously, as a result of stress, accompanied by excessive muscle tension that directly affects the larynx and vocal fold vibration. However other patients use elevated pitch and loudness levels simply out of habit.

C. Laryngeal lesions and dysphonias caused by trauma, phonotrauma, or chronic irritation

1. **Chronic laryngitis** is the term used to refer to any pathologic condition that is characterized by long-standing inflammation of the laryngeal mucosa secondary to laryngeal trauma. Chronic laryngitis should be distinguished from acute laryngitis, which is an inflammation of the larynx caused by infectious agents (see **I.C.4**).

   Hoarseness, lowered vocal pitch, and complaints of **vocal fatigue** are the most common vocal symptoms of the various forms of chronic laryngitis. Frequently, patients with chronic laryngitis use a more forceful voice than necessary in an attempt to overcome the effects of hoarseness. This effort, however, tends to increase glottal tension and, consequently, subjects the vocal folds to additional irritation.

   Although there are many factors that can individually or collectively cause chronic laryngitis, cigarette smoking, vocal abuse and misuse, industrial air pollution, and the drainage of chronic sinusitis are the most frequent. Alcohol is implicated in some individuals, especially when it is combined with cigarette smoking.

   Gastroesophageal reflux disease (GERD) is responsible for a particular form of chronic laryngitis in which the laryngeal tissues are chronically inflamed and irritated by acidic stomach secretions. Gastroesophageal reflux onto laryngeal tissue occurs during sleep because of a weakened or incompetent lower esophageal sphincter muscle. The individual may complain of morning hoarseness, bitter taste in the morning, and occasionally of heartburn (Sataloff, 1997b).

   In the early stages of chronic laryngitis, the vocal folds and the supraglottic larynx appear especially edematous due to vasodilation (dilation of a blood vessel) and hyperemia (blood engorgement) of the subepithelial tissues. Depending upon the constitution of the mucosal tissue involved, chronic laryngitis with vocal fold irritation can progress to the following:

   (1) **vocal fold thickening** or **hypertrophy of the laryngeal epithelium** along the glottal margins of the vocal fold, and

   (2) **extensive polypoid degeneration, or Reinke's edema** (Boone & McFarlane, 1994). Changes in the laryngeal mucosa are bilateral and symmetric in long-standing chronic laryngitis (Birrell, 1977).

   a. **Etiology**

   (1) **Cigarette smoking** is probably one of the most common causes of chronic nonspecific laryngitis.

   (2) **Phonotrauma,** especially coughing and throat clearing, excessive talking, vocal strain, yelling, screaming, and faulty singing technique are frequently implicated.

(3) **Persistent mouth breathing,** which results in inadequate humid-ification of inhaled air, may cause the laryngeal mucosa to become dried out and irritated.

(4) **Gastroesophageal reflux disease** is the cause in some cases of chronic laryngitis.

(5) L. D. Holinger (1976b) reports that a history of **abuse of mouth washes and gargles** is frequently found in patients with chronic nonspecific laryngitis.

b. **Symptoms.** A hoarse, dry, low pitched voice and a dry, nonproductive cough are the typical symptoms of chronic nonspecific laryngitis. Although patients may report neck or throat ache and tension when they use their voices for extended periods of time, they usually do not com-plain of generalized laryngeal pain.

c. **Laryngoscopic findings.** The vocal folds have lost their usual pearly sheen and are reddened and are often irregularly thickened. Small, dilated blood vessels can be seen on the superior surface of the folds. The vocal fold margins, which normally appear to have sharp edges during phonation, are more rounded, and vocal fold vibration is obviously asyn-chronous (Ballenger, 1977). The supraglottic laryngeal region may be edematous.

d. **Medicosurgical management** of chronic laryngitis is generally directed toward elimination of the principal sources of laryngeal irrita-tion, especially cigarette smoking and the excessive use of alcohol. If the laryngeal irritation is due to an airborne irritant, environmental man-agement is frequently necessary. Allergies or sinusitis, if present, should be evaluated and treated by a physician and may be managed by medi-cations that limit the amount of associated drainage. If the cause is gas-troesophageal reflux, the patient must carefully follow the prescribed dietary and pharmacologic regimen.

e. **Voice therapy management.** If the laryngeal irritation is caused by phonotrauma, a program of voice management that focuses on elimina-tion of poor vocal habits is the principal method of treatment (see Chap. 5, **II**).

2. **Reinke's edema,** sometimes known as **polypoid degeneration,** is char-acterized by the formation of diffuse polypoid swelling in Reinke's space, or the superficial layer of the lamina propria. When the vocal fold is profusely edematous in chronic laryngitis, the condition may be labeled as Reinke's edema, polypoid corditis, or polypoid degeneration (Sataloff, 1997a). The edema is more diffuse in polypoid degeneration than in a vocal fold nodule or polyp (Stemple et al., 1995) (see **C.5** and **C.6** in this chapter).

a. The majority of patients diagnosed with Reinke's edema **smoke cigarettes** or **use alcohol excessively.** Reinke's edema appears to be caused by vocal irritation such as cigarette smoking or heavy alcohol intake, although other factors such as hypothyroidism and phonotrauma may contribute (Sataloff, 1997b).

b. The **primary symptom** of Reinke's edema is severe and persistent hoarseness. The severity of the hoarseness may vary slightly, depending upon the degree of edema. Aphonia occurs occasionally, and vocal pitch is usually low. The polypoid masses usually extend along the full length of the vocal fold in Reinke's space.

c. **Laryngoscopic findings.** When examined laryngoscopically, Reinke's edema appears as multiple, usually bilateral, grayish-pink to red, symmetric, sausage-shaped masses projecting from the margins of each vocal fold. Because the swelling is profuse, the vocal folds may lie in close approximation and tend to obliterate the anterior portion of the glottis. The folds appear floppy and are often referred to as having an "elephant ear" appearance (Sataloff, 1997b).

d. **Medicosurgical management.** Although removal of the source of laryngeal irritation may well be all that is necessary to eliminate the polypoid masses in some patients, surgery may be required, followed by an intensive program of voice therapy. When surgery is indicated in Reinke's edema, it is usually performed on only one fold at a time. The surgeon will generally wait for the first fold to heal before operating on the second fold. The procedure for the first fold may result in an acceptable voice, and the patient may elect not to have the second procedure (Sataloff, 1997a). (see Chap. 5, **III**).

e. **Voice therapy management.** Patients with lesser degrees of Reinke's edema improve with removal of laryngeal irritants and with intensive voice therapy (see Chap. 5, **III**). Good vocal hygiene must be established in the patient to prevent the return of this trauma-induced lesion.

3. **Laryngitis sicca** is a specific form of chronic irritation of the vocal folds that is characterized by dryness and atrophy of the laryngeal mucosa, including the glandular structures. When chronic laryngitis is allowed to continue untreated, marked atrophy of the laryngeal mucosa, or laryngitis sicca, may result (Colton & Casper, 1996). The atrophic mucosal glands are unable to provide the larynx with its natural internal lubrication, which results in excessive dryness of the larynx. Laryngitis sicca is defined simply as dry voice.

a. **Etiology.** Laryngitis sicca may be caused by **irradiation therapy,** in which the larynx has been included in the field (Ballenger, 1977). Occasionally, a dry larynx follows protracted episodes of chronic nonspecific laryngitis. It may also occur as a result of prolonged use of drying agents such as antihistamines. In many patients, however, the etiology is not obvious.

b. The most persistent **symptoms** of chronic atrophic laryngitis are hoarseness, a persistent cough, and the complaint of a dry, tickly throat. The patient with a chronic dry larynx may have offensive breath odor as a result of the extreme dryness of the laryngeal interior (Ballenger, 1977; L. D. Holinger, 1976b). It is not uncommon for the patient with chronic dry larynx to also suffer from atrophic rhinitis.

c. **Laryngoscopic findings.** Upon laryngeal examination, the laryngeal mucosa appears to be rough, dry, and glazed. Crusts are usually present (similar crusts are found in the nasal passages of patients with atrophic rhinitis). If these crusts are removed by the laryngologist, a raw oozing surface remains, although actual ulceration is rare. Small, tenacious, thick mucous is typically present (Ballenger, 1977).

d. **Medicosurgical management** of laryngitis sicca is usually symptomatic, because the destroyed mucosal glands cannot be regenerated. The primary focus of management is to provide adequate humidification (lubrication and moisture) to the laryngeal interior through the use of mucolytic agents and increased levels of environmental humidity.

e. **Voice therapy management.** Because of the deleterious and permanent effects of a chronically dry larynx, voice therapy has little or no effect upon voice quality. Consequently, voice therapy for patients with atrophic laryngitis is usually not indicated.

4. **Acute laryngitis** is unrelated to chronic laryngitis. Whereas chronic laryngitis is a consequence of laryngeal trauma, acute laryngitis is a consequence of infection. Acute laryngitis may be one symptom of an upper respiratory tract infection or may occur as an isolated condition.

   a. **Etiology.** Acute laryngitis is a common illness that most frequently results from viral infections and occasionally from bacterial infections.

   b. The **symptoms** of acute laryngitis include sore throat, hoarseness, and a nonproductive cough. A mild fever may be present. Talking may exacerbate the throat discomfort.

   c. **Laryngoscopic findings.** A laryngeal examination reveals that the interior of the larynx is reddened and edematous. Vocal fold movement is normal.

   d. **Medicosurgical management** of acute laryngitis involves increased fluids, bed rest, and medication for symptomatic relief of fever, cough, and sore throat. Secondary bacterial infections can be treated with broad-spectrum antibiotics (Ballenger, 1977).

   e. **Voice therapy management** is contraindicated since the vocal symptoms will subside when the upper respiratory tract infection clears and vocal fold edema decreases. Vocal rest is indicated in acute laryngitis. If voice rest is not possible, then the patient should be made aware that they should use the voice as little as possible and with great care. They should speak softly, avoid lengthy phone conversations, avoid clearing the throat, singing, yelling, and so on.

5. **Vocal nodules** (singer's nodes, screamer's nodes) are a localized form of chronic laryngitis. The nodules are benign extensions of the epithelium occurring at the junction of the anterior one-third and posterior two-thirds of the true vocal folds (see Figure 4.1).

   The incidence of vocal nodules varies with age and sex. In children, vocal nodules are more frequent in active, young boys. Nodules in adults, however, are found predominantly in females, particularly those who sing frequently. This distribution may reflect cultural differences in vocal usage by males and females.

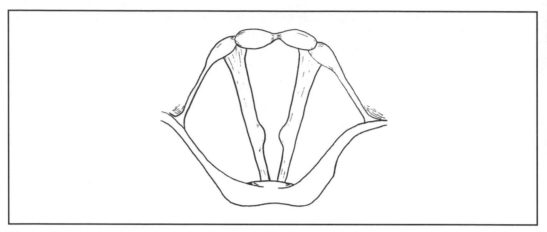

Figure 4.1. Vocal nodules.

a. **Etiology.** Vocal nodules are the result of vocal fold tissue reaction to the trauma and chronic physical stress of vocal hyperfunction. The same factors that cause chronic laryngitis (see **I.C.1**) also contribute to the development of vocal nodules.

Most authorities agree that the added mass of vocal nodules on vocal folds can contribute to a lowering of a patient's habitual pitch level. Opinions differ, however, as to whether vocal nodules are caused by the inappropriate use of a too high or too low habitual pitch level. Regardless of which opinion is correct, use of an inappropriate habitual pitch level, whether too high or too low, can only be maintained through the use of excessive laryngeal tension, which may serve as a factor in the development of the nodules.

b. **Symptoms.** The patient's voice quality is hoarse and breathy with a tendency toward low pitch. Patients with vocal nodules frequently report that their voice quality is best early in the morning and worsens as the day progresses. A nonproductive cough is also a common symptom.

Patients with vocal nodules may talk excessively (Mowrer & Case, 1982; Toohill, 1975) and frequently use a loud voice. These patients are often involved in occupations that demand much vocal usage. Although the patient with vocal nodules may use a low pitch when the speech–language pathologist first meets him or her, it was most likely laryngeal tension, hard glottal attack, and excessive talking that precipitated the formation of the nodules.

c. **Laryngoscopic findings.** Vocal nodules present themselves as bilateral and symmetrical extensions of the epithelium on the margins of the vocal folds at the junction of the anterior one-third and the posterior two-thirds portions. Vocal nodules vary in appearance depending upon their stage of maturity. Recently formed nodules appear soft, reddish, vascular, and edematous, whereas more mature nodules appear hard, white, thickened, and fibrotic. Children's nodules are usually soft and edematous, and are seldom fibrotic (Chagnon & Stone, 1996).

d. Medicosurgical management. Vocal rehabilitation rather than surgical removal is the primary method of treatment for vocal nodules. Frequently, the reduction of vocal fold trauma through voice therapy techniques that alter a patient's method of producing voice is sufficient to reduce the size of or eliminate vocal nodules. Even long-standing, fibrous nodules may be reduced or eliminated through use of a well-planned program of voice therapy. Occasionally, however, mature, fibrous nodules require both surgery and a period of voice therapy for complete resolution.

Because vocal nodules are caused by hyperfunctional vocal behaviors, they can recur after treatment if the vocal behaviors are not eliminated. Patients must understand that good vocal hygiene is the key to preventing the recurrence of vocal nodules.

e. Voice therapy management of vocal nodules is identical to the program previously outlined for chronic laryngitis. This program should include the following procedures:

  (1) A program of **vocal rest** (see Chap. 5, **I**) is optional, unless surgery has been performed, in which case a period of vocal rest is mandatory.

  (2) If a vocal rest program is not instituted, **voice usage should be reduced** for a more rapid regression of the vocal nodules.

  (3) A program of **vocal hygiene** (see Chap. 5, **II**) should be begun.

  (4) Vocal hyperfunctional behaviors, which are maintaining the vocal nodules, must be eliminated. **Voice therapy** for vocal nodules should be directed toward the following goals:

   (a) Elimination of hard glottal attack (see Chap. 5, **III.D.2.b**)

   (b) Increased breath support to permit the most efficient voice production

   (c) Reduced intensity (see Chap. 5, **III.D.2.a**)

6. Vocal polyps are benign extensions of the epithelium that appear on the free margin of the vocal folds secondary to vocal fold trauma. There are two types of polyps: (1) **sessile or broad-based polyps,** which can involve varying extents of the vocal folds (see Figure 4.2), and (2) **pedunculated** or **stem-based polyps,** in which the polyp mass is attached to the vocal fold by a stalk-like appendage (see Figure 4.3).

a. Etiology

  (1) Vocal fold trauma due to one or many episodes of phonotrauma

  (2) Vocal fold trauma induced by other than phonotrauma

  (3) Secondary reactions to:

   (a) Allergies

   (b) Thyroid imbalance

   (c) Upper respiratory tract infection

   (d) Excessive use of alcohol

   (e) Excessive cigarette smoking

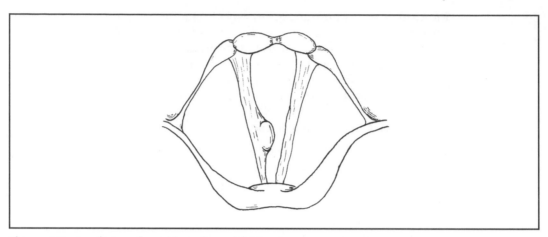

Figure 4.2. Sessile-type (broad-based) vocal fold polyp.

b. Symptoms

(1) Vocal polyps, whether sessile or pedunculated, are usually unilateral. As a result, a common vocal characteristic associated with this type of lesion is **diplophonia,** which is the audible perception of two distinct pitches during phonation (see Chap. 3, **The Voice Evaluation Process, VI.E.2**). Diplophonia in patients with vocal polyps is most likely caused by the increased mass that the polyp adds to just one fold.

(2) **Sudden voice breaks** are also commonly heard in patients with **pedunculated polyps.** These breaks occur because the polypoid stalk bends easily, which allows the body of the polyp to fall between the folds. This sudden insertion of the polyp body between the folds disrupts the pattern of vocal fold vibration and results in a sudden voice break.

(3) Patients with **sessile polyps** generally demonstrate **hoarse and breathy vocal qualities** because of the mass the polyp adds to the vocal folds. Because sessile polyps have broad bases, they are tightly connected to the folds and thus are prevented from bending over into the glottis during phonation. As a result, patients with this kind of polyp do not experience voice breaks. **Airway obstruction** occasionally occurs when the polyp enlarges sufficiently.

c. Laryngoscopic findings.
Examination usually reveals a unilateral vocal fold lesion. The polyp appears as a fluid-filled or blood-engorged sessile or pedunculated mass. Laryngeal polyps typically are found at the junction of the anterior and middle one-third of the vocal fold margin (the same location at which vocal nodules appear). Laryngeal polyps are also occasionally found on the superior and inferior surfaces of the vocal folds. Clinicians should note that physicians may refer to polyps as hemangiomas, fibromas, or myxomas (Andrews, 1995). A blood-filled or hemorrhagic polyp is often the result of a single, traumatic vocal event, and the

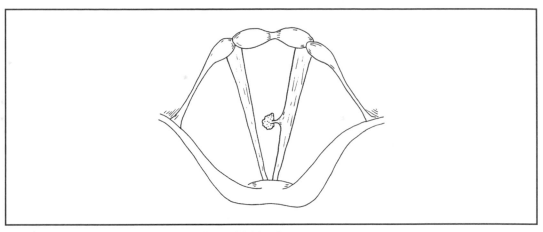

Figure 4.3. Pedunculated (stem-based) vocal fold polyp.

patient may report pain at the time of the precipitating vocal event (Casper, 1998).

d. **Medicosurgical management.** Polyps occasionally disappear without treatment, though surgical removal is often required. Use of lasers in surgery for voice problems remains controversial, but whether lasers or surgical instruments are used, the underlying lamina propria should be disturbed as little as possible (Sataloff, 1997a). Surgery may be delayed in cases of smaller polyps to see if voice therapy is effective in reducing the size of the lesion. Low dose oral steroids may resolve polyps in as little as 4 weeks for some patients (Sataloff, 1997b.)

e. **Voice therapy management.** Voice therapy is usually the initial treatment for small polyps. This therapy should be focused on establishing vocal behaviors in the patient that are conducive to reducing the size of the polyp. Small polyps may require as much as 2 to 6 months of voice therapy before there is any significant improvement in voice quality.

Voice therapy for the purpose of establishing improved vocal behaviors may also be indicated **following surgery.** This will help prevent recurrence of the polyp and eliminate any hoarseness or breathiness. Voice management of laryngeal polyps, like the management programs for other phonotrauma related lesions, should include the following procedures:

(1) A program of **vocal rest** (see Chap. 5, **I**) should be considered.

(2) A program of **vocal hygiene** (see Chap. 5, **II**) should be instituted, with the primary goal being identification of factors related to the individual patient's phonotrauma.

(3) The following examples of phonotrauma should be altered or eliminated:

(a) Hard glottal attack should be eliminated (see Chap. 5, **III.D.2**).

(b) Breath support should be increased.

(c) Vocal intensity should be reduced (see Chap. 5, **III.D.1**).

(d) Voice usage should be reduced.

7. **Vocal fold cysts** are fluid-filled lesions that have an epithelial case or shell around them causing them to be encapsulated.

   a. **Etiology.** Cysts may be congenital, or they may be the result of poor lymphatic drainage (Casper, 1998) possibly combined with phonotrauma (Andrews, 1995). Cysts are generally unilateral, but multiple cysts occur. When a cyst occurs bilaterally, it is not unusual for the patient to be given a diagnosis of vocal nodules (Stemple et al., 1995).

   b. **Symptoms.** The patient may be mildly to moderately dysphonic depending on the size and location of the cysts. The voice has been described as low pitched, hoarse, and "tired" (Colton & Casper, 1996). Large cysts may prevent glottic adduction, and a breathy quality may be heard (Sataloff, 1997b).

   c. **Laryngoscopic findings.** Cysts protrude onto the vibratory margin of the vocal fold, increasing mass and stiffness of the fold (Sataloff, 1997a). Stroboscopic findings can be helpful in diagnosing cysts, as the mass and stiffness characteristics of the fold with a unilateral cyst may be more pronounced than that of the opposite fold even if the opposite fold is thickened (Stemple et al., 1995).

   d. **Medicosurgical management.** Cysts must almost always be surgically removed, although occasionally a cyst will disappear spontaneously. The desired goal in surgical removal is to remove the encapsulated cyst with as little disruption as possible to the mucosa (Sataloff, 1997a).

   e. **Voice therapy management.** Trial voice therapy for a period of 4 to 6 weeks following diagnosis may preceed surgical removal, although surgery is usually required (Andrews, 1995; Sataloff, 1997a). Postsurgical voice therapy is also indicated (Stemple et al., 1995). Voice therapy procedures are similar to those discussed for nodules and polyps, with the goal of therapy being to help the patient find his or her best and healthiest voice.

8. **A contact ulcer (contact granuloma)** is a benign lesion that develops on the vocal process of the arytenoid cartilages, secondary to vocal abuse (see Figure 4.4). The ulceration may be unilateral or bilateral. As contact ulcers heal, they are soon replaced by granulated and, eventually, fibrous tissue.

   a. **Etiology.** A contact ulcer is caused by repeated hyperadduction of the vocal processes of the arytenoid cartilages. Traditionally, contact ulcers have been thought to be most prevalent in professional men, who may be characterized as ambitious, upwardly mobile, and very hard driven. Low pitch (sometimes as low as glottal fry), persistent hard glottal attack, and sudden, abrupt vocalizations appear to be etiologic.

   Gastroesophageal reflux disease (GERD) also contributes significantly to this disorder. Contact ulcer patients frequently have a history of stress-related gastrointestinal difficulties, such as hiatus hernia, heartburn, acidity, peptic or duodenal ulcer, and stress reaction in the abdomen. The

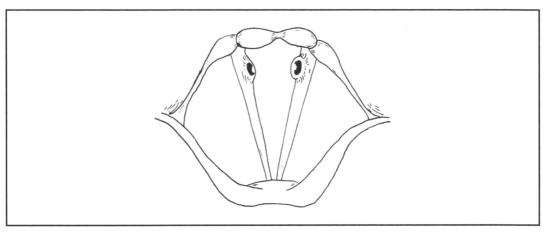

Figure 4.4. Bilateral contact ulcers.

contact ulcer may be complicated by gastric reflux during sleep, which further irritates the ulcer and retards healing.

b. **Symptoms.** Because contact ulcers occur on the tips of the arytenoids rather than on the vibrating vocal fold, patients with contact ulcers may not have vocal symptoms. Patients with contact ulcers most frequently complain of pain in the larynx (either unilateral or bilateral), vocal fatigue, and occasionally referred pain to the lateral neck area or the ear, especially during swallowing (L. D. Holinger, 1976b). The patient may also complain of a persistent tickling of the throat, a nonproductive cough, and a sensation of a lump in the throat (Ballenger, 1977). The patient's voice may be tense, slightly hoarse, low pitched, and breathy. This breathiness most likely results from the patient's efforts to avoid forming a tight contact between the arytenoids during phonation because of the pain that results.

As the ulceration begins to heal, it becomes granulated (contact granuloma). This granulated tissue eventually may become fibrous and large enough to interfere with vocal fold adduction. As a result, vocal quality is usually more affected in the later, rather than earlier, stages of the lesion.

c. **Laryngoscopic findings.** Laryngoscopic examination of a patient with a contact ulcer reveals a pale-colored, sessile lesion on the vocal process of each arytenoid cartilage. Although this lesion may be unilateral, it is most commonly bilateral. Granulated tissue may be observed on the perimeter of the ulcer.

d. **Medicosurgical management.** The primary method of treatment of contact ulcers at all stages is a program of voice therapy (Bloch & Gould, 1974; Bloch, Gould, & Hirano, 1981). If gastroesophageal reflux disorder is contributing to the problem, patients should be seen by a physician for dietary management and medication as indicated (Sataloff, 1997b). Surgery should be considered only after an intensive program of vocal hygiene and voice therapy has failed to reduce or eliminate the contact ulcer. Surgery for the removal of contact ulcers becomes progressively more complicated each time it is performed because the length of time for healing following surgery also increases with each surgical procedure (Ballantyne, 1971).

e. **Voice therapy management.** Prior to 1950, voice management of contact ulcers frequently included a period of vocal rest (Peacher, 1947). Since that time, a program of voice therapy without vocal rest has been the usual approach. Voice therapy without vocal rest has been shown to reduce or eliminate contact ulcers without causing the financial and emotional hardships that are often associated with vocal rest.

The core of a voice management program for patients with a contact ulcer should be a program of **vocal hygiene** (see Chap. 5, **II**). If gastroesophageal reflux contributes to the patient's problem, foods that can irritate the ulcer, such as hot liquids or spicy foods, should be eliminated from the patient's diet. The patient should also take medications as prescribed by his or her physician for gastroesophageal reflux. The diet should be further modified to decrease the patient's need to clear the throat. This can be done by eliminating foods or liquids that thicken saliva.

It has been suggested that patients should **not substitute whispering** for normal phonation, particularly when the individual is producing a forced whisper. Increases in expiratory muscle effort and airflow during forced whisper may suggest an accompanying increase in effort and possibly in muscular tension (Colton & Casper, 1996).

Therapy designed to alter a patient's method of voice production should proceed at a slow, relaxed pace, which should help to alleviate the patient's stress. As the voice is occasionally asymptomatic in patients with contact ulcers, a decrease in the amount of laryngeal pain may be the measure of success of the therapy program. Even though the vocal folds may evidence complete remission of the contact ulcer, voice therapy must continue until inefficient vocal behaviors are completely eliminated and habits of efficient voice production are well established. In addition, the patient's concept of what elements constitute efficient voice production should be altered. Most frequently, the elimination of hard glottal attack (see Chap. 5, **III.D.2**) and the elimination of an inappropriately low-pitched voice (see Chap. 5, **III.D.3**) should receive primary emphasis.

Another crucial component of voice management should be consideration of the **psychological component.** The patient and therapist should explore the relationship between the patient's voice and his or her self-concept. Stress reduction techniques, use of electromyograph (EMG) biofeedback to reduce muscle tension, and techniques of relaxation (see Chap. 5, **III.D.4**) may need to be taught to the patient.

9. **Keratosis of the larynx** is a term that is used to refer to laryngeal lesions that are characterized by abnormal growth or maturation of the epithelium. Abnormal epithelial development occurs as a response to (1) laryngeal trauma, especially cigarette smoking and other forms of vocal hyperfunction, and (2) protracted cases of chronic laryngitis. The terms **leukoplakia, hyperkeratosis,** and **keratosis** are used to refer to these lesions. The

major concern with these lesions is that some of them have been associated with laryngeal carcinoma.

In order to differentiate these lesions, a histologic examination by a pathologist is necessary. Although laryngologists may use these terms to describe laryngeal lesions they have viewed during laryngoscopy, no lesion can be considered premalignant until a pathologic examination has been performed.

Much confusion has arisen about the different types of lesions, particularly with regard to the exact relationship of each type to carcinoma of the larynx. The confusion is related to the issues of (1) which type, or types, of lesion actually represents a premalignant condition, and (2) how each type of lesion should be treated by the physician. The need for clarity regarding these issues is important, because greater clarity might prevent some patients from unnecessarily undergoing radical therapy and might ensure that patients with significant disease receive adequate treatment or follow-up.

a. Generally, **laryngeal hyperkeratosis** is considered to be the most benign in this spectrum of histologic lesions (Ogura & Thawley, 1980). It is characterized by an irregular piling up of a proteinaceous substance called keratin that produces reddened, verrucous (wart-like) lesions. Although laryngeal hyperkeratosis is found on rare occasions to be associated with laryngeal carcinoma (Andrews, 1995), the incidence of laryngeal hyperkeratosis becoming invasive carcinoma is only 3% (McGavran, Bauer, & Ogura, 1960).

  (1) **Etiologies.** Laryngeal hyperkeratosis results from trauma to the larynx, especially to the vocal folds. The trauma can be caused by the following:

   (a) Inhalation of dust and noxious fumes, particularly cigarette smoke

   (b) Excessive use of alcohol

   (c) Chronic infection of the sinuses and pharynx

   (d) Chronic laryngitis

   (e) Radiation injury

  (2) The chief **symptom** of laryngeal hyperkeratosis is vocal hoarseness, which is occasionally accompanied by lowered vocal pitch.

  (3) **Laryngoscopic findings.** Laryngeal hyperkeratosis appears as a plaque-like, irregular thickening of the laryngeal mucosa, usually on the true vocal folds. It may appear as a reddish papillary lesion or as a keratin-covered area of irregular mucosa (Ballenger, 1977). In addition, the vocal folds may show evidence of inflammation and generalized edema. Movement of the vocal folds is usually normal. A biopsy is required for conclusive identification of the lesion.

  (4) **Medicosurgical management.** When a histologic examination confirms a diagnosis of hyperkeratosis, a conservative course of therapy is usually followed. The patient is instructed to avoid exposure to laryngeal irritants (especially cigarette smoke) and to eliminate

vocal hyperfunctional behaviors. Many lesions will disappear if these measures are taken. Since laryngeal hyperkeratosis can, on rare occasions, be a premalignant condition, the patient should be carefully followed by a laryngologist.

(5) **Voice therapy management.** Instruct the patient with regard to the importance of eliminating any phonotrauma. A program of management that establishes good vocal hygiene should be initiated (see Chap. 5, **II**).

b. **Laryngeal leukoplakia.** The term **leukoplakia** is the name commonly given to white patches on mucous membranes anywhere in the body. Laryngeal leukoplakia, one form of the disease, occurs more often in males, although its incidence is increasing in females. This lesion often takes the form of a white patch of plaque-like cells appearing in the larynx. Laryngeal leukoplakia may be deemed premalignant if histologic evaluation reveals the presence of epithelial dyskeratosis.

(1) **Etiologies.** Laryngeal leukoplakia results from chronic irritation to the larynx. The etiologies are similar to those in hyperkeratosis (see **I.C.5.a.(1)** earlier in this chapter).

(2) **Symptoms.** Chronic vocal hoarseness is the primary symptom in cases where leukoplakia involves the vocal folds. Otherwise, the patient may be asymptomatic.

(3) **Laryngoscopic findings.** As the name leukoplakia (white plaque) suggests, an examination of the larynx reveals large, whitish patches on the mucosal tissue. The lesion is especially prominent on the anterior portion of the vocal folds. Histologic evaluation is required for an accurate diagnosis of leukoplakia.

(4) **Medicosurgical management.** If the lesion has been induced through chronic laryngeal irritation, removal of the irritant (which is often cigarette smoking) generally results in spontaneous regression of the leukoplakia. Severe lesions frequently require more extensive medicosurgical management. If histologic examination of leukoplakia reveals epithelial dyskeratosis (cellular atypia), then the leukoplakia should be considered premalignant and the physician should manage the patient accordingly.

Sometimes, laryngeal leukoplakia is confused with carcinoma in situ. Histologically, carcinoma in situ of the larynx represents a pathologic condition in which the squamous epithelium is replaced by cells that have a malignant morphologic pattern but do not extend beneath the basement membrane and into deeper layers (Ogura & Thawley, 1980). According to English (1976c), the histologic findings in carcinoma in situ are similar to the findings in cases of laryngeal leukoplakia with epithelial dyskeratosis.

The strobosocopic image may assist in ruling out carcinoma. Generally, in early keratosis and leukoplakia, there may be a fairly normal mucosal wave. However, in carcinoma, the mucosal wave may be limited, indicating deeper invasion of the tissue (Colton & Casper, 1996).

(5) **Voice therapy management.** Hoarseness due to leukoplakia is generally not responsive to voice therapy. Removal of the laryngeal irritant (including vocal abuse or misuse) and an optional program of vocal rest (see Chap. 5, **I**) should be the primary methods of treatment.

II. **Dysphonias Caused by Mechanical Trauma to the Larynx.** On rare occasions, the larynx can be traumatized by external assault to the anterior neck region. It might seem surprising that injuries from accidental blows to the anterior neck region do not occur more frequently than they actually do, especially considering that the region appears so poorly protected; however, the mandible and the sternum usually receive the major impact from any forceful assault (Sofferman & Hubbell, 1981). Other ways in which the larynx can be mechanically traumatized are improper use of endoscopic instruments and procedures, improperly placed nasogastric tubes, and improper tracheostomy.

Often, mechanical trauma results in direct injury to the highly distensible laryngeal submucosal tissue, which causes edema and hematoma formation. At other times, mechanical trauma can result in dislocation or fracture of the laryngeal cartilages. On occasion, laryngeal fractures and dislocations may go unnoticed in the rush of emergency room procedures, only to be discovered several days, or even weeks, later, when fibrosis and stenosis have already developed. Penetrating wounds of the larynx, on the other hand, are immediately noticeable.

The dysphonia that results from mechanical trauma may vary from a mild hoarseness to complete aphonia. If hoarseness develops following mechanical trauma to the larynx, it is indicative of injury to the vocal folds from edema, hematoma, laceration, presence of a foreign body, or paralysis (Templer, 1976).

A. **Sources of mechanical trauma to the larynx**

1. **External sources**

a. **Automobile accidents.** A common cause of mechanical injury to the adult and adolescent larynx are automobile accidents in which the neck region and larynx are thrust into the steering wheel, instrument panel, or a broken windshield. Most of these injuries could have been prevented if the driver and passengers had used seat belts and shoulder harness restraints. Laryngeal fractures and dislocated cartilages are the most common injuries associated with laryngeal trauma due to automobile accidents. Penetrating wounds of the larynx can also be caused by a piece of broken windshield or other sharp objects.

b. **Forceful assault from blunt objects.** Mechanical injury frequently occurs as a result of blunt objects striking the larynx with great force. One example of this type of accident is one in which a child runs or rides a bicycle into a tightly stretched wire. If the wire strikes at the level of the larynx, the laryngeal cartilages may be fractured or dislocated, or the trachea and larynx may actually be separated.

Another example of forceful assault to the larynx occurs in incidents in which the victim is hit in the laryngeal region by a baseball bat or other blunt club that is being used in recreational play. Fractures and dislocations of laryngeal cartilages are some of the most common injuries associated with forceful assault from blunt objects.

c. **Penetrating injuries to the larynx** usually result from automobile accidents or from gunshot or knife wounds.

d. **Complications of a too-high tracheostomy.** Because the cricoid cartilage is difficult to distinguish from a tracheal ring in young children, the tube used in a tracheostomy (surgical creation of an opening into the trachea through the neck) may be accidentally inserted through the cricothyroid membrane or occasionally through the cricoid cartilage itself. Adults may also be injured in this way during the rush of emergency room procedures. Serious injury is infrequent if the cricoid cartilage is not fractured and if the malpositioned tracheostomy tube is removed within 24 to 48 hours. If the high-positioned tracheostomy tube is allowed to remain for a longer period of time, or if the cricoid cartilage is badly damaged, perichondritis (inflammation of the connective tissue that covers all cartilage) of the cricoid cartilage, excessive granulation, and infraglottic stenosis (narrowing or constriction) frequently result. A too-high tracheostomy is a common cause of laryngeal stenosis (Ballenger, 1977).

2. **Internal sources**

a. **Improper endoscopic examination procedures.** Although the incidence of laryngeal injury due to endoscopy is decreasing as a result of improved endoscopic techniques, improved instrumentation, and an increasing awareness of this type of injury, it still sometimes occurs. The most common laryngeal injury of this type is dislocation of the cricoarytenoid joint (see **II.B.2.b** later in this chapter).

b. **Endotracheal intubation.** The presence of an endotracheal tube during lengthy surgical procedures can cause trauma to the thin mucosa that covers the vocal process of the arytenoid. This source of laryngeal injury is especially common in female patients because of the smaller size and structural relationships of the female larynx. When the endotracheal tube is passed through the female larynx, the small size of the larynx causes the tube to lie more posteriorly. In this position, the tube has a greater likelihood of irritating the mucosa that covers the arytenoids, thus causing an intubation granuloma to develop (see **II.B.1.a** later in this chapter).

c. **Indwelling nasogastric tubes.** Although nasogastric tubes are commonly used in medicine and surgery, complications develop in approximately 6% of patients intubated for more than 3 days (Friedman et al., 1981). As a nasogastric tube courses through the esophagus to the stomach, it passes just posterior to the lamina of the cricoid cartilage. If the tube is placed in the esophagus in the midline rather than lateral position, it can rub against the postcricoid mucosa during swallowing and phonatory movements, thus causing an ulceration of the postcricoid mucosa. Infection of the perichondrium and the cricoid cartilage itself often results, and cases of temporary bilateral vocal fold paralysis have been reported (Sofferman & Hubbell, 1981). The continued presence of infection can lead to perichondritis, chondral necrosis (death of cartilaginous tissue), and stenosis of the infraglottic region. Hoarseness and laryngeal pain that radiates to the ears are symptomatic of midline naso-gastric tube placement.

B. **Types of laryngeal lesions and injuries caused by mechanical trauma**

1. **Laryngeal lesions**

a. **Intubation granuloma** is a lesion that develops in the region of the vocal process of the arytenoids as a result of endotracheal tube trauma to the larynx. Although the lesion usually results from prolonged intubation during lengthy surgical procedures, it may also appear following short-term intubations. Fewer than 1% of all patients receiving endotracheal intubation develop an intubation granuloma (L. D. Holinger, 1976b). The lesion is more frequent in women and children, because the endotracheal tube tends to lie more posteriorly in the larynx of these patients due to the size and configuration of their larynges (Balestrieri & Watson, 1982; Ballenger, 1977).

Although bilateral lesions can occur, intubation granulomas are usually unilateral. Intubation granulomas are members of a group of nonspecific granulomas that also includes contact ulcers (see **I.C.4**) and granulomas secondary to gastroesophageal reflux.

(1) **Etiology.** Intubation granulomas develop as a consequence of assault to the larynx from either the introduction of an endotracheal tube or from the constant pressure the tube exerts on the vocal folds during surgery. The lesion begins as an ulceration, which then becomes infected. Infection tends to retard healing by preventing reepithelialization, so granulation tissue is soon formed.

(2) **Symptoms**

(a) Discomfort in the area of the larynx and, occasionally, pain referred to the ear (Ballenger, 1977).

(b) Persistent cough.

(c) Vocal hoarseness postoperatively.

(d) Because the size of the lesion may prevent complete approximation of the vocal folds, the voice may sound breathy.

(3) **Laryngoscopic findings** in a patient with an intubation granuloma vary depending on the stage of growth of the lesion. The lesion generally develops according to the following course (Snow, Hirano, & Balough, 1966):

(a) An **abrasion** or **irritation** of the vocal process of one or both arytenoids appears, varying in size from microscopic to easily visible.

(b) This irritated region soon becomes covered by granulated tissue and forms a **sessile-type lesion.**

(c) As healing occurs, the base of the granuloma becomes narrowed until the lesion becomes **pedunculated.** Autoamputation of the lesion may occur as the stalk atrophies.

(4) **Medicosurgical management** of intubation granulomas generally involves surgical removal of the lesion.

(5) **Voice therapy management.** A period of voice therapy following surgical removal of the granuloma may be necessary if a patient with intubation granuloma is to regain a normal voice (Boone & McFarlane, 1994).

b. **Traumatic laryngeal web.** As a consequence of trauma or infection, a small piece of connective tissue may form anteriorly between the vocal folds (see Figure 4.5). This tissue, which is called a laryngeal web, can have adverse effects on voice production and, occasionally, respiration.

(1) **Etiology.** Traumatic laryngeal webs are formed by laryngeal tissue in reaction to forceful mechanical trauma or chronic infection. Traumatic laryngeal webs are similar in appearance (but etiologically unrelated) to congenital laryngeal webs (see Chap. 7, **II.C**).

(2) **Symptoms**

(a) The effect that a traumatic laryngeal web has on the voice depends upon the extent of the web. Small webs located at the anterior commissure have little effect on voicing. Webs that are large enough to effectively limit the vibratory portion of the vocal folds can cause an **elevation in vocal pitch.**

(b) The patient's voice may also have a **hoarse** quality due to asynchronous vibration of the vocal folds as a result of the web.

(c) The patient may experience no difficulty with quiet, at-rest breathing, but **stridor and difficulty with breathing** may occur during forceful respiration if the web occludes the airway sufficiently.

(3) **Laryngoscopic findings.** The laryngoscopic examination reveals a web of connective tissue that partially occludes the larynx. These

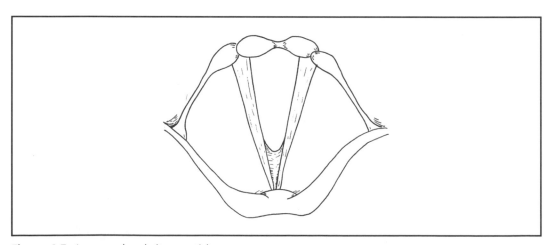

Figure 4.5. Laryngeal web (traumatic).

webs are located at the anterior commissure and grow posteriorly. The thickness of the web varies from patient to patient.

(4) **Medicosurgical management** of traumatic laryngeal webs may initially include repeated attempts to dilate the web using a broncho-scope. If repeated attempts at dilation fail, the web must be surgically separated and the raw edges cauterized. To prevent the surgically separated halves of the web from reuniting, the surgeon usually places a thin keel between the vocal folds temporarily until the raw surfaces where the web was divided have healed.

2. **Dislocation of the articulating joints of the laryngeal cartilages.** Dislocation of the cricoarytenoid joint can be caused by external or internal sources of trauma. The dislocation is rarely bilateral.

a. **Etiology.** In some instances, a **strong blow** to the anterior neck forces the cricoid cartilage posteriorly, resulting in an anterior dislocation of the cricoarytenoid joint. In other instances, **dislocation of the joint** occurs as a consequence of improper endoscopic examination procedures.

b. **Symptoms.** At the time of injury, pain and hoarseness will be present. If edema becomes severe and narrows the airway, **dyspnea and stridor** will develop. Hoarseness is a common vocal symptom because the dislocated arytenoid cannot move and vocal fold adduction is prevented or limited.

c. **Laryngoscopic findings.** Laryngoscopic examination reveals a flaccid, bowed vocal fold in association with an anteriorly displaced arytenoid. Vocal fold approximation during phonation is incomplete.

d. **Medicosurgical management** frequently involves the following (Ballenger, 1977; Benninger & Gardner, 1998; Casiano & Goodwin, 1991):

(1) **Direct manipulation** of the arytenoid into correct alignment with the cricoid cartilage

(2) **Injection of collagen, fat, or other substances** into the affected vocal fold to improve vocal quality if arytenoid reduction is not possible or if the arytenoid does not regain adequate adductor function

e. **Voice therapy management.** If medicosurgical techniques are unable to restore arytenoid function and if injection into the affected fold is required, voice therapy techniques directed at increasing glottal tension may be required to improve voice quality (see Chap. 8, **VII.E.4.a–b**).

3. **Fractures of the laryngeal cartilages.** Fractures of the larynx and the hyoid bone do occur; however, the incidence is relatively low.

a. **Etiology.** Laryngeal fractures are most often the result of automobile accidents in which the patient's neck is thrust into the steering wheel or dashboard.

b. **Symptoms.** Stridor and cyanosis may develop following a laryngeal fracture, and such fractures usually necessitate a tracheostomy to provide an adequate airway for the patient. If airway obstruction is developing, the patient's voice may sound muffled.

c. **Laryngoscopic findings.** Laryngeal fractures are often accompanied by swelling and tears in the laryngeal mucosa, which results in narrowing or obstruction of the laryngeal airway. The epiglottis may be displaced posteriorly, thus covering the laryngeal lumen. Unilateral or bilateral vocal fold paralysis may be present.

d. **Medicosurgical management** of laryngeal fractures typically includes resectioning of the fractured part, the insertion of an indwelling plastic stent to maintain the laryngeal airway, and occasionally a skin graft at the site of the injury.

e. **Voice therapy management** directed at improving glottal closure (see Chap. 8, **VII.E.4.a–b**) may be beneficial; however, the voice will usually remain breathy and hoarse due to the permanently altered conditions of the larynx.

III. Dysphonias Caused by Burns to the Larynx

A. **Thermal burns of the larynx** are often seen in firefighters and members of rescue squads.

1. **Etiology.** Thermal burns of the larynx are usually caused by the inhalation of hot air or gases. Burns of the interior of the larynx can also occur secondary to the ingestion of hot foods or liquids. First-degree and second-degree burns are more common than third-degree burns, and burns of the supraglottic larynx are more common than those of the lower airway (Casiano & Goodwin, 1991). Healing is usually relatively rapid, and chronic stenosis rarely develops as a result of thermal burns.

2. **Symptoms.** The patient's voice is hoarse and severe pain accompanies the patient's attempts to phonate. Stridor and respiratory obstruction may be present.

3. **Laryngoscopic findings.** The false folds appear red and edematous, and the true vocal folds are burned over the anterior two-thirds (Ballenger, 1977).

4. **Medicosurgical management** includes the following:

   a. Emergency **tracheostomy** for laryngeal obstruction due to edema, although the edema usually subsides rapidly.

   b. Administration of **antibiotics** to prevent infection.

   c. **Humidification of laryngeal tissue** to promote healing.

5. **Voice therapy management** generally includes a period of vocal rest (see Chap. 5, **I**). Hoarseness usually resolves spontaneously as the edema subsides; therefore, direct voice therapy techniques are contraindicated.

B. **Chemical burns of the larynx** occur most frequently in children.

1. **Etiology.** Chemical burns of the larynx are caused by ingestion of corrosive chemicals.

2. **Symptoms.** First-, second-, and third-degree burns are common. The esophagus and hypopharyngeal region are also frequently burned. Often, ulcera-

tion and infection occur, followed by the development of granulated and fibrotic lesions. The voice is characterized as hoarse and breathy, or the patient may be aphonic.

3. **Laryngoscopic findings.** An indirect laryngeal examination reveals that the supraglottic structures are reddened and edematous. With severe burns, there will be actual charring, with the mucous membrane appearing gray-black. If the epithelial surface of the epiglottis has been denuded by the burn, it will appear white (Ballenger, 1977).

4. **Medicosurgical management** typically includes the use of antibiotics and steroids to prevent infection and fibrosis; however, chronic supraglottic stenosis frequently results despite this treatment regimen.

5. **Voice therapy management** directed at improving glottal closure (see Chap. 8, **VII.E.4.a–b**) may be beneficial; however, severe scarring and cicatricial stenosis (narrowing due to the formation of scar tissue) resulting from adhesions between the false folds usually prevents much improvement in voice quality.

Chapter 5
Voice Therapy Treatments for Phonotrauma

♦ ♦

Voice therapy management for dysphonias related to laryngeal hyperfunction (phonotrauma) involves the use of techniques that are designed to reduce vocal fold hyperfunction, to reduce muscle tension in the laryngeal and pharyngeal regions, and to restore normal tone to affected speech muscles. Voice therapy techniques will not guarantee the patient a good voice. Rather, they are intended to assist the patient in producing the best possible voice in the clinical setting, with the expectation that the patient will eventually abandon the actual techniques while retaining the improvements in voice made possible by the techniques.

Laryngeal hyperfunction (phonotrauma), which may be associated with vocal misuse, typically results in pathologic laryngeal conditions (e.g., chronic laryngitis, vocal nodules, and vocal polyps) that are usually reversible with the cessation of laryngeal hyperfunction. Voice therapy management must, therefore, incorporate programs that assist the patient in identifying and eliminating those vocal activities that are characterized by laryngeal hyperfunction. In addition, for some patients, a program of vocal rest may be required, at least for a limited period of time. While the benefits of voice rest as a therapy are unproven, anecdotal information suggests that it has value in certain situations.

I. **Program of Vocal Rest.** Vocal rest, either modified or total, is a program in which the patient's use of the larynx is restricted for a specified period of time. Vocal rest is usually prescribed for a period of 4 to 7 days, but it is rarely prescribed for longer than 7 days (Sataloff, 1997a).

A. **Indications for vocal rest.** Speech–language pathologists and laryngologists typically prescribe vocal rest in three situations:

1. Mandatory vocal rest is frequently prescribed to promote the healing of surgically traumatized tissues following various forms of **laryngeal surgery**, especially surgery involving the margins of the vocal folds. The benefit of vocal rest in these cases is that, by eliminating phonation and other laryngeal activities, it prevents the irritation caused by vocal fold vibration and vocal fold adduction.

2. Vocal rest is important as the initial treatment of **some lesions of the larynx,** including vocal fold hemorrhage and mucosal tear. Elimination of the irritating effects of vocal adduction through a program of vocal rest frequently permits these lesions to regress and lessens the severity of any associated dysphonia.

3. A program of **modified vocal rest** (i.e., speaking only when absolutely essential and using healthy vocal strategies) may be valuable when the patient is experiencing an acute inflammation of the voice such as with a cold, or following development of vocal nodules or vocal fold edema.

B. **Advantages and disadvantages of a vocal rest program.** Use of vocal rest in a program of voice rehabilitation is controversial. Some professionals believe that a program of vocal rest should not be used for voice management purposes because it places too many unrealistic demands and hardships on the patient. Others advocate the use of vocal rest in certain situations because of its therapeutic effects and because of the diagnostic and prognostic information it can provide (Sataloff, 1997a). The controversy that surrounds the question of whether or not to use vocal rest hangs on whether or not the benefits to the patient outweigh the hardships. The following are some of the advantages and disadvantages of a program of vocal rest.

1. **Advantages**

   a. Vocal rest usually allows a rapid **reduction in size and severity of the laryngeal lesion,** which is accompanied by a concomitant decrease in the severity of the associated dysphonia.

   b. A properly followed program of vocal rest can give the patient an opportunity to easily identify those situations in his or her life that promote misuse. **Identification of situation-specific vocal behavior** is the first step in enabling the patient to modify the situations that promote vocal misuse.

   c. Use of a program of vocal rest also allows the speech–language pathologist to **determine a patient's commitment to the process of voice improvement.** If a patient is unable to complete the assignment of a 4 to 7 day voice rest, the question must be raised as to whether the patient is able to make the commitment necessary to change his or her vocal habits.

2. **Disadvantages**

   a. Patients who use their voices professionally may find it **financially impossible** to complete a vocal rest program.

   b. It is an extremely **difficult task** for the average person to adhere to a program of vocal rest, and an even more difficult task for people who misuse their voice, as these patients frequently have very "talky" personalities. Instructing a patient to reduce talking slightly while using a manner of voice production that does not harm the vocal mechanism is probably a more realistic goal than having a patient go from an unusually large amount of talking to no talking at all.

   c. Some patients become depressed with continued vocal rest. Because some forms of vocal misuse are related to emotional or personality disturbances, the additional burden of **depression** secondary to vocal rest has the potential to seriously compromise the patient's state of mental well-being.

C. **Description of vocal rest programs.** There are essentially two different programs of vocal rest: the first is a program in which complete vocal rest is followed, and the second is a modified program in which voice use is significantly reduced but not completely eliminated. In each program it is important that the patient understand that whispering is not an alternative to voice rest, as it may result in increased laryngeal dryness (Colton & Casper, 1996) and effort.

1. **General procedures.** Using simple diagrams, the patient should be given an explanation of normal vocal fold functioning and an explanation of the effects of vocal behaviors on the folds. The explanation may have to be rephrased into several different versions until it is certain that the patient thoroughly understands the concept of how abusive vocal activities result in vocal fold trauma. When the patient is familiarized with the typical vocal activities that result in laryngeal trauma (see Chap. 4, **I.A & B**), a recording of the patient's voice should be made using a standard reading passage (see Chap. 3, **The Voice Evaluation Process, II.B**). Replay the recording of the patient's voice and discuss with him or her the characteristics that are present in the voice. Several replays of the recording may be necessary before the patient can identify the various disturbed parameters of the voice. Also ask the patient to rate the severity of the recorded voice sample and make note of this severity rating for later analysis.

2. **Program of complete vocal rest.** The patient is instructed to eliminate all activities that either adduct the vocal folds into forced approximation with each other or that cause the vocal folds to vibrate and result in the production of sound (e.g., talking, singing, coughing, laughing). The patient should be given the following guidelines, with instructions to follow them explicitly (see also the informational handouts in Appendix B).

   a. **Activities to avoid.** The patient should be instructed to avoid the following activities, which result in vocal fold adduction:

      (1) Speaking

      (2) Singing

      (3) Humming

      (4) Whispering

      (5) Coughing

      (6) Throat clearing

      (7) Laughing

      (8) Lifting or pushing heavy objects

      (9) Forceful effort during bowel movements

   b. The patient should be instructed to cough and clear the throat only with the following **method of silent coughing and throat clearing** (Zwitman & Calcaterra, 1973):

      (1) **Procedure.** Instruct the patient to push as much air as possible from the lungs in short, blast-like bursts. Tell the patient that the only sound produced should be a quiet rush of air.

(2) **Benefits.** The silent cough method prevents vocal fold adduction during coughing and throat clearing and reduces the duration of throat clearing.

3. **Program of modified vocal rest for adults** (see informational handouts in Appendix B). A program of modified vocal rest provides the adult patient with a slightly less rigid program than full vocal rest by allowing some talking under controlled conditions.

   a. **Conditions under which vocalization is permitted.** With the modified vocal rest program, conversational rules are strictly followed:

      (1) Conversation should be limited to a total time of no more than 15 minutes per day.

      (2) Each period of talking must be limited to no more than 5 minutes in duration.

      (3) Conversations must be on a one-to-one basis and in an environment that has a minimum level of background noise.

   b. **Activities to avoid.** As in the program of complete vocal rest, the patient should not sing, whisper, or hum. Lifting, pushing, and forceful elimination (all of which forcefully adduct the vocal folds) should be avoided.

   c. **Conditions under which coughing and throat clearing are permitted.** Coughing and throat clearing are permitted as long as the silent cough or throat clearing method (see **I.C.2.b**) is used.

4. **Program of modified vocal rest for children** (see informational handouts in Appendix B). Attempting to reduce the talking time of an adult patient is difficult at best, but trying to quiet a noisy youngster is an even greater challenge. While the primary goal of the modified vocal rest program for children is to reduce talking time by one-half or more, children often find it more difficult than adults to refrain from talking. As a result, their periods of vocal rest are often less

   A vocal rest program can only be used with a child who understands what has caused his or her laryngeal lesion (see Chap. 4, **I.A & B**). If the child is too young or cannot understand the responsibility of vocal rest, then vocal rest should be avoided as a therapy approach with the child.

   Children who are able to understand and to take responsiblity should be told that the responsibility for changing their vocal behavior belongs to them alone, and not to mother, father, grandmother, or anyone else. For this treatment to work, the child *must* understand and accept the responsibility for limiting his or her talking during the initial clinical session. Do not cut short the discussion of the child's responsibility and how that responsibility is the most important part of improving the voice.

   Explain to the child that the first step in the program is reducing the amount of talking that she or he does for a period of 7 days. It is important to explain to the child that talking is restricted for *only* 7 days.

Parental support and encouragement are vital to the success of the vocal fold program with children. Some children might benefit from setting up a **reward** system as an incentive for them to follow through with the modified vocal rest program. In these cases, the child's parents can be encouraged to establish a behavioral contract with the child and decide on a special reward for successful completion of the program. The reward should be one that the child values enough to work for diligently.

Another way to promote even more success with the program is to **involve *all* members of the child's family.** Choosing a reward that the child can share with his or her siblings is one way this involvement can be encouraged. A trip to the beach, a trip to a favorite amusement park, or a special camping trip are examples of rewards that can be easily shared and enjoyed by the entire family. There is no doubt that the desirability of the reward is a major factor in promoting some children's full participation in the modified vocal rest program. Because not all children and their parents are able to adhere to the rules of a modified program of vocal rest, the child/family candidates for a modified vocal rest program must be selected carefully.

a. **Guidelines for the child to follow** (also see informational handouts in Appendix B). Instruct the child that some talking will be permitted during the 7-day period, but only under the following conditions, which have been adapted from a program by F. B. Wilson and Rice (1977):

   (1) The child can to talk *quietly* to the parents in the morning before going to school.

   (2) The child is allowed to answer questions in the **classroom** but should be excused from activities that require talking to large groups of people (e.g., giving speeches and acting in plays). Moreover, no singing is permitted.

   (3) The child must not talk during **recess, lunch, or physical education class.** These are environments that frequently have a high background noise level, which necessitates shouting just to be heard. Recess, lunch, and physical education class are also situations where the child is most likely to go from talking to shouting simply because of the nature of the activities that are carried out in these settings. By prohibiting talking during these situations, the chances for the child to accidentally slip into a shout are greatly reduced. Helping the parents devise a plan—perhaps in conjunction with the child's teachers—for assisting the child from refraining from talking during these activities will be critical, especially for young children.

   (4) The child is permitted to talk quietly to the parents **after school,** but only for a brief period. After this time, no more talking is allowed until mealtime.

   (5) The child is allowed to talk quietly to the entire family at mealtime. The family should be encouraged to **model** quiet talking habits so that a supportive conversational atmosphere can be provided for the child during the meal. In some families, mealtime is a battleground for verbal competition. Each child in this type of situation tries to obtain the attention of the rest of the family by talking louder than anyone else. For vocal rest to have a chance to work, parents should eliminate verbal competition. If verbal competition at mealtimes is not eliminated, the child who is on a vocal rest program will be placed in an untenable situation that will likely result in the failure of the program.

(6) The child's talking time during the **evening hours** should be as limited as possible.

b. **A healthy vocal technique children can use to get attention.** One of the primary ways in which many children abuse their vocal mechanisms is by shouting to get attention. Children yell and scream to each other from one end of the block to the other, from far right field to home plate, and from room to room in the house. There are also many times when children feel that it is necessary to compete vocally to get the attention of teachers and parents. If a program of vocal rest is to succeed, the child who is on the program must be provided with a surefire method of getting the attention of playmates, siblings, parents, and teachers.

One technique that has been used successfully in helping the child who is on a modified vocal rest program to get attention is to give the child a **whistle** that can be worn around the neck at all times. The child is instructed to use the whistle instead of yelling whenever it becomes necessary to attract someone's attention. The novelty of the whistle is usually sufficient to encourage its use. Advise parents to purchase a good quality whistle at a sporting goods store as soon as possible. Moreover, tell them that a little noise from a whistle is a small price to pay in order to help their child successfully complete a program of vocal rehabilitation.

D. **Selecting patients for a program of vocal rest** involves critical evaluation of many facets of the patient. The advantages and disadvantages of a program of vocal rest must be carefully matched with each patient's individual circumstances of occupational voice use, motivation, voice history, and personal schedule when deciding whether or not to initiate the program.

The speech–language pathologist cannot simply tell the patient to stop talking and expect a successful period of vocal rest to follow. Unless the clinician conveys a seriousness of purpose in prescribing a program of vocal rest and carefully plans and helps the patient execute the program, it most likely will fail. Counseling the patient before actually beginning the vocal rest program is extremely important; if this step is neglected or slighted, the chances for failure increase. Vocal rest programs can work, but they must not be carelessly prescribed for every patient with phonotrauma. The following are a few of the factors that should be considered in deciding which patients should be placed on a program of vocal rest:

1. The patient's **occupational requirements for voice use** and the effects of possible lost time at work should be evaluated. Many occupations place heavy demands on the vocal mechanisms. Talking is the principal activity of receptionists, real estate agents, salespersons of all types, telemarketers, teachers, and singers, among others. Patients in these occupations are much less apt to accept a program of vocal rest than are patients who use their

voices very little in their work. The effect of a vocal rest program on the patient's job must be thoroughly explored. Any patient who is reluctant or unable to alter on-the-job vocal requirements for 4 to 7 days should not be considered a candidate for a vocal rest program.

Some patients may be able to use personal-leave or sick-leave time if it is necessary for them to be absent from work during the period of vocal rest. A vocal rest program may cause undue financial hardship for patients who must take time off from work without pay. Patients who are worried about the consequences of lost wages are poor candidates for a program of voice rest.

2. The patient's **motivation** to follow through with the vocal rest program should be evaluated. It is often possible to get a sense of the patient's motivation to improve her or his voice while obtaining the case history. However, no matter how highly motivated the patient may be, he or she must understand that the speech–language pathologist has no magic wand or little pink pill that can miraculously change vocal behaviors. All patients must understand that the difficult task of altering vocal behaviors is one that they themselves must take responsibility for and that the speech–language pathologist's role is simply one of guidance.

    The most highly motivated patients usually have no difficulty following through with the requirements of a vocal rest program. Patients with low motivation, however, can benefit most from hearing the dramatic voice improvement that a 4- to 7-day period of vocal rest can effect. There is nothing more exciting to the dysphonic patient than hearing the improved voice that results from rest, especially if the patient has been dysphonic for a long time. If poorly motivated patients are able to follow through with the vocal rest program, the improvement in voice that results frequently raises their motivational level and thus makes it more likely that a program of vocal rehabilitation will succeed.

    If, however, the patient fails to adhere to the restrictions of the vocal rest program, it is an indication that the patient may not have sufficient motivation or the personal commitment that is required to change a pattern of vocal hyperfunction. The patient who fails the first attempt at a vocal rest program should be given a second opportunity. If the second attempt also meets with failure, the patient should be counseled about the personal commitment required to change vocal behaviors. He or she should then be introduced to voice rehabilitation strategies other than voice rest in an attempt to determine an approach that would be more likely to succeed.

3. Explore any **signs of reluctance** in the patient. Patients who are highly motivated and very willing to make whatever vocal changes are required to eliminate hyperfunctional behaviors may appear reluctant to enter into a program of vocal rest. With some patients, the reasons for the reluctance can be examined through discussion, resolved, and the vocal rest program can proceed. Other patients, however, remain reluctant or unwilling even following candid discussion. These patients should not enter into a vocal rest program because of the dangers of experiencing failure at an early stage of the vocal rehabilitation process.

Patients who are highly motivated to participate in a vocal rehabilitation program, but reluctant to attempt vocal rest, can usually be started on a program of vocal improvement with the goal of establishing a soft, easy, breathy manner of voice production. Although the size of the patient's vocal fold lesion may not be reduced as quickly as it might under a program of vocal rest, the establishment of a soft, easy, and breathy voice will nonetheless reduce the size of the vocal fold lesion over the course of time. It is better not to attempt a vocal rest program at all than to attempt one and fail.

4. Evaluate the patient's **personal calendar** before initiating a vocal rest program. The patient may have an upcoming, out-of-the-ordinary event that would make it impossible for him or her to follow through with the vocal rest program. If this is the case, delay the starting date until the particular event has occurred.

   Some patients insist that they have personal calendars that are so full that there is no time during which the vocal rest program can be scheduled. This type of patient is a poor candidate for a vocal rest program and should most likely begin a program of vocal improvement to establish a soft, easy, breathy manner of voice production.

5. Because use of the larynx can prevent healing, patients who have had recent **laryngeal surgery** may have no choice but to participate in a program of vocal rest. The length of the vocal rest period depends on the type and extent of surgery, and the patient should not resume vocal use until clearance is given by the laryngologist (usually 4 to 7 days following most surgical procedures).

II. **Program of Vocal Hygiene** (see informational handouts in Appendix B). A vital prerequisite to successful voice rehabilitation for patients with histories of vocal hyperfunction is a program of vocal hygiene. The primary purpose of such a program is to first identify and then modify or eliminate causative factors.

   A. **Development of listening skills.** A necessary first step in any vocal hygiene program is the development of listening skills in the patient. It is important that the patient learn to identify those vocal behaviors that harm and strain the larynx. The patient should not only be able to identify sounds and behaviors indicative of hyperfunction in the vocal behaviors of others, but also in his or her own vocal behaviors. This process of auditory discrimination is most easily taught to the patient using the following guidelines:

      1. Using live and prerecorded samples, the clinician should demonstrate and contrast appropriate and hyperfunctional vocal patterns. Ask the patient to discriminate between the two, and discuss the characteristics of each.

      2. Demonstrate the hyperfunctional vocal patterns that the patient uses to heighten the patient's awareness of these vocal patterns.

   B. **Identification of the patient's hyperfunctional vocal patterns.** One of the most important aspects of the vocal hygiene program is to identify the patient's hyperfunctional vocal behaviors and the times and situations in which they occur. Virtually no improvement in voice can realistically be expected until the behaviors that are traumatizing the larynx are eliminated. A little vocal hyperfunction goes a long way in maintaining dysphonia.

Teaching **children** to identify hyperfunctional behaviors is particularly diffi-cult. Unlike the adult, who frequently refers himself or herself for voice ther-apy, children are typically unaware of any dysphonia that they may have. Because they are unaware of the dysphonia, it is often necessary to help the child become aware of and concerned about the dysphonia before instituting the program. Then the child may be sufficiently motivated to engage in the pro-cess of identification of hyperfunction.

1. **Defining and isolating hyperfunctional vocal behaviors.** The initial step in identification of vocal hyperfunction is to define and isolate the behaviors. Adolescents or adults should initially be given demonstrations of typical vocal hyperfunction by the speech clinician. The patient and clini-cian should then discuss how closely the demonstrated vocal behaviors match any of the patient's behaviors. Some patients can readily recognize the vocally hyperfunctional behaviors that have been demonstrated as their own, whereas others cannot.

   Sometimes a picture of the patient's vocal hyperfunction can best be obtained by having the patient give a description of his or her voice usage during a typical day, including a description for a typical weekend day. If you find that the patient is engaging in activities that are especially conducive to phonotrauma, make note of any such instances.

   With children it is usually necessary to enlist the assistance of others who are familiar with the child's vocal behavior. Parents, teachers, siblings, and friends can often assist the child and clinician in obtaining an accurate assessment of the frequency of occurrence of hyperfunctional vocal behav-iors in different situations throughout a day.

2. **Maintaining data on frequency of phonotrauma.** Once it is clear that the patient understands and recognizes hyperfunctional behaviors, he or she should be asked what causes the behaviors. This initial impression of causation should be noted and saved for later comparison after the patient has had ample opportunity to examine personal vocal behaviors.

   The patient should then be asked to maintain data on the frequency of occurrence of the vocal behaviors for at least 1 week. Have the patient keep an absolute tally of the number of times the hyperfunctional behaviors were performed, as well as separate tallies reflecting the number of occurrences of vocal hyperfunction while at work or school, during recreation, and dur-ing evening hours.

   The speech–language pathologist and the patient should attempt to dis-cover the sources of or the circumstances surrounding phonotrauma. This may, in part, be accomplished through the speech–language pathologist's observation of the patient during the initial interview as well as during the diagnostic evaluation. Particular attention should be focused on any epi-sodes of hyperfunctional vocal behavior and on what circumstances precip-itated this behavior.

   Following the 1-week period in which the patient maintains a tally of hyper-functional behaviors, ask the patient what factors he or she believes to be the causes of the phonotrauma. A comparison of these causes with those initially named by the patient can be helpful in evaluating how she or he has learned to analyze her or his vocal hyperfunction. Keeping a record of hyperfunctional behaviors is beneficial in helping the patient and clinician determine the situations that promote the patient's poor vocal habits. The speech–language pathologist may need to interview other reliable sources, such as the patient's spouse or parent, to obtain an even clearer picture of the patient's vocal patterns.

3. **Explanation of the effects of vocal hyperfunction.** Once the specific behaviors have been identified and baseline data have been obtained for all of the patient's daily activities, describe to the patient the physiological effect these patterns have on normal voice production. Next, explain what voice therapy techniques are recommended and what changes can be expected from voice therapy.

The patient should continue to chart his or her hyperfunctional vocal behaviors until they are eliminated. Maintaining data helps the patient develop a heightened awareness of the effects that these behaviors have on the voice. The continuous feedback of the frequency of the behavior in general, as well as in specific situations, should result in a significant decrease in the number of times phonotrauma is committed.

C. A **program of good vocal hygiene** consists of the patient's strict adherence to healthy vocal behaviors. See Appendix B for reproducible vocal hygiene handouts that may be given to patients to guide them in using healthy voice habits. Patients should be instructed to follow these general guidelines:

1. **Limit amount of talking time.** Patients should limit their amount of talking time, particularly when they have an upper respiratory tract infection. It is important that patients use their optimal pitch when talking and speak with adequate loudness.

2. **Do not compete vocally with excessive background noise.** When talking to groups of people, the patient should be situated in the center of the group. The patient should be cautioned to never attempt to "talk over" other people, loud machinery, or other loud noises. All hyperfunctional uses of the voice, including shouting, screaming, excessively loud laughter, reverse phonation, or strenuous vocal activities such as singing, should be avoided. The speech–language pathologist may be able to help the patient find healthy substitutes for many of these behaviors.

3. **Do not use strained vocal productions.** The patient should be cautioned to avoid phonating while lifting or exerting pressure, as this causes hyperadduction of the vocal folds due to the glottal effort closure reflex. Furthermore, the patient should avoid straining the muscles of the face, neck, throat, and shoulders, particularly while talking.

4. **Avoid excessive coughing or throat clearing.** Caution the patient to eliminate excessive throat clearing or coughing. Encourage the patient to use the method of silent coughing/throat clearing instead (see **I.C.2.b.(1)** earlier in this chapter). Advise the patient to avoid foods and liquids that tend to thicken saliva or to which the patient is allergic, as they create the need for excessive throat clearing.

5. **Avoid airborne laryngeal irritants.** Instruct the patient to eliminate as many laryngeal irritants as possible from his or her environment. Caution the patient to avoid dusty or smoky areas and to limit the use of tobacco and alcohol products, which may irritate the vocal folds. Instruct the patient to breathe through the nose and not through the mouth, as the nasal cavity is a natural filtration system.

III. **Program of Voice Therapy.** The vocal characteristics of dysphonias caused by laryngeal trauma can vary, depending on the size and location of the lesion. Lesions that do not affect the vocal folds will leave the voice asymptomatic. Lesions that increase the mass of the vocal folds, however, typically result in a dysphonia that is characterized as low pitched, breathy, and hoarse. Other common vocal characteristics of patients who use vocal hyperfunction are increased vocal loudness and use of a hard glottal attack.

A. **Goals.** Following an optional program of vocal rest and after the patient has been placed on a permanent program of vocal hygiene, a program of voice therapy should be initiated to improve the patient's trauma-related dysphonia. Such a program of voice therapy often includes techniques that are directed at remediating particular symptoms or characteristics of the disorder. These include the following: (1) eliminating the cause of phonotrauma, (2) softening the patient's glottal attack, (3) reducing vocal intensity, and (4) adjusting the patient's pitch to an appropriate level. Not every patient requires improvement in all areas, so the treatment program should be custom-tailored to each patient by choosing and applying those therapeutic techniques that are appropriate for the individual patient. A patient who follows an appropriate program of voice therapy may be able to improve his or her voice and reduce or eliminate a vocal pathology, thus avoiding more costly surgical intervention.

B. **Recent trends in voice therapy.** Recently there has been a trend toward holistic or eclectic (Stemple, 1997) voice therapies, rather than therapies designed to remediate a particular vocal symptom (National Center for Voice & Speech, 1994). These more holistic therapies are based upon three assumptions: (1) that voice therapy is at least as much an art as a science, (2) that the health of the entire person impacts voicing, and (3) that voicing requires a balance of the subsystems of respiration, phonation, and resonation. These **holistic therapies offer the following advantages and disadvantages**:

1. They will strengthen and improve the health of virtually any voice, not just the voices of patients with dysphonia.

2. They are designed as healthy alternatives to a symptomatic therapy approach and are directed at improving the health of the entire system, not just toward eliminating a dysphonic symptom.

3. They have the disadvantage that they can be somewhat complicated for the patient to learn.

4. They require a commitment on the part of the patient to participate wholeheartedly in the method, which includes body movements and required home practice.

C. Holistic voice therapies.

1. **Vocal function exercises (VFE)** (including associated **frontal focus** and **dynamic range exercises**) are intended for any disorders that result in weakness, strain, or imbalance in the vocal mechanism. The VFE program (Stemple et al., 1995) treats the voice as a physical therapist might treat any other muscle group of the body. VFE offers the following **advantages:**

   a. Laryngeal muscles can become weak, strained, or imbalanced just like a knee or any other muscular part of the patient's body. VFE seeks to restore balance to the entire mechanism through stretching, strengthening, and balancing the **entire** muscle system (Breiss, 1959).

   b. VFE, practiced for many years by Stemple (Stemple et al., 1995), has been shown to be particularly effective for professional or performing voices (Sabol, Lee, & Stemple, 1995). In addition, these same authors report that VFE can be used to improve normal voice function in most patients with hyperfunctional voice disorders if the program is followed carefully by the patient.

   c. **VFE procedures.** After completing the diagnosis and describing the problem to the patient, teach the patient the following four exercises (Stemple et al., 1995) to be completed at home, two times each, two times per day. Impress on the patient that the success of the program depends upon his or her compliance with home practice.

      (1) **Warm-up exercise.** Sustain the vowel /i/ for as long as possible on the musical note F above middle C for females and F below middle C for males. The goal is for your patient to sustain the /i/ for an amount of time equal to the longest /s/ that they are able to sustain. Placement of the tone should be in an extreme forward focus (see the following frontal focus exercises). All exercises should be produced softly and without breathiness.

      (2) **Frontal focus exercises.** These exercises may be necessary to help your patient establish proper placement of the tone before beginning VFE. The poor focus or backward focus results as the voice becomes increasingly strained in an attempt to override the effects of problems by tensing and pushing the voice in talking. As the inappropriate focus becomes a habit, it is common to need to reintroduce a more ideal and healthy focus. The following exercises, adapted from Stemple (1997), will help the patient establish a healthier, more forward focus:

         • **Patient education.** Resonation and placement of the voice are explained through vocal practice and play, such as having the patient change her or his voice to sound like others or imitating a nasal "twang." Then demonstrate a tight, constricted, back-focused phrase and have your patient try to imitate your production. Next, demonstrate a breathy, poorly focused tone, followed by a very nasal exaggerated forward focus. Again, have your patient try to imitate your productions, and explain that this last production is closest to the desired placement.

- **Nasalized productions.** The patient should slowly and softly chant the following phrases at a comfortable pitch slightly above their normal fundamental frequency (F_0):

  Oh my

  Oh me

  Oh no

  Oh my no

  Oh me oh my

  Instruct the patient to use an exaggerated forward resonance and to feel the resonance in her or his face, nose, lips, and so on. Use audiocasette recordings to provide auditory feedback. Once the tone is appropriately forward, have the patient alternate between backward focus and forward focus (negative practice) to determine that the concept is firmly established (use the same simple phrases).

- **Intensity and rate variations.** Using the same phrases, have the patient practice each phrase multiple times following this progression (have the patient concentrate on maintaining forward focus while varying rate and loudness):

  very slow-very soft

  faster-louder

  fast-loud

  slower-softer

  very slow-very soft

- **Inflected phrases and normal speech.** Phrases may be modified from a single pitch to a more "sing-song" or inflected voicing, and then finally to production of a normal spoken phrase:

  soft and slow

  louder-faster

  exaggerated inflections

  normal speech

- Monitor the **proper focus of tone** throughout. Some patients will catch on to the desired focus very quickly, whereas some will require many therapy sessions to habituate the new, desired focus. Your final step is to expand your patient's ability to produce a forward focus from the practice phrases to conversational phrases, sentences, and paragraph reading.

(3) Once the patient has a well-established and forward-focused tone, have the patient proceed with the vocal function exercises. The patient should glide from the lowest note he or she can produce, to

the highest note on the word *knoll*. The goal is no voice breaks. Even if the voice breaks at the high end of the range, have your patient continue to glide without hesitating. The glide may even be continued if the voice "cuts out" completely at the top because the vocal folds will continue to stretch.

(4) Have the patient glide from his or her highest note to the lowest note on the word *knoll*. Some patients may find it easier to do the downward glide before the rising glide. Regardless of which the patient does first, it is important to do a slow, systematic downward glide. Again, the goal is no voice breaks.

(5) Have the patient sustain the musical notes C-D-E-F-G for as long as possible on the vowel /o/. Have the patient start at middle C for females and one octave lower for males (this can be varied up or down to fit a particular voice). The goal is the same as for the warm-up exercise—the number of seconds you determined in the warmup exercise would be your goal (holding the vowel as long as the unvoiced /s/).

(6) All exercises are done as softly as possible. Soft tones require more control and give a much better vocal "workout." Times for sustained phonations will increase as the efficiency of vocal fold vibration increases. Take extra care to teach production of an extremely forward tone lacking in tension.

(7) Some patients experience mild laryngeal "aching" as they begin the program. As with all exercise programs, this will subside with continued practice. The estimated time of completion of the program is 6 to 10 weeks.

(8) **VFE maintenance program.** Patients may begin the maintenance phase of VFE when they have been doing the full program two times each, two times per day, and when they have been maintaining at least 85% of their targeted goal (a soft, frontally placed tone that can be sustained for at least 85% of the time identified in the warm-up exercise). The patient then continues the maintenance program in the following progression:

- Full program two times each, one time per day.
- Full program one time each, one time per day.
- Exercise #5, two times each, one time per day.
- Exercise #5, one time each, one time per day.
- Exercise #5, one time each, three times per week.
- Exercise #5, one time each, one time per week.

2. **Dynamic range exercise (DR).** Occasionally, a patient will improve phonation time, vocal balance, and so on through use of VFE, but still complain of lack of power in the voice. The dynamic range (DR) exercise (Stemple, 1997) may be particularly beneficial for professional voice users who place extra demands on their voice daily. DR is a low impact, isometric exer-

cise for the voice. *It should only be used after the patient has closely approximated his or her VFE goals.*

a. Use the DR exercise following a thorough vocal warmup like VFE, as it is a very vigorous vocal exercise.

b. Have the patient sustain the five vowels (*a, e, i, o, u*) from very soft to reasonably loud on the musical note F above middle C for females, and F below middle C for males (or the note you have chosen if you have varied it for your patient's voice). Instruct the patient to sustain the vowels two times each, two times per day.

c. Instruct the patient to use an extreme forward focus and no laryngeal tension for all DR practice.

d. Instruct the patient to stop the DR exercises if the voice breaks or becomes disengaged. This exercise is only for an accomplished VFE patient.

e. Slight laryngeal aching may occur during the first few days of DR practice, but should cease after a few days.

3. The **accent method (AM)** (Kotby, 1995; Stemple, 1997) is intended for patients with a wide range of voice disorders, including vocal hyperfunction; paralysis and weakness not requiring surgical intervention; and chronic and acute laryngitis. This approach works well for essentially any disorder not requiring medical or surgical intervention. The accent method offers several advantages:

   • The method, based on earlier work by Smith and Thyme (1976), follows the principles of the myoelastic–aerodynamic theory of voice production. In research using the accent method, subjects have shown an increase in airflow with a resultant increase in subglottal pressure. The focus on airflow eliminates two faulty phonation patterns: patterns with excessive glottal waste and those with excessive glottal tightness.

   • The AM is much like melodic intonation therapy in that it is a holistic or integrated approach to total body communication, and thus is beneficial across disorder types, such as voice disorders, fluency disorders, dysarthrias, and so on.

   • The expected result of the AM is automatic regulation and balance of the voice through balance of respiration, phonation, and articulation.

   a. The Accent Method includes three major components: **breathing exercises, phonatory exercises,** and **movement exercises.**

      (1) **Breathing exercises.** The therapist and patient stand side by side with the back of their hands on each other's abdomens. Practice slow, deep inhalation, and exhalation with equal time spent on both. Then, practice faster inhalation and exhalation with equal time spent on both. Alternate between fast and slow (slow in, fast out, fast in, slow out). Add rhythmic breathing with voiceless consonants /f/, /s/, /ʃ/, /θ/, and so on.

(2) **Phonatory exercises.** Ask the patient to use a **largo rhythm** (largo is a slow, relaxed 3/4 time, with an initial short, unstressed segment followed by a long, accentuated segment) to produce vowels, then voiceless consonants, then voiced consonants. That is, the patient would first produce an unstressed vowel or consonant followed by a stressed version of the same phoneme. The result would be, for instance, /a 'a/ or /z 'z/. Once the patient can produce this unstressed, stressed combination, instruct her or him to follow these steps:

(a) Change and vary the vowels.

(b) Add voiceless consonants.

(c) Add voiced consonants.

(d) Add body movement of easy, relaxed swaying backwards and forwards (this addition constitutes the **movement exercises** component of the accent method).

(e) Add arm movements to the swaying.

(f) At the second and third levels of the phonatory exercises, have the patient change to **andante rhythm** (an initial quick segment followed by three accented beats, v VVV, as in the first measure of "Deep in the Heart of Texas") or **allegro** (initial quick segment followed by five accented beats, v VVVVV, as in the first measure of "The Farmer in the Dell").

  • With the andante rhythm, have the patient turn her or his body side-to-side rhythmically, with the arms swinging side-to-side.

  • With the **allegro** rhythm, the patient's body is much more free to "dance" to the rhythm, and the arm motions can be much more individualized.

(g) For each rhythm, follow the progression in (a) through (e).

(h) With all rhythms, vocal pitch and loudness can be varied once the basic rhythm set is mastered.

(i) Carryover to speech follows a typical hierarchy through words, phrases, sentences, and so on.

(j) Arm and hand movements continue throughout therapy to intensify the sense of rhythm.

b. **Termination of the accent method.** According to Kotby (1995), therapy using the accent method can be terminated when:

(1) The patient has mastered abdominal/diaphragmatic breath support.

(2) The patient consistently uses a soft glottal attack.

(3) The patient consistently uses no glottal fry.

(4) The patient consistently uses appropriate pitch range and loudness.

(5) The patient consistently uses rhythmic intonations in speech.

(6) The patient is satisfied with his or her voice in everyday speaking situations.

(7) There is an improved perceptual judgment of the patient's voice.

(8) There is an improved visual appearance of the vocal folds.

(9) There is improvement on objective voice measures.

c. **Other considerations in using the accent method.**

(1) Patients who are motivated and naturally rhythmic or musical will generally do best with this approach.

(2) Hearing impairment may interfere with the patient's ability to use this method.

(3) Sometimes age may prevent a patient from finding success with this approach.

(4) The speech–language pathologist will need to be willing to serve as a vocal model for the patient. The goal is to create a "ping-pong" type of interaction, with the patient imitating your productions.

(5) Most patients will succeed with the initial breathing exercises within one therapy session. The rest of the therapy can be very individualized.

(6) For this method to work, patients should be seen twice per week for at least 30 minutes, and they should practice at home two times per day for 20 minutes.

(7) The expected result of the accent method is automatic regulation and balance of the voice through balance of respiration, phonation, and articulation.

4. **Confidential voice therapy** is intended for patients with swelling-based vocal problems, such as vocal fold nodules and polyps. This technique, for problems of vocal hyperfunction, has been well explained by Colton and Casper (1996) and has also been discussed by Verdolini-Marston, Burke, Lessac, Glaze, and Caldwell (1995) in their article comparing this approach with resonant voice therapy (see next section).

a. Confidential voice therapy involves having the patient concentrate on **speaking as quietly as possible and in a breathy voice,** as if he or she were speaking in confidence or telling a secret.

b. The patient is instructed to speak with the **softest intensity she or he can produce,** as if telling a confidence to a friend.

c. If the patient cannot produce the confidential voice from instructions, try **practicing the yawn–sigh or sigh** to get the patient started.

d. It is not enough for the patient's voice to be lowered in loudness; it must be **noticeably breathy** (the "Marilyn Monroe voice," but not whispered).

The breathiness must be easy, without any evidence of pushing or forcing out air.

e. The patient **should not reduce mouth opening nor lower her or his pitch.**

f. The patient should **use his or her voice in this method for all speaking throughout the period of therapy,** because this technique reduces the number of syllables/breath the person can say. Because confidential voice therapy also tends to dry the throat, instruct the patient to increase fluid intake.

5. **Resonant voice therapy (RVT)** (Verdolini-Marston et al., 1995) has its foundations in singing and acting and is based on earlier work by Lessac (1967). It is intended for any patient for whom vocal fold adduction is a critical problem—that is, either hyperadduction or hypoadduction. In a study by Verdolini-Marston et al. (1995), nodule patients who used either RVT or confidential voice therapy approach showed roughly the same benefit from therapy, regardless of method. Because RVT is more complicated to teach, there may be some implied advantage in confidential voice therapy. The **main goal of RVT** is a frontal tone focus (similar to Stemple's frontal focus exercises). RVT is based on the following considerations:

a. Because the patient is instructed to produce voice with slightly abducted vocal folds, the patient is highly **unlikely to misuse or abuse the voice** using RVT (Colton & Casper, 1996).

b. The patient is taught to develop a sense for an oral or facial "ring" or "twang" and to take the focus off the larynx, thus producing a **more efficient phonation.**

c. RVT is not a therapy the patient can learn from reading a book; instead, it depends on her or his willingness and ability to sense vibrations in the facial "mask," which can be located by using the hands to gently cover the cheeks and eyes with the lips lightly touching together in the closed position. Hum directly into the palms of the hands, feeling the vibrations produced by the voice (Raphael & Sataloff, 1997).

6. **Other less traditional or symptomatic voice therapy approaches are being used with anecdotal success.** Two widely used techniques that focus on body awareness and movement training are being used in voice training. The **Alexander Technique** and the **Feldenkrais Method** are body awareness techniques that help individuals become aware of how they use their bodies and help them make better choices in body posture and breathing (Verdolini, 1998b). There is little research to date to support the efficacy of these approaches in voice therapy. However, techniques that foster better general health can certainly be of benefit when combined with a comprehensive voice therapy program.

7. **Voice training designed for the theater or for singers.** Many speech–language pathologists have begun incorporating techniques such as breath control and efficiency, posture control, and using a resonant "placed" tone free from tension. In addition, some clinicians are referring patients to experts in classical singing or theatrical singing techniques. Verdolini

[handwritten margin note: "Can be used for both" with a brace spanning items a–c]

(1998b) provides descriptions of these techniques, developed by such master teachers of the theater as Arthur Lessac and Kristin Linklater, who have developed systems for "freeing or opening" natural voices. Speech–language pathologists may find that their patient's voice will continue to improve after the voice injury has healed if, in addition to voice therapy, the patient is referred to someone who is well schooled in classical singing or theater training techniques.

D. Traditional approaches in voice therapy. Some patients may not respond well to the holistic approaches previously discussed. For example, they may not be able to appreciate the importance of the somewhat uninhibited requirements of the accent method or a frontal focus placement, or they simply may not follow through with the amount of home practice required. Other patients may simply respond better to the identification and treatment of one or two vocal symptoms at a time.

Boone and McFarlane (1994) have provided the most comprehensive collection of therapy techniques in their list of 25 facilitating techniques for patients with vocal hyperfunction. Though some of the facilitating techniques were previously described by other authors, Boone and McFarlane combined them in a comprehensive and commonly recognized list.

Use of facilitating techniques or traditional voice therapy techniques does not necessarily guarantee that a patient's voice will improve, anymore than use of the holistic techniques can guarantee improvement. The techniques described in the following pages are simply those that will facilitate the patient's attempts at producing a good voice through modification of specific vocal symptoms. As a particular technique is attempted, listen carefully—along with your client—for changes in the pitch, quality, and loudness characteristics of the patient's voice. If voice production improves while the patient is using one of the techniques, the speech–language pathologist should immediately point out the improvement and praise the patient for the good voice production.

Improvements in voice production are often fleeting at first. Consequently, the speech–language pathologist must be quick to identify, evaluate, and reinforce each instance of improvement. In addition, it is best to record the entire therapy session with an audiocasette so that the patient's productions can be replayed immediately.

1. **Monitoring of productions.** The patient's auditory feedback channel must also be heightened, as tactile and proprioceptive feedback are poor channels for monitoring the larynx. The importance of helping the patient develop the auditory skills necessary to monitor the quality of voice productions cannot be overstated. The patient's ability to eventually maintain the production of a good voice will depend almost entirely on his or her ability to self-monitor through hearing.

   As the patient becomes gradually more adept at recognizing improved vocal productions, he or she will need to learn how to manipulate the vocal mechanism in order to duplicate the improved productions. The voice therapy techniques that follow should help facilitate this vocal manipulation.

2. The following **voice therapy techniques** are specifically designed to help the patient reduce hyperfunctional vocal behaviors, reduce vocal intensity,

soften a hard glottal attack, and establish a comfortable pitch level. Some techniques focus on improving specific voice parameters, whereas other techniques focus on improving several parameters simultaneously. The choice of which techniques to use is based on the nature of the patient's pathology, her or his preference or comfort level with a particular approach, and the speech–language pathologist's determination of the efficacy of any given approach. As a result, the clinician and patient collaborate to choose the combination of approaches best suited to each the patient.

a. **Techniques to facilitate reduction of vocal loudness.** Before initiating specific techniques to reduce a patient's vocal loudness, the patient should be given a **hearing evaluation.** The results should be analyzed to determine whether the patient's increased vocal loudness is related to a hearing loss. After hearing loss has been ruled out as the cause of increased vocal loudness, one or several of the following techniques can be used for reduction of vocal loudness:

(1) **Discussion with the patient about vocal loudness.** Before actually initiating specific steps to reduce vocal loudness, discuss with the patient the nature of vocal loudness and its role in communication. The following questions should be raised and discussed with the patient:

(a) **What factors determine how loud the voice should be?** Probably the most important factor in determining how loudly to speak is intelligibility, or how easily speech can be understood. Two factors determine how loudly a person has to speak to be intelligible:

- It is necessary to talk at a level that is **loud enough** to surpass the level of competing background noise. Conversation in a quiet living room requires much less vocal loudness than conversation on the corner of a busy city street. The adjustment that people make in vocal loudness in response to varying degrees of competing background noise is fairly automatic.

- The second factor that is related to how loudly people talk is the **physical distance** between the speaker and the listener. The greater the distance, the greater the vocal loudness level that is required to transport the vocal signal through the air to the receiver. Shorter distances dictate reduced vocal loudness.

People who misjudge the **level of background noise** or the distance between the speaker and the listener speak with inappropriate loudness. Some patients have great difficulty in accurately evaluating these factors and making appropriate vocal loudness adjustments. These patients require voice therapy that is specifically directed at developing a greater sensitivity for vocal loudness as it relates to background noise and the physical distance between speaker and listener. Other patients, however, are able to make adjustments in their vocal loudness levels as soon as they have been informed that their loudness level is inappropriate in many circumstances.

(b) **Psychological space and how it affects the vocal loudness level.** Just as there is measurable physical distance between two people, there is also a region around each person that can be defined as psychological space. This space is considered an extension of the person, and each individual attempts to control the movement of other people into and out of it.

The size of this psychological space varies across cultures, from person to person, and from moment to moment in the same person. There are times when an individual feels comfortable with other people entering into his or her space, while there are other times when an individual regards entry into his or her space as an intrusion. It is most likely intrusion into this space that causes some people to feel uncomfortable when they find themselves caught in large crowds of people or on crowded elevators.

Similarly, most people feel discomfort when their space is invaded in nonphysical ways, as when they are in the presence of an overbearing, uncomfortably loud, and dominating voice. A person who perceives that his or her psychological space is being intruded upon by a too-loud voice has a natural tendency to back away from the voice until a comfortable distance exists between the intruding voice and the personal self.

Patients who have voices that are too loud frequently find other people withdrawing from them. These patients are similar to patients who have difficulty in judging the amount of vocal loudness necessary for a given distance from the listener and should participate in voice therapy that is directed at developing a sensitivity for personal space. Some patients are able to make an adjustment in their vocal loudness level as soon as they are informed that they are perceived by others as being vocally intrusive.

(2) **Developing auditory discrimination for vocal loudness.** One of the difficulties of using an audiocasette recorder for developing patient awareness of vocal loudness is that loudness can be controlled on playback by means of the volume control. If a recording of an especially loud patient is replayed at a comfortable listening level, the actual vocal loudness level is masked.

The audiocasette recorder or video recorder can best be used as a tool for developing a patient's auditory discrimination ability for vocal loudness if several *other* voices are recorded along with the patient's voice. In this way, a comparison of the relative loudness of the various voices can be made. In order to prevent any loudness effects of proximity, the recording should be made with all speakers sitting at the same distance from the recording microphone.

A playback of the recording and frank discussion with the patient should be sufficient to raise the patient's awareness of vocal loudness differences. If other speakers are included on the recording, the speech–language pathologist should ask the patient to rank the various speakers in order of vocal loudness level and then discuss the accuracy of the patient's ratings.

(3) **Reduction of the patient's vocal loudness level** can be accomplished most simply by using various reading materials and an audiocasette recorder or a video recorder. Have the patient read sample phrases or sentences at varying levels of overall loudness. Then have the patient read the materials using different vocal loudness levels on different words or phrases in order to vary vocal emphasis. Discussion accompanied by recorded feedback is one of the best methods of helping a patient to monitor his or her own vocal loudness. Because the patient's vocal loudness level can be positively influenced by an atmosphere of reduced vocal loudness during the therapy session, model a comfortable vocal loudness level for the patient.

(4) **Visual monitoring of vocal loudness.** Electronic devices that provide instant visual feedback of vocal loudness are commercially available. Baseline measurements of the patient's vocal loudness level should be made at the beginning of the first voice therapy session. Depending on the mode used for visual feedback on the particular device being used, such as the CSL Pitch program or a VU meter on an audiocasette recorder, mark the range of appropriate vocal loudness to indicate for the patient the acceptable upper and lower limits of loudness. Instruct the patient to read a series of phrases and sentences while watching the vocal loudness monitor and trying to maintain vocal loudness within the limits of acceptability. After a limited period of practice, the patient should be able to reproduce an acceptable vocal loudness level without the aid of the monitoring device.

b. **Techniques for reduction of hard glottal attack.** Hard glottal attack is a manner of phonating characterized by adducting the vocal folds tightly until they are actually blown apart by increased subglottic air pressure. Techniques that facilitate a gradual approximation of the vocal folds can result in a softening of hard glottal attack. Consistent practice of such techniques disrupts the pattern of hard glottal attack, facilitates a softened glottal attack, and allows the patient to adopt a different and less harmful manner for initiating vowel production.

(1) **Developing auditory discrimination for hard glottal attack.** Using an audiocasette or vidotape recorder, record samples of the patient's voice while he or she is reading a paragraph and during conversation. Replay the recording for the patient and point out the abrupt, staccato-like vocalizations that characterize the hard glottal attack. In particular, note the hard, biting quality of the patient's voice on words that begin with a vowel. Compare this recording of the patient's voice with prerecorded audiocasettes or tapes of voices that are good models of either a normal or a softened glottal attack.

(2) **The chewing technique** was devised by Froeschels (1952). This technique is based upon the assumption that normal, relaxed muscle

tonicity and muscle balance of the tongue, jaw, neck, and larynx can be naturally induced when the patient is engaged in the act of chewing. Better vocal fold approximation and optimum muscular adjustment of the vocal folds are specific physiologic improvements that result from this technique. Therefore, if the patient is engaged simultaneously in the acts of chewing and speaking (articulating and phonating), the improved muscle balance and tonicity associated with chewing should result in conditions that effect improved voice production. The muscular adjustments that are facilitated by the chewing approach usually result not only in a reduction of hard glottal attack, but also in simultaneous improvements in loudness, pitch, and vocal quality. Use the following steps to instruct the patient in the use of the chewing method:

(a) Explain to the patient that you are going to use a technique called the chewing method. Tell the patient that the technique is a means of obtaining muscle balance in the vocal mechanism. Advise the patient that you understand that he or she may feel awkward or silly when first trying the technique, but that the technique is, nonetheless, very useful. Also advise the patient that the exaggerated mouth movements associated with the technique in no way resemble the manner in which the voice will be produced in later stages of therapy.

(b) Have the patient sit facing a mirror. Ask the patient to pretend he or she is chewing a chunk of cotton candy. Tell the patient to chew in a relaxed, open-mouthed, exaggerated manner, and to pretend to move the cotton candy around in the mouth with exaggerated movements of the tongue. Comment upon the exaggerated movements as they are observed in the mirror. Do not rush this stage of the technique, and do not proceed until the patient is capable of producing a natural and exaggerated manner of chewing.

(c) While the patient is engaged in exaggerated chewing, ask him or her to start phonating softly. It may be necessary to model this for the patient. Be certain that a variety of vowel-like sounds are produced (Boone & McFarlane, 1994). Be alert for monotonous repetitions retaining the tongue on the floor of the mouth and therefore not moving the tongue vigorously enough. It is important to encourage the patient to use relaxed, exaggerated tongue movements.

(d) After the patient has become adept at using a relaxed method of chewing and phonating, ask him or her to inhale deeply and to chew and phonate the outgoing airstream. Encourage the patient to let the vocal pitch vary erratically. Have the patient practice chewing and phonating until a relaxed voice is produced.

(e) Next, the patient should be told to simultaneously chew, phonate, and articulate brief two- or three-word combinations that begin with vowels (e.g., "I am in," "I am over," "I am up"). At first, the patient should move back and forth between chewing/phonating vowels and chewing/phonating short phrases. Vocal pitch, loudness, and quality should not vary between chewed vowel productions and chewed phrase productions. The relaxed vocal postures that develop with the production of vowels should carry over to the production of short phrases.

(f) When the patient begins to demonstrate relaxed phonation with short phrases, additional stimulus materials can be introduced. Practice drills should progress to include chewing sentences at various pitch and loudness levels. Daily practice with the chewing technique should continue until the patient begins to demonstrate diminished laryngeal dysfunction in conversational speech.

(3) Techniques that utilize prephonation glottal airflow. Because hard glottal attack is characterized by the explosive release of air as phonation begins, any technique that establishes a gentle airflow through the glottis prior to phonation should prevent air stoppage and soften glottal attack. There are several techniques that utilize this principle to facilitate the reduction of hard glottal attack.

(a) One technique involves **production of words beginning with the fricative /h/,** which is produced by sending air through the glottis. The patient is instructed to gently produce the phoneme /h/ in isolation several times. Then the patient should be instructed to produce the /h/ followed by a vowel sound. Listen carefully to be sure that there is no "vocal catch" just as the vowel is initiated. To illustrate the acoustic differences between a soft and hard glottal attack, it may be necessary for the speech–language pathologist to demonstrate, and for the patient to imitate, the difference between the gentle onset of the vowel in a production such as /ha/ and the abrupt onset of the vowel in a production such as /ʔa/.

As the patient becomes able to produce various /h/ + vowel combinations without hard glottal attack, a list of one- and two-syllable words that begin with /h/ should be substituted as the stimulus material. Again, the patient can better develop an awareness of the difference between a gentle and hard onset if he or she produces these /h/ words followed by the same words produced without the initial /h/ phoneme. This contrastive exercise should continue throughout all levels of practice stimuli. Additional stimulus materials, which initially consist of one- and two-syllable words beginning with unvoiced fricatives, should be used later and developed into phrase, sentence, and monologue drills.

(b) Breathy technique (see **III.C.4** earlier in this chapter). Various descriptors of the target voice quality (e.g., "Marilyn Monroe voice," "bedroom voice," or "confidential tone voice") may evoke connotations that make it easier for the patient to identify and, consequently, to produce an unstrained vocal quality. Use of this type of voice production can correct several defective aspects of voice simultaneously, because it tends to reduce vocal intensity, soften glottal attack, normalize vocal pitch, and provide for a generally relaxed voice-producing mechanism. The patient should use this easy tone initiation with a breathy voice initially, and then gradually eliminate the breathiness without resuming the production of hard glottal attacks.

(4) **Chant talk technique.** A technique that is particularly useful for the reduction of hard glottal attack, called the chant talk technique, has been described by Boone and McFarlane (1994). The patient is taught to reduce hard glottal attack by using a phonatory style that sounds like a religious chant.

(a) Play either a recording of a religious chant or model a chant for the patient. Explain to the patient that the chanting is only a temporary measure, which will be modified later to resemble normal speech.

(b) While using various reading materials, have the patient practice alternately using the chant voice and his or her normal voice. Tape record these productions and replay them for discussion of the differences between the chanted and the normal voices. As the patient becomes more skilled at using the chant, drills should be directed at achieving a style of voice production that is characterized by a softened glottal attack.

(5) **The yawn–sigh technique.** Another excellent approach to establishing easy, relaxed phonation in a patient is to use a normal, vegetative function—the yawn—that puts the vocal tract musculature into a relaxed state prior to phonation. A yawn is composed of a sustained inhalation accompanied by a relaxed widening of the mouth and pharynx. As a consequence of vocal tract relaxation, the easy phonation (vocal sigh) that may accompany the exhalation phase of a yawn is produced with normal vocal resonance, optimal vocal pitch, and reduced muscle hyperfunction (Boone & McFarlane, 1994). Instruct the patient to use the following steps to achieve vocal tract relaxation:

(a) Demonstrate a yawn to the patient, making sure to prolong the inhalation and exhalation phases. Produce a gentle, voiced sigh during the exhalation phase.

(b) Ask the patient to try to produce a similar yawn with an accompanying sigh. Have the patient repeat the yawn followed by a sigh several times.

(c) After the patient has produced several yawn and sigh combinations, instruct him or her to yawn and then to say one of the following syllables: /ha/, /ho/, or /hu/.

(**d**) When the patient becomes adept at producing these syllables with good oral resonance following a yawn, the yawn should be eliminated and the patient should attempt to produce the syllables when they are preceded by a simple, gentle inhalation.

(**e**) As soon as the patient demonstrates normal, relaxed phonation for the practice syllables, additional practice materials, such as words, phrases, and sentences, can then be attempted.

(6) **Visual monitoring.** The CSL Pitch Program is a computer-based instrument that can be used to train a patient to soften his or her glottal attack (see Appendix C for more information). The integrated hardware/software, PC-based system provides simple, innovative real-time displays of important speech/voice parameters for visual feedback and the ability to make quantitative measurements to track therapy progress. The CSL Pitch Program has high-fidelity audio playback, the ability to perform quantitative measurements, delayed auditory feedback (DAF), innovative games for children, and clinical protocols that automate specific therapy tasks with convenient prompts for easy use. The CSL Pitch Program has a split-screen picture that allows for patient modeling. Through repeated practice, the patient can use the CSL Pitch Program to provide visual feedback to assist in reduction of hard glottal attack.

c. **Techniques for normalization of vocal pitch.** There is great controversy among speech–language pathologists regarding whether a patient's vocal pitch should be changed, or whether there is an optimum pitch that should be targeted in therapy. The available data seem to reject the notion of an optimum pitch as it is presently used in clinical intervention (Colton & Casper, 1996). Often, a patient's vocal pitch is not actually changed as a result of therapy, but is *perceived* as changed because of alterations in loudness, vocal effort, and vocal quality (Murry, 1982). Raising perceived pitch may make a patient's voice sound less breathy or hoarse, but the resultant strain on the larynx may produce long-term damage. If the habitual pitch is accidentally raised too high, laryngeal tension will be increased at a time when increased tension could further irritate already sensitive vocal folds. Usually, as laryngeal muscle balance and tone begin to normalize through procedures designed to reduce vocal loudness, there is accompanying normalization of vocal pitch. The effort in therapy should be directed toward healthy voice habits, including reduction of loudness if indicated. However, it is probably best not to work directly on changing vocal pitch.

d. **Techniques for development of relaxation and reduction of laryngeal tension.** Most authorities agree that the voice produced by any individual is heavily influenced by his or her emotional state of being. We are all familiar with the subtle changes that occur in our own voices when we feel elated, bored, indifferent, or sad. Our voices are frequently an automatic indicator of our psychological and emotional conditions.

Quite often, muscular hypertension of the larynx occurs as a reaction to emotional stress, which is frequently related to life problems. Emotional conflicts in the patient's life may initially cause undue general body tension, which can later become focused on the larynx.

Vocal fold approximation, then, is adversely affected in patients with chronic hypertension of the muscles of the larynx as a reaction to emotional stress. It is not understood why some patients focus their tension on their backs and develop backaches, why others focus their tension on their faces, scalps, and neck muscles and develop headaches, and why other patients focus their tension in the region of the neck and larynx and become dysphonic. The degree to which the voice is affected can range from slight to severe, depending on how well the individual is able to manage increased levels of stress.

Patients with tension of the muscles in the upper body, neck, and laryngeal region typically develop a voice in which vocal strain and tension are audible. This audible tension is most likely related to limitations in vocal fold excursion resulting from hypertension of the intrinsic laryngeal muscles and hypercontraction of the muscular walls of the pharynx. Vocal pitch is usually slightly raised, hard glottal attacks are common, and the patient's voice may vary from hoarse to strident as he or she attempts to phonate through the hyperfunctional larynx and vocal tract.

Excessive muscular tension usually results in an elevation of the entire larynx and hyoid bone sling. Typically, the space between the hyoid bone and the superior margin of the thyroid cartilage decreases due to muscular overcontraction. The net effect of all this hypertension is to cause the larynx to be fixated in the neck so that it is very resistant to being moved manually in either a vertical or lateral direction. The extent to which the larynx is affected is related to the degree of muscle hypertension and the length of time that the state of laryngeal hypertension has existed.

Patients with laryngeal hypertension often complain of difficulty in swallowing, feeling like something is caught in their throats, or acute episodes of pain, which are described as radiating from the larynx to the ear or chest region. If the clinician attempts to manually lower the patient's larynx into the neck, the patient may express feelings of discomfort or extreme pain.

Voice therapy management of dysphonias with accompanying tension of the larynx as a symptom may include procedures to reduce hypertension and muscle imbalance. These include laryngeal massage or indirect approaches such as relaxation therapy (see **III.D.4.d.(2)** later in this chapter), the chewing technique (see **III.D.2.b.(2)** earlier in the chapter), the chant talk technique (see **III.D.2.b.(4)**), the yawn technique (see **III.D. 2.b.(5)**), or instrumental biofeedback of laryngeal tension.

(1) **Laryngeal massage** can be used to improve the dysphonia and relieve the discomfort or pain associated with laryngeal hypertension. In this procedure, the laryngeal region is manually massaged to reduce laryngeal tension and improve muscle balance within the larynx. One of the most noticeable results of decreased laryngeal

tension and improved muscle balance is improvement in the pitch and quality characteristics of the patient's voice.

The degree to which any single patient will respond to laryngeal massage cannot be predicted accurately. Some patients demonstrate improvement within several minutes, while others take several hours or perhaps repeated sessions of the therapy before the effects of direct laryngeal massage are evidenced. Some patients never benefit from these procedures and require other methods to reduce muscular hypertension of the larynx and the associated dysphonia. Roy, Bless, Heisey, and Ford (1997) and Roy and Leeper (1993) investigated the effects of laryngeal massage on the voices of patients with muscle tension dysphonia. Muscle tension dysphonia (MTD) is a problem caused by overactivity of the laryngeal muscles with accompanying voice fatigue and discomfort. It is known to be particularly responsive to laryngeal massage (Verdolini, 1998b). Results indicated that most patients had marked vocal improvement following one therapy session, although some patients did experience a relapse afterwards.

Massage generally starts at the hyoid bone and proceeds downward. The hyoid bone and the larynx are moved in the same direction. The patient should be asked to gently sustain the production of the vowel /a/ while he or she is being massaged. The effects of laryngeal massage on the voice, if any, consist of improvements in pitch and quality characteristics. Once the quality of the sustained vowel production improves, the patient should be encouraged to produce syllables and words and, finally, to converse under the conditions of decreased laryngeal tension. The techniques for laryngeal massage are as follows (Aronson, 1985):

(a) The clinician should begin by locating the patient's thyroid notch with his or her index finger. Situated just above the notch is the hyoid bone. Using the thumb and middle finger, the clinician should then massage the hyoid bone with small, circular movements while progressively moving in an anterior to posterior direction along the hyoid bone. As the tips of the major horns of the hyoid bone are reached, the clinician should slow down and watch the patient's face for any signs of undue discomfort or pain.

(b) The next region below the hyoid bone that requires massage is the thyrohyoid space. Often, this space is reduced in size or absent in patients with excessive laryngeal tension, and the hyoid bone appears to rest upon the superior margin of the thyroid cartilage. Again using the thumb and middle finger, the clinician should massage the thyrohyoid space with small, circular movements while progressing in an anterior to posterior direction. As muscle tension decreases, the clinician should feel an increase in the distance between the hyoid bone and the superior margin of the thyroid cartilage, and the vocal strain and tension heard in the patient's sustained production of /a/ should decrease.

(c) Finally, the thyroid cartilage should be encircled by the thumb and middle finger, which are placed on the upper margin of the cartilage. Slow, circular, downward, or lateral movements should then be used to manipulate the larynx lower into the patient's neck while the patient sustains the vowel /a/.

(2) **Relaxation therapy** involves techniques that the patient can use to promote general relaxation of the body, as well as specific relaxation of the pharynx and laryngeal area. While the methods for achieving relaxation may vary, the final goal of all the methods should be a vocal tract free from excessive muscle tension and a larynx in which proper muscle balance results in the production of a normal voice. Two methods that can be used to achieve pharyngeal and laryngeal relaxation are described below.

(a) A technique that has often been used to facilitate head, neck, and laryngeal relaxation is the **head roll.** However, evidence suggests that the circular head rotation may not be beneficial to the intervertebral disks, and thus **should be avoided** (Nagler, 1987).

(b) Another method of relaxation, called **progressive relaxation,** was developed by Jacobson (1978). This technique involves instructing the patient to focus on a particular part of the body and then to tense that body part as much as possible while concentrating on how the tension feels and simultaneously keeping the other body muscles relaxed. After the body part has been maintained in a state of tension for 10 to 15 seconds, the patient should then be instructed to relax the body part and concentrate on how the relaxation feels in contrast to the previous state of tension.

This procedure typically involves tensing and relaxing the limbs first and then progressively tensing and relaxing more proximal body parts. To focus on relaxation of the pharynx and larynx, the following sequence can be used: forehead, eyes, nose, jaw, and finally the larynx. The general goal of this procedure is to give the patient the ability to consciously relax a specific body region by controlling the tensed and relaxed states of various muscle groups.

(3) **Inhalation phonation** has been used with success in patients who have developed excessive muscular tension dysphonia accompanied by tight adduction of the ventricular folds. Rarely, some patients with this type of muscle tension dysphonia may develop true ventricular fold phonation. Phonation on inhaled air is always produced by the true vocal folds (Lehmann, 1965). Boone and McFarlane (1994) give the following procedure for inhalation phonation in their list of facilitating techniques:

(a) The therapist should first demonstrate the technique by initiating an inhaled high-pitched hum while raising the shoulders. Raising the shoulders helps the patient visualize the difference between exhaled air (shoulders down) and inhaled air (shoulders raised).

(b) The patient is then asked to produce an inhalation phonation with the accompanying raised shoulders.

(c) The therapist demonstrates a inhaled–exhaled "set" in which a high-pitched hum is produced on inhalation with raised shoulders, followed by the same high-pitched tone produced on exhaled air with lowered shoulders. The patient then imitates the inhaled–exhaled combinations exactly as demonstrated.

(d) The therapist then demonstrates the inhaled–exhaled combination again, but this time the therapist sustains the high-pitched exhale and "sweeps down" (Boone & McFarlane, 1994) from the high-pitched voice to the regular speaking or chest register pitch. The patient then attempts to imitate this shift to the lower register. If the patient cannot make the shift to the lower register, the therapist should repeat the steps of the procedure from the beginning.

(e) Once the patient is able to produce the exhaled phonation in the lower speaking register, she or he may then continue to use the exhaled hum phonations in the speaking or chest register until he or she is comfortable initiating the "new voice" with the hum. The patient may then proceed to single-syllable word lists and drop the associated shoulder movements. The therapist may want to explain to the patient that the new voice is working well because the vocal fold mechanism is now working the way it should. This approach places the blame on the mechanism rather than the patient (Boone & McFarlane, 1994). Inhalation phonation may help the patient find and use the true vocal folds again, but it is likely that the patient will need additional therapy to identify the causes of the vocal hyperfunction and to habituate a healthy voice.

IV. **Special Considerations for the Professional Voice User.** The professional voice user is any person whose voice is the primary instrument for performing his or her work. Professional voice users include singers, actors, teachers, ministers, attorneys, radio and TV personalities, auctioneers, and telemarketers, to name just a few. For these individuals, voice problems or loss of voice are devastating professionally and financially. Even a brief period of laryngitis may mean a cancelled seminar or performance and the loss of considerable income. Although vocal health is important for everyone, professional voice users have special voice needs and demands that require them to prevent vocal dysfunction.

A. **Prevention of vocal dysfunction** (see informational handouts in Appendix B).

1. **Whole body health, warm-ups, and stretching.** Professional voice users should be instructed to make whole body stretches and warm-ups part of

their daily routine. Each day the professional can warm up the body and the voice (whether performing that day or not) with the simple protocol that follows (McCorvey & Lugo,1998; Raphael & Sataloff, 1997). The following are usually done while standing:

a. Begin warm-ups by **physically loosening up and stretching** *for at least 5 minutes.* Loosen clothing (ties, belts, etc.). Do genuine, whole body yawns with full stretches.

b. Gently **shake the body** (arms, legs, hands, etc.) for a few moments to release tension (time is an individual preference here) until the body begins to feel loose and relaxed. Some individuals prefer to dance to music, do yoga exercises, or other similar activities.

2. **Breathing and alignment exercises.** The next steps in the warm-up progression are breathing and body posture and alignment maneuvers (McCorvey & Lugo, 1998; Raphael & Sataloff, 1997):

a. **Slowly inhale** with a "softened belly" to permit an effortless inhalation, then allow the air out again easily and gently. Place the palm of the hand on the abdomen for the first few breaths, which gives kinesthetic feedback to encourage air to move out completely with no shoulder or spinal (postural) collapse. Let the exhaled air out on a gentle, relaxing sound ("ahhhhhhhhhhhhhhh" or "fffffffffffff"). Inhale again completely, without shoulder elevation or tension. Repeat the cycle four or five times and then allow the arms to drop to the sides and continue the relaxed inhale/exhale cycle for **2 or 3 minutes.**

b. Slowly and gently let the **head lead and roll gently** down the spine. Bend (roll) forward only as far as is comfortable. Stay in that position for a few seconds, feeling the gentle stretch of the trunk and spine as they are allowed to "go with" gravity. Slowly rebuild posture by rolling back up the spine into an upright position. Very slowly and gently roll the head back upright until the effort "turns off" as the head is naturally aligned straight atop the spine. Repeat at least three or four times. Remain quiet, making sure to feel the moment when the effort "turns off" as the head sits in proper, comfortable alignment. Continue for **at least 2 or 3 minutes.**

c. While seated or standing, slowly and gently let the **head drop to the chest** in a completely relaxed fashion (as though nodding off to sleep). Let the head relax for a 5- to 10-second count. Slowly lift the head into an upright position. Very slowly and gently bring the head back upright until the effort "turns off" as the head is naturally aligned straight atop the spine. Repeat with the head relaxed first to the right shoulder (as though pouring water from the ear), and then with the head relaxed to the left shoulder. Repeat front, right, left, several times with a gentle realignment of the head into the upright position after each position (i.e., front, upright; right, upright; left, upright) and repeat.

d. Sataloff (1997a) provides a particularly outstanding collection of breathing, alignment, and vocal warm-up exercises focusing on the professional voice user. It is important to remember that the point of these exercises is to warm up the body for the professional voice tasks required of it.

Tasks should be chosen that gently stretch, relax, and warm up muscles of the body, head, neck, and larynx. While it is important that the professional be physically healthy, aerobic exercises, weight lifting, and similar activities will generally *not* serve as effective warm-ups for the body and voice (see **(1)** through **(8)** below). The professional can vary breathing and alignment exercises in any manner that is comfortable but **does not** result in the following:

(1) **Effortful closure of the glottis including hard glottal attack.** This would also include any exercise that results in grunting, groaning, or excessive vocal use (such as counting the numbers of aerobic repetitions).

(2) **Muscle strain or tension**

(3) **Extreme fatigue**

(4) **Excessive dryness of the mouth and throat or excessive thirst**

(5) **Inhalation phonation**

(6) **Talking over background noise**

(7) **Loud laughing**

(8) **Throat clearing or coughing**

3. **Vocal warm-ups and stretching** should also be a part of the professional's daily routine. For the most effective results, the professional should do warm-up routines (including the body and breathing exercises discussed earlier) for *at least 20 minutes* or more before each rehearsal and performance. General vocal health will likely be improved if these activities are done daily.

   a. Vocal warm-ups are always started in the **relaxed, most comfortable midrange** of the professional's voice.

   b. It is best to start the vocals with something like **tongue trills** (raspberries), **lip trills** (Bronx cheers), or **humming.** All of these types of phonation place the attention and emphasis in the front of the face and lift the voice off of the larynx. This is sometimes referred to as tone focus or forward focus as opposed to back focus. A back-focused voice (effort directly on the larynx) quickly results in laryngeal fatigue and strain.

   c. Chant or sing the word "hummmmmmm" at a comfortable pitch and loudness level in the middle of the range. Make this phonation light and airy (like a sigh). Make sure to start with a very breathy "h" in "hum," as that allows the vocal folds to turn on through a soft, airy voiceless breath, followed by the "mmmmmmm" that can easily be felt in the facial mask (see **III.C.5.c** earlier in this chapter; Andrews, 1995). Hold the word "hum" for several seconds, feeling the vibrations of the "mmmmmmm" in the facial mask. Repeat three to five times, letting the voice swell gently with each successive "hum."

   d. Maintain the lightness and forward focus of the "hum" and slide the "hum" *up* to a second note (no higher than four or five notes) and back to the first. Slide the "hum" *up* a full octave and back to the first note. Repeat three to five times.

e. Repeat the "hum" while sliding down to a second note (no lower than four or five notes) and back to the first. Slide the "hum" *down* a whole octave and back to the original note. Repeat several times.

f. Slide *up* an octave using first /a/, then /i/, then /u/. Then go *up* the octave step by step, using each of the same vowels preceded by /θ/. Go *up* the octave step by step again, this time using each of the vowels preceded by /m/. Repeat going *down* an octave rather than *up,* using the same procedure.

g. Go *up* the octave step by step, using each of the same vowels (/a/, /i/, /u/) preceded by /j/. Go *down* an octave step by step using each of the same vowels preceded by /j/. Exaggerate and feel the relaxed jaw opening and closing (like chewing the tones) as you sing /ja/, /ji/, or /ju/. Repeat several times.

h. Warm up the articulators using tongue twisters such as these: "A big black bug bit a big black bear and made the big black bear bleed blood;" "A Tudor who toots the flute tried to tutor two tooters to toot;" "Old oily Ollie oils old oily autos;" and "Lily ladles little Letty's lentil soup" (Staley, 1999). These will loosen up the articulators and the brain. There are many books of tongue twisters available in print. In addition, there are pages of public domain tongue twisters available on the World Wide Web (see Staley, 1999).

i. Using as many vowels and consonants as possible, sing (or say, or chant) a series of relaxed scales with a consonant preceding a vowel. For example, sing "/mi/" up the scale one step at a time, and back down the scale one step at a time (1-2-3-4-5-6-7-8-7-6-5-4-3-2-1). Use consonants that vary place of articulation, such as bilabials, labiodentals, velars, and so on, and varying vowels, such as front, back, and so on. Extend the scales beyond one octave as level of comfort permits. Extending beyond one octave may be necessary for a professional singer but not for a professional speaker. The decision of whether to extend the voice through its entire range should be based on the patient's comfort level and her or his professional vocal requirements.

j. Sing another series of the scales listed in the previous passage, but with the vocal effort cut in half and with no whispering or voicelessness. Try to cut the vocal effort in half again.

k. Finally, gradually increase the loudness and fullness of the sounds from Section **i.** Vocalize the entire range of the voice using relaxed, full resonance. Check for vibrations in the facial mask periodically to be sure that the tone is staying forward and focused.

4. A routine can be varied to meet the individual needs of any performer. Professionals should stop and take a break anytime they feel tired or the voice feels tired or strained. For the most effective results, the patient should be instructed to break during the warm-up exercises after about each 5 to 10 minutes of activity. At each break the professional should walk around, stretch, and get a drink of water so that the voice is well hydrated before actually beginning a demanding vocal task (McCorvey & Lugo, 1998). The performer should remember to drink a minimum of eight glasses of water a day to maintain hydration.

V. **Voice Changes Associated with Gender Reassignment.** The speech–language pathologist may be called upon to assist in modification of an individual's voice characteristics during gender reassignment. Brodnitz (1988) has indicated that voice therapists are seeing more individuals for gender identification therapy. Female-to-male changes are usually managed through use of masculinizing hormones. The hormone regimen results in an increase in laryngeal mass size and lowered fundamental frequency (Colton & Casper, 1996). However, in male-to-female changes, administration of hormones does not reduce the mass size of the vocal folds, and thus voice therapy may be beneficial in helping to develop strategies for effective communication.

A. **Management of pitch changes for male-to-female gender reassignment.**

1. **Test the entire frequency range of the voice** (see pitch range assessment in Chapter 3) to determine a comfortable, functional range.

2. **Counsel the client** that there is considerable overlap in frequency range between male and female speakers (Andrews, 1995). Morrison and Rammage (1994) suggest that a F_0 of approximately 160 Hz lies in a region referred to as "gender ambiguous."

3. **Help the client to identify a new F_0** that is comfortable and does not result in laryngeal tension.

4. **Use feedback devices** such as CSL Pitch to help the client monitor the new pitch.

5. It may be beneficial to **teach the patient a light, breathy voice quality with a slightly retracted tongue.** The retracted tongue tends to elevate the larynx and provide additional feminine quality to the voice (Stemple et al., 1995).

6. Andrews (1995) also notes that it is beneficial for speakers to **use more stereotypically feminine intonation patterns.** For example, tentative or rising inflections at the ends of utterances are more common in females. Wolfe, Ratusnik, Smith, and Northrop (1990) found that subjects who had a higher percentage of upward inflections and a lower percentage of downward inflections were more likely to be rated as female speakers.

7. **Speakers should attempt to develop "head resonance" versus "chest" resonance,** as women reportedly use head resonance while men use chest resonance (Looking Glass Society, 1997). Head resonance is accomplished by opening the mouth more, using more air, and "placing" the voice into the face and head.

8. **Falsetto voice should be discouraged.** While falsetto is higher in pitch, it is not perceived as a natural feminine voice style. A lower pitch voice with other distinctly feminine attributes (e.g., the voice of Lauren Bacall) is more authentic.

9. There are several **surgical techniques** that have been used to assist in elevation of vocal pitch. The most commonly used procedure is called **cricothyroid approximation.** In cricothyroid approximation, the thyroid cartilage is pushed downward to approximate the cricoid cartilage, and the cartilages are sutured together in that position. This procedure is also referred to as a **Type IV Thyroplasty** procedure (Case, 1996). The procedure results in an increase in pitch and pitch range for some clients. Other surgeons have attempted laser resection of the thyro-arytenoid muscle to elevate vocal pitch. Reportedly this procedure has met with limited success (Lawrence, 1999).

B. **Management of other speech and voice characteristics to facilitate male-to-female gender identification.** Pitch is a very important consideration in gender reassignment, but not the only one. Female voices can still be identified as female even when the stereotypical pitch differences are removed (Coleman, 1976). This finding suggests that other factors, such as stress, intonation, and timing, are important in gender identification (Colton & Casper, 1996).

1. Male-to-female gender change speakers must learn to speak more softly and adopt a phrasing pattern that is legato or connected, rather than staccato or abrupt and disconnected (Andrews, 1995). Günzburger (1995) found that transsexual speakers using their female mode used a softer voice as well as a higher F_0 and increased pitch range.

2. Speech rate and pause time are both slightly increased in female speakers. Female speakers show about a two- to three-word per minute faster overall rate when compared with male speakers (Walker, 1988). However, females also show slightly increased pause time in connected speech, indicating that actual speaking time may be considerably faster than for male speakers.

3. Attention to articulation may be indicated, as female speakers tend to use more precise articulation than male speakers.

4. Linguistic style is different in female speakers, who show greater use of terms such as *can, will, may,* or *shall* (Case, 1996), and greater use of indirect speech acts (e.g., saying "Do you think it is warm in here?" rather than "Turn off the heat") (Andrews, 1995).

5. Female speakers tend to emphasize feelings and relationships in their communicative interactions, using more qualifiers and disclaimers and tending to deemphasize literal, factual, direct strategies (Andrews, 1995).

6. Body language and gestural strategies are softer in female speakers. There is more touching, smiling, and leaning or inclining toward the other speaker. There is also more eye contact in female speakers than in male speakers (Andrews, 1995). Podrouzek and Furrow (1988) found increased eye contact in female speakers as early as 2½ years of age.

7. Speakers who wish to sound more feminine should avoid use of throat clearing, low-pitched vocalized pauses, and coughing, which are more common in male speakers (Stemple et al., 1995).

8. Frequent use of videotape feedback will be critical in gender identification therapy. The client must be able to see if the end product is the image that she or he had hoped for, including voice, speech, and gestural characteristics.

9. Gender reassignment clients should be encouraged to use the resources available to them to answer their questions. Andrews (1995) has an especially helpful section on gender reassignment that addresses all aspects of communication. In addition, there are many outstanding resources on the World Wide Web that address gender reassignment. Lawrence (1999) has an outstanding collection of resources for transsexual clients and speech–language pathologists on her web site. The site maintains a collection of current peer-reviewed literature about male-to-female gender reassignment, speech, and voice. The Looking Glass Society (1997) also has an excellent Web page addressing male-to-female speech and voice techniques.

Chapter 6
Functional, Psychogenic, and Spasmodic Dysphonias

◆ ◆ ◆ ◆ ◆ ◆ ◆ ◆ ◆ ◆ ◆ ◆ ◆ ◆ ◆ ◆ ◆ ◆ ◆

P recise coordination of the laryngeal muscles is necessary for proper adduction of the vocal folds. A reciprocal balance among all of the phonatory muscles results in vocal fold adduction that is neither too tense nor too lax. Many voice disorders are caused by faulty approximation of the vocal folds. In some disorders, the vocal folds are overadducted because of excessive laryngeal tension, resulting in dysphonias with specific characteristics. In other disorders, the vocal folds are hypoadducted because of lax laryngeal muscles and thus fail to approximate each other sufficiently, resulting in dysphonias with another set of characteristics. Spasmodic dysphonia, an often severe approximation disorder, is also discussed in this chapter.

Problems of vocal fold approximation that are organic in origin usually manifest as conditions of hypoadduction or insufficient approximation. Frequently, the faulty approximation is caused by vocal fold lesions or interarytenoid growths that preclude complete closure of the vocal folds. Laryngeal lesions that prevent complete vocal fold approximation are described in Chapters 4 and 7. Insufficient vocal fold approximation may also be related to paresis or paralysis of the vocal folds (see Chap. 8, **I.A**).

In addition to vocal fold approximation problems associated with laryngeal lesions or paralysis, there are vocal fold approximation problems associated with functional or psychogenic disorders and disorders resulting from specific neurological deficits known as focal dystonias. In these disorders, the vocal folds are either tensed and hyperadducted or lax and hypoadducted. These disorders of vocal fold approximation are discussed in this chapter. These voice disorders range from conditions of complete aphonia to conditions in which the higher-pitched voice of prepubescent males continues into adolescence or adulthood.

I. **Ventricular dysphonia (dysphonia plicae ventricularis, false fold phonation)** is a rare voice disorder in which the ventricular folds (false folds) are approximated and may be used for phonation while the true vocal folds are usually held in a slightly abducted position. Occasionally, simultaneous vibration of the false folds and the true vocal folds occurs, resulting in a double-pitched voice that is called **diplophonia.** Mass loading of the false folds onto the true folds may occur, with the false folds actually resting or sitting on the true folds. This mass loading effect results in dampened true fold vibration and a significantly lowered and dysphonic fundamental frequency. In our experience, it is unusual for the false vocal folds to actually vibrate. More often than not, there is considerable tension and approximation observed in the false cords, but actual vibration is rare (S. M. Archer, personal communication, 1998; Boone & McFarlane, 1994).

A. Etiology. Ventricular dysphonia may develop as a consequence of excessive muscular tension in the laryngeal region. Ventricular dysphonia may also develop as a substitute voice for patients who have a severely debilitating disease or paralysis of the vocal folds. Occasionally, the use of ventricular phonation as a substitute phonatory source by these patients should be encouraged and, perhaps, improved through voice therapy. However, when ventricular phonation is a consequence of excessive laryngeal tension, it should be eliminated.

B. Symptoms. The voice of the patient with ventricular dysphonia can be described as low pitched, restricted in vocal range, reduced in loudness, and hoarse. These vocal symptoms are directly related to the vibratory characteristics of the false folds.

The low vocal pitch occurs because the false folds contain more mass than the true vocal folds, and consequently are not able to vibrate as rapidly. The large mass of the false folds also makes it very difficult for the patient to keep the false folds vibrating, thus making it appear as if the patient is speaking under considerable strain. Because the patient has little or no conscious control over the tenseness of the false folds, the pitch range is severely limited.

C. Laryngoscopic findings. Laryngeal examination during quiet, relaxed breathing will reveal that the false folds are in the normal, abducted position, although the false folds are often thickened (hypertrophied). When the patient is asked to phonate, the false folds approximate and begin to vibrate (Fred, 1962).

D. Medicosurgical management of ventricular dysphonia is generally contraindicated unless the dysphonia is the consequence of a primary vocal fold defect that has caused the patient to adopt ventricular phonation as a substitute. In such cases, medicosurgical management to eliminate the defect may enable the patient to regain use of the true vocal folds for speaking purposes.

E. Voice therapy management. The goal of voice therapy for the patient with ventricular dysphonia is dependent upon the etiology of the dysphonia. Voice therapy goals for patients who inappropriately use ventricular phonation when their true vocal folds are capable of producing normal phonation are much different than voice therapy goals for patients who develop phonatory use of the false folds when their true vocal folds are severely diseased or paralyzed.

1. **Patients who are capable of voice production using the true vocal folds.** The principal goal of voice therapy for the patient with normally functioning vocal folds is to eliminate phonation produced by the false folds and retrain the true vocal folds to assume this function once again. The prognosis for regaining use of the true vocal folds is good to guarded, depending upon the patient's level of motivation and the length of time that ventricular phonation has been used (Cooper, 1973). The following techniques in the manner of Boone and McFarlane (1994) may be helpful in enabling the patient to regain function of the true vocal folds:

   a. First, the patient should be given a detailed explanation of how the false folds are substituting for the true vocal folds. Detailed drawings of the anatomic relationship of the true and false folds may make it easier for the patient to understand the explanation.

b. Next, ask the patient to slowly inhale and exhale several times and then try to phonate while trying to inhale (inhalation phonation). If the patient is unable to do this, it may be necessary for the clinician to demonstrate. Following a demonstration, most patients should be able to produce an inhalation phonation.

c. When the patient is able to consistently produce phonation during inhalation, ask the patient to produce inhalation phonation and then quickly try to exhale and match the pitch produced during exhalation with the pitch produced during inhalation. If the patient is able to match the two pitches, the clinician can be reasonably certain that the voice is being produced by the true vocal folds, since pitch control of the false folds cannot be consciously controlled to any great extent by the patient.

d. After the patient is able to consistently match pitches produced during inhalation and exhalation, the inhalation phonation should be eliminated. Then, ask the patient to reproduce the pitch once again, but only during exhalation. If the patient is successful, ask the patient to phonate the vowel /a/ at the same pitch. Once the patient is able to consistently produce /a/ at that pitch, have him or her vary the pitch (remember, only when vowels are produced by the true vocal folds can the pitch be varied significantly). Control of the true vocal folds can be further improved by having the patient **practice various vowels, words, phrases, and sentences.**

2. Patients who develop ventricular phonation to compensate for true vocal folds that are incapable of producing voice. The principal goal for the patient with ventricular dysphonia who has diseased or paralyzed true vocal folds is to improve the characteristics of the ventricular phonation, because normal phonation is no longer possible. Occasionally, the loudness and pitch aspects of ventricular phonation can be improved to a limited degree. Loudness may be improved by having the patient gain greater control over exhalation and by using a relaxed, more open mouth posture. Vocal pitch and pitch variability may also be improved through the patient's increased control over expiration, but it should be remembered that only slight control of pitch characteristics of ventricular phonation can be obtained by most patients.

II. Conversion voice disorders (conversion dysphonia, conversion aphonia, conversion muteness) consist of the total or partial loss of phonatory ability due to a conversion reaction. The result may be either complete **mutism** (the patient neither whispers nor attempts to articulate), **aphonia** (the patient can whisper, but no vocal fold vibration occurs), or **dysphonia** (the patient has varying degrees of hoarseness). Other terms that have been used to describe this type of loss of voice are hysterical aphonia, functional aphonia, and psychogenic aphonia.

A. Etiology. Conversion voice disorders result from a problem known as a **conversion reaction.** The primary manifestations of conversion reactions are either interruption of a channel of sensory feedback or the inability to perform certain voluntary muscle movements. In both cases, there is no organic pathology to explain the symptoms.

B. Symptoms. The voice symptoms associated with conversion voice disorders range from a mild disruption of vocal function to complete loss of the voice. All aspects of the voice pitch, loudness, and quality may be affected. Conversion voice disorders are frequently associated with the following characteristics:

1. Even though volitional control of the voice may be affected, the vegetative vocal functions, such as coughing, sighing, laughing, and crying, are unimpaired.

2. Some patients, however, may develop conversion voice disorders in combination with a dysphonia that is related to a laryngeal pathology. These patients, however, frequently exhibit voice symptoms that are much more severe than would normally be expected for a patient with such a laryngeal pathology (e.g., a patient with mild laryngitis would not be expected to demonstrate extreme breathiness).

3. In the initial stages, patients may experience temporary bouts of dysphonia, with the voice returning to normal. In later stages, the dysphonia may be continuously present.

4. Patients often describe a history of emotional stress or mental conflict.

5. It is not uncommon for some patients to identify and attribute the onset of the dysphonia with a particular emotional event or crisis.

6. Onset of the vocal symptoms is usually sudden, occurring within seconds, minutes, or perhaps hours.

7. The majority, perhaps as many 80%, of patients with conversion voice disorders are women (Andrews, 1995; Aronson, 1980).

C. Laryngoscopic findings. Examination reveals a normal-appearing laryngeal structure, with the vocal folds abducted in the normal position (intermediate) for quiet breathing. When the patient is instructed to phonate, the vocal folds may do one or more of the following:

1. Abduct to a more lateral position than they were at rest (Boone, 1983)

2. Partially adduct into a lax approximation

3. Adduct completely for coughing

D. Medicosurgical management of conversion voice disorders is contraindicated because they are psychogenic in origin.

E. Voice therapy management. The principal goal of therapy for a patient with a conversion voice disorder is to reestablish normal vocal fold function by slowly shaping the patient's unaffected vegetative vocal functions into a usable voice. Often, the patient does not associate vegetative vocal functions with the speaking voice and can be guided into voice recovery by a speech–language pathologist who is skillful enough to catch any of the patient's fleeting examples of good voice production and then shape those productions into useful speech.

In the beginning, most patients with conversion voice disorders do not give up trying to communicate; they just experience a partial or total loss of voice. These patients usually converse casually with others using whispered or dysphonic speech. As time passes, patients with conversion voice disorders tend to develop a mental block against speaking, even though they have retained the *ability* to speak, and go through day-to-day experiences without attempting to phonate.

While answering questions during the taking of the case history, the patient may recount episodes of emotional stress and mark the onset of the voice disorder with one of those events. Some patients believe that the emotional event actually caused the loss of voice. Other patients recall that the event and loss of voice occurred at the same time, but do not believe that the event caused the voice loss. The best course for the clinician is to focus on the voice itself, because dwelling on the events leading up to the disorder may cause emotionally negative feelings to temporarily develop that might interfere with voice therapy.

The **prognosis** for a patient with a conversion voice disorder is guarded to good. Quite often, the degree to which a patient responds to voice therapy depends on how vividly the patient remembers the emotional stress or event that precipitated the voice loss. Clinically, we have found that patients who seek voice rehabilitation months or even years after the onset of the conversion voice disorder are no longer adversely affected by the emotional stress or event and have a much better prognosis than those patients whose precipitating crisis occurred more recently in their lives.

Others have suggested that when a considerable period of time has passed between the development of the vocal symptoms and the initiation of therapy, prognosis for improvement is decreased (Case, 1996). Apparently some patients develop the dysphonia as a habituated way of speaking, and that habit pattern or set can be quite resistant to change. Conversely, some patients, particularly if they are completely aphonic, may be anxious for help and more receptive to therapy if they have been without voice for a considerable period of time before consulting a speech–language pathologist (Freeman, 1986). Patients who are completely aphonic also apparently improve more quickly than patients who retain some voice, because patients who have voice find ways to communicate and "get by," which the patient who has aphonia cannot do.

Prognosis for improved voice is also enhanced if the patient can regain good voice production in the first session. The clinician should be persistent and keep trying to elicit good voice from the patient, even if it means that the initial therapy session must last for several hours. Because of the psychogenic nature of the voice disorder, enormous benefits can result if the patient can regain good voice before the therapy session ends. Some patients may require only one therapy session to establish good voice and one follow-up visit to evaluate whether the patient is maintaining adequate voice production. Other patients may require several therapy sessions before a productive voice is achieved.

Frequently, patients with a conversion voice disorder have been examined by a laryngologist before coming to the speech–language pathologist. The amount of information that the patient is given about the voice disorder varies with the individual physician. Some laryngologists prefer to tell their patients that the voice loss is due to emotional stress and that the voice will return when the patient is ready for it to return (these patients often interpret the physician's statement to mean that the voice loss is just "in the patient's head"). Physicians who use this method of informing their patients about a conversion voice disorder frequently prescribe tranquilizers to aid in voice rehabilitation. Other laryngologists assure their patients that there is no organic reason for the voice loss and then go on and explain that perhaps the patient has just temporarily lost control of the voice, much like many other patients that the physician has seen before.

To tell a patient with a conversion voice disorder that, in effect, the problem is "in your head" does little to help the patient regain use of the voice. No matter how many times patients are told that there are psychological reasons that they are experiencing voice loss, it does nothing to help patients who believe that the physician does not understand that the loss of voice control is real and not imagined. In fact, patients who have been informed about their voice disorder in this way often come to the speech–language pathologist for assurance that they are not, as these patients frequently state, "crazy."

No single technique can be guaranteed to work with all patients with a conversion voice disorder. The following steps should be used and modified for the needs of the individual patient:

1. Explain to the patient that this particular type of voice disorder is not unusual and that therapy will involve rediscovering use of the old voice. It is very important to show an extremely positive attitude when working with patients who have conversion voice disorders and to reassure them that they will, indeed, regain use of the voice. The patient should be given a simple physiologic explanation of how the loss of voice is related to the fact that the vocal folds are not coming together properly. It is better to avoid discussion with the patient about the psychological reasons that the vocal folds are not approximating, and instead focus the discussion on how voice therapy techniques will aid the patient in getting the vocal folds back together once again.

2. Begin by asking the patient to gently attempt one of the following vocal activities, which should be audiocasette recorded:

   a. Cough or clear the throat

   b. Hum

   c. Yawn and then sigh

   d. Laugh

   e. Phonate on inhalation

3. If the patient is able to produce any voice using one of the above methods, ask him or her to repeat the vocal activity several times. Tell the patient to perform the activity gently so that it does not "catch" in the throat. When voice is produced using any of the methods, the clinician can point out to the patient that the rudimentary tone required for voice production is available and that this is evidence that the vocal folds can actually come together.

4. After the patient can consistently produce a tone, have him or her produce the tone once again and sustain and shape it into the vowel /a/ or /o/. When the patient is successful at producing these two vowels, attempt the production of other vowels. As soon as vowel production begins to stabilize, have the patient attempt to produce the vowels *without* using one of the vegetative voice activities as a crutch for initiating phonation.

5. After the patient has demonstrated successful vowel production, have him or her attempt productions of nonsense syllables. Nonsense syllables that start with the consonant /h/ are usually the easiest for the patient to produce. It is important to have the patient attempt nonsense syllables before attempting to produce words, because the patient may have a mental block that temporarily makes it difficult to produce real words. If the patient should, at any time during the session, develop a block against voice production, have the patient use one of the vegetative vocal activities to regain spontaneous voicing ability.

6. When the patient demonstrates competence at producing a series of nonsense syllables, ask him or her to repeat words that begin with a vowel. Have the patient repeat these and other lists of words beginning with consonants before advancing to phrase and sentence practice exercises.

7. If the patient is accompanied by another person (e.g., spouse, friend), invite that person into the therapy room and have the patient engage in conversation with this person. Conversation with persons who are personally close to the patient tends to stabilize the patient's voicing ability. If the patient has come to the clinic unaccompanied, ask him or her to telephone a friend or family member who is familiar with the voice disorder and who can help motivate the patient to keep the newly rediscovered voice after leaving the therapy situation.

8. At least 50% of conversion voice disorder patients can be treated in one or two extended-length therapy sessions. The other half of this group may require several weeks or months of voice therapy before an adequate voice returns. A small proportion of patients with conversion voice disorders may have emotional problems that are severe enough to require a long-term program of psychotherapy, even when the voice therapy program requires only several weeks before the voice returns to an acceptable level of production.

   Although long-term psychotherapy may be indicated for some patients, Aronson (1990, p. 321) cautions that **premature referral** of patients experiencing conversion voice disorders to psychiatry and psychology may almost guarantee failure to improve voice. He recommends that patients first be seen by otolaryngology to rule out organic causes, then be seen for symptomatic voice therapy, and then be referred to psychiatry or psychology if indicated.

III. **Mutational falsetto (puberphonia)** is the failure to eliminate the higher-pitched voice of prepubescence and substitute the lower-pitched voice of postpubescence and adulthood in the presence of a structurally normal larynx. Because the amount of vocal pitch change that occurs at puberty is about one octave for males and only three to four semitones in females, mutational falsetto is a voice problem found primarily, but not exclusively, in postpubescent and adult males.

The social consequences for males who exhibit falsetto voice are many. In some cultural groups, males with falsetto voices are thought of as being effeminate, passive, and immature, and they may endure much teasing from schoolmates. Gender confusion on the telephone (in which the listener may mistakenly identify the falsetto speaker as a female) is also a common occurrence.

A. **Etiology.** Mutational falsetto is the persistence of a higher-pitched voice into adulthood, even when the larynx is physically capable of producing the normal lower pitch of adult males.

1. The use of mutational falsetto beyond the time of normal voice change frequently results from **psychosocial factors.** Although little research has been done to support this belief, many speech–language pathologists hold the notion that the patient with mutational falsetto may be embarrassed about the newly developing low-pitched voice or reject the responsibilities and roles of adulthood and consequently maintain the voice of childhood into adulthood. As in other types of voice disorders, talking in a high-pitched voice today will build a mental set that will perpetuate talking with a higher-pitched voice in future days.

2. Factors other than psychosocial factors may be etiologic. They include the following (Aronson, 1980):

   a. In some cases, laryngeal development is delayed because of an **endocrine disorder.** If the development of a larynx capable of producing an adult pitch is delayed too long, however, it may be very difficult for the patient to abandon the high-pitched voice.

   b. Loss of control over the developing lower-pitched voice may be caused by a **severe hearing loss,** which prevents the person from perceiving the changes that are occurring in the voice.

   c. **Neurologic disease** during puberty that causes weakness of the vocal folds or the muscles of respiration may cause persistence of falsetto voice.

   d. A **debilitating disease** during puberty may be so severe as to affect respiration sufficiently enough to interfere with the development of a lower-pitched voice.

B. **Symptoms.** The voice of the patient with mutational falsetto is high pitched, breathy, and hoarse. These patients usually report that there are occasions when the vocal pitch level drops, especially when they shout or attempt heavy lifting.

   The higher-pitched voice is produced by a larynx that is elevated high in the neck and tilted downward. This laryngeal posture puts the vocal folds in a state of laxity. As the individual attempts phonation, the arytenoids adduct so tightly that the posterior portion of the vocal folds is prevented from vibrating and the thyroarytenoid muscle fails to contract. This particular phonatory posture tends to reduce the mass of the vocal folds and permits only the thin glottal edge to vibrate.

C. **Laryngoscopic findings.** Laryngeal examination reveals a structurally normal larynx.

D. **Medicosurgical management** of mutational falsetto is contraindicated because of the psychogenic etiology of the dysphonia.

E. **Voice therapy management.** Prognosis for improved voice is excellent for patients with mutational falsetto; most of these patients can be successfully treated in several therapy sessions. The principal goal of voice therapy for patients with mutational falsetto is to shape a vegetative vocal production, such as coughing, clearing the throat, or grunting, into a normal voice. The following procedures should be used in therapy:

1. Ask the patient to take a deep breath and then clear the throat or cough sharply. This should result in the production of a lower-pitched voice. Be sure to point this lower-pitched voice out to the patient and tell him that it is the target voice that you are after.

2. If the patient is unable to produce a lower pitch level using any vegetative vocal production, it may be necessary to alter the position of the larynx. Because the larynx is usually held very high in the neck in patients with mutational falsetto, manipulation of the larynx into a lowered neck position may facilitate the production of a lower-pitched voice. Ask the patient to cough sharply once again while holding the larynx lower in the neck manually. This should result in a lower-pitched production.

3. After the patient has produced several lower-pitched coughs or grunts, have the patient produce a cough and blend it into the production of the vowel /a/. Again, keep pointing out the lower pitch of the voice that is being produced (an audiocasette recorder can be very beneficial at this point).

4. After the patient has produced several different vowels using the cough as a facilitator, the cough should be eliminated and isolated vowel productions should be attempted. The ability of the patient to make consistently low-pitched productions determines how quickly the patient should move on to syllable, word, phrase, and sentence practice exercises.

5. The most difficult part of voice therapy with mutational falsetto patients is getting them accustomed to their new, low-pitched voice. During the therapy sessions, the patient may frequently refer to how strange the new voice sounds. Reassure the patient that the strangeness of the voice is only temporary and occurs because the patient has been listening to his old, higher-pitched voice for such a long time.

   Even though the patient may be able to demonstrate good, lower-pitched voice production in the clinic, do not assume that he is easily able to use the voice outside of the clinical situation. One of the most difficult tasks that a patient with mutational falsetto must do is face family and friends with his "new voice." It may be necessary for the clinician to assist the patient in using his new voice in different speaking environments.

   Occasionally, a patient with mutational falsetto is able to use the low-pitched voice in the clinical setting, but unable to use the voice outside the clinic. Careful counseling with these patients can reveal whether the patient should receive supportive, psychological management. Frequently, these patients return for voice therapy after a period of psychological counseling.

[handwritten note: know 3 types]

[handwritten checkmark] **IV. Spasmodic Dysphonia (adductor, abductor, and mixed spasmodic dysphonia).** The term **spastic** (rather than spasmodic) **dysphonia** has historically been used to refer to a group of voice disorders that are characterized by severe and spasmodic problems of vocal fold approximation. The term **spasmodic dysphonia,** however, is more descriptive and is used more frequently by health professionals to better differentiate two specific forms of this dysphonia from the dysphonia associated with spastic (pseudobulbar) dysarthria (see Chap. 8, **II**).

Spasmodic dysphonia is one of a group of neurologic disorders called dystonias. A **dystonia** is a movement disorder characterized by forceful, inappropriate contraction of muscle groups. In spasmodic dysphonia, the intrinsic laryngeal muscles are involved. There are **two primary types of spasmodic dysphonia.** The most common type is **adductor dysphonia.** This occurs when the thyroarytenoid muscles, which close the vocal folds, contract with excess force, causing tight, strained, strangled phonation. **Abductor dysphonia** occurs when random opening of the vocal folds is caused by contractions of the posterior cricoarytenoids. The resultant voice is randomly breathy and whispered (Gaut, 1997).

Adductor spasmodic dysphonia is the term used to describe a voice disorder in which the vocal folds are approximated so tightly that it is impossible to produce sustained vocal fold vibration. The term **abductor spasmodic dysphonia** refers to a type of severe breathy dysphonia in which the vocal folds episodically abduct to the lateral position (Hartman & Aronson, 1981). It is generally accepted that the abductor type of spasmodic dysphonia is probably etiologically unrelated to the adductor type. Symptoms and management techniques differ for both types of the disorder.

There are also **three subtypes of spasmodic dysphonia.** One subtype is **mixed dysphonia,** a combination of adductor and abductor spasm, while a second subtype occurs as **spasmodic dysphonia symptoms accompanied by voice tremor.** The third subtype consists of a **severe voice tremor with adductor phonation spasm during the tremors** (National Spasmodic Dysphonia Association [NSDA], 1998).

A. **Etiology.** The exact etiology of spasmodic dysphonia is unknown, but it was first described by Traube in 1871. For many years, spasmodic dysphonia was thought to be psychogenic in origin. Readers of voice disorders literature may be aware that the prevailing historical reason offered for many disorders was psychological. More recently, our technology and research have allowed us to discover other contributing factors. Perhaps a clearer awareness will create "kinder, gentler" voice therapists who are aware that "psychological origin" may mean simply what it says (not something mysterious), or it may mean that we do not yet have the technology to know a disorder's true etiology. Knowing this may make professionals more holistic as therapists, more likely to offer all reasonable therapies, and less likely to rush to judgments that may stop thought and stigmatize patients.

Spasmodic dysphonia is not caused by stress and is not a psychological disorder. It is now known that spasmodic dysphonia is one of several neurological conditions called **focal dystonias.** Spasmodic dysphonia is a focal dystonia affecting the vocal muscles of the larynx. Like other forms of dystonia, it is characterized by abnormal involuntary muscle movements. The causes of spasmodic dysphonia are not fully known, but it is thought to be due to abnormal functioning in an area of the brain called the **basal ganglia.** The basal ganglia help to coordinate movements of the muscles throughout the body. In spasmodic dysphonia, the normally smooth coordination of the vocal cords is disrupted, resulting in an abnormal voice pattern.

Spasmodic dysphonia is slightly more common in women than in men. It is usually an adult-onset disorder, beginning between approximately at 30 to 50 years of age. A genetic factor is suspected in some patients because other family members may have signs or symptoms of dystonia involving some other segment of the body (Dystonia Medical Research Foundation, 1999).

B. **Symptoms** of spasmodic dysphonia vary, depending on the type of the disorder. The following are characteristics associated with the two different types:

1. **Symptoms of the adductor type.** Adductor spasmodic dysphonia is the more common of the two general types.

   a. **Vocal symptoms.** Onset of the disorder is characterized by a nonspecific hoarseness with associated "vocal catches" pitch and phonation breaks that eventually evolve into complete laryngospasms. The voice of the patient with an advanced form of adductor spasmodic dysphonia has been described as a strained, squeezed, staccato phonation (Aronson, 1980; Luchsinger & Arnold, 1965), produced with extreme phonatory effort that nevertheless results in little vocal loudness. The general impression that one gets when listening to a patient with adductor spasmodic dysphonia speak is that great vocal effort is being expended for little acoustic output. Sustained phonation is very difficult because the true vocal folds, and occasionally the false folds and pharyngeal musculature, intermittently overadduct (laryngospasms) so tightly as to prevent vocal fold vibration from occurring (Borenstein, Lipton, & Rupick, 1978; McCall, Skolnick, & Brewer, 1971; Parnes, Lavorato, & Myers, 1978). Instead, phonation occurs as abrupt, staccato, vocal explosions. The vocal symptoms are most noticeable when the patient attempts to communicate with others; laughing, singing, shouting, and noncommunicative vocalizations are often unaffected (Boone, 1983; Salassa, DeSanto, & Aronson, 1982).

   Several key features help **differentially diagnose spasmodic dysphonia** from other muscle tension or hyperfunctional dysphonias. Patients with spasmodic dysphonia report dysphonia patterns that are different from those associated with other dysphonias. Abrupt voice breaks are common with spasmodic dysphonia (both with the adductor and abductor types), but not usually with hyperfunctional dysphonia. Spasmodic dysphonia is generally not intermittent; that is, it rarely goes away altogether once it begins. Patients with spasmodic dysphonia may report a good voice for a brief period of time when they first arise in the morning. This is because, like other dystonias, spasmodic dysphonia disappears during sleep. Also, they may report that their voice improves somewhat when they are relaxed, for example, when drinking alcoholic beverages (Koufman, 1998a).

Although patients with either type of dysphonia appear to expend considerable effort in speaking, patients with adductor spasmodic dysphonia seem to tire because they are pushing the voice through a tight opening, whereas patients with the abductor type seem to tire because so much air is being wasted in phonatory attempts.

Differences in vocal behavior when reading a sentence that is totally voiced versus a sentence that contains both voiced and voiceless consonants can assist the speech–language pathologist in differentiating a patient with abductor spasmodic dysphonia from a patient with adductor spasmodic dysphonia.

(1) A patient with the abductor type of spasmodic dysphonia would have little difficulty saying the following all-voiced sentence (i.e., no voiced/voiceless phoneme transition required), whereas a patient with the adductor type would experience difficulty:

> "Early one morning a man and a woman were ambling along a one-mile lane running near Rainy Island Avenue" (Dedo & Shipp, 1980).

(2) Patients with abductor or adductor spasmodic dysphonia both experience difficulty saying the following voiced/voiceless sentence:

> "He saw half a shape mystically cross a simple path at least fifty or sixty steps in front of his sister Kathy's house" (Dedo & Shipp, 1980).

(3) Spectral (or spectrographic) analysis reportedly offers valuable additional information in the differentiation of adductor dysphonia from other muscle tension or hyperfunctional dysphonias. The acoustic characteristics of muscle tension dysphonias include no abrupt voice breaks, excessive high frequency noise, and indistinct formant patterns. By comparison, the characteristics of adductor dysphonia are abrupt voice breaks, irregular wide-spaced vertical striations, some high-frequency noise, and distinct well-preserved formants (Koufman, 1998a).

b. **Nonvocal symptoms.** In addition to the vocal symptoms associated with adductor spasmodic dysphonia, difficulty in breathing and muscle pain in the upper chest are common symptoms that are also related to the struggle to speak. Facial grimacing, neck contractions, synkinetic eye blinking, and exaggerated chest and abdominal wall contractions are common (Salassa et al., 1982), and patients who exhibit the more severe forms of the dysphonia typically experience bulging neck muscles and bulging veins in the neck as they struggle in their attempts to phonate against the glottal resistance.

2. **Symptoms of the abductor type.** Abductor spasmodic dysphonia is not as common as the adductor type. The voice of the patient with abductor spasmodic dysphonia has been described as having intermittent moments of aphonia and breathiness, with impairment of voiced/voiceless phoneme distinctions (Hartman & Aronson, 1981; Zwitman, 1979). Typically, the patient with abductor spasmodic dysphonia has the most difficulty with the transi-

tion from a voiceless consonant to a vowel in a stressed syllable. The patient is frequently unable to initiate laryngeal valving following the voiceless consonant, and a glottal-widening, abductor-type laryngospasm then occurs.

The laryngeal characteristics of abductor spasmodic dysphonia are exactly opposite to those of the adductor type. Whereas adductor spasmodic dysphonia is characterized by laryngospasms that result in highly constricted, overadducted vocal folds, abductor spasmodic dysphonia is characterized by laryngospasms in which the vocal folds approximate briefly and then abruptly and randomly abduct, thus preventing vocal fold vibration and causing episodic breathiness.

C. **Laryngoscopic findings** of spasmodic dysphonia differ with each type of the disorder. The following are descriptions for each type:

  1. **Laryngoscopic findings in the adductor type.** The larynx appears normal when at rest; however, closer inspection may reveal minute "quivering" (Bastian, 1998). When the patient is asked to phonate, the true vocal folds and the false folds may be seen to hyperadduct in intermittent and irregular spasms.

  2. **Laryngoscopic findings in the abductor type.** The larynx appears normal when at rest. The vocal folds will, however, approximate and then abruptly abduct widely as the patient attempts to phonate.

D. **Medicosurgical management.**

  1. Currently the treatment of choice for spasmodic dysphonia is **injection of botulinum toxin A (Botox)** into the appropriate laryngeal muscle. Botulinum toxin A was first recognized as a safe and effective treatment for spasmodic dysphonia in the 1980s. Although treatment techniques vary from center to center, most centers employ a multidisciplinary approach with an otolaryngologist, a speech–language pathologist, and a neurologist. Botox injections for adductor spasmodic dysphonia are performed either percutaneously using EMG, or perorally using fiberoptic visualization. Injections may be either unilateral or bilateral. Percutaneous injection is the most common approach in use today. In this approach, the injection is placed through the cricothyroid membrane into the thyroarytenoid muscle of the right or left vocal fold using EMG or fiberoptic localization. Two potential advantages of the EMG localization method are that virtually all patients can be injected, and effective thyrovocalis muscle localization is virtually assured (Koufman, 1998a).

  The dosage employed also varies with the technique of injection and the vocal needs of the patient. Bilateral injection seemingly has one potential advantage; that is, a good result may still be obtained even if one of the injections is suboptimal. The patient having a unilateral injection usually receives more Botox than the patient having bilateral injections (Koufman, 1998a). Ludlow (1995) suggests that 5.0 units be administered in each of three locations for unilateral injections. For bilateral injections, the recommended dosage is 2.5 units per side in a single location. Patients will typically require reinjection every 2 to 6 months. Patients with adductor spasm who have received Botox typically report a postinjection period of weak and breathy voice that may last from 3 to 7 days. They then have a period of "good voice," which may last from several weeks to months. Patients are encouraged to stay on their periodic injection schedule so that their spasmodic symptoms will not return to initial severity levels (Colton & Casper, 1996). Long-term effects of injection of Botox are virtually unknown, as the procedure has only been performed since the 1980s. The patients with tremor, abductor type, or mixed dystonias are more difficult to treat. In the case of the abductor type, the posterior cricoarytenoid muscle is generally the muscle that is injected, but results are less predictable than with adductor dysphonia.

An occasional patient is seen who appears to be "cured" with a single Botox injection. This type of patient most likely actually suffered from a functional voice disorder—that is, a muscle tension or hyperfunctional dysphonia. This type of dysphonia has been referred to as "pseudo spasmodic dysphonia" (Koufman, 1998a).

The following is a summary of screening procedures used prior to the patient attending a Botox clinic for an injection. It is essential that a thorough assessment of the patient's vocal characteristics be done prior to the procedure. Specifically, the patient with adductor spasmodic dysphonia must be distinguished from the patient with abductor spasmodic dysphonia in order for the otolaryngologist and the Botox team to determine the site of injection. It is also essential to gather baseline voice data prior to Botox treatment to help determine the efficacy of the individual patient's dosage and injection schedule.

a. A complete **voice examination** (see Chap. 2, **The Voice Evaluation Process**) should have been done at the first meeting to obtain baseline acoustic and behavioral characteristics of the patient for later comparison. Most important, videotape and audiocasette recordings, including the videoendoscopic examination of the patient, should have been made and maintained as baseline data. Voice screenings should then be performed each time the patient attends a Botox clinic. Minimally, the voice screening should include an audio recording of conversation and of a standard reading passage. Patients should be asked about the quality of their voice postinjection, including their estimate of the length of time that they have had "good voice" since their last injection and how long it took postinjection before they obtained "good voice."

b. Patients should be counseled at each Botox clinic that they may experience dysphagia or swallowing problems following the injection. On each clinic day, all patients should be questioned concerning any swallowing difficulties they may have experienced following their last injection. Each patient may need to be taught strategies, such as the supraglottic swallow, if he or she is experiencing difficulty after a Botox injection. To perform the supraglottic swallow, the patient is told to (1) inhale and to hold her or his breath tightly (or "clamp down"); (2) swallow while holding the breath; and (3) cough following the swallow (Logemann, 1998). If patients are experiencing enough swallowing difficulty to warrant use of the supraglottic swallow, the physician may decrease the dosage of subsequent injections to prevent continued swallowing problems and vocal weakness (R. B. Owens, personal communication, 1998).

c. An important part of each Botox clinic is critical listening by the trained ear of the speech–language pathologist and comparison of preinjection perceptual data (e.g., audiocasette and videotape recordings or the patient's postinjection voice). At each Botox clinic, the skill of the speech–language pathologist is vital in listening for improvement in the patient's voice or for changes in the voice that might indicate the need for a modification of dosage (e.g., a weak breathy voice). Critical listening is an important part of the overall assessment of the patient's progress with Botox therapy.

2. **Recurrent laryngeal nerve section** has been controversial since its introduction by Dedo in 1976. One of the problems with surgical management in adductor dysphonia is that the dysphonia recurs in over 50% of patients within 5 years after surgery. Others have reported that 3 years following sectioning of the recurrent laryngeal nerve, 64% were not improved and 48% were worse than before surgery (NSDA, 1998). It has been speculated that the recurrence of the dysphonia is due to a worsening or resetting of the dystonia symptoms on the unoperated side. This occurrence is characteristic of the dystonias (Koufman, 1998a). Generally, surgical techniques should be considered as an alternative to Botox only in carefully selected patients for whom Botox injection is ineffective.

For abductor dysphonia patients, bilateral medialization surgery has been attempted to push the vocal folds together so that the abductor voice breaks cause less air wasting. The result of this surgery has been a dramatic temporary improvement in most cases; however, in no case has the improvement lasted for more than 5 years. Fat injection into the vocal folds has also been employed to achieve a similar effect. The results of this procedure have also been variable (Koufman, 1998a; Murry & Woodson, 1996).

E. **Voice therapy management.** Voice therapy management for spasmodic dysphonia has generally had a poor history of success, as voice therapy is not the appropriate primary management technique for spasmodic dysphonia. However, in some situations, behavioral voice therapy has been reported to have variable success for management of spasmodic dysphonia.

1. The patient with early or mild symptoms of spasmodic dysphonia may benefit from voice therapy alone or voice therapy combined with Botox injection. Cooper (1998) reports success with voice therapy alone using neutral, relaxed phonations that are then expanded and generalized into words, phrases, and sentences. These voice therapy successes are not universally reported in the literature, however. Also reported are humming activities designed to place the voice in the facial mask and to remove effort from the laryngeal area (Iskowitz, 1998). Voice therapy may be the therapy of choice for patients when Botox or surgical procedures are contraindicated or refused.

2. Voice therapy appears to be useful in maximizing the patient's good voice, and extending the time the patient experiences good voice between Botox injections (B. Smith, 1998).

3. Voice rehabilitation techniques that might be useful for adductor dysphonia in either of the above therapy situations include the following methods for reducing laryngeal tension and associated symptoms of the dysphonia: (1) the chewing technique (see Chap. 5, **III.D.2.b**), (2) the chanting technique (see Chap. 5, **III.D.2.d**), (3) the yawn–sigh technique (see Chap. 5, **III.D.2**), (4) biofeedback, and (5) techniques that expose and desensitize the patient to a series of speaking situations arranged by order of communicative stress. Simple environmental manipulations such as using a voice amplifier when talking on the phone may be beneficial to improve intelligibility and to reduce the tendency to put effort into phonations.

Another technique, the frontal focus exercise approach (Stemple, 1997), may also be used to take effort off the larynx and improve quality. Stewart (1997) reports that slightly elevated pitch during speaking helps spasmodic dysphonia patients increase vocal loudness, and that inhalation phonation exercises practiced regularly may improve voice quality and ease of speaking. Patients with adductor spasmodic dysphonia may be able to start their voices more easily by using /h/ phonations (see Chap. 5, **III.D.2.**), whereas abductor patients may use humming to turn their voices on more easily before speaking (Stewart, 1997).

Stewart (1997) also reports that all spasmodic dysphonia patients should be taught to warm up the vocal cords in the morning as a way of getting their voice started for the day. Warm-up techniques might include relaxed humming for 2 or 3 minutes before speaking, or singing a relaxed scale of "raspberries" (tongue and lip trills) or "Bronx cheers" (lip trills) in a comfortable, midrange of voice for 2 or 3 minutes. These techniques may be used singly or in combination with each other. Therapy is aimed at not only improving the patient's voice quality, but at identifying and reducing any compensatory strategies that the patient may have developed in an attempt to improve speaking (B. Smith, 1998).

V. **Paradoxical vocal fold motion (PVFM) (Vocal cord dysfunction [VCD] or Paradoxical vocal cord motion [PVCM])** is a disorder that is frequently mistaken for asthma. It also may be misdiagnosed as exercise-induced bronchospasm (Landwehr, Wood, Blager, & Milgrom, 1996). The primary characteristic of the disorder is airway obstruction due to vocal fold closure, even when the patient is inhaling (Colton & Casper, 1996). The disorder appears to be chronic in nature, with patients reporting their symptoms generally over a period of several years, often in spite of aggressive treatment as uncontrolled asthmatics. It has been estimated that it may be present in as many as 40% of patients who are seen for asthma diagnosis (Landwehr et al., 1996).

A. **Etiology.** The cause of PVFM is not known; however, Bless and Swift (1995) have reported that PVFM may be a disorder with multiple causes, including the following: (1) psychological causes, (2) airway hyperreactivity, (3) possible neurogenic causes, (4) pharmacological, or (5) other unspecified medical problems. Prior to Bless and Swift's comments, the prevailing thought about PVFM was that it was of psychological origin. Several authors have reported PVFM to be a form of conversion disorder (Christopher, Wood, Eckert, Blager, Raney, & Souhrada, 1983; Martin, Blager, Gay, & Wood, 1987).

B. **Symptoms.** The primary symptoms of concern in PVFM are nonvocal. Patients may come to the physician with throat tightness, wheezing, chest tightness, shortness of breath, and cough (Landwehr et al., 1996). Patients with PVFM are often diagnosed with asthma and may have been aggressively but unsuccessfully treated for asthma or airway obstruction with corticosteroids and occasionally with tracheotomy. Reported vocal symptoms range from breathy and weak phonation to hoarse voice. Inspiratory stridor is common. There are varying symptoms or types of PVFM, with some patients reporting consistent airway obstruction and others reporting a more paradoxical pattern in which the vocal folds adduct during attempted inspiration and partially abduct during expiratory attempts. Some patients may report difficulty swallowing and others may use strategies such as a cough or throat clear to open the airway (Blager, 1996).

C. **Laryngoscopic findings.** During a spasm, the true—and sometimes the false—vocal folds may be seen to adduct during the entire respiratory cycle with both inhalatory and exhalatory stridor (Colton & Casper, 1996; Jacobson, Stemple, Glaze, & Gerdeman, 1998). In another variation of PVFM, the vocal folds appear to adduct during inspiration and slightly abduct during exhalation. There are periods of remission from PVFM in which the patient is symptom free.

D. **Medicosurgical management.** Therapeutic use of inhalation of a helium-oxygen (heliox) mixture of 70% helium and 30% oxygen successfully relieves acute symptoms of PVFM, and may effectively reduce symptoms even after the treatment is discontinued (Blager, 1996; Colton & Casper, 1996). Helium is a less dense gas than air and is easier for the patient to breathe. This relieves the acute dyspnea and usually the acute symptoms in general (Martin et al., 1987). The patient then may be directed through a protocol with heliox and relaxed breathing techniques (see **E.** in this chapter) in which the patient begins with periods as long as 5 minutes using the heliox mask, working toward increased time without the mask and decreased times with the mask (Blager, 1996). If they have been taking large amounts of corticosteroids prior to the diagnosis of PVFM, patients may also need close physician supervision to determine the appropriate course of management. Patients also often require psychotherapy in addition to medical and voice therapy management. Because many of these patients often have spent several years being treated unsuccessfully for asthma, being afraid that they were going to suffocate, or undergoing multiple hospitalizations and tests, they may continue to need supportive psychological or psychiatric care.

E. **Voice therapy management.** According to Blager (1996), the speech–language pathologist should direct the patient through a systematic program that offers the following: (1) slow direction, which acknowledges the very real nature of the respiratory distress the patient has been experiencing; (2) specific behavioral exercises, which are performed during "normal" periods to help the patient prepare for attacks; (3) use of diaphragmatic breathing to help focus respiration away from the larynx; (4) wide-open throat breathing to create another relaxed focus of breathing away from the larynx; (5) focus on exhalation in which the patient counts up to a number determined in therapy while exhaling, thus preventing shallow respirations; (6) self-awareness and ownership of the step-by-step breathing sequence; and (7) interruption of effortful breathing patterns in which the patient is made aware that following these steps will help his or her breathing happen in a natural and relaxed fashion (Blager, 1996; Martin et al., 1987).

Blager (1996) also teaches patients a **relaxed throat breath,** which they are to use at any sign of laryngeal stridor or of airway tightness. To perform the relaxed throat breaths, the patient should do the following: (1) sit with the hand on the abdomen; (2) be aware that the abdomen goes out with inhalation and in with exhalation; (3) inhale with a relaxed throat while the tongue lies relaxed in the floor of the mouth with the lips very gently closed; and (4) exhale easily on a sibilant /s/. This relaxed breath protocol is used in a progression with the patient doing at least five of these breaths several times per day and at any sign of tension, tightness, or stridor. The patient learns that these relaxed, systematic breathing techniques can help her or him through constriction, tightness, and situations that previously provoked attacks.

Chapter 7
Congenital Dysphonias

♦ ♦ ♦ ♦ ♦ ♦ ♦ ♦ ♦ ♦ ♦ ♦ ♦ ♦ ♦ ♦ ♦ ♦ ♦ ♦

Congenital anomalies of the larynx are characterized by three groups of symptoms: (1) respiratory difficulties due to airway obstruction, (2) hoarseness or a weak or aphonic cry, and (3) dysphagia. Congenital laryngeal anomalies are of interest to the speech–language pathologist because dysphonias may appear consequent to the anomaly. Although the primary management of infants with congenital laryngeal anomalies is medicosurgical, these children should be carefully monitored for the possible development of dysphonia. Congenital laryngeal anomalies are manifested primarily as either mass lesions or structural anomalies.

I. Congenital Mass Lesions of the Larynx

A. **Congenital subglottic hemangiomas** appear in children as large, purplish-red, sessile tumors that tend to be subglottic. These lesions are relatively rare, but when they do occur they are usually curable. The presence of congenital hemangiomas in the trachea may cause episodes of airway obstruction in infants. These tumors may also, upon occasion, extend submucosally into other regions of the larynx. Although hemangiomas are thought to be congenital, symptoms may not appear until 2 to 3 months following birth, often following the infant's first upper respiratory tract infection (Snow, 1979). The usual course of development is for the tumor to enlarge for 6 to 12 months and then to spontaneously regress (English, 1976b). Laryngeal hemangiomas may also be found in adults.

1. **Symptoms.** Some infants with subglottic hemangiomas are asymptomatic because the lesion does not affect vocal fold vibration and does not obstruct the airway. In other cases, infants are asymptomatic only when they are held upright, with symptoms appearing as they are placed in a reclining position.

   a. **Inspiratory stridor** is the most common presenting problem (Cotton & Richardson, 1981).

   b. **Dyspnea and cyanosis** may occur if airway obstruction becomes more severe (Cotton & Richardson, 1981).

   c. **Hoarseness** may appear occasionally, but since the vocal folds are usually not involved, the cry is usually normal.

   d. **Excessive coughing** is common.

   e. **Dysphagia** may occur.

   f. About half of patients with congenital subglottic hemangiomas have **hemangiomas of the face, head, and neck** as well (Andrews, 1995).

2. **Endoscopic findings.** Because congenital laryngeal hemangiomas are usually subglottic, they are not easily diagnosed with laryngoscopy (unless the patient is anesthetized); however, hemangiomas can be seen using endoscopy. Congenital subglottic hemangiomas are large, sessile masses that are generally found subglottally in the space between the true vocal folds and the lower edge of the cricoid cartilage. A frequent characteristic of this type of lesion is a reduction of the cross-sectional area of the trachea by the mass, which projects from the lateral wall and into the lumen (opening) of the trachea (Holder, Leape, & Ashcraft, 1973).

3. **Medicosurgical management.** Tracheostomy may be required if the hemangioma becomes large enough to obstruct the airway, as it does in 30% to 50% of cases (Birrell, 1978; Wood & Northern, 1979). Because congenital subglottic hemangiomas usually regress spontaneously by the age of 2 (Birrell, 1977; Kummer & Marsh, 1998), the use of surgery or radiation is generally delayed or avoided if at all possible. In the event that the tumor does not spontaneously regress, the following medicosurgical procedures for treatment or removal of the lesion may be used:

   a. **Laser surgery** (Kummer & Marsh, 1998).

   b. **Surgical excision** is reserved for those patients whose hemangiomas have either enlarged or failed to show signs of regression by the age of 2 (Cotton & Richardson, 1981).

   c. **Steroid therapy** (Snow, 1979).

   d. **Tracheostomy** (Andrews, 1995).

4. **Voice therapy management.** Since congenital laryngeal hemangiomas are usually subglottic, the vocal folds are not typically involved, and as a result the infant's cry is usually unaffected. Persistent hemangiomas in children, however, may enlarge sufficiently to affect vocal fold mass or movement, which can result in a hoarse voice quality. Voice therapy is usually not indicated as a primary treatment for patients with hemangiomas, but voice therapy procedures may be required to eliminate any persistent hoarseness following medicosurgical removal of the tumor.

B. **Congenital laryngeal papilloma (papillomatosis)** is the most common laryngeal growth found in children (although it is rare within the entire spectrum of laryngeal disease). Although laryngeal papilloma has been found in the neonate, most children will acquire papilloma between the ages of 2 and 4 (Kummer & Marsh, 1998). The tumor may on rare occasions appear in adults.

The juvenile form of laryngeal papilloma usually begins as a benign epithelial tumor that appears at the anterior portion of the vocal folds and then spreads across the laryngeal epithelium to include, either singly or in combination, the aryepiglottic folds, the ventricular folds, and various subglottic regions (see Figure 7.1). Although papillomas can be removed by medicosurgical methods, they frequently recur after being removed, sometimes in as short a time as 2 weeks (English, 1976b). Because the rate of growth of the tumor is often very rapid, papillomas must be monitored carefully to prevent airway obstruction.

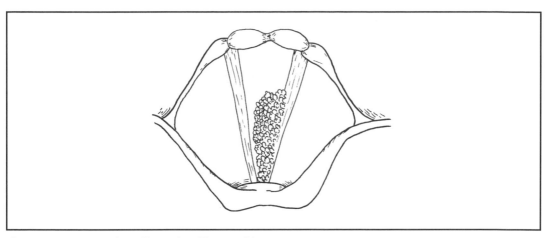

Figure 7.1. Laryngeal papilloma (papillomatosis).

1. **Etiology.** This wart-like growth of the larynx and tracheobronchial tree is thought to be caused by the human papillomavirus (HPV) (Ford, 1996). This virus tends to be specific to the laryngeal region and appears to be unrelated to other types of papilloma that are found in the nose, mouth, and paranasal sinuses (L. D. Holinger, 1976b). Support for the hypothesis that papillomas are caused by a virus can be found in the following data:

   a. There is a high incidence of papilloma in children born of women who have condylomata acuminatum (genital warts) (Boles, 1975b).

   b. Patients tend to respond to treatment that is directed at enhancing the body's immune response.

2. **Symptoms**

   a. Voice quality is **hoarse** if the papilloma involves the vocal folds.

   b. **Aphonia** may result if vocal fold involvement is severe.

   c. **Respiratory stridor** is common.

   d. **Dyspnea** may occur.

3. **Laryngoscopic findings.** Laryngeal papillomas arise from the anterior part of the larynx and may spread to involve supraglottic or subglottic regions. The lesions rarely arise from the posterior part of the larynx. In appearance, the lesions are sessile or pedunculated and exhibit numerous wart-like papillae. They may resemble a raspberry or a small grape-like cluster and are pale pink or red in color.

4. **Medicosurgical management.** The primary treatment of laryngeal papilloma is medicosurgical removal of the lesions. Since the lesions tend to frequently recur, repeated surgery is common in order to maintain an adequate airway. Because of the repeated surgery, the vocal folds are frequently left with a roughened free margin. Consequently, a surgeon's consideration of the method of tumor removal often includes an evaluation of which method

will result in the least amount of tissue damage. The following are other medicosurgical methods that have been used with varying results:

a. **CO₂ Laser surgery** is the most common approach for the surgeon in managing laryngeal papilloma (Shapsay, Rebeiz, Bohigian, & Hybels, 1990). However, these techniques should be used with caution. The development of anterior commissure webs and posterior interarytenoid scarring, which limit vocal fold adduction, have resulted from laser surgery, especially in small larynges (McCabe & Clark, 1983).

b. **Cryosurgery** has also been used with success.

c. **Photodynamic therapy (PDT)** has been studied in the treatment of laryngeal papilloma. A photosensitive agent is administered intravenously 2 to 3 days before photoactivation surgery using an argon-pumped or gold-vapor laser (Ford, 1996).

d. **Interferon injection** for the treatment of papillomatosis has had limited success, with the most disappointing finding being the regrowth of significantly reduced papillomas after interferon treatment has been discontinued (Haglund, Lundquist, Cantell, & Strander, 1981).

5. **Voice therapy management.** Because the primary treatment of laryngeal papilloma is medicosurgical, voice therapy is indicated only if hoarseness persists following surgery, which occurs in approximately 20% of cases (Szpunar, 1977). Persistent hoarseness may result from surgery, which leaves vocal folds with a roughened free margin.

II. Congenital Structural Anomalies of the Larynx

A. **Laryngomalacia** (congenital chondromalacia and inspiratory stridor) is the most common congenital laryngeal anomaly in which symptoms appear during infancy and is the cause of 75% of cases of congenital stridor (Andrews, 1995; Birrell, 1978; Cotton & Richardson, 1981; Wood & Northern, 1979). It is characterized by excessive flaccidity of the supraglottic larynx, which is accompanied by inspiratory stridor. The prognosis for spontaneous recovery in 12 to 18 months is good (Cotton & Richardson, 1981; L. D. Holinger, 1976a; Wood & Northern, 1979).

1. **Etiology. Laryngomalacia** (or chondromalacia of the larynx) may be caused by insufficient or delayed calcium deposition in infants, which results in excessive flaccidity of the cartilaginous superstructure of the larynx. The lack of calcium provides inadequate support for the cartilaginous epiglottis (which is omega-shaped in these patients), which consequently collapses over the glottis during inspiration (Ward, 1973) (see Figure 7.2). A reduction of calcium may also be present in the tracheal cartilages. Similar airway symptoms have been seen in older children with central nervous system problems (Andrews, 1995).

2. **Symptoms.** The symptoms of laryngomalacia are usually present at birth, but in 30% of cases the symptoms go unnoticed until several weeks after the infant has left the hospital (Birrell, 1978). The following are the symptoms associated with this congenital laryngeal anomaly:

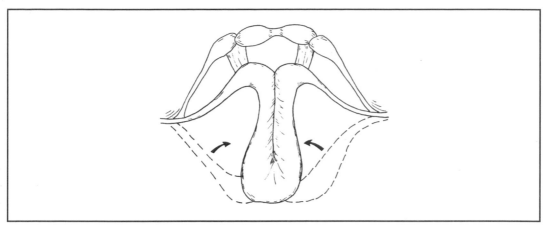

Figure 7.2. Laryngomalacia (congenital laryngeal stridor). The dashed lines indicate the normal position of the epiglottis before it collapses over the glottis during inspiration.

    a. The primary symptom is a **noisy inspiratory stridor** that sounds like "crowing." Stridor may be accompanied by suprasternal and intercostal retraction during inspiration (Cotton & Richardson, 1981; Ward, 1973).

    b. Because supine or feeding positions frequently allow the flaccid epiglottis to block the airway, infants in these positions may exhibit **dyspnea** or **cyanosis.**

    c. The **cry is normal.**

  3. Laryngoscopic findings. Because inspiratory stridor so commonly accompanies laryngomalacia, thereby making the diagnosis clear, direct laryngoscopy is deferred or omitted in most cases (Boles, 1975b). If laryngoscopy is performed, however, examination will reveal an omega-shaped epiglottis that is collapsed over the glottis during inspiration. The aryepiglottic folds are in close approximation to each other and are usually sucked into the glottis during inspiration and blown away from the glottis on expiration. If the laryngoscope is passed under the epiglottis, the stridor usually decreases or ceases (Birrell, 1978).

  4. Medicosurgical management. Infants with severe cases of laryngomalacia frequently require observation in the hospital, although they can usually be cared for at home. Dyspnea can be eliminated by placing the child in the prone position (Boles, 1975b). Having the infant pause frequently during feeding to take a breath is also helpful. Intubation or tracheostomy is rarely required.

  5. Voice therapy management. Because the vocal folds are unaffected by laryngomalacia, the voice is asymptomatic and requires no voice therapy management. In severe cases in which a tracheostomy is required and complete remission of symptoms extends beyond 12 to 18 months, the child's development of expressive language skills should be carefully monitored. Alternative forms of communication (e.g., gestural and augmentative systems) may be temporarily required until the symptoms have completely regressed and the tracheostomy has been closed, thus allowing the production of voice.

B. **Cri-du-chat syndrome** (Cat's cry syndrome, Lejeune syndrome) is so named because of the presence of a characteristic weak, wailing cry like that of a kitten. The larynx has the identical appearance of laryngomalacia (see **II.A** earlier in this chapter).

1. **Etiology.** Cri-du-chat syndrome is caused by the partial deletion of chromosome number 5 (Dirckx, 1997).

2. **Symptoms.** In addition to the distinctive, high-pitched, kitten-like cry found in infants and the weak, high-pitched voice accompanied by vocal fold aperiodicity in older children, cri-du-chat syndrome is also characterized by the following distinctive combination of features (Birrell, 1978; Dirckx, 1997):

   a. **Mental and physical retardation**

   b. **Beak-like profile** with a micrognathic (undersized) jaw

   c. **Microcephaly** (small-sized head)

   d. **Hypotonia**

   e. **Hypertelorism** (widely spaced eyes)

   f. **Antimongoloid palpebral fissures** (downward slanting eyes)

   g. **Epicanthal folds** (a vertical fold of skin on either side of the nose)

   h. **Strabismus** (asymmetrical eye movement)

   i. Medial **oral clefts**

   j. Various **visceral anomalies**

   k. Severe to moderate **articulation delay**

   l. **Language delay,** although most patients develop functional communication skills.

3. **Laryngoscopic findings.** Examination reveals a larynx that looks identical to the larynx in cases of laryngomalacia. The epiglottis is omega-shaped and collapsed over the glottis. The aryepiglottic folds are in close approximation to each other and are sucked into the glottis during inspiration and blown away during expiration.

4. **Medicosurgical management** for patients with cri-du-chat syndrome focuses mainly on their failure to thrive at an early age. No specific medicosurgical techniques are required for management of the patient's voice.

5. **Voice therapy management.** Spectrographic analysis reveals that the cry and speaking voice of patients with cri-du-chat syndrome is typically weak, high pitched, and accompanied by vocal fold aperiodicity. Voice therapy may be difficult with these patients because they present with so many problems (Andrews, 1995). Most patients with cri-du-chat syndrome make greater gains in overall communicative ability if therapy focuses on a program of

simultaneous manual and oral expression, with major emphasis on improving intelligibility through heightened articulation skills.

C. **Congenital laryngeal webs and laryngeal atresia** represent varying degrees of laryngeal occlusion that are caused by webs of connective tissue in subglottic, glottic, and supraglottic regions (Cotton & Richardson, 1981) (see Figure 7.3). If the webbed tissue completely occludes the larynx at birth (congenital laryngeal atresia), immediate action must be taken to provide an airway or the infant will die (Cotton & Richardson, 1981; English, 1976b). Congenital webs of the larynx represent lesser degrees of laryngeal atresia and have negative effects on both respiration and phonation.

1. **Etiology.** Laryngeal atresia and webs result from a failure of the vocal fold primordia (embryologic tissue) to partially or completely separate during the first trimester of embryologic development.

2. **Symptoms** associated with laryngeal webs vary depending upon the location and the extent of the opening in the web. Seventy-five percent of all laryngeal webs are interglottic (Birrell, 1978; Cotton & Richardson, 1981; English, 1976b) Laryngeal webs that are at the level of the glottis affect vocal fold vibration; consequently, they usually affect phonation. Laryngeal webs at any level in the larynx (subglottic, glottic, or supraglottic) may have an effect on respiration, depending upon the extent of the opening in the web. The following phonatory and respiratory symptoms are typically associated with laryngeal webs:

   a. **Phonatory symptoms**

      (1) The voice may be asymptomatic if the web is not located at the level of the glottis.

      (2) The effect that an interglottic laryngeal web has on **vocal pitch** varies with the extent of the web. Small webs located at the anterior commissure have little, if any, effect on vocal pitch. Larger webs, which involve greater degrees of the vocal folds, can cause significant elevation of pitch. Elevation of pitch occurs because the effective

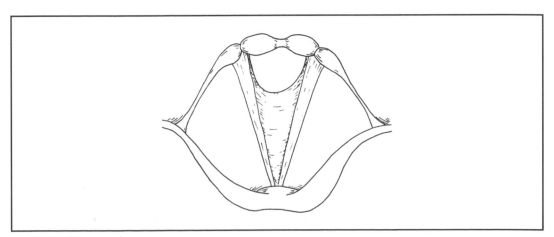

Figure 7.3. Laryngeal web (congenital).

vibrating portion of the vocal folds is shortened due to the presence of the web.

Some infants present a high-pitched cry at birth, which generally indicates laryngeal webbing. Some small laryngeal webs at the anterior commissure go unnoticed for years, only to be discovered when the patient's voice fails to lower following puberty (Ballenger, 1977).

(3) If the web causes asynchronous vocal fold vibration, the voice may be hoarse.

(4) Aphonia will result if the web is extensive. Aphonia is always accompanied by severe stridor and dyspnea.

b. **Respiratory symptoms** (Ward, 1973)

(1) Stridor

(2) Cyanosis

(3) Restlessness or other **signs of respiratory distress** in the infant

3. **Laryngoscopic findings.** Inspection of the larynx reveals a web of connective tissue that partially occludes the larynx. Laryngeal webs at the level of the glottis are located at the anterior commissure and grow posteriorly. The thickness of the laryngeal web varies, with some webs being extremely thick and others appearing thin and transparent (Cotton & Richardson, 1981).

4. **Medicosurgical management.** Removal of a web is performed surgically using either a laser or scalpel (Kummer & Marsh, 1998). After the laryngeal web has been removed, a keel is usually placed between the vocal folds and sutured in place to prevent the vocal folds from approximating. The keel is kept in place for a period of several weeks to prevent the recurrence of webbing. The patient must remain on vocal rest while the keel is in place (Boone & McFarlane, 1994), because the presence of the keel prevents vocal fold vibration.

5. **Voice therapy management.** Because the primary treatment of congenital laryngeal webs is medicosurgical, voice therapy is contraindicated. However, if medicosurgical management leaves the patient with a roughened free margin on the vocal folds, voice therapy for the elimination of any postsurgical dysphonia should then be initiated.

D. **Congenital subglottic stenosis** refers to a narrowing of the airway between the glottis and the first tracheal ring. Subglottic stenosis is the third most common congenital disorder of the larynx, although it accounts for only 6% of all congenital laryngeal lesions (L. D. Holinger, 1976a; P. H. Holinger & W. T. Brown, 1967). It occurs almost twice as often in females as males (Holder et al., 1973). Only 1 mm of swelling can reduce the airway opening by 35% (Andrews, 1995). Acquired stenosis frequently is a result of prolonged intubation (Andrews, 1995).

1. **Etiology.** Subglottic stenosis can result from the following:

a. Thickening of subglottic tissue and, occasionally, the vocal folds.

    b. Cartilaginous narrowing of the cricoid cartilage in an anterior to posterior direction, leaving a small posterior opening.

2. **Symptoms** of congenital subglottic stenosis may be intermittent and are as follows:

    a. Inhalatory and exhalatory stridor, with or without an accompanying cyanosis, is present in severe cases (Cotton & Richardson, 1981).

    b. Less severe cases of stenosis may masquerade as recurrent episodes of croup (Holder et al., 1973).

    c. Phonation is generally normal, although it may be reduced in intensity if the stenosis severely limits airflow.

3. **Laryngoscopic findings.** The following may be observed in the subglottic region of the larynx (L. D. Holinger, 1976a):

    a. Soft tissue stenosis appearing as concentric narrowing or bilateral subglottic swelling.

    b. Cartilaginous stenosis appearing anteriorly with a small posterior opening.

4. **Medicosurgical management.** Mild stenoses generally resolve with growth of the larynx (Boles, 1975; L. D. Holinger, 1976a). Tracheostomy may be required in as many as 80% of cases (Fearon & Ellis, 1971), although some authors (P. H. Holinger, Kutnick, Schild, & L. D. Holinger, 1976) report a less frequent need to perform a tracheostomy on these patients. Surgical reduction of the stenosis may be performed if laryngeal growth is insufficient for resolving the stenosis.

5. **Voice therapy management.** The voice is usually unaffected by congenital subglottic stenosis because the vocal folds are not involved.

E. **Laryngocele (congenital). A laryngocele** is an air-filled or fluid-filled dilation or herniation of the anterior appendix of the laryngeal ventricle, the space between the false and true vocal folds (see Figure 7.4) (Ogura & Biller, 1973). The laryngocele sac has a small opening directly into the interior of the larynx, which allows the laryngocele to become inflated. Approximately 80% of laryngoceles remain asymptomatic and undiagnosed until adulthood, when they may become symptomatic (Andrews, 1995).

There are three types of laryngoceles, which are described by their extent of dilation (Ballenger, 1977; Cotton & Richardson, 1981; Ogura & Biller, 1973): (1) **internal** type, in which the inflated sac remains entirely within the thyroid cartilage; (2) **external** type, in which the sac protrudes above the thyroid cartilage, through the thyrohyoid membrane, and presents itself externally as a lateral bulge on the patient's neck; and (3) a **combination** type, which has features of both the internal and external types.

1. **Etiology.** Laryngoceles result from a congenitally enlarged laryngeal ventricle that is further enlarged by activities that increase intralaryngeal air pressure, including the following (Ballenger, 1977; L. D. Holinger, 1976a; Snow, 1979):

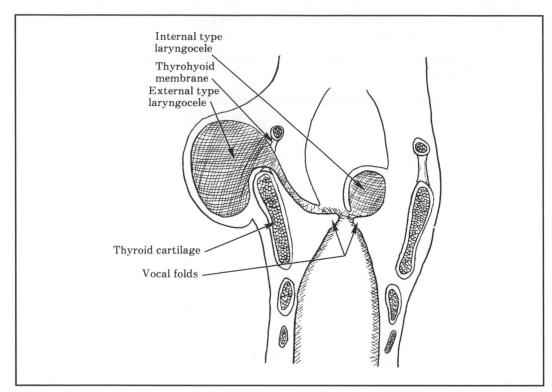

Figure 7.4. Laryngocele (internal and external types). This frontal section through the larynx illustrates the positions of the two types of laryngoceles. Note that the internal type remains entirely within the thyroid cartilage and that the external type protrudes above the thyroid cartilage and through the thyrohyoid membrane.

    a. Straining

    b. Coughing

    c. Vocal abuse

    d. Playing wind instruments

    e. Glassblowing

2. **Symptoms.** Laryngoceles are usually asymptomatic in infancy. Symptoms normally appear in adulthood, almost exclusively in males, usually in their fifties (Ballenger, 1977). Common symptoms of laryngoceles include the following:

    a. Hoarse voice or cry if the internal type of laryngocele is present and is affecting vibration of the true vocal folds.

    b. Inspiratory stridor.

    c. An **external bulge in the neck** may be present with the external and combination types of laryngocele. The mass tends to fluctuate in size as intralaryngeal pressure increases; direct pressure on the neck frequently decreases the size of the mass. As the mass is pressed on, a small rush of air or a gurgling sound may be heard in the hypopharynx as the sac deflates (Ogura & Biller, 1973).

    d. **Dysphagia** may occur if the laryngocele is sufficiently large (Birrell, 1978; Ogura & Biller, 1973).

3. **Laryngoscopic findings.** The larynx may appear normal if there is only an external component to the laryngocele (Ogura & Biller, 1973). However, external components are frequently accompanied by an internal component that appears as marked swelling of the false folds and the aryepiglottic folds.

4. **Medicosurgical management.** Laryngoceles are managed medically or surgically if intervention is indicated (Andrews, 1995). The patient may undergo repeated aspiration of the laryngocele, or incision and drainage may be necessary. Occasionally, tracheostomy is necessary if there is significant respiratory obstruction.

5. **Voice therapy management.** Voice therapy is not indicated for the hoarseness that is a symptom of laryngoceles. Instead, vocal hoarseness may be temporarily reduced by using the hand to apply direct pressure to the bulge on the neck in order to reduce a combination or external type laryngocele. However, if the internal component cannot be sufficiently reduced and continues to affect the true vocal folds, hoarseness will remain until the internal component is medicosurgically reduced.

F. **Congenital laryngeal cysts** are small fluid-filled sacs that are found in the larynx, primarily in the ventricle. Congenital laryngeal cysts are related to congenital laryngoceles (see **II.E** in this chapter) and have a similar origin. The primary difference between a cyst and a laryngocele is that a cyst does not have an opening directly into the interior of the larynx (Donegan, Strife, & Seid, 1980; L. D. Holinger, 1976a).

1. **Etiology.** A laryngeal cyst results from a congenital saccule that progressively enlarges due to an accumulation of secretions from glands in the submucosa of the saccule.

2. **Symptoms.** Laryngeal cysts may be asymptomatic unless they enlarge sufficiently to displace the true and false vocal folds and obstruct the supraglottic region of the larynx. Enlarged laryngeal cysts will result in the following:

    a. **Hoarseness** if the true vocal folds are displaced.

    b. **Inspiratory stridor** if sufficient airway obstruction occurs.

3. **Laryngoscopic findings.** Laryngeal cysts are located primarily in the ventricle and appear as marked swellings of the false vocal folds, aryepiglottic folds, or arytenoids.

4. **Medicosurgical management.** Laryngologists find that aspiration of laryngeal cysts is useful only for the purpose of diagnosis. Surgical removal of the cyst wall is generally required for cure (Cotton & Richardson, 1981; L. D. Holinger, 1976a).

5. **Voice therapy management.** Until medicosurgical therapy is completed, voice therapy for hoarseness is not indicated. Although removal of the cyst generally results in improved voice quality, voice therapy for residual dysphonia may be required.

G. **Laryngeal cleft.** A laryngeal cleft is a vertical opening between the larynx (cricoid cartilage) and the esophagus. The cleft may be limited to the region of the larynx or it may form a complete laryngotracheoesophageal cleft.

1. **Etiology.** A laryngeal cleft results from failure of dorsal fusion of the cricoid lamina (signet portion) (L. D. Holinger, 1976a; Stemple et al., 1995).

2. **Symptoms.** A laryngeal cleft is frequently associated with other congenital anomalies. Symptoms appear shortly after birth, when the infant chokes and perhaps aspirates during the first feeding. Other symptoms include the following (Aronson, 1990; Cotton & Richardson, 1981; L. D. Holinger, 1976a):

   a. Respiration obstruction

   b. Weak cry or aphonia

   c. Repeated pneumonia

3. **Laryngoscopic findings.** A laryngeal cleft appears as an obvious vertical cleft located between the arytenoids and extending into the lamina of the cricoid cartilage.

4. **Medicosurgical management.** A laryngeal cleft is usually closed surgically as soon as possible.

5. **Voice therapy management.** The extent of voice therapy depends upon the structural adequacy of the laryngeal mechanism for phonation following surgical repair.

Chapter 8
Neurogenic Dysphonias

◆　◆　◆　◆　◆　◆　◆　◆　◆　◆　◆　◆　◆　◆　◆　◆　◆　◆

T he production of voice requires the precise coordination of the many muscles that constitute the respiratory, resonatory, and phonatory systems of the voice-producing mechanism. Impairments in the innervation of these muscles, impairments in the function of the muscle itself, and impairments of neurologic motor planning (all considered to be neurogenic) often result in a defect in voice production. All aspects of voice pitch, loudness, and quality can be affected to varying degrees if the neurologic or muscular integrity of the vocal tract is violated.

Disturbances of the motor supply of the muscles of the speech mechanism result in a group of speech disorders called **dysarthrias.** Dysarthrias are characterized by disturbances of phonation, as well as by disturbances of articulation, resonance, and respiration. Each of the dysarthrias and its associated dysphonia results from various abnormal neuromuscular conditions. These conditions include abnormalities of muscle strength or muscle tone and excessive, involuntary muscle movements. Table 8.1 provides a summary of the various types of dysarthrias.

Motor disturbances can result from lesions of the motor pathways or of the muscles themselves. When a motor disturbance occurs, muscle strength is reduced, resulting in a paresis (weakness) or paralysis (immobility) of the affected muscles (Brookshire, 1997).

Abnormalities of muscle tone frequently accompany changes in muscle strength due to motor disturbances. Normal muscle tone is the result of continuous, mild muscular contraction, which requires an intact motor supply. When at rest, a normal muscle does not become flabby, but retains a certain resilience. Abnormal muscle tone, however, appears clinically as one of three different conditions of tone: **flaccidity, spasticity,** or **rigidity.** The presence of any one of these abnormal conditions of muscle tone in the speech mechanism results in dysarthria.

Some dysarthrias are characterized by **excessive movement** of the speech muscles resulting from damage to the extrapyramidal system (especially the basal ganglia). These increased movements may be overlaid on purposeful movements or they may preclude normal voluntary movement until they have diminished or ceased. These excessive movements result from a mechanism known as **release phenomenon.** Because the basal ganglia and related structures normally inhibit spontaneous rhythmic movements initiated by the cortex, disease to those structures results in the release of excessive movements (Chusid, 1976). These movements can appear as (1) choreiform, athetoid, or dystonic movements; (2) tremors; (3) tics; or (4) myoclonus. Each of these abnormal movements results in a distinctive dysarthria.

Andrews (1995) cautions that human vocalization should be considered in context as one complex, integrated neurological system. However, classification schemes serve as effective and convenient aids in understanding how neurological disruptions affect

Table 8.1. Motor Speech Disorders

Dysarthria Type	Neuropathology Location	Associated Neurological Condition	Speech Characteristics
Flaccid	Lower Motor Neuron	Bell's palsy, myasthenia gravis, muscular dystrophy, bulbar palsy, poliomyelitis	Phonatory and resonatory weakness; imprecise consonants; marked hypernasality; frequent nasal air emission; continuous breathiness; audible inspirations
Spastic	Upper Motor Neuron	Multiple CVAs, pseudo-bulbar palsy, spastic cerebral palsy	Strained–strangled voice quality; harsh voice; very imprecise articulation; low pitch; some hypernasality; reduced stress
Ataxic	Cerebellum	Cerebellar ataxia, cerebellar CVA, ataxic cerebral palsy, Friedrich's ataxia, toxic effects	Excess and equal stress; phoneme and interval prolongation; dysrhythmia of speech and syllable repetition; some loudness and variations; harsh voice quality
Hypokinetic	Extrapyramidal System	Parkinson's disease	Monopitch; monoloudness; reduced overall loudness; short rushes of speech; some inappropriate silences; imprecise consonants
Hyperkinetic	Extrapyramidal System	1) *Quick:* Huntington's disease, Tourette's syndrome	1) Imprecise articulation; sudden variations in loudness; sudden tic-like barks, growls, corprolalia
		2) *Slow:* Athetosis, drug-induced dyskinesia dystonia	2) Unsteady loudness; phoneme and interval prolongation; articulatory inaccuracy; highly variable characteristics; prosodic excess
		3) *Tremor:* Organic voice tremor	3) Involuntary, rhythmic alteration in pitch and loudness; some complete voice stoppages
Mixed	Multiple Motor Systems	1) Amyotrophic lateral sclerosis (Lou Gehrig's disease)	1) Grossly defective articulation; extremely slow, labored; marked hypernasality; severe harshness; nearly disruption of prosody
		2) Multiple sclerosis	2) Impaired control of loudness; harshness; possible defective articulation; speech may be normal, ataxic, or spastic/ataxic
		3) Wilson's disease	3) Reduced stress; monopitch; monoloudness; similar to Parkinsonian dysarthria except no short rushes of speech; tremor; rigidity

phonation (Colton & Casper, 1996). The classification scheme for the dysarthrias (and the dysphonia associated with each dysarthria) that we use in this chapter is adapted from the classic work of Darley, Aronson, and Brown (1975), as shown in the summary in Table 8.1. In this scheme, dysphonias are categorized according to the site of the lesion that causes the dysarthria with which it is associated. Major sections in this chapter include dysphonias associated with lower and upper motor neuron disorders, cerebellar disorders, extrapyramidal system disorders, disorders of multiple motor systems, and disorders resulting from a neurologic loss of volitional control. Each section comprises a general description of a specific dysarthria and its associated dysphonia, its etiologies, its symptoms (including motor speech symptoms described in Dworkin's [1978] landmark article), the laryngoscopic findings, and medicosurgical and voice therapy management techniques.

I. **Dysphonias Associated with Disorders of the Lower Motor Neuron, Myoneural Junction, and Muscle. Flaccidity** (muscular hypotonia) refers to a reduction in muscle tone resulting from a loss of motor supply to the muscle due to peripheral neuromuscular disorders, such as damage to lower motor neurons, myoneural junction pathologies, or myopathies. As a flaccid limb is moved passively, no resistance to the movement is felt because of reduced muscle tone. Flaccid muscles often appear flabby. Fasciculations (small, visible twitchings beneath the skin due to a loss of motor nerve supply) and severe muscle atrophy are common coexisting symptoms.

Approximately 90% of all vocal fold paralyses are due to peripheral causes and result in flaccid dysphonia (Portlock & Goffinet, 1980). Flaccid dysphonias are characterized neurologically by laryngeal weakness or paralysis, a reduction in the strength of reflexes in affected muscles, and muscular hypotonia. Laryngeal paralysis is frequently a component of a more generalized flaccid dysarthria that can affect all of the cranial nerves that innervate the speech musculature. Isolated lesions of the cranial nerve X (vagus nerve) can also cause laryngeal weakness or paralysis, but this dysphonia is unaccompanied by flaccid dysarthria of the speech muscles innervated by other cranial nerves.

A. **Flaccid dysphonias due to isolated lesions of the vagus nerve.** Perhaps the easiest way for the student of voice to understand the effects of lesions located at various sites along the vagus nerve is to imagine this cranial nerve and its nerve branches as a system of water pipes that serve the palatopharyngeal and laryngeal musculature. Within this system, the right and left vagus nerves serve as the principal water mains from which the various branches separate (see Figure 8.1). These two water mains arise from their separate reservoirs (nuclei), which are located in the medulla. The right and left mains course downward through the neck, past the larynx, and into the upper chest, where they abruptly reverse their course and return to terminate at the larynx.

Two pipes branch off from each of the water mains as the mains descend through the neck. The first pair of branches—one from the left main and one from the right—supplies the palatopharyngeal area and is called the pharyngeal branch. Each of the next pair of branches, called the superior laryngeal branch, subdivides into two smaller branches, one of which serves as a sensory route for the interior of the larynx (the internal branch), and the other of which

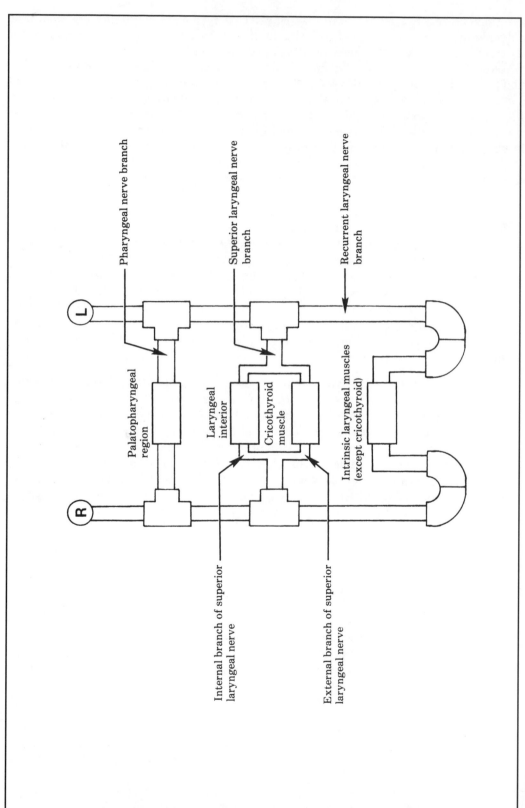

Figure 8.1. Vagus nerve innervation of the laryngeal and palatopharyngeal areas conceptualized as a system of water pipes.

serves as a motor supply to the cricothyroid muscle on its respective side (the external branch).

Blockages or ruptures (lesions) of the two mains or any of the branches can reduce or completely stop the flow to parts of the system beyond that point. For example, a blockage in the right water main above the point where any of the branches separate would prevent any flow beyond that point, thus affecting all branches on that side (indicated by the string of triangles in Figure 8.2A). On the other hand, a blockage of the right pharyngeal branch itself would prevent the flow from reaching the right palatopharyngeal area, but the remainder of the system would operate normally (see Figure 8.3A). As can easily be seen, the flow in both sides of the same system can be interrupted only if there are also blockages or ruptures on both sides (see Figures 8.2B and 8.3B).

The flow of neural impulses along the vagus nerve and its branches is very similar to the water pipe system that has been described. Lesions anywhere along the vagus nerve or any of its branches produce predictable muscular deficits, depending upon the specific site of the lesion. When neural flow is blocked in any one segment of the system, the muscles that are supplied by that segment of the system are also adversely affected (Figures 8.2 through 8.7 demonstrate the losses of neuromuscular function that result from lesions located at differing sites along the pathway of the vagus nerve).

1. **Vagus nerve lesions above the level of the pharyngeal nerve branch (adductor paralysis with associated palatopharyngeal paralysis).** Because a lesion at this level lies above the point where the pharyngeal, superior laryngeal, and recurrent laryngeal branches separate from the vagus nerve (see Figure 8.3), all three nerve branches are affected. Consequently, the functioning of all speech muscles supplied by the vagus (soft palate muscles, pharyngeal muscles, and all intrinsic laryngeal muscles) is also affected. The specific effects of this type of lesion are adductor paralysis of the larynx (an inability to adduct the vocal folds) with an associated palatopharyngeal paralysis (an inability to close the velopharyngeal port).

   a. **Etiology.** Unilateral and bilateral adductor paralysis of the larynx with an associated palatopharyngeal paralysis occurs as a result of vagus nerve lesions above the level of the pharyngeal nerve branch. Most often, bilateral adductor paralysis results from a brainstem (medulla) lesion that involves both of the intramedullary vagus nerve nuclei, rather than from bilateral damage to the extramedullary and extracranial portions of the nerve. Unilateral adductor paralysis, however, can result from unilateral damage to the intramedullary, extramedullary, or extracranial segment of the vagus nerve. Vagus nerve lesions can be caused by the following (Aronson, 1980; Darley et al., 1975; DeWeese & Saunders, 1977; Hageman, 1997):

      (1) **Traumatic injury** to the vagus nerve from forceful assault upon the neck, usually resulting from an automobile or motorcycle accident

      (2) **Vascular disorders** such as thrombosis (the formation of a blood clot), hemorrhage (bleeding), and arteriovenous malformation

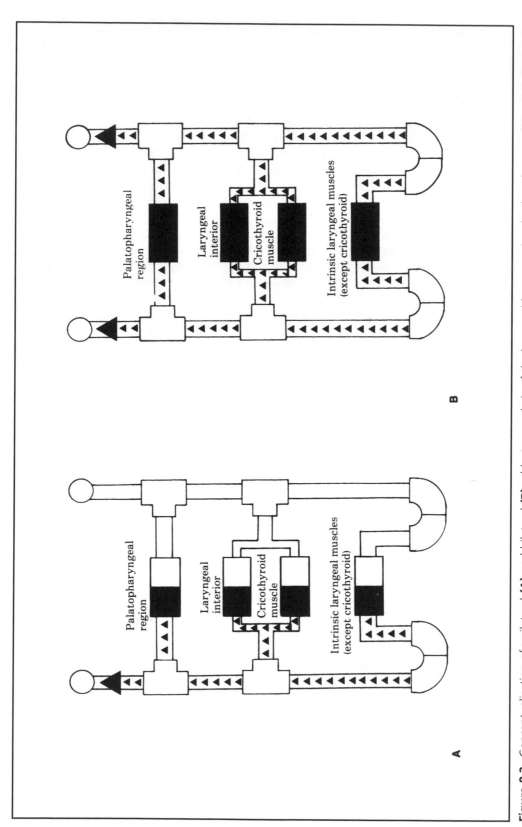

Figure 8.2. Conceptualization of unilateral **(A)** and bilateral **(B)** adductor paralysis of the larynx with an associated palatopharyngeal paralysis (**large triangles** indicate sites of blockage, **small triangles** indicate route where flow is interrupted, and **blackened areas** indicate the extent of paralysis).

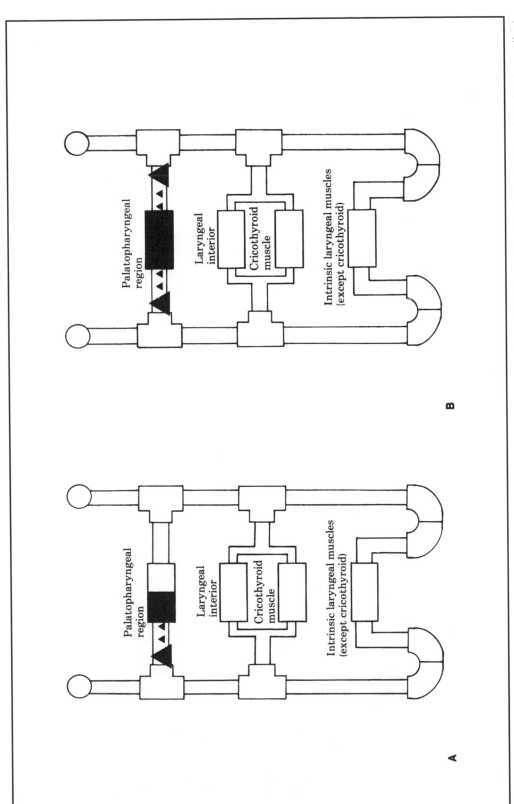

Figure 8.3. Conceptualization of unilateral **(A)** and bilateral **(B)** isolated palatopharyngeal paralysis (**large triangles** indicate sites of blockage, **small triangles** indicate route where flow is interrupted, and **blackened areas** indicate the extent of paralysis).

(3) **Malignant neoplasms** that have originated near or metastisized (spread) to the vagus

(4) **Metabolic disease,** particularly myasthenia gravis

(5) **Inflammatory disorders** such as:

(a) Poliomyelitis

(b) Guillain-Barre syndrome (an inflammation of the nerves, and occasionally the spinal cord, that is of unknown etiology but which most often occurs following an upper respiratory or gastrointestinal tract infection)

(6) **Degenerative neurologic disease** such as amyotrophic lateral sclerosis (ALS)

(7) **Poisons** (alcohol, metallic, such as arsenic, lead)

(8) **Idiopathic disorders** (disorders of unknown cause or spontaneous origin). It has been estimated that 30% to 35% of vocal fold paralysis is idiopathic (Willatt & Stell, 1991).

(9) **Multiple sclerosis**

(10) **Diphtheria**

(11) **Tetany**

b. **Symptoms.** Because a vagus nerve lesion that occurs above the level where the various nerve branches separate from the vagus affects all of the branches, the muscles that are innervated by these branches are, consequently, also adversely affected. As a result, a vagus nerve lesion above the point of bifurcation of the pharyngeal nerve branch results in (1) an inability to elevate the soft palate and constrict the muscles of the pharynx because of pharyngeal branch involvement; (2) an inability to stretch the thyroarytenoid muscle (via the action of the cricothyroid muscle) because of superior laryngeal nerve branch involvement; and (3) an inability to tense the intrinsic laryngeal muscles for the purpose of adducting the vocal folds because of recurrent laryngeal nerve involvement (hence, the paralysis is called the adductor type). Because of this particular pattern of neuromuscular involvement, the following symptoms, which vary in intensity or kind depending upon whether the lesion is unilateral or bilateral, may be observed:

(1) **Motor speech symptoms**

(a) **Dysphonia due to a unilateral lesion of the vagus nerve above the level of the pharyngeal branch** is characterized by the following:

(i) **Symptoms associated with impaired velopharyngeal function:** (1) a mild to moderate **hypernasal** voice quality results because the soft palate can elevate on only one side; (2) **nasal emission** may also be heard due to incomplete velopharyngeal closure; (3) the **palatopharyngeal gag reflex** is reduced or absent because vagus nerve lesions above the level where the superior laryngeal nerve separates can cause sensory deficits.

(ii) **Symptoms associated with impaired laryngeal function:** (1) a **breathy voice quality or whispered voice** occurs because unilateral paralysis of the intrinsic laryngeal muscles prevents the fold on the affected side from adducting to the midline; (2) **hoarseness** develops because of the asynchronous vibratory patterns of the intact and paralyzed vocal folds; (3) **reduced vocal loudness** results because of inefficient glottal closure due to the unilateral vocal fold paralysis; (4) **low vocal pitch** with possible pitch breaks.

(b) **Dysphonia due to a bilateral lesion of the vagus nerve above the level of the pharyngeal nerve branch** is characterized by the following:

(i) **Symptoms associated with impaired velopharyngeal function:** (1) moderate to severe **hypernasality** is common because both sides of the soft palate are unable to elevate sufficiently for velopharyngeal closure; (2) **nasal emission** may also result from incomplete velopharyngeal closure; (3) the **palatopharyngeal gag reflex** is reduced or absent because vagus nerve lesions above the level where the superior laryngeal nerve separates can cause sensory deficits.

(ii) **Symptoms associated with impaired laryngeal function:** (1) **marked breathiness** or **whispered voice** results because both vocal folds are unable to approximate the midline, thus causing the outgoing airstream to flow through the larynx with little or no glottal resistance; (2) a **"mushy" cough** or **weak glottal attack** is present because of the reduced or absent ability of the vocal folds to approximate each other; (3) **markedly reduced loudness**; (4) **aphonia** will result if the bilateral paralysis is total.

(2) **Associated symptoms** may be present to varying degrees depending on the severity of neuromuscular weakness and whether the involvement is unilateral or bilateral.

(a) Many patients experience **difficulty swallowing** due to involvement of the palatal and pharyngeal muscles.

(b) **Nasal regurgitation** of foods or liquids may occur because of inadequate velopharyngeal closure.

(c) **Aspiration of secretions** may also occur because of palatopharyngeal and laryngeal involvement. A tracheostomy may be necessary if aspiration becomes a problem for the patient.

c. **Laryngoscopic findings**

(1) **Unilateral lesions.** During phonation, the vocal fold on the affected side is fixated at the abducted, intermediate position while the fold

on the unaffected side approximates the midline (see Figure 8.4). Because the soft palate is only unilaterally innervated, it is pulled toward the unaffected side during phonation.

(2) **Bilateral lesions.** Both vocal folds are fixated at the intermediate position while at rest and during attempts to phonate. The soft palate is also paralyzed, rests close to the posterior surface of the tongue, and does not move during phonation.

d. **Medicosurgical management** of adductor paralysis of the larynx with an associated palatopharyngeal paralysis generally includes procedures that are directed primarily at protecting the patient's airway and secondarily at improving phonation:

(1) In cases of bilateral adductor paralysis, **protection of the airway is of primary concern.** Patients may need to be fed by gastrostomy tube to prevent aspiration, and an artificial larynx may be necessary to aid voicing (Stemple et al., 1995).

(2) In cases of unilateral adductor paralysis, **autologous fat** may be injected into the paralyzed fold to improve glottal closure by making the paralyzed fold large enough so that the intact fold can approximate it. In addition to injection of autologous fat, **laryngeal framework surgery,** also known as vocal fold medialization or Type I thyroplasty, has had very good results. In Type I thyroplasty, the vocal fold on the affected side is pushed toward the midline or medialized.

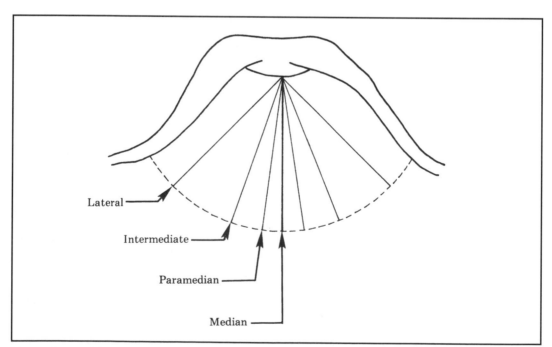

Figure 8.4. Paralytic positions of the vocal folds. *Note.* Adapted from *Speech Pathology: An Applied Behavior Science* (2nd ed.), by W. H. Perkins, 1977, St. Louis: Mosby.

In a recent modification of the medialization procedure, surgeons at Johns Hopkins University School of Medicine have developed an implant called **Vocom (vocal cord medialization)** from calcium-based synthetic bone material. The implants have been developed in five different sizes. The patient remains awake during the medialization procedure, and the surgeon inserts different sizes of the implant until the patient indicates that he or she is satisfied with the sound of their voice (St. John-Kelly, 1998). Because the surgeon focuses specifically on improving the sound of the patient's voice, this type of surgery is referred to as **phonosurgery,** or surgery performed primarily to improve the voice rather than just to improve the structure of the larynx (Case, 1996).

Otolaryngologists usually wait a period of 6 to 12 months after the onset of vocal fold immobility before surgical intervention (Benninger & Gardner, 1998). Voice therapy is indicated in the interim to prevent development of excessive muscular tension and to help the patient develop the most efficient voice possible (Sataloff, 1997a).

(3) **Injectable teflon** can be placed in the posterior pharyngeal wall (pharyngeal implant), or a palatal lift prosthesis (see **VII.C.3.a**) can be used to improve velopharyngeal competence.

(4) Another **surgical procedure** for unilateral adductor paralysis is one in which a nerve-muscle pedicle from the omohyoid muscle is implanted into the thyroarytenoid muscle to reinnervate it for the purpose of improved voice production (Tucker, 1977). As the implant begins to take, the effects of this type of surgery gradually become apparent over the course of the first 4 postoperative months (Tucker & Rusnov, 1981), with the patient showing improved adductor function, which results in improved pitch control and increased vocal loudness. This procedure may be more effective in combination with a medialization or Type I thyroplasty technique, which can be performed using the same incision (Sataloff, 1997a).

e. **Voice therapy management**

(1) **Prognosis** for improved phonation in patients with flaccid dysphonias due to CN X lesions is related to the following:

(a) The **etiology** of the paralysis greatly affects the patient's chances of recovery. Paralyses due to degenerative peripheral nervous system diseases have a poorer prognosis than those due to static lesions. Paralyses due to idiopathic disorders may improve spontaneously.

(b) The **position in which the paralyzed folds are fixed** often determines the degree of phonatory improvement to be expected. The closer the paralyzed fold is to the midline, the better the prognosis for voice improvement.

(c) Unilateral paralyses respond better to voice therapy than do bilateral paralyses.

(2) **Basic principles of voice therapy for unilateral adductor paralysis.** Three basic voice therapy techniques have been used for patients with unilateral adductor paralyses. The first two techniques involve two different methods by which the patient can be taught to use forceful adduction of the intact vocal fold to approximate the paralyzed fold in order to compensate for the paralysis (see **VII.E.4.a–b** in this chapter). Forceful adduction techniques should be used with extreme caution to avoid development of excessive tension. The third technique, which should be taught along with the techniques of forceful adduction, utilizes the respiratory system through a process of controlled exhalation (Rosenbek & LaPointe, 1978) to provide the patient with the best possible voice (see **VII.E.4.c** in this chapter).

In addition, vocal function exercises (Stemple, 1997) offer promise as a holistic voice therapy approach to unilateral adductor paralysis. Use of the vocal function exercises may result in better approximation of the vocal folds while balancing and improving the entire vocal mechanism (see Chapter 5).

(3) **Management of hypernasality and nasal emission.** Hypernasality and nasal emission commonly accompany CN X lesions that affect all speech muscles supplied by the vagus (soft palate muscles, pharyngeal muscles, and all intrinsic muscles of the larynx). Therapy for hypernasal resonance includes (1) development of the patient's awareness of hypernasality (see **VII.C.2** in this chapter and Chap. 9, **I.D.2**), (2) prosthetic management (see **VII.C.3.a**), and (3) surgical management (see **VII.C.3.c** in this chapter).

(4) **Basic principles of voice therapy for bilateral adductor paralysis.** Voice therapy for bilateral adductor paralysis with associated palatopharyngeal involvement is generally contraindicated because it is physiologically impossible for the patient to effect sufficient approximation of the paralyzed vocal folds for the purpose of phonation. However, if the paralysis should begin to diminish, the following measures can be used in an effort to improve phonation:

(a) All of the **voice therapy methods** suggested for cases of unilateral paralysis (see **(2)** a few passages earlier) may be attempted for cases of bilateral paralysis; however, the voice usually remains unimproved unless some spontaneous recovery occurs.

(b) Utilization of a **larger mouth opening** (see **VII.E.2.b** in this chapter) and pushing exercises (see **VII.E.4** in this chapter) may increase the intensity of the patient's whispered speech.

(c) **Alaryngeal speech** or a **nonvocal communication aid** (see Chap. 10) may be used to provide the patient with a means of communication if the patient finds whispered speech insufficient for most communication settings.

2. **Vagus nerve lesions below the pharyngeal nerve branch** but above the level where the superior laryngeal nerve separates from the vagus

(adductor paralysis with no associated palatopharyngeal paralysis). A vagus nerve lesion below the pharyngeal nerve branch but above the superior and recurrent laryngeal nerve branches affects all intrinsic muscles of the larynx; palatal and pharyngeal muscles are unaffected, however, because the lesion is below the level where the pharyngeal nerve branch bifurcates from the vagus nerve (see Figure 8.5).

a. **Etiology.** Adductor paralysis without an associated palatopharyngeal paralysis occurs most often as a result of lesions caused by the following (Darley et al., 1975):

(1) **Surgical trauma** to the vagus nerve (thyroidectomy, thoracic surgery, cervical fusion, endarterectomy) (Sataloff, 1997a)

(2) **Infections** in the vicinity of the vagus nerve

(3) **Idiopathic disorders**

b. **Symptoms.** Because the superior laryngeal and recurrent laryngeal branches of the vagus nerve are both affected by a lesion located below the pharyngeal branch but above the superior laryngeal nerve branch, the laryngeal symptoms for this type of dysphonia are nearly identical to those of adductor paralysis of the larynx with an associated palatopharyngeal paralysis (see **I.A.1.b** in this chapter). The only difference between these two dysphonias is that there is no velar or pharyngeal involvement (palatopharyngeal paralysis), nor any hypernasality or nasal emission associated with the dysphonia under discussion; hence, this dysphonia is referred to as adductor paralysis of the larynx with no associated palatopharyngeal paralysis.

c. **Laryngoscopic findings**

(1) **Unilateral lesions** result in the vocal fold on the affected side fixating at the intermediate position (see Figure 8.4). Soft palate movement during phonation is normal.

(2) **Bilateral lesions** result in bilateral vocal fold fixation at the intermediate position (see Figure 8.4). Soft palate movement during phonation is normal.

d. **Medicosurgical management** generally includes the same procedures used with adductor paralysis of the larynx with an associated palatopharyngeal paralysis (see **I.A.1.d** in this chapter), except that with this form of paralysis the management of velopharyngeal involvement is not necessary.

e. **Voice therapy management** considerations are nearly identical to the procedures discussed for the other form of adductor paralysis of the larynx (see **I.A.1.e**), except that no procedures are required for management of velopharyngeal incompetence.

3. **Vagus nerve lesions affecting only the superior laryngeal nerve** (isolated paralysis of the superior laryngeal nerve). A CN X lesion that affects only the superior laryngeal nerve branch can occur (see Figure 8.6). The superior laryngeal nerve divides into two subbranches—the internal

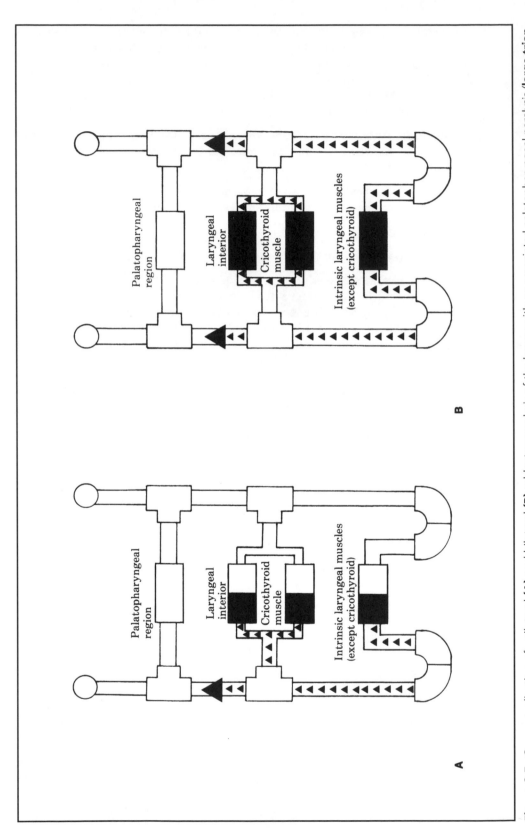

Figure 8.5. Conceptualization of unilateral **(A)** and bilateral **(B)** adductor paralysis of the larynx with *no* associated palatopharyngeal paralysis (**large triangles** indicate sites of blockage, **small triangles** indicate route where flow is interrupted, and **blackened areas** indicate the extent of paralysis).

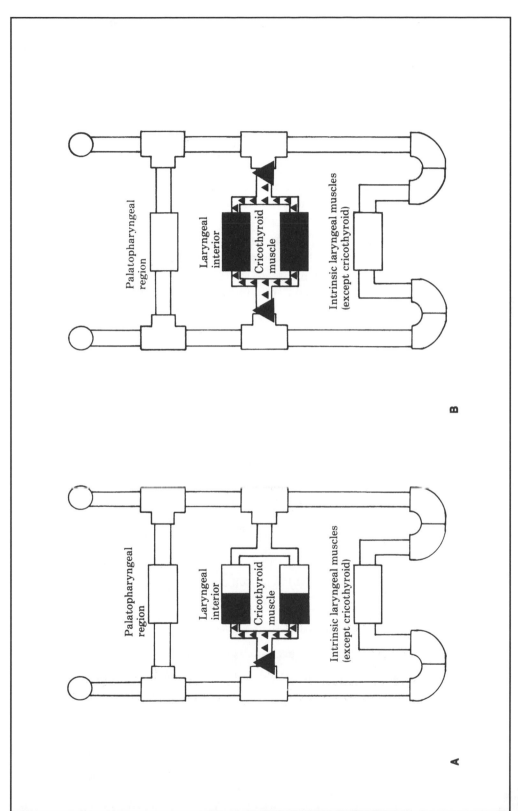

Figure 8.6. Conceptualization of unilateral **(A)** and bilateral **(B)** isolated paralysis of the superior laryngeal nerve (**large triangles** indicate sites of blockage, **small triangles** indicate route where flow is interrupted, and **blackened areas** indicate the extent of paralysis).

and external. The internal branch is sensory from the larynx, while the external branch is motor to the cricothyroid muscle.

a. Etiology. Isolated paralysis of the superior laryngeal nerve occurs most often as a result of CN X lesions due to the following:

  (1) Surgical trauma is the most common cause of damage to the superior laryngeal nerve.

  (2) Accidental trauma to the neck, often as a result of an automobile or motorcycle accident, is also a common cause of this dysphonia.

  (3) Benign thyroid disease can affect the superior laryngeal nerve because of the proximity of the gland and the nerve.

b. Symptoms. Because the pharyngeal and recurrent branches of the vagus nerve are spared with this type of paralysis (see Figure 8.6), the soft palate and all the intrinsic muscles of the larynx function normally. The only muscle that is paralyzed is the cricothyroid muscle. Because of this paralysis, the thyroid cartilage cannot be tilted with respect to the cricoid cartilage, and the patient's ability to stretch and tense the vocal folds is therefore impaired.

  (1) Motor speech symptoms

   (a) Dysphonia due to a *unilateral* lesion is characterized by the following laryngeal symptoms:

    (i) Breathiness, which is usually mild.

    (ii) Mild hoarseness.

    (iii) Normal or slightly reduced vocal loudness.

    (iv) The ability to **vary pitch** is affected; however, it is often only noticeable when the patient attempts to sing.

    (v) The patient may complain of **vocal fatigue** (Stemple et al., 1995).

   (b) Dysphonia due to a *bilateral* lesion is characterized by the following laryngeal symptoms:

    (i) Mild to moderate breathiness.

    (ii) Mild to moderate hoarseness.

    (iii) Reduced loudness is common.

    (iv) The patient's ability to **alter pitch is markedly affected,** with the patient being unable to sing up and down the musical scale.

    (v) The patient may complain of **vocal fatigue** (Stemple et al., 1995).

  (2) Associated symptoms. Laryngeal anesthesia due to the loss of innervation of the internal branch of the superior laryngeal nerve can result in a mild postdeglutition cough, choking, or aspiration, or a mild cough after swallowing; however, because these symptoms are often not constant or obvious, the patient may not report them as problems.

c. **Laryngoscopic findings**

(1) **Unilateral lesions** result in the following:

(a) A shortened and flaccid vocal fold on the affected side.

(b) An asymmetrical shift of the epiglottis and anterior larynx toward the intact side during phonation.

(c) One fold may lag the other in adduction, and the larynx is tilted (Sataloff & Spiegel, 1993).

(2) **Bilateral lesions** result in the following:

(a) An absence of tilt of the thyroid cartilage with respect to the cricoid cartilage.

(b) An overhanging epiglottis, which makes it difficult to observe via indirect mirror laryngoscopy.

(c) Shortened vocal folds due to a loss of cricothyroid muscle function, which prevents the folds from being stretched out to their normal at-rest length.

(d) Bilateral vocal fold bowing, because the loss of the cricothyroid muscle function relaxes the tension on the folds and thus allows them to bow.

d. **Medicosurgical management.** Medicosurgical management techniques for the treatment of patients with an isolated paralysis of the superior laryngeal nerve are not usually performed because of risk of worsening the patient's voice (S. M. Archer & S. Shotts, personal communication, 1999).

e. **Voice therapy management.** The most noticeable effects of isolated paralysis of the superior laryngeal nerve are on the singing voice rather than the speaking voice. Specifically, the ability to vary vocal pitch is impaired. Because there are no alternative means by which the vocal folds may be stretched, there is little that can be done to improve the patient's singing voice. As patients with this type of paralysis usually experience only a very mild dysphonia, symptomatic voice therapy management is usually unnecessary. The symptoms of the dysphonia are often more pronounced in patients with bilateral lesions, but, again, there are no voice therapy techniques that can be used to increase vocal fold length in the absence of cricothyroid muscle function.

4. **Vagus nerve lesions that affect only the recurrent laryngeal nerve (abductor paralysis of the larynx).** A vagus nerve lesion that affects the recurrent laryngeal nerve branch only (see Figure 8.7) can occur. Left recurrent laryngeal nerve paralysis occurs 10 times more frequently than does right recurrent laryngeal nerve paralysis. This type of lesion will result in paralysis of all the intrinsic muscles of the larynx except the cricothyroid

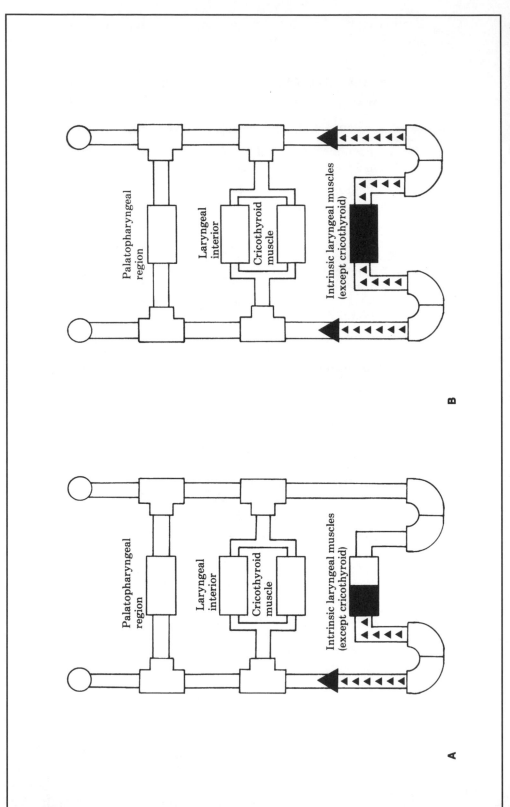

Figure 8.7. Conceptualization of unilateral **(A)** and bilateral **(B)** abductor paralysis of the larynx (**large triangles** indicate sites of blockage, **small triangles** indicate route where flow is interrupted, and **blackened areas** indicate the extent of paralysis).

muscle (the cricothyroid muscle is innervated by the superior laryngeal nerve branch).

The principal neuromuscular effect of this type of paralysis is loss of the ability to abduct and adduct the vocal folds. However, because the cricothyroid muscle still functions, it contracts and stretches and pulls on the vocal folds until they are drawn to a midline position. Once the folds reach the midline, the paralyzed abductor muscles are unable to pull the folds apart and widen the glottis; hence, this type of paralysis is referred to as abductor paralysis of the larynx.

a. Etiology

   (1) Etiology of unilateral abductor paralysis. Unilateral abductor paralysis of the larynx occurs most often as a result of lesions caused by the following (Darley et al., 1975; DeWeese & Saunders, 1977):

   (a) Intrathoracic malignant neoplasms that involve the recurrent laryngeal nerve or structures near the nerve as it passes through the thorax before changing course and returning to innervate the larynx.

   (b) Aneurysms (balloon-like bulges in the wall of a blood vessel) that impinge upon the vagus nerve and thus disrupt its function.

   (c) Mitral stenosis, which causes the left auricle to enlarge and thus, in some cases, stretch the left recurrent laryngeal nerve.

   (d) Trauma to the neck due to surgery or accidents.

   (e) Idiopathic disorders. Approximately 80% of cases of idiopathic unilateral abductor paralysis regress spontaneously within 6 to 12 months following onset of the nerve lesion (DeWeese & Saunders, 1977).

   (2) Etiology of bilateral abductor paralysis. Bilateral abductor paralysis is most often caused by lesions that result from the following:

   (a) Surgical trauma, such as thyroid surgery (thyroidectomy)

   (b) Trauma to the neck due to accidents

   (c) Tumors that affect the nerve itself or that impinge upon the nerve

   (d) Infection

   (e) Idiopathic disorders

b. Symptoms. Patients with abductor paralysis of the larynx primarily complain of an inability to draw a sufficiently large breath, especially when they are engaged in physical activity. This inability is due to the narrowed airway at the glottis, which results from the paralysis. Ironically, because the vocal folds are fixated near the midline (paramedian position) (see Figure 8.4), phonation is usually unaffected.

   (1) Motor speech symptoms vary depending upon whether the dysphonia is due to a unilateral or bilateral lesion.

(a) **Dysphonias due to *unilateral* lesions**

   (i) The paralyzed vocal fold is usually fixated at the paramedian position because of the effects of the intact nerve supply to the cricothyroid muscle. As a result, the patient's voice may show few if any signs of disability, because the unaffected vocal fold can approximate the paralyzed fold normally. If the voice is affected, the quality is mildly breathy and mildly hoarse, with slightly reduced loudness and occasional diplophonia being present.

   (ii) Quiet, at-rest breathing is generally unaffected, although the patient with unilateral abductor paralysis may experience shortness of breath during physical activity due to the narrowed airway.

(b) **Dysphonia due to *bilateral* lesions**

   (i) Because paralysis of the abductors prevents widening of the glottis upon inhalation, inhalatory stridor is a prominent symptom of bilateral abductor paralysis.

   (ii) With bilateral lesions, both of the vocal folds are paralyzed. However, because both vocal folds are fixed near the median position, phonation is virtually normal. This paradox is due to the fact that both vocal folds remain weakly adducted in a position where they can be vibrated passively, but equally, by the outgoing airstream.

(2) **Associated symptoms**

   (a) **Unilateral paralysis**

      (i) Because of the marginal airway that results from the abductor paralysis, the patient may experience **difficulty in breathing,** but usually only during periods of deep respiration.

      (ii) The patient's **voice is usually unaffected.**

      (iii) The patient may have a **weak cough or glottal attack.**

   (b) **Bilateral paralysis**

      (i) The patient may experience severe **difficulty with inhalation** for life purposes. A tracheostomy is often necessary.

      (ii) **Inhalatory stridor** may be present because of the marginal airway.

c. **Laryngoscopic findings** (Arnold & Stephens, 1980)

   (1) **Unilateral lesions** result in the vocal fold on the affected side fixating in the paramedian position.

   (2) **Bilateral lesions** result in bilateral fixation of the vocal folds in the paramedian position.

d. Medicosurgical management

   (1) Any decision about medicosurgical management of *unilateral* **abductor paralysis of the larynx** is generally delayed until 6 to 12 months have elapsed to allow for spontaneous recovery of recurrent laryngeal nerve function or for a gradual movement of the paralyzed fold to a more open position. Rarely is surgery indicated in management of unilateral abductor paralysis (Boone & McFarlane, 1994).

   (2) Medicosurgical management of *bilateral* **abductor paralysis of the larynx** generally includes the following:

   (a) **Tracheostomy** to provide a safe and adequate airway for reasonable day-to-day exertion.

   (b) **Arytenoidectomy** (the removal of one arytenoid) (Woodman & Pennington, 1976) or arytenoidopexy (the surgical fixation of an arytenoid and its associated vocal fold) (Biller & Lawson, 1980) to provide an airway without the need for tracheostomy by either removing the vocal fold or lateralizing it permanently. Surgical fixation of the arytenoid has been less successful than arytenoidectomy in providing an adequate airway (Sataloff, 1997a).

   (c) **Reinnervation surgery** (Tucker, 1976, 1977, 1980) may be attempted if the patient presents with a fair voice and at least a borderline airway (Sataloff, 1997a).

e. Voice therapy management

   (1) Prognosis for improved voice in *unilateral* **abductor paralysis** is very good. This type of laryngeal paralysis generally does not require voice therapy. The voice may show few if any signs of disability. Patients who use their voices professionally may require instruction in methods of increasing breath control (see **VII.D** and **VII.E.4.c** later in this chapter), increasing intensity, and maintaining a relaxed vocal tract (see Chap. 5, **III.D.4**).

   (2) Ironically, voice quality in patients with **bilateral abductor paralysis** is usually very good, as the vocal folds are paralyzed in a position in which they are sufficiently approximated for phonation to occur (see Figure 8.4). However, because surgery or tracheostomy to provide an adequate airway for life-sustaining purposes is often required, prognosis for improved voice following an arytenoidectomy or arytenoidopexy in bilateral abductor paralysis is poor.

   Because medicosurgical techniques are generally required to reestablish an adequate airway, voice therapy must not be initiated unless medical clearance is given. Consultation with a surgeon regarding the reconstructed airway's ability to withstand the stress of voice therapy is essential. If the physician recommends them, hyperadduction and controlled exhalation techniques may be used to improve the quality of the patient's voice (see **VII.E.4**).

B. **Flaccid dysphonia due to myasthenia gravis.** Myasthenia gravis and the less common Eaton-Lambert myasthenic syndrome (Muscular Dystrophy Association, 1999) are autoimmune disorders of the neuromuscular junction characterized by excessive fatigability of muscles that undergo repetitive stimulation or activity. Myasthenia gravis is the most common of the neuromuscular junction diseases (Brookshire, 1997). The head and neck, or bulbar muscle group, are the muscles most involved early in the disease, with the extrinsic ocular muscles being particularly affected (Snead et al., 1980). Most patients are young to middle-age women (Drachman, 1978). A flaccid dysphonia can occur as a dysarthric component of myasthenia gravis.

1. **Etiology.** Myasthenia gravis is caused by the production of autoantibodies resulting in destruction of acetylcholine receptors at the myoneural junction (Newman & Ramadan, 1998; Reeves, 1981). Because of reduced availability of acetylcholine at these junctions, transmission of neural impulses from the motor end plate is reduced or prevented.

2. **Symptoms**

   a. **General neuromuscular symptoms.** In general, patients with myasthenia gravis complain that they fatigue easily during the course of a day and that they feel most energetic upon awakening. The initial symptoms in approximately one half of patients with myasthenia gravis are ocular problems; one third report difficulty with speaking, swallowing, and chewing; and one fifth report limb weakness (Brooke, 1977). Patients with generalized myasthenia gravis decline from normal health to severe weakness with respiratory insufficiency in a matter of weeks. During the endurance-testing portion of the general voice evaluation (see Chap. 3, **The Voice Evaluation Process, IX**), the patient with myasthenia gravis will experience reduced loudness and increasingly greater degrees of breathiness, hypernasality, nasal emission, and articulatory imprecision. Because of the depletion of acetylcholine at the motor end plates, the patient is often nearly aphonic before she or he can count to 200.

   b. **Motor speech symptoms** vary according to the anatomic component being evaluated.

      (1) The patient's **lips** function normally during the initial portion of the examination, but weakness appears after stressful or prolonged speaking activities. The patient's smile may be asymmetrical.

      (2) The **mandible,** like the lips, functions normally during the initial portion of the examination. Weakness appears after stressful, repetitive mandibular movement.

      (3) **Velopharyngeal mechanism**

         (a) Bilateral effects of muscular weakness are evidenced in the **bilateral lowering of the soft palate.**

         (b) **Bilateral velar immobility** appears after a period of stressful or prolonged speaking.

         (c) **Hypernasality and nasal emission** increase during stressful or prolonged speaking activities.

(4) The **tongue** functions in a normal manner at the beginning of a period of stressful or prolonged speaking but then becomes weakened, and articulatory precision decreases.

(5) After stressful use of the **larynx,** the following symptoms appear:

(a) Breathiness and hoarseness, which are often the leading symptoms of myasthenia gravis, increase during a sustained speaking activity, such as counting to 200 (see Chap. 3, **The Voice Evaluation Process, IX**).

(b) Inhalatory stridor results because the weakened vocal fold abductors are unable to open the glottis sufficiently.

(c) Reduced loudness results because the weakened vocal fold adductors are inadequate to effect efficient laryngeal closure.

(d) Monopitch is present due to reduced function of the cricothyroid muscle.

c. **Associated symptoms**

(1) Dysphagia due to weakened palatal and pharyngeal muscles may occur.

(2) Nasal regurgitation of food and liquids may result from weakening of palatal muscles.

(3) Complaints of **general body fatigue** are frequent.

(4) Progressive dysphonia is the only symptom of myasthenia gravis in approximately 6% of all patients (Grob, 1958; M. Rontal, E. Rontal, Leuchter, & Rolnick, 1978; Stuart, 1965).

3. **Diagnosis of myasthenia gravis.** Because the voice symptoms of myasthenia gravis may exist in the presence of a normal laryngeal examination, the speech–language pathologist may erroneously diagnose myasthenia gravis. The progressive degradation of all aspects of speech production (i.e., phonation, resonation, and articulation) during prolonged speaking activities is a classic finding characteristic *only* of myasthenia gravis.

Medical confirmation of the diagnosis of myasthenia gravis can be accomplished by intravenous administration of Tensilon (edrophonium chloride). The diagnosis of myasthenia gravis is confirmed if:

a. Within 20 to 60 seconds of Tensilon injection (according to Falconer, Patterson, Gustafson, & Sheridan, 1978, and to Vogel & Carter, 1995, the duration of the action of Tensilon is 2 to 10 minutes) there is a transient improvement in muscle strength resulting in marked speech improvement, including elimination of hypernasality and nasal emission along with significant articulatory improvement.

b. When compared with pre-Tensilon spectrograms, post-Tensilon voice spectrograms show (M. Rontal et al., 1978):

(1) Significant improvement in the periodicity of the vocal folds

(2) Reappearance of normal formant structure

(3) Reduction of breathiness

4. Laryngoscopic findings

a. The vocal folds may appear normal in patients with **mild cases** of myasthenia gravis.

b. In more **advanced cases,** there is bilateral restriction of vocal fold adduction and abduction.

c. Bowing of the vocal folds may occur.

5. Medicosurgical management of myasthenia gravis generally includes the following:

a. The administration of **anticholinesterase drugs** such as pyridostigmine is used to delay destruction of acetylcholine at neuromuscular junctions, thus allowing a sufficient amount of the transmitter chemical to build up, which in turn makes muscle stimulation and contraction possible (Asperheim & Eisenhauer, 1977; Newman & Ramadan, 1998; Walshe, 1982).

b. More advanced cases of myasthenia gravis are managed through **immunosuppression** with drugs like the corticosteroids or with cyclosporin (Newman & Ramadan, 1998).

c. **Thymectomy** (removal of the thymus gland) is effective in over 50% of patients (Muscular Dystrophy Association, 1999; Walshe, 1982).

d. **Plasmapheresis** to remove destructive antibodies is used in cases of myasthenic crisis when respiration is compromised and the patient's life is in danger (Vogel & Carter, 1995).

6. Voice therapy management

a. The greatest improvement in voice can generally be obtained through the patient following a medical regimen of anticholinesterase therapy or through surgical removal of the thymus. Voice therapy for myasthenia gravis is generally contraindicated.

b. Hypernasality and nasal emission may be successfully managed through the use of a **palatal lift prosthesis** (see **VII.C.3.a** later in this chapter).

c. Techniques of vocal fold hyperadduction (see **VII.E.4.a–b**) should not be used, as they greatly fatigue the patient's use of the speech musculature.

C. **Flaccid dysphonia due to myotonic muscular dystrophy.** The muscular dystrophies are inherited diseases characterized by progressive weakness and atrophy of the affected muscles. There are several different forms of muscular dystrophy, each of which is classified by its pattern of muscle involvement, for example **pseudohypertrophic (Duchenne), oculopharyngeal,** and **myotonic muscular dystrophy (Steinert's Disease)** (Muscular Dystrophy Association, 1999; Ward, Hanson, & Berei, 1981). Onset is usually during adolescence or early adulthood, and the disorder occurs equally in males and females. Progression of the disease is slow.

Myotonic muscular dystrophy is the most common form of adult muscular dystrophy, and also one of the most common of the neuromuscular diseases affecting adults. It is characterized by myotonia and marked weakness of the facial and neck muscles. Flaccid dysarthria with an associated flaccid dysphonia is common with myotonic muscular dystrophy.

1. **Etiology.** The myotonic type of muscular dystrophy is a **hereditary myopathy** in which the speech musculature is particularly affected. The inheritance is autosomal dominant. Some patients reach old age with only minimal symptoms. The gene responsible for myotonic dystrophy was identified in 1992. The defect has proved to be a region of unstable genetic material (DNA) on chromosome 19 (Muscular Dystrophy Group, 1999).

2. **Symptoms**

   a. **General neuromuscular symptoms** of myotonic muscular dystrophy are not usually noticed until adolescence or adulthood. In general, the earlier the illness appears, the more severe the bulbar musculature involvement will be. Myotonic muscular dystrophy follows a progressive course and is characterized by ptosis, marked facial weakness, wasted sternocleidomastoid muscles, weakness in muscles supplied by the cranial nerves, and myotonia.

      Myotonia, which is a common characteristic of all forms of muscular dystrophy, is a phenomenon in which relaxation of a muscle following contraction is prolonged over several seconds. Myotonia accounts for several of the neurologic symptoms associated with myotonic muscular dystrophy, such as difficulty in relaxing handgrip or difficulty in relaxing a persistently contracted tongue.

   b. **Motor speech symptoms** of the dysarthria associated with myotonic muscular dystrophy are characterized by effects on the following anatomic areas:

      (1) **Face and neck.** The following characteristics have been used to describe patients with myotonic muscular dystrophy (Brooke, 1977):

         (a) A **drawn and lugubrious appearance,** which is a classic characteristic of the disease in adults

         (b) **Hollowing of muscles around the temples and jaws**

         (c) **Bilateral ptosis**

         (d) **Marked wasting of the sternocleidomastoid muscles**

      (2) **Lips**

         (a) **Thin and weak circumoral musculature**

         (b) **Reduced range of movement**

      (3) **Velopharyngeal mechanism**

         (a) **Hypernasality** is present because of flaccidity and weakness of the soft palate muscles.

(b) **Nasal emission** occurs because of velopharyngeal incompetence, which results from weakness of the palatopharyngeal muscles.

(4) Larynx

(a) **Breathiness,** which is due to weakness of the vocal fold adductors, is a common symptom.

(b) **Inhalatory stridor** is present because the weakened laryngeal abductors are unable to maintain an adequate glottal opening.

(c) **Reduced loudness** results because of reduced efficiency of laryngeal valving.

c. **Associated symptoms.** Myotonic muscular dystrophy is a systemic disorder with concomitant medical problems which include the following (Jablecki, 1982; Newman & Ramadan, 1998):

(1) Aspiration pneumonia

(2) Cardiac arrhythmias or heart failure

(3) Cataracts

(4) Dysphagia

3. **Laryngoscopic examination** reveals the following:

a. Bilateral restriction of the vocal folds during adduction and abduction.

b. Bowing of the vocal folds may occur due to weakness of the cricothyroid and thyroarytenoid muscles.

4. **Medicosurgical management** of myotonic muscular dystrophy generally includes the following:

a. **Physical therapy** for improved general body muscle tone and for gait maintenance.

b. **Mechanical devices** (e.g., ankle supports) for gait maintenance as distal weakness develops.

c. **Respiration care** to prevent the development of a shallow breathing pattern.

d. **Genetic counseling,** as there is 50% chance that any child born to an affected parent will develop the disease.

5. **Voice therapy management.** Because the progression of the disease is slow, management of the various voice symptoms will have to be initiated as the symptoms appear.

a. **Management of hypernasality and nasal emission.** Hypernasality and nasal emission may be successfully managed through the use of a palatal lift prosthesis (see **VII.C.3** later in this chapter).

b. **Management of reduced loudness and breathiness.** Vocal loudness and quality can generally be improved through the cautious use of hyperadduction and controlled expiration techniques (see **VII.E.4**).

      c. **Management of respiration.** Because respiration is often affected, it may be necessary to instruct the patient in the use of an efficient abdominal–diaphragmatic breathing technique (see **VII.D**).

II. **Dysphonia Associated with Disorders of the Upper Motor Neuron.** Central nervous system (upper motor neuron) causes of dysphonia are infrequent and account for only approximately 10% of all neurologically based dysphonias. The upper motor neuron supply to the vagus nerve (and other cranial nerves) consists of the motor strips from both sides of the cerebral cortex and the corticobulbar fibers, which descend to synapse with the right and left vagus nerves at the level of the brainstem. Although the majority of the corticobulbar fibers decussate (cross) to innervate the vagus nerve on the contralateral side, there is still considerable innervation of the vagus nerve on the ipsilateral side. In effect, the nucleus of the vagus nerve receives bilateral innervation from upper motor neuron sources.

Because of this bilateral innervation, a unilateral lesion of the motor area or its associated corticobulbar tract will have virtually no demonstrable effect on laryngeal function. Because the motor areas are widely separated, only bilateral cortical lesions that are sufficiently massive or exactly symmetrical can result in a dysphonia. However, as such lesions are ordinarily life threatening, this type of dysphonia is rarely seen (DeWeese & Saunders, 1977).

Spasticity (muscular hypertonia) is found in disorders of the upper motor neuron. Even though a limb may be weak or paralyzed, muscle tone in the limb can be so greatly increased that the limb cannot be moved passively with ease. This is called spastic weakness. With spasticity, there is increased resistance to sudden passive movements, and upon further pressure there may be a sudden decrease in resistance (this is called the **clasp knife phenomenon**). In some cases, the degree of spasticity may be so great that it is impossible to move the limb.

An upper motor neuron dysphonia that has spasticity as its primary muscle characteristic (spastic dysphonia) can result from small bilateral lesions that occur just above the nucleus of the vagus nerve where the corticobulbar fibers decussate. Spastic dysphonia is frequently a component of a more generalized spastic (pseudobulbar) dysarthria and rarely occurs without the associated dysarthria. Spastic dysphonia should not be confused with adductor spasmodic dysphonia (see Chap. 6, **IV**).

A. **Etiology.** Spastic dysarthria results from lesions of the corticobulbar tracts that supply the motor nuclei of the cranial nerves involved in speech production. These lesions may be due to the following (Aronson, 1980; DeWeese & Saunders, 1977; Murdoch, Thompson, & Theodoros, 1997; Portlock & Goffinet, 1980):

    1. Cerebrovascular accident

    2. Tumor

    3. Cerebral palsy

    4. Traumatic brain injury

    5. Infection

    6. Multiple sclerosis

    7. Poliomyelitis

B. **Symptoms**

1. **Motor speech symptoms** of spastic dysarthria are characterized by effects on the following anatomic areas:

a. **Lips**

(1) **Weakness and spasticity** can be observed in the lip muscles.

(2) AMRs (alternate motion rates) involving the lips are slow and irregular.

b. **Mandible**

(1) **Bilateral weakness** can be observed in the muscles of mastication when the patient attempts to lower the mandible against the examiner's resistance.

(2) As the patient depresses the mandible, it may **deviate** to either side.

(3) **Asymmetrical elevation** of the mandible is common.

c. **Velopharyngeal mechanism**

(1) The effects of bilateral muscular weakness can be observed in the soft palate, which hangs lower than normal when it is in the at-rest position.

(2) **Spasticity** can be observed in the movements of the velopharyngeal musculature.

(3) A **hyperactive palatopharyngeal gag reflex** is present.

(4) **Hypernasality** is heard as a result of the weakness and spasticity associated with the soft palate.

d. **Tongue**

(1) Evidence of **bilateral muscular weakness** can be observed during tongue movements.

(2) The tongue may appear **smaller than normal.**

(3) **Spasticity** can be observed in movements of the tongue.

(4) AMRs (alternating motion rates) are slow and irregular.

(5) **Articulatory defects** are heard.

e. **Larynx**

(1) **Strained–strangled phonation** is common as patients attempt to phonate through hyperadducted vocal folds. Hyperadduction of the vocal folds is most likely caused by destruction and subsequent loss of control of inhibitory neurologic signals from the cortex. The strained–strangled voice quality is often the least responsive motor speech system to therapy (Murdoch et al., 1997)

(2) **Harsh voice quality** also results from the hyperadduction.

(3) Excessively **low pitch and reduced loudness** are common.

2. Associated symptoms

    a. Articulatory imprecision results from weakened and spastic conditions of the jaw, lips, and tongue.

    b. Slow rate of speech is common.

    c. A frequent symptom of spastic dysarthria is an **uncontrollable laugh or cry** (sometimes referred to as emotional lability), which can occur suddenly and without cause (although normal emotional events can also trigger their appearance) (Kreindler & Pruskauer-Apostol, 1971). The laugh or cry usually occurs in the absence of the emotions that are normally associated with each behavior. Some patients may, on occasion, rapidly alternate between a pseudobulbar laugh and a pseudobulbar cry without any ability to stop or modify the outbursts. Uncontrollable laughing and crying often makes patients with spastic dysarthria appear to be emotionally unstable when in fact they are emotionally normal.

C. Laryngoscopic findings

    1. The vocal folds appear to be structurally normal.

    2. Normal bilateral adduction of the true and false vocal folds may occur, although some patients present evidence of vocal fold spasticity.

D. Medicosurgical management is usually focused on reducing spasticity and generally includes the following:

    1. Dantrium and Lioresal (antispasmodics)

    2. Valium (a skeletal muscle relaxant)

    3. Peripheral nerve block with a local anesthetic to reduce severe spasticity

E. Voice therapy management

    1. The strained–strangled phonation associated with the dysphonia of spastic dysarthria does not generally affect the patient's **intelligibility.** Consequently, symptomatic voice therapy is usually not attempted with these patients.

    2. Management of hypernasality. Management of hypernasality with a palatal lift prosthesis (see **VII.C.3.a** later in the chapter) is contraindicated when the soft palate is extremely spastic.

    3. Management of reduced loudness. Techniques of vocal fold hyperadduction (see **VII.E.4.a–b**) should not be attempted in the management of reduced vocal loudness associated with the spastic dysphonia of spastic dysarthria. These techniques are contraindicated because they may reduce even further the patient's ability to speak.

    4. Management of strained–strangled voice quality. The use of a breathy phonatory onset may slightly reduce the strained–strangled quality of the voice (see Chap. 5, **III.D.2.b**).

III. Dysphonia Associated with Disorders of the Cerebellar System. The major function of the cerebellum is inhibitory modulation of all motor activity, including regulation of muscle tone and coordination of muscle activity. **Ataxic dysarthria**

is a cerebellar dysfunction resulting in a breakdown of the rhythmic, coordinated muscle patterns of speech production, as well as general body incoordination (Newton, 1977). Phonation is frequently normal in less severe cases of ataxia; abnormally low pitch and a voice tremor are associated with more severe cases. Ataxic dysarthria is characterized chiefly by disturbances of intonation and rhythm (Kent & Nestell, 1975) and articulatory imprecision resulting in slurred, slow speech production (J. R. Brown, Darley, & Aronson, 1970; Lechtenberg, 1982).

A. **Etiology.** Ataxia has been found to result from left cerebellar hemispheric lesions (Allen & Tsukahara, 1974; Cannito & Marquardt, 1997; Lechtenberg & Gilman, 1978) due to the following:

1. Cerebrovascular accidents

2. Cerebellar tumor

3. Congenital conditions, such as cerebral palsy

4. Infection

5. Toxic effects

6. Traumatic brain injury

7. Metabolic disorders

B. **Symptoms**

1. **General neuromuscular symptoms.** Lesions of the cerebellum result in (Reeves, 1981) the following:

   a. A **kinetic-type tremor** that is rhythmic (3 to 8 per second) and disappears with posturing or at rest. Severity of the tremor increases with increased stress or anxiety.

   b. **Muscular hypotonia**

   c. **Ataxia** (incoordination of voluntary muscle movement), which is characterized by:

      (1) Impaired ability to maintain balance and equilibrium.

      (2) Incoordination of gross and fine motor skills.

      (3) Great difficulty in regulating the range of movement.

      (4) Tremors accompanying volitional movements of a limb and increasing toward the end of the movement.

2. **Motor speech symptoms** of ataxic dysarthria, when present, are characterized by effects on the following anatomic areas:

   a. **Lips**

      (1) AMRs are slow and irregular.

      (2) **Articulatory defects** can be heard.

   b. **Tongue**

      (1) The tongue appears to be structurally normal.

(2) AMRs are slow and irregular.

(3) Lateral tongue movements are slow and appear incoordinated.

(4) Articulatory defects can be heard.

c. **Larynx**

(1) The voice of the patient with ataxic dysarthria is often normal.

(2) Occasionally, a **hoarse or harsh voice quality** may be found in patients with ataxia.

(3) **Abnormally low pitch** is usually found only in the more severe cases of ataxia.

(4) The following vocal behaviors, which are the consequences of the effects of ataxia upon laryngeal and respiratory muscle coordination, may be heard (Aronson, 1980; Cannito & Marquardt, 1997):

(a) **Monopitch**

(b) **Monoloudness**

(c) **Inappropriate and imprecise stress patterns**

(d) **Harshness**

(e) **Overall excessive loudness** as well as irregular, uncontrolled bursts of loudness

(f) **Abnormally unsteady phonation** or **coarse voice tremor** that is most noticeable on sustained productions

C. **Laryngoscopic findings**

1. The vocal folds appear to be structurally normal.

2. Normal bilateral abduction and adduction of the vocal folds are observed.

D. **Medicosurgical management** of ataxia is nonspecific and has been disappointing. Some surgery may decrease postural instability and dysarthria, but with accompanying serious side effects (Vogel & Carter, 1995).

E. **Voice therapy management**

1. **Management of abnormally low pitch.** The abnormally low pitch of the dysphonia of ataxia does not generally affect the patient's intelligibility. If the pitch of the patient's voice is judged to need improvement, techniques for elevating vocal pitch (see Chap. 5, **III.D.2**) may be used.

2. **Management of vocal loudness.** The patient can be helped to develop kinesthetic feedback for vocal loudness by learning to recognize the degree of effort required to sustain a normal loudness level during conversation. The cautious use of vocal fold adduction techniques with controlled exhalation (see **VII.E.4** in this chapter), the use of abdominal–diaphragmatic respiration (see **VII.D**), and the use of increased mouth opening (see **VII.E.2.b**) will help increase vocal loudness. A loudness-level meter, the CSL Pitch Program, the VideoVoice Speech Training System, or other instrumentation can

be used to teach the patient to self-monitor vocal loudness (see Chap. 5, **III.D.2** and also Appendix C).

3. **Management of inappropriate stress patterns.** Contrastive stress drills may help to reduce the patient's use of inappropriate and imprecise stress patterns (see **VII.B.1**).

4. **Management of dysarthric intonation patterns.** The clinician can initiate contrastive intonation contour drills to improve the patient's dysarthric intonation patterns (see **VII.B.2**).

5. **Management of articulatory imprecision.** The patient's level of intelligibility can be increased immensely if articulatory accuracy is improved (see **VII.A**).

IV. **Dysphonias Associated with Disorders of the Extrapyramidal System.** A principal function of the basal ganglia is to control automatic motor behavior, (e.g., postural control). This control is regulated by the presence of several neurotransmitter systems within the basal ganglia. Dopamine, a neurotransmitter found in the basal ganglia, is converted from levodopa in the pigmented cells in the substantia nigra. In addition to the dopamine system, the basal ganglia also contains the cholinergic (acetylcholine-utilizing) system. These two neurotransmitter systems must be in equilibrium for neurologic function to be normal.

An imbalance in these two systems is the theoretic basis for parkinsonism, chorea, and other movement disorders related to basal ganglia dysfunction. Parkinsonism, which is characterized by rigidity and bradykinesia, results from idiopathic degeneration of the basal ganglia, especially a loss of neurons in the substantia nigra. Degeneration of the substantia nigra causes a concurrent depletion of dopamine in the basal ganglia and results in a relative excess of cholinergic activity. Based upon this hypothesis, Parkinson's disease treatments have been directed at development of agents that enhance the dopamine system or reduce the acetylcholine activity in the striatum (Lechtenberg, 1982). More recently, there have been significant refinements in levadopa therapy (Adams, 1997).

The *hypokinetic* characteristics (rigidity and bradykinesia) of parkinsonism appear to be counterbalanced by the *hyperkinetic* characteristics of chorea. The neurologic characteristics of these two disorders cannot be present to any significant degree simultaneously.

Evidence for dysequilibrium between the dopaminergic and cholinergic systems has been obtained by analyzing the effects of drugs on each of these movement disorders. The earliest pharmacologic treatment for parkinsonism involved drugs that were directed at the cholinergic system and were designed to deplete acetylcholine. These drugs, in effect, balanced the dopaminergic and cholinergic systems by depleting the level of acetylcholine relative to the level of dopamine. However, because of the side effects of these early anticholinergic drugs, **levodopa,** a drug directed at the dopaminergic system by inducing excess dopamine formation or reducing dopamine destruction, was developed. Administration of levodopa to patients with parkinsonism appears to decrease related symptoms by restoring depleted dopamine levels in the basal ganglia. In summary, a relative excess of the dopaminergic system leads to chorea, and a depletion of this system leads to parkinsonian symptoms. Similarly, a relative excess of the cholinergic system leads to parkinsonism, whereas a depletion of this system leads to chorea.

A. **Dysphonia associated with parkinsonism.** A hypokinetic dysphonia can occur as a dysarthric component of parkinsonism, a disorder of the basal ganglia. Onset of this movement disorder typically occurs after the fourth decade of life. Parkinsonism is characterized by the combination of rigidity and bradykinesia and frequently includes a resting tremor, a disorder of posture and balance, and, to a lesser degree, dementia (Broe, 1982).

The underlying pathophysiology of the clinical symptoms of this extrapyramidal system movement disorder is depletion of dopamine in the striatum, secondary to a slow degeneration of the substantia nigra of the basal ganglia (Asperheim & Eisenhauer, 1977; Wiederholt, 1982). There are several forms of the disorder that may produce the clinical symptoms of parkinsonism. The most common form is called **Parkinson's disease;** this term applies only if the movement disorder is caused by idiopathic degeneration of the basal ganglia. In addition, there are several less common symptomatic varieties, which include the postencephalitic, neuroleptic-induced, and manganese poisoning-induced forms.

1. **Etiologies**

   a. **Idiopathic degeneration of the substantia nigra** of the basal ganglia, or Parkinson's disease (PD), which impairs either the production of dopamine or its transport to the corpus striatum, is the most common form of parkinsonism (Adams, 1997; Wiederholt, 1982). The degree of dopamine deficiency correlates with the severity of the symptoms (Lloyd & Hornykiewicz, 1972).

   b. Another form of parkinsonism can result from a disturbance of the basal ganglia due to the **therapeutic use of neuroleptic (tranquilizing) drugs,** such as piperazine phenothiazines (e.g., trifluoperazine), butyrophenones (e.g., haloperidol), and reserpine (Broe, 1982; Goetz, Dysken, & Klawans, 1980; Marsden, Tarsy, & Baldessarini, 1975; Reeves, 1981). The signs and symptoms of this form are dose related and usually disappear within 3 weeks to several months after the drug dosage is lowered or the drug is stopped (Lechtenberg, 1982). This form of parkinsonism has a high incidence in persons over 70, in whom the normal loss of up to 50% of the substantia nigra neurons (R. L. McGeer & E. G. McGeer, 1978) goes unnoticed until medications further deplete already significantly lowered dopamine levels.

   c. Parkinsonian features and dementia can develop as a consequence of **manganese poisoning,** which is usually caused by occupational exposure to the metal (Wiederholt, 1982).

   d. Postencephalitic parkinsonism is a rare disorder that occurs most often in younger patients. Although it may follow any **viral encephalitis,** it most frequently follows encephalitis due to an influenza virus (Lechtenberg, 1982). It is easy to distinguish this form of parkinsonism from the idiopathic variety because postencephalitic parkinsonism is characterized by oculogyric crises (a condition in which the patient's eyes remain turned upward for minutes to hours). An additional characteristic of the postencephalitic form of the disorder, especially when it occurs in children, is hyperkinetic behaviors (e.g., excessive restlessness and purposeless activity) superimposed on parkinsonism; abstract thinking may also be impaired (Lucas & Goodlund, 1978).

e. Parkinsonian-like features are also characteristic in **Wilson's disease.** Wilson's disease is an inherited disorder in which excessive amounts of copper accumulate in the body. Although the accumulation of copper begins at birth, symptoms of the disorder may not appear until as late as 40 years old (National Institutes of Neurological Disorders and Stroke, 1996).

f. **Parkinsonism induced by MTPT** (meperidine, an illegally produced drug) and arteriosclerotic parkinsonism are also Parkinson-like, rigid, movement disorders (Adams, 1997; Dirckx, 1997).

2. **Symptoms**

a. **General neuromuscular symptoms** (Vogel & Carter, 1995)

(1) **Rigidity,** which is characterized by steady resistance to passive movement, regardless of how fast or strong that movement is, is a classic sign of basal ganglia disorders. Sometimes, when a limb is being passively moved, the rigidity is rhythmically jerky. This intermittent and rhythmic alteration of resistance to passive movement is called "cogwheel rigidity" (Lechtenberg, 1982).

(2) Another clinical feature of parkinsonism is **bradykinesia.** Bradykinesia is not actually a slowness of movement as much as it is an inability to initiate or to perform voluntary movements even though the pyramidal system is intact (Reeves, 1981). When a movement is finally initiated, it is often performed more rapidly than normal. Included under bradykinesia are the loss of movements such as arm swinging while walking, the inability to smile voluntarily, the inability to initiate mandibular movement, and hesitations and seemingly false starts in speech.

(3) Parkinsonism is sometimes characterized by a **resting tremor,** particularly in the distal portions of the extremities. This 3 to 6 cycles-per-second (cps) tremor is most commonly seen in the fingers or hands, where it is described as "pill rolling" because the patient appears to be rolling a pill between the thumb and index finger. The resting tremor appears during complete relaxation and disappears when the patient makes an intentional movement. It is absent during sleep. As the disease progresses, the patient may begin to develop an intention tremor (7 to 12 cps), which most likely results from involvement of the cerebellar system. These resting and intention tremors may increase in severity when the patient becomes anxious or stressed (Reeves, 1981).

(4) Patients with PD may also develop **problems related to posture and balance.** It is characteristic for these patients to have difficulty adjusting to postural change. This causes them great difficulty in

tasks such as rising from a chair or turning from one side to the other while reclining. In order to compensate for the difficulty with balance, they often stand in a stooped manner with the arms flexed. When they are pushed backwards they fall easily (retropulsion). When the patient attempts to turn the body, the head and trunk turn together as if they were fused into a single block (turning en bloc). Patients walk with a shuffling gait in which the range of movement is small but the speed of movement is rapid; initiating or stopping walking is difficult.

b. **Motor speech symptoms** of the hypokinetic dysarthria associated with PD are characterized by effects on the following anatomic areas:

(1) Face and cheeks

   (a) Rigid, mask-like appearance with sunken and hollow cheeks

   (b) Reduced eye blinking and a prominent stare

   (c) Slight drooling

(2) Lips

   (a) Smiling, when it occurs, is usually very slow and deliberate due to rigidity and bradykinesia.

   (b) Lip movements during speech and nonspeech activities are slow, limited in range, and asymmetrical because of the neuromuscular rigidity.

   (c) AMRs become progressively slower, although at times they may occur as rapid, small-range repetitive movements (Darley et al., 1975).

   (d) Range of lip movement is reduced during AMR testing due to the effects of rigidity.

(3) Mandible

   (a) Reduced range of movement due to rigidity

   (b) Reduced speed of movement due to bradykinesia; however, speed of movement may be fast at times, particularly after movement is initiated (Pengilly, 1999).

(4) Tongue

   (a) Resting tremor may occasionally be present.

   (b) AMRs are usually slow, although they may be fast and irregular at times.

   (c) Range of movement is reduced during AMR testing due to rigidity.

(5) Larynx. All of the following laryngeal symptoms occur as a result of the neuromuscular rigidity of PD (Darley et al., 1975; Pengilly, 1999):

   (a) Monopitch

        (b) Monoloudness

        (c) Reduced loudness

        (d) Reduced stress

        (e) Harsh voice quality

        (f) Breathy voice quality

c. Speech symptoms. Speech may or may not be impaired. Estimates are that 60% to 80% of patients with PD develop speech symptoms as the disease progresses (Adams, 1997). If it is impaired, the features associated with the hypokinetic dysarthria of PD suggest that the respiratory, phonatory, and articulatory systems are all adversely affected. The most typical symptoms are marked restriction in the range of individual movements, impairments in the automaticity of movement, and reduced loudness.

  (1) Due to the effects of the disease upon **respiratory function,** the patient's overall loudness level is reduced. As the disease progresses, the patient may become completely inaudible. Speech is produced as a series of short phrases that are separated by inappropriate pauses. Usually, the rate of speech is slow and deliberate, although, at times, the patient hurriedly produces a string of words in an effort to get them out before running out of air.

  (2) Because of the dysarthric effects on the larynx, **mobility of the vocal folds** is reduced. The voice is usually monopitched, and pitch range is limited. The patient's voice is breathy and hoarse in the initial stages of the disease. In the later stages, the patient may be aphonic. Because of decreased automaticity of response, the patient may have difficulty in initiating phonation simultaneous with articulatory movements.

  (3) The effects of the hypokinetic dysarthria on **articulation** are also prominent. A large percentage of patients with PD demonstrate difficulty with rate of speech (Adams, 1997). AMRs for the tongue and lips are usually slowed. During repeated movements the articulators produce discrete articulation on the first few productions, and then articulatory contact becomes incomplete and the sounds or syllables appear to run together, producing a continuant sound. At other times, the patient appears to freeze up and cannot initiate any sound production (Canter, 1965). These patients may also demonstrate palilalia, which is the repetition of a word or phrase with increasing rapidity (Boller, Albert, & Denes, 1975).

  (4) The **articulation of consonants** in patients with PD is imprecise due to reduced range, force, and speed of articulatory movements. Diminished vocal loudness, articulatory imprecision, and respiratory insufficiency may cause the patient to end many utterances unintelligibly.

d. Associated symptoms

(1) **Dementia, memory loss, and depression may** occur in more advanced stages of PD (Adams, 1997; Broe, 1982; Wiederholt, 1982).

(2) **Other symptoms** that may be associated with PD include the following:

(a) Dysphagia

(b) Drooling

(c) Seborrhea of the face

(d) Progressive difficulty with writing

(e) Decreased facial expression (National Parkinson Foundation, 1999)

3. **Laryngoscopic findings** in parkinsonism.

a. The at-rest appearance of vocal folds may be normal.

b. Stroboscopic laryngoscopy and spectrography reveal irregular pitch periods due to asymmetrical abductor and adductor movements (Schley, Fenton, & Niimi, 1982), and closure during phonation is often incomplete, which results in breathiness and reduced loudness.

c. Patients with **postencephalitic parkinsonism** exhibit a greater degree of tremor in the laryngeal muscles than do patients with other forms of parkinsonism (Ward et al., 1981).

d. Patients with **idiopathic Parkinson's disease** reveal a normal range of motion of the arytenoids but are not able to tense the folds, which occasionally results in a bowing of the vocal folds and a resultant inability to vary vocal pitch (Ward et al., 1981). D. Hanson, Gerratt, and Ward (1984) observed bowed vocal folds in 30 of 32 patients with PD.

4. **Medicosurgical management** of parkinsonism generally includes the following procedures:

a. Long-term treatment with levodopa (L-dopa) in a combination form, which acts to reduce rigidity and to control tremors and dysphagia, is generally indicated. Approximately 80% of patients taking levodopa experience symptomatic improvement; however, no medication alters the progression of the disease. Virtually all patients are treated with levodopa in a form combined with a dopa-decarboxylase inhibitor that blocks the peripheral systemic side effects of levodopa (Vogel & Carter, 1995). Although levodopa dosage can easily be adjusted in most patients, symptoms of a too-high dosage include the following (Broe, 1982):

(1) Anorexia

(2) Vomiting

(3) Postural hypotension

(4) Mental changes (e.g., confusion, delirium, hallucinations, and psychosis)

b. Sinemet, Madopar, and Prolopa are drugs consisting of a combination of levodopa and carbidopa. These are often prescribed because these combination levodopa drugs eliminate many of the unpleasant side effects of levodopa.

c. Surgery of the pallidum (pallidotomy) or thalamus may be performed to control rigidity and tremors.

d. Tremor control implants are also being used to control the tremors of parkinsonism. The implant wires are surgically inserted into an area such as the thalamus. The implant control unit is then implanted into the patient's chest, much like a cardiac pacemaker. When activated, the unit sends a high frequency stream of electrical pulses to the brain, resulting in blockage of the tremors (U.S. Department of Health and Human Services, 1997).

e. A controversial treatment for parkinsonism involves **implantation of fetal tissue** into areas of the brain that control movement. The fetal tissue experiments have used tissue from both human and pig fetuses. The underlying principle is that the newly transplanted cells replenish the dopamine deficiency (Baker, Ramig, Johnson, & Freed, 1997; Stein & Glasier, 1995). To date, this approach remains controversial and experimental.

5. **Voice therapy management**

   a. **Prognosis.** Advances in drug and surgical treatments and use of a new voice therapy protocol described in the following section have positively affected the outlook for voice rehabilitation in parkinsonism.

   b. **Management of loudness**

      (1) The Lee Silverman Voice Treatment program (LSVT) (Ramig, Countryman, Thompson, & Horii, 1995) has been shown to be an effective treatment approach for increasing loudness and improving overall intelligibility. In the LSVT approach, patients attend four intensive, individual treatment sessions per week for 1 month. Patients learning LSVT focus on increasing vocal loudness by increasing phonatory or respiratory effort. The actual techniques used in LSVT include common voice treatment approaches such as pushing (Froeschels, Kastein, & Weiss, 1955) to achieve greater vocal fold adduction and loudness. The approach is kept simple and straightforward; patients are encouraged to "think loud, think shout" (Ramig, 1997). The simple, easy-to-self-monitor approach allows the patient to "calibrate" (Ramig, 1997) or develop self-awareness and self-monitoring of the level of effort required to generalize the new patterns of speaking. Training and certification in the LSVT technique are offered at a number of workshops held across the nation.

      (2) Respiration training has been used in the past to increase loudness and simultaneously reduce the speaking rate. However, Ramig et al. (1995) concluded that LSVT treatment was more effective than respiration treatment alone in improving communication in parkinsonism. Based on the results of this investigation, LSVT appears to be

significantly more effective for treatment of the communication deficits of parkinsonism than respiration training alone.

(3) If techniques to improve loudness are not effective, it may be desirable to fit the patient with a portable amplification unit in order to achieve loudness sufficient for everyday communication (Greene & Watson, 1968).

c. W. Hanson & Metter (1980) demonstrated that **the short rushes of speech** typical of parkinsonism could be reduced and intelligibility improved by establishing a reduced speaking rate through the use of a portable delayed auditory feedback (DAF) device.

d. **Management of inappropriate stress patterns and intonation.** Perceptual self-ratings of the effects of monopitch and monoloudness in the speech of the patient with parkinsonism were improved following use of LSVT (Ramig et al., 1995). Though contrastive stress drills and contrastive intonation contour drills (see **VII.B.2** in this chapter) traditionally have been used to reduce the effects of monopitch, monoloudness, and reduced stress (see **VII.B.1**), improvement in monopitch and monoloudness appears to occur as a result of LSVT.

B. **Dysphonia associated with chorea.** Chorea is a disease of the basal ganglia and is manifested by purposeless, irregular, fleeting, and involuntary movement of the limbs or axial muscles, which includes muscles of the face, jaw, and tongue. Limb tone is usually either hypotonic or normal (Reeves, 1981), not rigid or spastic. It is characterized by degeneration and destruction of the striate nucleus (caudate and putamen) and subthalamic nuclei. The forms of chorea of greatest interest to the speech–language pathologist are (1) Huntington's disease, an inherited, degenerative disorder that affects the basal ganglia and cerebral cortex; (2) Sydenham's chorea, a self-limiting form of chorea that occurs primarily in children; and (3) chorea gravidarum, another self-limiting form, which occurs only in pregnant women.

Chorea results in a hyperkinetic dysarthria in which movements of the speech muscles are quick, jerky, and irregular. These choreiform movements can also disrupt the function of the laryngeal and respiratory musculature, thus resulting in a dysphonia.

1. **Etiology.** Chorea is caused by lesions that damage the striate nucleus of the basal ganglion, which results in an imbalance of dopamine and acetylcholine in the striate nucleus. Based upon the fact that patients with parkinsonism who are given high doses of levodopa develop chorea, it has been speculated that chorea may result from an excess of dopamine and a lack of acetylcholine.

Although every variety of chorea results from damage to the striate nucleus, the exact etiology of each form of chorea is different. Huntington's disease is a rare, autosomal dominant disease that is characterized by degeneration of the striatum (caudate and putamen) and widespread cortical neuronal degeneration. Huntington's is now known to be caused by an expansion of an area on chromosome 4 (Newman & Ramadan, 1998). Sydenham's chorea, which occurs primarily in children, most likely results from a previous group A streptococcal infection associated with acute rheumatic fever (Casey, 1977; Klawans, Goetz, Paulson, & Barbeau, 1980; Klawans, Goetz, & Perlik, 1980). Chorea gravidarum most likely results from the normal hormonal changes associated with pregnancy, which in some cases can adversely affect the sensitivity of the basal ganglia to normal levels of dopamine (Lechtenberg, 1982). Chorea gravidarum patients may have a history of Sydenham's chorea.

2. **Symptoms**

   a. **General neuromuscular symptoms.** Chorea is characterized by irregular, rapid, and involuntary movements of the limbs and axial muscles. Because choreic movements are superimposed on normal voluntary movements, the patient with chorea is in constant motion.

      (1) **Huntington's disease (HD)** is characterized by limb and axial chorea and progressive dementia. In the initial stages, choreic movements are minimal; likewise, mental changes (e.g., lability of mood, withdrawal, increased anxiety) are subtle. After the first few symptoms appear, the course of the disease is progressive, and the patient never stabilizes. As the disorder progresses, intellectual problems (e.g., impaired problem-solving ability and recall) begin to appear, and the patient begins to develop a profound dementia (Newman & Ramadan, 1998; Wiederholt, 1982). Later neurologic signs include numerous and obvious movements (gait problems and dysarthria) that progress until athetoid movements and dystonic posturing predominate. Patients eventually become totally dependent. The disease is generally fatal within 15 to 25 years. Suicide is not uncommon (Kevles & Hood, 1999).

      (2) In the initial stages of **Sydenham's chorea,** the movements are subtle and generally interpreted as signs of restlessness or fidgetiness (Wiederholt, 1982). Within days to weeks, choreiform symptoms become more noticeable. About 40% of the children who develop Sydenham's chorea have symptoms of hyperkinetic dysarthria (Naidu & Narasimhachari, 1980; Nausieda, Grossman, Koller, Weiner, & Klawans, 1980). This form of chorea is self-limiting.

      (3) **Chorea gravidarum** begins as restlessness and anxiety followed by jerking movements of the arms and/or legs within days or weeks (Ichiwaka, Kim, Givelber, & Collins, 1980). The movements are usually limited to just one side of the body (hemichorea). Involuntary mouth and tongue movements may occur. This form of chorea terminates with the end of pregnancy.

   b. **Motor speech symptoms** of the dysarthria associated with chorea affect the following anatomic areas:

      (1) **Face and cheeks**

         (a) Irregular, quick, and jerky facial grimaces

         (b) Drooling

         (c) Reduced ability to puff out the cheeks

(2) **Lips**

   (a) Slow and irregular AMRs

   (b) Unpatterned lip movements when lips are at rest

   (c) Bilateral lip weakness

   (d) Articulatory defects

(3) **Mandible.** There are involuntary and asymmetric movements of the mandible when the mandible is at rest or in motion.

(4) **Velopharyngeal mechanism**

   (a) The velopharyngeal mechanism appears to be structurally normal.

   (b) Intermittent hypernasality can be heard.

(5) **Tongue**

   (a) Appears structurally normal.

   (b) Slow and irregular AMRs.

   (c) Unpatterned movements in the tongue when the tongue is at rest.

   (d) Bilateral weakness of the tongue.

   (e) Articulatory defects.

(6) **Larynx**

   (a) Characteristic intermittent harsh voice quality.

   (b) Strained–strangled phonation.

   (c) Transient breathiness.

   (d) Extremely limited pitch and loudness range.

   (e) Inappropriate and imprecise stress patterns.

   (f) Sudden variations in loudness (going from normal loudness to excessive loudness).

   (g) Sudden forced inspirational and expirational sighs.

c. **Dysarthric symptoms.** Chorea typically results in a hyperkinetic dysarthria characterized by disturbances of the normal prosody of speech. The patient talks in short, irregular segments, with pauses of variable length occurring between the segments. Articulation is variably imprecise, and the patient's voice is characterized by irregular episodes of hypernasality, breathiness, harshness, and loudness variation (Darley et al., 1975).

All aspects of speech production—respiration, phonation, articulation, and resonation—are affected by chorea. The choreiform movements that affect the speech muscles occur with no consistent pattern; consequently, disruptions of speech are highly variable and unpredictable. For example, a phrase may be spoken unintelligibly because of the effect of choreic movements on the articulators, only to be spoken immediately following that episode with precise articulation. Similarly, vocal loudness may be erratic, such as when an increase in loudness due to an uncontrolled exhalation is followed by complete aphonia due to respiratory arrest. As the patient attempts to compensate for these disruptions of speech production, speech rate and prosody are adversely affected.

3. **Laryngoscopic findings**

   a. The vocal folds appear to be structurally normal.

   b. There is normal bilateral abduction and adduction of the vocal folds.

4. **Medicosurgical management** of chorea varies, depending upon the form of the disorder. The various management strategies include the following:

   a. Management of **Huntington's disease** includes pharmacologic treatment with a dopamine receptor blocker, which is administered to the patient during the early stages of the disorder; nothing, however, can be done to stop the progression of the disease. Psychological counseling may be required to assist the patient in managing the progressive dementia and the severe depression that frequently accompany this movement disorder. In addition, family counseling may be beneficial to family members.

   Because each child born to an affected parent has a 50% chance of inheriting the disease, genetic counseling is essential. However, because the disease does not usually manifest itself until the third or fourth decade of life, most affected individuals are beyond the child-bearing years when they are first diagnosed. The gene for Huntington's disease was discovered in 1993. People suspecting that they may be at risk for the disease can now be tested by a blood test to determine if they carry the HD gene (Huntington's Disease Society of America, 1998).

   As in Parkinson's disease, a controversial treatment for Huntington's disease involves implantation of fetal tissue into the brain to provide a source of healthy, new brain cells. The fetal tissue experiments have used tissue from both human and pig fetuses.

   b. Because of the side effects of neuroleptic drugs and because it is a self-limiting disease, Sydenham's chorea is generally not treated. Recovery usually occurs within 3 to 4 months.

   c. Because **chorea gravidarum** disappears with the termination of pregnancy, it is generally not treated.

5. **Voice therapy management**

   a. Prognosis. Prognosis for improved phonation in patients with chorea is generally poor. If phonation does improve, it is generally due to an improvement in articulation and prosody.

   b. Management of harshness. Voice therapy, if attempted for a trial period, generally includes techniques to reduce the harsh voice quality, transient breathiness, and strained–strangled phonation. The techniques to reduce harsh, strained phonations are discussed later in this chapter (see **VII.E.5**).

c. **Management of prosodic alterations,** which are associated with chorea, should include contrastive drills for stress and intonation (see **VII.B.1–2** in this chapter).

d. **Management of involuntary orofacial movements.** The clinician may initiate a trial period of therapy to evaluate whether involuntary orofacial movements can be inhibited before beginning articulation therapy (see **VII.A.4**).

C. **Dysphonia associated with myoclonus.** Myoclonus can result in a hyperkinetic dysarthria characterized by brief episodes of abnormal speech production (particularly during sustained vocal activity) due to short, shock-like, rhythmic muscular contractions of the velum, pharynx, and larynx (palatopharyngeolaryngeal myoclonus).

1. **Etiology.** Myoclonic jerks affecting the velar, pharyngeal, and laryngeal muscles result from lesions in the pathways connecting the red nucleus, the olivary bodies of the medulla, and the dentate nucleus of the cerebellum (Chusid, 1976). Other signs of a brainstem lesion may be present.

2. **Symptoms**

   a. **General neuromuscular symptoms.** Palatopharyngeolaryngeal myoclonus is characterized by rhythmic movements of the soft palate, the pharyngeal wall, and the larynx. Simultaneous myoclonic jerks may be observed in the facial muscles. These rhythmic jerks occur at a rate of 1 to 4 per second (Darley et al., 1975; Zraick & LaPointe, 1997).

   b. **Motor speech symptoms** of palatopharyngeolaryngeal myoclonus are characterized by effects on the following anatomic areas:

      (1) **Velopharyngeal mechanism**

         (a) The soft palate elevates and drops in an abrupt and rhythmic manner and in synchrony with myoclonic laryngeal movements.

         (b) The lateral pharyngeal walls move medially and laterally in an abrupt and rhythmic manner and in synchrony with myoclonic laryngeal movements.

         (c) Temporary hypernasality may be detected during a myoclonic episode.

      (2) **Tongue.** Upon initial examination at rest, the tongue appears unaffected. If the patient can open the mouth and hold it steadily open for several minutes, myoclonic movement of the tongue may be seen. Myoclonic movements of the tongue may be also seen when the tongue is protruded and during phonation (Darley et al., 1975).

      (3) **Larynx**

         (a) Momentary voice arrest may occur during a myoclonic episode; however, voice arrest is generally undetected in contextual speech unless myoclonus is severe. Voice arrest is most noticeable during vowel prolongation and while the patient is singing.

(b) Laryngeal and palatal myoclonus often occur simultaneously.

(c) Myoclonus may affect the diaphragm and thus cause rhythmic voice arrests by interfering with respiration.

c. Associated symptoms

(1) Contraction of the pharyngeal muscles may cause the orifice of the eustachian tube to open and close, thus producing a clicking noise that can be heard emanating from the patient's ear.

(2) The patient may complain of a clicking sensation or a sensation of spasm in the larynx.

(3) Articulation is generally normal; however, the patient may exhibit some irregular articulatory breakdowns during myoclonic episodes.

(4) Myoclonic movements may be present at rest as well as during phonation.

(5) Subcutaneous upward and downward movements of the larynx and pharynx may be observed on the external surface of the patient's neck.

3. Laryngoscopic findings reveal that the vocal folds have rhythmic bilateral adductor movements, which occur at a rate of 1 to 4 per second. These adductor movements may interfere with inspiration by producing complete adduction before inhalation is completed.

4. Medicosurgical management of myoclonus is nonspecific.

5. Voice therapy management of myoclonus is generally unnecessary because myoclonic jerks of the larynx typically go unnoticed in contextual speech. Myoclonic episodes will be most noticeable during sustained vocal activity, such as singing.

D. Dysphonia associated with Gilles de la Tourette's syndrome consists of brief episodes of uncontrolled, abnormal speech production due to rapid, tic-like movements and involuntary vocalization. The movements (tics) observed in Tourette's syndrome are quick, coordinated, and repetitive, in contrast to the irregular, nonrepetitive movements that are characteristic of chorea. The onset of this disorder is insidious, and the disorder follows a waxing and waning course (Lechtenberg, 1982).

1. Though the **etiology** of Tourette's syndrome is unknown, it is currently considered a neurological movement disorder.

2. Symptoms

a. Motor speech symptoms of Tourette's syndrome are unremarkable.

b. Associated confirmatory symptoms

(1) The initial symptom of Tourette's syndrome is a single tic, usually involving the eye. The tics are generally first noted before 18 years of age (Shapiro, Shapiro, & Wayne, 1973; Tourette Syndrome Foundation of Canada, 1999). As the disorder progresses, the tics are characterized by various involuntary movements, including kicking, biting, squatting, and scratching or touching different parts of the body.

(2) **Dysfluency, throat clearing, and coprolalia** (the uncontrolled use of obscene language, which is used without any provocation) develop as the disorder progresses.

(3) In later stages, massive involuntary contractions of limb and trunk muscles may cause bizarre movements and inappropriate noises.

(4) Echolalia may be demonstrated.

3. **Differential diagnosis of Tourette's syndrome** is difficult, as the characteristic movements and sounds of the disease often overlap with appropriate cultural behaviors. Clinical evidence suggests that the administration of methylphenidate hydrochloride (Ritalin) to children with previously hidden cases of Tourette's syndrome can temporarily exacerbate the symptoms, thus facilitating correct diagnosis.

4. **Laryngoscopic findings**

   a. The vocal folds appear to be structurally normal.

   b. Normal bilateral abduction and adduction of the vocal folds are observed.

5. **Medicosurgical management.** Haloperidol (Haldol) has been used, but its frequent side effects have limited its success (Abuzzahab & Anderson, 1974). Pimozide (Orap) and clonidine (Catapres) have also been used to control the tics and abnormal movements of Tourette's syndrome (Vogel & Carter, 1995).

6. **Voice therapy management.** The value of voice therapy for the dysphonia resulting from Tourette's syndrome is questionable. Treatment with medication generally controls the phonatory symptoms.

E. Dysphonia associated with athetosis. Athetosis is a rare movement disorder characterized by involuntary, unpatterned, and arhythmic wriggling and writhing movements of the head, neck, torso, and extremities. These movements are overlaid on and interfere with voluntary body movements. Because erratic choreiform components are frequently associated with athetosis, the term choreoathetosis is often used to describe the neuromuscular symptoms (Helme, 1982).

1. **Etiology.** Athetosis may be congenital or acquired, or it can be a clinical symptom of a form of Wilson's disease that occurs in children. At one time a common cause of athetosis was hyperbilirubinemia (kernicterus), which damaged the basal ganglia and cerebral cortex and resulted in mental retardation and cerebral palsy with choreoathetosis (Reeves, 1981). Today's medical and technical advances have significantly reduced the incidence of kernicterus from hyperbilirubinemia. Kernicterus is completely preventable if jaundice is treated promptly (Pershyn, 1999).

   a. The **congenital form of athetosis** is a type of cerebral palsy that can be caused by trauma or anoxia in the perinatal period.

b. Athetosis acquired at a later age may be attributable to the following:

(1) Neuronal degenerative disease

(2) Encephalitis

(3) Cerebral arteriosclerosis

(4) Hyperthyroidism (Fischbeek & Layzer, 1979)

2. **Symptoms**

a. **Motor speech symptoms** of athetosis are characterized by effects on the following anatomic areas:

(1) **Face and cheeks**

(a) Facial grimaces accompanied by slow, writhing movements of the musculature

(b) Drooling

(c) Reduced ability to puff out the cheeks

(2) **Lips**

(a) Slow and irregular AMRs

(b) Bilateral lip weakness

(c) Articulatory defects

(3) **Mandible.** There are involuntary, slow, writhing movements of the mandible at rest and in motion.

(4) **Tongue**

(a) Slow and irregular AMRs

(b) Bilateral tongue weakness

(c) Articulatory defects

(d) Involuntary, slow, writhing, and random movements of the tongue when the tongue is at rest and in motion

(5) **Larynx**

(a) Hoarse voice quality with the degree of hoarseness varying slowly and continuously

(b) Breathiness

(c) Monopitch and monoloudness

(d) Inappropriate and imprecise stress patterns

(e) Sudden, uncontrolled increases in vocal loudness level

b. **Associated symptoms.** Respiratory anomalies are very common in patients with athetosis and may contribute to the following characteristics (Hardy, 1964; Love, 1992; McDonald & Chance, 1964; Palmer, 1952; Westlake & Rutherford, 1961), which tend to be aggravated by nervousness and tension:

(1) Abdominal breathing, which is normal in infants, is common due to weak flexors of the neck and shoulders.

(2) Breathing rate is typically excessively rapid.

(3) Patients with athetosis tend to experience difficulty in inhaling deeply or controlling a prolonged exhalation.

(4) Diaphragmatic–abdominal and thoracic movements are often antagonistic.

(5) Vital capacity of the lungs appears to be significantly reduced due to incoordination of the respiratory musculature.

(6) Involuntary movements of the respiratory musculature interfere with normal respiration.

3. **Laryngoscopic findings**

   a. The vocal folds appear to be structurally normal.

   b. Normal bilateral abduction and adduction of the vocal folds are observed during nonspeech moments.

4. **Medicosurgical management** of athetosis is nonspecific.

5. **Voice therapy management**

   a. **Prognosis.** Prognosis for improved phonation in patients with athetosis is generally poor. If phonation does improve, it is generally due to improvement in articulation and prosody.

   b. **Management of harshness.** Voice therapy, if attempted for a trial period, generally includes techniques to improve the patient's harsh voice quality, transient breathiness, and strained–strangled phonation. Techniques to assist in improving these aspects of phonation are discussed later in this chapter (see **VII.E.5**).

   c. **Management of respiration.** The use of rhythmic abdominal–diaphragmatic respiration (see **VII.D** in this chapter) and controlled exhalation (see **VII.E.4.c**) should provide improved respiratory support and improved intelligibility.

   d. **Prosodic alterations** associated with athetosis may improve with use of contrastive drills for stress and intonation (see **VII.B**).

   e. **Management of involuntary orofacial movement.** Before attempting articulation therapy, a trial period of therapy should be initiated to evaluate whether involuntary orofacial movements can be inhibited (see **VII.A.4**).

F. **Dysphonia associated with dystonia.** Dystonia is characterized by slow, involuntary movements and severe postural deformities resulting from fixed muscle contractions. Dystonic movements and dystonic posturing may affect only one part of the body (focal or segmental dystonia) or they may develop into a more generalized form that affects the entire body (dystonia musculorum deformans).

Hyperkinetic dysarthria is a common symptom in approximately 50% of patients with the more generalized forms of dystonia and in nearly 100% of patients with a form of dystonia called **tardive dyskinesia** (Wiederholt, 1982). Tardive dyskinesia is a specific dystonia that appears following long-term use of neuroleptic drugs (Crane, 1980; Portnoy, 1979; Wolf, Santana, & Thorpy, 1979). It is characterized by irregular mouthing movements.

1. **Etiology**

   a. **Dystonia** results from damage to the extrapyramidal system, secondary to (Wiederholt, 1982):

   (1) Encephalitis

   (2) Degenerative basal ganglia diseases

   (3) Trauma

   (4) Intoxication

   (5) Unknown causes

   b. **Tardive dyskinesia** develops from disordered basal ganglia function following long-term use of neuroleptic drugs. Tardive dyskinesia is most commonly caused by the long-term use of neuroleptic drugs, particularly those that block dopamine production. Patients with Parkinson's disease may develop dyskinesias following high doses of levodopa (Vogel & Carter, 1995). Piperazine, phenothiazines, and butyrophenones are also likely to cause tardive dyskinesia (Lechtenberg, 1982).

2. **Symptoms**

   a. **General neuromuscular symptoms.** The neuromuscular characteristics of dystonia predominantly affect the muscles of the torso, neck, and proximal limbs (Darley et al., 1975). With focal dystonia, the symptoms are confined to a specific region of the body.

   Tardive dyskinesia is characterized primarily by abnormal movements affecting the mouth, such as lip, tongue, and mandible protrusion (Freedman, 1973). One of the first symptoms to develop in this dyskinesia is a writhing motion of the tongue on the floor of the mouth (Marsden et al., 1975). In the later stages of tardive dyskinesia, the trunk and limb muscles also become involved.

   b. **Motor speech symptoms** of the dysarthria associated with dystonia are characterized by effects on the following anatomic areas (Darley et al., 1975):

   (1) **Lips**

       (a) Abnormal movements

           (i)   Inappropriate lip rounding

           (ii) Inappropriate pursing movements

           (iii) Inappropriate protrusion movements

           (iv) Inappropriate lateralization movements

      (b) Slow and irregular AMRs

      (c) Articulatory defects

  (2) Mandible

      (a) Slow elevation and depression

      (b) Slow and irregular lateral movements of the mandible

  (3) Tongue

      (a) Appears structurally normal

      (b) The following abnormal tongue movements can be observed at rest and during speech:

        (i) Protrusion

        (ii) Rotation

        (iii) Lateralization

      (c) Slow and irregular AMRs

      (d) Articulatory defects

  (4) Larynx

      (a) Intermittent harsh, strained–strangled phonation

      (b) Transient breathiness

      (c) Limited pitch and loudness ranges

      (d) Inappropriate variations in loudness

      (e) Inappropriate and imprecise patterns of stress

      (f) Sudden, forced inspirations and expirations

c. Associated symptoms

  (1) Neuromuscular symptoms

      (a) Sustained, involuntary, writhing movements predominantly affecting the muscles of the trunk, head, neck, and proximal extremities

      (b) Variable muscle tone, fluctuating between hypertonic and hypotonic conditions

      (c) General slowness of movement

      (d) Dysphagia in approximately 20% of patients (Musson, 1998; Wiederholt, 1982)

  (2) Dysarthric symptoms (Aronson, 1980)

      (a) Markedly imprecise articulation

      (b) Disturbances of speech due to the patient's attempts to prevent a momentary breakdown of speech. Such disturbances of speech are as follows:

> **(i)** Prolonged intervals between words or syllables
>
> **(ii)** Variable rate of speech
>
> **(iii)** Inappropriate silences
>
> **(iv)** Prolonged phonemes
>
> **(v)** Short phrases

3. **Laryngoscopic findings**

   a. The vocal folds appear to be structurally normal.

   b. Normal bilateral abduction and adduction of the vocal folds are observed.

4. **Medicosurgical management.** No consistently effective therapy has been found, although many drugs have been tried. Management of the dystonias is highly individualized and depends on the type of dystonia. Severe dystonia may be eliminated through surgery of the thalamus, which is known as a thalamotomy (Young & Delwaide, 1981). Other dystonias may be managed through surgery directed at the globus pallidus, which is known as a pallidotomy (Dystonia Medical Research Foundation, 1999).

5. **Voice therapy management**

   a. Prognosis for improved phonation in patients with dystonia is usually poor. The tide-like ebb and flow of the laryngeal spasms and uncontrollable pitch changes associated with dystonia do not respond well to symptomatic voice therapy. A combination of voice therapy, pharmacological, and surgical treatments may be required (Zraick & LaPointe, 1997). If improvement does occur, it generally has less effect on overall intelligibility than on specific articulatory and prosodic elements.

   b. Management of involuntary orofacial movement. Before attempting articulation therapy with the patient, the clinician should initiate a trial period of therapy to evaluate whether involuntary orofacial movements can be inhibited (see **VII.A.4** later in this chapter).

G. **Essential tremor** is a finely oscillating tremor that appears in normal individuals. It may appear as familial tremor, which is an autosomal dominant inherited form, or it may occur idiopathically, in which case it is called essential tremor (Newman & Ramadan, 1998). The rate of the tremor, which only appears with movement, is 5 to 12 cycles per second. Severity of the tremor is aggravated by stress, whereas alcohol can significantly reduce or eliminate the tremor. Phenobarbital and Valium can limit the tremor. Current treatment includes beta blockers such as propranolol, or anticonvulsants such as primidone (Newman & Ramadan, 1998).

Essential tremor is one of the most commonly occurring movement abnormalities (Wiederholt, 1982). It has an estimated incidence of over 400 per 100,000 people (Haerer, Anderson, & Schoenberg, 1982). Although it may start at any age, it is most common in 30- to 50-year-old patients. Tremors of the head and voice (essential voice tremor) are common. Essential voice tremor results in a dysphonia characterized by quavering intonation or voice arrest.

1. **Etiology.** Essential voice tremor results idiopathically or from an involuntary, benign, hereditary tremor of the larynx. Neither the gene for the familial form nor the site of lesion have been identified.

2. **Symptoms**

    a. **Motor speech symptoms** of essential voice tremor are characterized by effects on the following anatomic areas:

    (1) **Lips**

        (a) The lips generally appear to be structurally and functionally normal.

        (b) A **lip tremor,** which is synchronous with the laryngeal tremor, may be present.

    (2) **Mandible**

        (a) The mandible generally appears to be structurally and functionally normal.

        (b) A **mandibular tremor,** which is synchronous with the laryngeal tremor, may be present.

    (3) **Velopharyngeal mechanism**

        (a) The velopharyngeal mechanism generally appears to be structurally and functionally normal.

        (b) A **soft palate tremor,** which is synchronous with the laryngeal and pharyngeal tremors, may be present.

    (4) **Tongue**

        (a) The tongue appears structurally normal in the at-rest position.

        (b) During sustained phonation, a **tongue tremor,** which is synchronous with the laryngeal tremor, may be observed.

    (5) **Larynx**

        (a) **Quavering intonation** is heard due to a 5- to 12-cycles-per-second rhythmic alteration of vocal pitch and loudness (Brown & Simonson, 1963; Critchley, 1949).

        (b) **Voice arrests** characterized by visible, vertical oscillations of the larynx will occur (Darley et al., 1975). The voice arrest occurs at the apex of the oscillation, when the larynx assumes its highest position in the neck.

        These periods of voice arrest are frequently misdiagnosed as the voice arrests and laryngeal spasms that are typical of adductor spasmodic dysphonia (Aronson, Brown, Litin, & Pearson, 1968b) (see Chap. 6, **IV**). However, the voice arrests associated with essential voice tremor are more regular than the voice arrests and laryngeal spasms of adductor spasmodic dysphonia (Aronson & Hartman, 1981).

    b. Associated symptoms. Articulation is generally unaffected, although incoordinated, irregular articulatory breakdowns may occur.

    3. Differential diagnosis. Essential voice tremor should be differentiated from tremors associated with parkinsonism, thyrotoxicosis, anxiety, and cerebellar disease (Brown & Simonson, 1963). Essential voice tremor is faster, is not present at rest, and is not accompanied by other neurologic symptoms other than unilateral or bilateral head or hand tremors (Wiederholt, 1982).

    4. Laryngoscopic findings

        a. The vocal folds appear to be structurally normal.

        b. Abductor and adductor oscillations that are synchronous with the voice tremor occur.

        c. Vertical oscillations of the larynx may be observed, with the patient experiencing voice arrest at the apex of the oscillation.

    5. Medicosurgical management of essential voice tremor, until recently, had been limited in reducing the tremor, although propranolol hydrochloride (Inderal), an antiarrhythmic agent that acts as a beta-blocker (Asperheim & Eisenhauer, 1977), had been tried (Tolosa & Loewenson, 1975). Current treatment includes the use of beta-blockers such as propranolol, or anticonvulsants such as primidone (Newman & Ramadan, 1998). The tremor, which can be reduced in amplitude but not frequency, is rarely eliminated completely.

    6. Voice therapy management. Because most patients with mild to moderate essential voice tremor are intelligible, the prognosis for intelligible speech is good. Symptomatic voice therapy has not been shown to be effective in reducing the voice tremor.

V. Dysphonias Associated with Dysarthrias of Multiple Motor Systems. Some dysphonias are a component of a mixed flaccid-spastic-ataxic-hypokinetic dysarthria. However, the degree to which the various flaccid, spastic, ataxic, and hypokinetic symptoms contribute to the dysarthria depends upon the nature of each particular disease. As a result, the dysphonia associated with these dysarthrias may exhibit characteristics running the gamut from flaccidity to spasticity to ataxia to hypotonicity.

    A. Dysphonia associated with the mixed flaccid-spastic dysarthria of amyotrophic lateral sclerosis. Amyotrophic lateral sclerosis (ALS, sometimes called Lou Gehrig's disease) is a progressive, degenerative, debilitating disease of the anterior horn cells, cranial nerve motor nuclei, and the corticobulbar and corticospinal tracts, resulting in a mixed dysarthria. A related condition (sometimes described as a form of ALS) affects only the lower motor neurons of speech and swallowing. This form is known as progressive bulbar palsy. The dysphonia component of ALS may have both spastic and flaccid characteristics. The disease begins in middle to late life, with the median age of onset in the mid-50s. The disease is more common in males than in females (Newman & Ramadan, 1998). The disease is inevitably fatal, with an average life expectancy of less than 3 years from the time of diagnosis.

The primary characteristics of ALS are wasting and weakening of muscles due to bulbar muscular involvement; spasticity and hyperreflexia may appear as a result of damage to upper motor neurons (Brooke, 1977). Pseudobulbar affect may be noted, with forced laughing and inappropriate crying (see **II.B.2.c** earlier in this chapter). On occasion, extrapyramidal tremor and rigidity may be noted.

Once the initial symptoms have appeared, the disease progresses within weeks or months to involve all muscles of the body. The patient is usually confined to a wheelchair within 12 to 18 months and bedridden and unable to move or talk as the disease progresses. Death occurs, on average, in less than 3 years after onset of symptoms. However, approximately 10% of patients may survive 10 to 20 years (Vogel & Carter, 1995).

1. **Etiology.** Most cases of ALS appear sporadically and without known cause; however, the generally accepted theory is that a viral agent is the cause. In Guam, where there is a very high incidence of ALS, it has been speculated that a plant toxin may be associated with development of the disease (Vogel & Carter, 1995). A small percentage of cases is thought to be hereditary.

2. **Symptoms**

   a. **Motor speech symptoms.** Because the effects of either the spastic or the flaccid dysarthria may predominate at any one time in a given patient, the effects of the disease are nearly impossible to predict for the individual patient. The following motor speech symptoms of the mixed flaccid-spastic dysarthria of ALS may appear with varying degrees of severity in any individual patient (Aronson, 1980; Brooke, 1977; Carrow, Rivera, Mauldin, & Shamblin, 1974):

      (1) The **face,** with the exception of the eyes, may exhibit slight muscular weakness.

      (2) **Lips**

         (a) Reduced lip strength

         (b) Significantly reduced AMRs

      (3) **Mandible**

         (a) Reduced mandibular strength

         (b) Reduced AMRs

      (4) **Velopharyngeal mechanism**

         (a) Possible asymmetric soft palate elevation

         (b) Reduced posterior pharyngeal wall movement

         (c) Hyperactive palatopharyngeal gag reflex

         (d) Hypernasality and nasal emission may be heard if palatal weakness is present.

      (5) **Tongue**

(a) The tongue may be abnormally small and have scalloped edges due to atrophy.

(b) Tongue fasciculations may be noted.

(c) Tongue movements are slow and stiff and accompanied by a synkinetic movement of the mandible.

(d) AMRs for speech and nonspeech movements are reduced.

(6) **Larynx**

(a) If the larynx is affected primarily by **spastic components,** the following effects will be heard (Aronson, 1980; Carrow et al., 1974):

(i) Strained–strangled phonation

(ii) Hoarse or harsh vocal quality

(iii) "Wet" or "gurgly" voice sounds due to an accumulation of saliva on the vocal folds and in the pyriform sinuses as a result of a reduction in the frequency and strength of swallowing.

(b) If the larynx is affected primarily by **flaccid components,** the following effects will be noted:

(i) Breathiness

(ii) Low vocal pitch

(iii) Restricted pitch and loudness ranges

(iv) Inhalatory stridor is possible, but will usually occur only in more severe cases.

(v) "Mushy" cough

(c) Some patients have a hyperactive cough reflex, which can be triggered by simply talking or breathing cold air (Brooke, 1977).

b. **Associated symptoms**

(1) Articulation is characterized by the following:

(a) Imprecise production of consonants

(b) Slow speaking rate

(2) Flaccid paralysis symptoms are frequently noted in the patient's limbs.

(3) Pseudobulbar crying and laughing (see **II.B.2.c**)

(4) Frequent arousals from sleep and nightmares due to mild anoxia are common in the latter stages of the disorder.

3. **Laryngoscopic findings**

a. The vocal folds appear to be structurally normal.

b. Spastic laryngeal components may result in bilateral hyperadduction of the folds; however, unilateral hyperadduction may also occur.

c. Flaccid laryngeal components may result in reduced range of abductor and adductor movements.

4. **Medicosurgical management** of ALS is generally nonspecific because there is no treatment that alters the course of the disease. A combination of medications may be needed, including neurotransmitters and medications to manage symptoms such as spasticity. Supportive devices (e.g., walkers, wheelchairs, braces) may be used to keep the patient mobile for as long as possible. A portable suction device may be required to prevent the problems created by the pooling of saliva in the pharynx. Because of patients' difficulties with swallowing solid foods, blended foods may be necessary. Psychological and family counseling for terminal illness may be required.

5. **Voice therapy management**

   a. The clinician should be prepared to offer **emotional support** after the patient with ALS has been informed that treatment will not reverse or arrest the effects of the disease.

   b. Therapy to **improve velopharyngeal valving or a palatal lift prosthesis** may be indicated to improve VP closure.

   c. The clinician should implement functional treatment procedures designed to heighten **auditory, proprioceptive, kinesthetic, and tactile feedback** for the purpose of temporarily offsetting the progressive effects of the disease. The clinician should also work with the patient's family and friends to identify strategies to prolong functional communication as long as possible. A voice amplifier may be needed as the disease progresses.

   d. **Nonvocal communication aids** are a necessity in the final stages of the disorder, because the patient becomes aphonic due to progressive bulbar weakness.

B. **Dysphonia associated with the mixed dysarthria of multiple sclerosis.** Multiple sclerosis (MS) is a demyelinating disease characterized by variable-sized plaques of demyelinization. These plaques can occur anywhere in the white matter of the central nervous system (CNS); peripheral nerves are not affected (Reeves, 1981). A prominent characteristic of MS is fluctuations in its clinical course. Neuromuscular deficits may last for hours or days, stabilize for 1 to 2 weeks, and then remit slowly over the next 1 to 6 weeks (Reeves, 1981). As the lesions accumulate, the remissions become less complete and are of shorter duration.

MS may result in a dysarthria of multiple motor systems, depending on the individual patient's specific pattern of neurologic involvement. When the dysphonia associated with MS does occur, it may exhibit characteristics of ataxic or spastic involvement.

Onset of MS generally occurs around age 30, but never before age 10 and rarely after age 50. The disease occurs more frequently in women by a ratio of about 3:2 (National Multiple Sclerosis Society, 1998; Romine, 1982). The average length of survival after initial diagnosis is approximately 15 to 20 years. Features of the disease used to confirm a medical diagnosis of multiple sclerosis include well-defined exacerbation and remission of symptoms that follow an overall progressive course and multiple lesions in the white matter of the central nervous system.

1. The **etiology** of MS is unknown; however, it is now generally accepted that MS is an autoimmune disorder in which an abnormal immune response is directed against the central nervous system (National Multiple Sclerosis Society, 1998).

2. **Symptoms**

   a. **General neuromuscular symptoms.** The nature of the neurologic deficits of MS depends on the location and the size of the demyelinating plaques. No two patients are exactly alike. The general features of the neurologic deficit can include the following (Romine, 1982):

      (1) Muscular weakness and spasticity due to corticospinal tract lesions

      (2) Spasticity of lower extremities accompanied by painful flexor spasms

      (3) Gait and limb ataxia

      (4) Hyperreflexia

      (5) Hemiparesis

      (6) Paraparesis

      (7) Quadraparesis

      (8) Monoparesis

   b. **Motor speech symptoms** of the mixed ataxic-spastic dysarthria of multiple sclerosis are characterized by effects on the following anatomic areas:

      (1) **Lips**

         (a) The lips appear to be structurally normal.

         (b) AMRs are slow.

      (2) **Mandible**

         (a) The mandible appears to be structurally normal.

         (b) AMRs are slow.

      (3) **Velopharyngeal mechanism**

         (a) The soft palate elevates symmetrically and completely during sustained vowel production.

         (b) The ability to impound intraoral air is unaffected.

         (c) Hypernasality and nasal emission are often present.

      (4) **Larynx**

(a) Sustained phonation of vowels may be severely reduced due to poor respiratory patterns or inappropriate laryngeal movement.

(b) Reduced pitch and loudness ranges are common.

(c) A harsh voice quality may be heard.

c. **Associated symptoms**

(1) Articulation errors

(2) Neuromuscular coordination for respiration is adversely affected.

(3) Below average vital capacity due to neuromuscular complications

(4) Nystagmus

d. **Dysarthric symptoms.** The dysarthria associated with multiple sclerosis is characterized by both spastic and ataxic neurologic features. Approximately 60% of patients will have essentially normal speech, and 10% to 15% will have only minimal speech problems (Case, 1996). The severity of the dysarthria is related to the severity of neurologic involvement. The most prominent speech deviations are as follows (Darley et al., 1975):

(1) Inappropriate loudness levels

(2) Harsh voice quality

(3) Articulatory defects

(4) Prosodic alterations

3. **Laryngoscopic findings**

a. The vocal folds appear to be structurally normal.

b. Normal bilateral abduction and adduction of the vocal folds are observed.

4. **Medicosurgical management** of MS generally includes the use of adrenocorticotropic hormone (ACTH) or corticosteroids to shorten the duration of acute exacerbations; however, no medical treatment currently available has been found to significantly alter the course of the disease. More recent treatments include administration of high doses of beta interferon, which appears to actually decrease the demyelinating activity, and oral administration of bovine myelin, which appears to stimulate remission and prevent exacerbation (National Multiple Sclerosis Society, 1998; Vogel & Carter, 1995). Anecdotal reports have suggested that remission of symptoms may occur through use of bee venom therapy (BVT). Patients voluntarily self-inflict multiple honeybee stings on a several-time-per-week schedule. Clinical trials are now underway to investigate the efficacy of BVT (Norris, 1998).

5. **Voice therapy management**

a. **Timing of management.** Because periods of exacerbation and remission of symptoms are a primary characteristic of multiple sclerosis, voice therapy will be most effective during a period of remission.

b. **Prognosis** for significant improvement in a short period of time is good if the patient experiences no intellectual decline.

c. **Presenting symptoms.** Movement disorders and the acoustic characteristics of the voice vary according to whether upper motor neurons, lower motor neurons, or the cerebellum are involved.

d. **Management of loudness.** Respiration training may be used to increase loudness (see **VII.D** in this chapter). Further increases in loudness may be obtained through the cautious application of vocal fold hyperadduction with controlled exhalation (see **VII.E.4**) and the use of increased mouth opening (see **VII.E.2.b**).

e. **Management of prosodic alterations** associated with multiple sclerosis should include contrastive drills for stress and intonation (see **VII.B**).

f. **Management of pitch range.** The restricted pitch range characteristic of the dysphonia of multiple sclerosis does not generally affect the patient's intelligibility. If the pitch of the patient's voice is judged to need improvement, techniques for increasing pitch range (see Chap. 5, **III.D.3**) may be attempted for a trial period.

C. **Dysphonia associated with the mixed ataxic-hypokinetic-spastic dysarthria of Wilson's disease.** Wilson's disease (progressive lenticular degeneration or hepatolenticular degeneration) often results in a mixed ataxic-hypokinetic-spastic dysarthria with a dysphonic component. Other signs of CNS involvement include dysphagia, tremors, dystonia, rigidity, and emotional lability (Helme, 1982). Onset of the disease is generally between the ages of 10 and 40 (Haymaker & Schiller, 1969), and death from hepatic failure occurs within 2 to 3 years of onset unless the disease is treated (Trauner, 1982). The disease affects approximately one in 30,000 persons (American Liver Foundation, 1997).

1. **Etiology.** Wilson's disease results from inadequate processing of dietary copper due to a rare, inherited autosomal recessive disorder. Deposits of copper occur most frequently in the brain and liver.

2. **Symptoms**

a. **General neuromuscular symptoms**

(1) **Emotional lability and severe depression** are sometimes the initial symptoms, although most patients are seen initially because of liver disease.

(2) **Parkinson-like symptoms** are a prominent early sign and they remain throughout the course of the disorder if untreated (Berry, Darley, Aronson, & Goldstein, 1974).

(3) A **tremor,** which is both a resting and kinetic tremor, is present (Helme, 1982). The tremor usually involves the arms, but may extend to the head and tongue.

(4) **Choreoathetoid movements** may be present in all limbs (Cartwright, 1978).

(5) **Dystonic posturing and spasticity** are late-appearing symptoms (Cartwright, 1978).

b. **Motor speech symptoms** of the mixed dysarthria of Wilson's disease are characterized by effects on the following anatomic areas:

(1) **Face**

(a) The face appears to be structurally normal in the **earlier stages** of the disease.

(b) A rigid, mask-like appearance of the face is present in **advanced stages** of the disease.

(2) **Lips**

(a) At rest, the lips appear to be structurally normal.

(b) AMRs are slow.

(c) There is restricted range of movement due to spasticity and rigidity.

(3) **Mandible**

(a) AMRs are slow.

(b) There is restricted range of movement due to spasticity and rigidity

(4) **Velopharyngeal mechanism**

(a) The soft palate elevates symmetrically during sustained vowel phonation. Range and speed of movement of the soft palate may be reduced due to spasticity and rigidity.

(b) Hypernasality is heard due to incoordination or spasticity and rigidity.

(5) Larynx

(a) Reduced range of vocal pitch and loudness

(b) Low pitch

(c) Harsh voice quality

c. **Associated symptoms**

(1) **Progressive liver disease**

(2) **Kayser-Fleischer rings** of the cornea (gray-green to red-gold pigmented rings at the outer margin of the cornea) due to depositing of excess copper

(3) Increased pigmentation over the anterior portion of the lower legs (Lechtenberg, 1982)

(4) Transverse bluish-green lines may appear across the fingernails (Lechtenberg, 1982)

(5) Occasional **renal dysfunction**

(6) Typical **characteristics of the disease in younger patients** include rapid progression of the following (Helme, 1982):

(a) Athetosis

(b) Rigidity

(c) Dystonia

(d) Myoclonus

d. **Dysarthric symptoms.** Speech symptoms of the mixed ataxic-hypokinetic-spastic dysarthria associated with Wilson's disease include the following (Darley et al., 1975):

(1) Reduced stress

(2) Monopitch

(3) Monoloudness

(4) Imprecise consonants

(5) Irregular articulatory breakdowns, as in ataxic dysarthria

(6) Hypernasality, as in spastic dysarthria

(7) Inappropriate silences, as in hypokinetic dysarthria

3. **Laryngoscopic findings**

a. The vocal folds appear to be structurally normal.

b. Bilateral hyperadduction of the folds occurs during phonation.

4. **Medicosurgical management** of Wilson's disease is successful if treatment is initiated promptly. With treatment, neurologic symptoms improve, the corneal rings disappear, and progressive hepatic destruction is halted. The disease is frequently managed with the following (Berry, Aronson, Darley, & Goldstein, 1974; Vogel & Carter, 1995):

a. **Chemotherapeutic treatment** with D-penicillamine has been the most frequently used pharmacologic approach. More recently the U.S. Food and Drug Administration (FDA) has approved zinc acetate (Galzin). The zinc acetate appears to deplete accumulated copper and also prevents its reaccumulation (Wilson's Disease Association International, 1998).

b. **Reduced intake** of dietary copper.

c. Patients with severe liver damage may require a **liver transplant.**

5. **Voice therapy management**

a. **Prognosis.** The client with Wilson's disease should be advised that strict adherence to the prescribed dietary and drug regimens often reverses many symptoms of the dysarthria. While intelligibility significantly improves after a 36-month regimen of dietary and chemical therapeutics, the following features may still need voice therapy management (Berry, Aronson, et al., 1974):

(1) Harsh voice quality

(2) Hypernasality

(3) Low vocal pitch

b. **Voice therapy.** The clinician should initiate a trial period of voice therapy using the following procedures:

(1) The patient's harsh voice quality can be managed by using techniques of breathy phonatory onset (see Chap. 5, **III.D.2.c**).

(2) Hypernasality due to muscular incoordination or weakness may be managed through the use of a palatal lift prosthesis (see **VII.C.3.a** later in this chapter), visual feedback devices (see **VII.C.2**), and techniques designed to decrease the amount of perceived hypernasality (see Chap. 9, **I.D.8**). If the soft palate is extremely spastic or rigid, management with a palatal lift prosthesis is contraindicated.

(3) Management of an abnormally low vocal pitch may be facilitated through pitch elevation techniques (see Chap. 5, **III.D.2**).

VI. **Dysphonias Associated with Neurologic Loss of Planned, Volitional Control of Phonation.** Dysphonias can occur due to a loss of volitional control of phonation. These dysphonias are neurologic, not psychologic, in origin.

A. **Dysphonia associated with apraxia of phonation. Apraxia** of speech is characterized by disrupted motor speech programming, which results in abnormal voice, respiration, and articulation. There is no paresis or paralysis of the musculature. Apraxia of phonation may be just one component of a more generalized apraxia of speech. Aphasia and dysarthria often occur in conjunction with apraxia.

1. **Etiology.** Apraxia results from a lesion that disconnects Broca's area from the motor association area responsible for organizing intentional actions, often a cerebrovascular accident (CVA).

2. **Symptoms**

a. **Motor speech symptoms** of apraxia are characterized by effects on the following anatomic areas:

(1) **Lips**

(a) Irregular voluntary movements

(b) Slow sequential motion rates (SMRs)

(c) Articulatory defects in which the errors are highly inconsistent; most errors resemble the target sound, and there are predictable error patterns (Brookshire, 1997).

(2) **Tongue**

(a) The tongue appears to be structurally normal.

(b) Irregular voluntary movements

(c) Slow SMRs

         (d) Articulatory defects (the errors are highly inconsistent)

    (3) Larynx

         (a) Apraxic phonation and respiration can occur as one of the three basic clinical scenarios that can result from an inability to recall neuromuscular integration for respiration and phonation. The three different possible clinical pictures are the following (Aronson, 1980):

            (i) Complete aphonia with no movement of the articulators

            (ii) Phonatory whisper with articulatory movement

            (iii) No voluntary or imitative respiration (although reflexive respiration is unaffected) with articulatory movement

         (b) The **ability to cough** when commanded to do so may be impaired, although the patient is able to cough reflexively.

    b. Associated symptoms

         (1) Motor programming for articulation is often impaired and is characterized by:

            (a) **Impaired phoneme production,** which occurs in the context of slow, labored speech

            (b) High frequency occurrence of **substituted** rather than distorted consonants that are seen in dysarthria

            (c) *Marked* **inconsistency in the production of phonemes**

            (d) Errors resemble the target sound

            (e) Predictable patterns of error (Brookshire, 1997)

         (2) Stutter-like blocks or hesitations are often apparent in the speech of patients with apraxia as they attempt through trial and error to coordinate the muscles for accurate speech production.

3. Laryngoscopic findings

    a. The vocal folds appear to be structurally normal.

    b. Normal bilateral abduction and adduction of the vocal folds are observed during reflexive activity (coughing or throat clearing).

    c. Incoordinated movement of the vocal folds may be observed during volitional activity (phonation).

4. Medicosurgical management for apraxia is nonspecific and is related to the neurologic problem that caused the apraxia, as in, for example, CVA.

5. Voice therapy management. The patient's intelligibility will depend on the severity of the effects of the apraxia upon the articulators.

    a. Muscle strengthening is contraindicated because neurologic deficits in motor programming, not deficits in muscle strength or endurance, account for the apraxic symptoms (Rosenbek, 1978).

b. Voice therapy management program. The voice therapy program of choice is one that emphasizes reeducation or reintegration of the functions of respiration and phonation.

   (1) Using motor learning principles, instruct the patient to cough or clear the throat upon command.

   (2) Then instruct the patient to extend coughing or throat clearing into a relaxed, sustained hum.

   (3) Have the patient try to shape the hum into various vowels.

   (4) Finally, help the patient shape the vowel productions into syllables, words, phrases, and sentences.

B. Dysphonia associated with akinetic mutism. The mutism resulting from extensive cerebral and brainstem lesions is referred to as **akinetic mutism.** It is a subacute or chronic state of altered consciousness in which the patient appears intermittently alert but is not responsive due to a variety of types of cerebral lesions (Dirckx, 1997). With this syndrome, the patient exhibits little or no interaction with his or her surroundings (Gelenberg, 1976). This condition has been noted in patients with Pick's disease and Alzheimer's disease.

1. Etiology. Akinetic mutism results from deep, widespread cerebral and brainstem lesions, which can be caused by the following (Klee, 1961):

   a. Anoxia

   b. Metabolic diseases

   c. Subdural hematomas with compressions

   d. Cerebrovascular accidents

   e. Tumors

2. Symptoms

   a. Motor speech symptoms of akinetic mutism are unremarkable.

   b. Associated confirmatory symptoms

   (1) The akinetically mute patient (Aronson, 1980; Cairns, Oldfield, Pennybacker, & Whitteridge, 1941):

   (a) Fails to respond to questions or comments unless he or she is prodded.

   (b) Is alert, has eyes open, yet tends to look away from others.

   (c) Performs few if any voluntary movements.

   (d) May exhibit sucking movements.

   (2) When the patient with akinetic mutism does speak, the voice is usually normal.

   (3) When voice function begins to return, usually after a long latency period, the patient often speaks:

   (a) In monosyllabic words or short phrases.

      (b) In a monotone voice.

    The mutism may return for intervals of minutes or months.

  3. Laryngoscopic findings

    a. The vocal folds appear to be structurally normal.

    b. Normal bilateral abduction and adduction of the vocal folds are observed.

  4. Voice therapy management. Prognosis for return of phonatory function in the patient with akinetic mutism is guarded. Return of function is generally varied and can occur within days or months. Symptomatic voice therapy is contraindicated.

VII. Therapy Procedures for Speech Rehabilitation. Because the term **dysarthria** implies that all aspects of speech production—respiration, phonation, resonation, and articulation—may be disrupted, the selection of management techniques for speech rehabilitation depends on the specific set of neuromuscular and speech symptoms each patient presents. The effect that any one or a combination of the techniques has on improving the dysarthria is dependent on many factors, such as the severity of neuromuscular involvement and the patient's ability to compensate, whether or not the neuromuscular disorder is progressive, how early in the course of the disorder therapy is started, the level of patient motivation, and the patient's skill at using the techniques effectively and efficiently.

Although each of the dysarthrias that has been discussed often has dysphonia as a component characteristic, it is usually imprecise articulation and disturbed prosody that contribute most to the patient's difficulty with intelligibility and ultimately to his or her ability to communicate effectively. Therefore, articulation and prosody should probably receive the initial thrust of therapy, with vocal rehabilitation being considered secondarily. There are, however, dysarthrias in which the dysphonia is so severe that the greatest improvement in overall intelligibility is most easily obtained by focusing therapy primarily on phonatory rehabilitation.

With the loss of normal neuromuscular function, the patient loses the ability to produce speech quickly and automatically. Therefore, regardless of which therapy technique is being used, the patient has to understand that what was once automatic will now require conscious and deliberate effort. As a result, it is imperative that the patient be taught to draw upon every type of sensory feedback system available (visiual, tactile, auditory, kinesthetic, and proprioceptive) for the purpose of monitoring all speech productions.

With most dysarthrias, neuromuscular dysfunction results in slowed and weakened movement of all speech muscles. Because muscular movement is slowed, the patient requires more time for speech production than was required before the dysarthria. Therefore, the patient's former rate of speech (in which several syllables per second were generated) will be reduced to a slower, syllable-by-syllable pace. The utterance of an unintelligible phrase at a normal rate is not communicative if the listener is unable to decipher the patient's message. Some patients can adopt this new manner of speaking quite easily; for others, it may require considerably more adjustment.

  A. Articulation. Because disorders of articulation have the highest incidence in the various dysarthrias and because articulatory precision is so closely related to intelligibility, articulation therapy must be considered in managing patients with dysarthria. The patient's intelligibility and articulatory accuracy can usually be increased by the following measures (Darley et al., 1975):

1. A patient should **speak slowly** enough to enable the tongue to make full excursions to all points within the oral cavity. However, many patients are unable to move the tongue through its full range due to neuromuscular involvement, even though a reduced speaking rate allows adequate time.

2. A **syllable-by-syllable manner of speaking,** in which every syllable is produced individually and with the greatest accuracy possible, is used. Syllable-by-syllable speech may sound unnatural, but Yorkston, Hammen, Beukelman, and Traynor (1990) argued that dysarthric speech may already be so unnatural sounding that rate change will not have a further detrimental effect. The loss of naturalness is overcome if the patient's speech is functionally intelligible.

3. **Overexaggerated productions of consonants,** which help to prevent the patient from omitting medial or final consonants, may be useful (Farmakides & Boone, 1960).

4. With disorders such as chorea, athetosis, and dystonia, involuntary movements of the articulators (i.e., lips, tongue, and mandible) are usually so severe that they seriously interfere with the patient's ability to perform the fine and precise movements required for articulation. As a result, a trial period of articulation therapy should be initiated to evaluate whether use of an acrylic bite block to **inhibit involuntary mandibular movement** will increase the patient's intelligibility sufficiently to warrant its use.

   The **bite block** is a custom-fitted acrylic or hard rubber device that is held between the upper and lower teeth (Yorkston, Beukelman, & Bell, 1988), with a string attached to prevent it from accidentally being swallowed. Some improvement in articulation should result because the bite block effectively eliminates interfering movements of the mandible, and with the mandible firmly fixed, there is usually a reduction in extraneous lip and tongue movements as well, which also results in greater articulatory precision.

B. **Prosody.** Disturbed prosody in patients with dysarthria results when neuromuscular defects cause the patient to use abnormal stress and intonation patterns. Typically, the patient tends to eliminate stress on words that should be stressed and to emphasize the less important words or syllables. Similarly, the meaning of the patient's utterances can be obscured by abnormal pitch contours, such as a disturbed monopitch/monoloudness pattern or a pattern in which the melodic intonation is erratic.

   Because word or syllable emphasis and phrase or sentence meaning are signaled by subtle variations in intensity, pitch, and duration, management techniques for disturbed prosody must incorporate opportunities for the patient to practice these variations singly and in combination. Because neuromuscular symptoms vary among individuals, some patients may find that they are able to vary only a single parameter of production (e.g., pitch, loudness, or duration) in order to signal changes in word stress or meaning. Other patients may be able to use two or all three parameters efficiently and effectively. The following exercises may be used to improve stress and intonation patterns in the patient with dysarthria:

1. **Contrastive stress drills** consist of stimulus materials in which a difference in meaning depends on which word or group of words in the phrase or sentence receives primary stress.

   a. Notice in the following examples (adapted from Fairbanks, 1960; Rosenbek & LaPointe, 1978) how stress differences for words or groups of words relate to the expression of meaning.

      (1) *Bob* hit Sam.

      Bob hit *Sam.*

      (2) *Now* they will go away.

      Now, they will go *away.*

      (3) *Why,* Bill?

      Why, *Bill!*

      (4) Blue bird.

      Bluebird.

      (5) Light house.

      Lighthouse.

      (6) It's the *new* fad.

      It's *the* new fad.

   b. Stress variations such as the following examples (adapted from Fairbanks, 1960; Rosenbek & LaPointe, 1978) can be introduced by asking the patient various questions in the following manner:

      (1) Stimulus: Bob hit Sam.

      Question 1: Who did Bob hit?

      Response: Bob hit *Sam.*

      Question 2: What did Bob do?

      Response: Bob *hit* Sam.

      (2) Stimulus: I almost hit the dog.

      Question 1: What did you almost hit?

      Response: I almost hit the *dog.*

      Question 2: What did you almost do to the dog?

      Response: I almost *hit* the dog.

2. **Contrastive intonation contour drills** can be used to improve the patient's dysarthric intonation patterns. Arrows should be used to indicate

to the patient whether the contour should be an upward intonation (↑) or a downward intonation (↓) (Fairbanks, 1960).

a. Use drills, such as the following, which consist of stimuli that differ in meaning because of a **difference in intonation contour.**

(1) I want it (↓).

I want it (↑)?

(2) Feed the cat tomorrow (↓).

Feed the cat tomorrow (↑)?

b. Contrastive intonation drills, such as the following, can be used to **differentiate between a general request for information and confirmation or denial of a statement.**

(1) She isn't eating the cake, is she (↑)?

She isn't eating the cake, is she (↓)?

(2) They are funny, aren't they (↑)?

They are funny, aren't they (↓)?

c. Contrastive intonation drills, such as the following, can be used to **differentiate between an inclusive yes/no or a choice.**

(1) Are you eating cake (↑) or ice cream (↑)?

Are you eating cake (↑) or ice cream (↓)?

(2) Will they buy the dog (↑) or the cat (↑)?

Will they buy the dog (↑) or the cat (↓)?

C. Resonance. The most frequent forms of disturbed resonance in the various dysarthrias are hypernasality and nasal emission. The hypernasality is a result of the neurologic involvement of the palatopharyngeal muscles rather than anatomic tissue deficiencies (e.g., cleft palate).

1. Blowing, sucking, and swallowing exercises. During the last several decades, speech–language pathologists have attempted to use therapy methods that use blowing, sucking, and swallowing activities to indirectly increase palatal movement; however, the results have been disappointing. Even direct palatal stimulation (Cole, 1971) has been found to be generally ineffective, except perhaps for those patients with a very slight velopharyngeal gap. Current research indicates that voice therapy is not beneficial in the presence of physiologic velopharyngeal dysfunction (Morris, 1991).

2. Use of feedback devices to develop awareness of hypernasality.

a. Perhaps one of the best methods for reducing hypernasality is to teach the patient to identify hypernasal resonance, and consequently to make whatever modifications of the vocal tract are necessary to reduce the hypernasality. Although identification of hypernasality is primarily dependent on the patient's ability to develop auditory skills for monitoring speech, a feedback device, called See-Scape, that utilizes visual feedback paired with auditory feedback has been found to be an effective method for teaching the patient to accurately detect the presence of hypernasality in his or her voice (Shprintzen, McCall, & Skolnick, 1975). See Appendix C for more information on the See-Scape.

The device consists of a clear plastic cylinder containing a styrofoam piston. One end of the cylinder is fitted with a piece of flexible tubing. The other end of the tubing is fitted with a glass or plastic "nasal olive" designed to fit into and occlude the patient's nostril. The device is very sensitive to any airflow, which causes the styrofoam piston to rise when it enters the cylinder. The patient can be taught to monitor his or her degree of velopharyngeal closure during speech or related nonspeech activities by watching the rise and fall of the piston.

Instruct the patient to place the nasal olive, which is attached at one end of the tubing, into his or her nostril. While watching the styrofoam piston in the cylinder, the patient should either begin blowing air out of the mouth or begin whistling and then adding phonation so that either blowing and phonation or whistling and phonation occur simultaneously. Once the patient can perform one of these tasks with no nasal emission, he or she should be instructed to eliminate the blowing or whistling and in its place produce a continuous, nonnasal phonation (perhaps the vowel /i/ or /u/). While visually monitoring the height of the piston, the patient should progress through productions of CVC words (single syllable words consisting of a prevocalic consonant [C], a vowel [V], and a postvocalic consonant [C] containing no nasal consonants) to productions of short nonnasal sentences.

b. A feedback device such as the Nasometer (Kay Elemetrics, 1993; see also Appendix C) can also be used. During speech, the Nasometer uses both oral and nasal microphones to extract an acoustic ratio that is termed nasalance. The Nasometer is an excellent method for reducing hypernasality because it provides instantaneous feedback regarding the oral/nasal ratio of speech (see Chap. 3, **The Voice Evaluation Process, VIII.C.2**), and normative nasalance data are available for standardized passages (Kay Elemetrics, 1993). The patient should be encouraged to pay particular attention to how it feels to produce nonnasalized speech. After being repeatedly presented with instrumental feedback of productions with a good oral/nasal ratio, most patients begin to develop an internal model of what is required to speak with oral resonance.

3. **Techniques to decrease hypernasality.** There are also several techniques the patient may use to decrease the amount of perceived hypernasality, even though the actual velopharyngeal gap remains the same. These techniques, which are designed to facilitate the development of orally, rather than nasally, directed airflow, are presented in Chapter 9 (see **I.D.8** in that chapter). If these techniques are ineffective in sufficiently reducing the hypernasality, the patient may require the following management techniques, which are designed to actually decrease the velopharyngeal gap:

a. **Palatal lift prosthesis.** The clinician should assess the severity of hypernasality during the general voice evaluation (see Chap. 3, **The**

Voice Evaluation Process, VIII.C.2.a) as it relates to the patient's overall intelligibility. If hypernasality is consistent and moderately severe or severe, a palatal lift prosthesis may result in improved intelligibility (Gibbons & Bloomer, 1958; Gonzalez & Aronson, 1970; Hardy, Netsell, Schweiger, & Morris, 1969; Johns & Salyer, 1978; Kerman, Singer, & Davidoff, 1973). A palatal lift prosthesis is a speech appliance that is designed to assist in velopharyngeal closure by elevating the paralyzed velum higher into the nasopharynx so that the lateral pharyngeal walls can approximate it. The palatal lift prosthesis consists of a maxillary section and the palatal lift section. The speech–language pathologist and the prosthodontist work together to determne the final shape of the palatal lift to obtain the best possible resonance and speech (Light, 1995). The prosthesis is usually attached to the patient's teeth and has a support that extends posteriorly into the oropharynx for the purpose of maintaining the paralyzed soft palate in the elevated position.

(1) When velopharyngeal incompetency is due to neurogenic rather than anatomic insufficiency, a palatal lift prosthesis is often preferred and gives better speech results than surgery (Gonzalez & Aronson, 1970; Hardy et al., 1969). After a patient has been fitted with the appliance, it may be necessary to instruct the patient in the use of increased auditory, tactile, and kinesthetic feedback (see **VII.C.2** in this chapter and Chap. 8, **I.D.2**) for the purpose of eliminating any residual hypernasality and nasal emission. The speech–language pathologist plays the primary role in determining the adequacy of the prosthesis for speech. The prosthodontist constructs the maxillary and palatal portions of the prosthesis and modifies the size and length of the nasopharyngeal bulb section based on the speech–language pathologist's recommendations (Light, 1995). Together they determine the size and shape of the prosthetic device that will provide the best speech.

(2) A palatal lift prosthesis may be used temporarily as a component in a treatment program that will eventually culminate in surgical correction of hypernasality.

(3) Use of a palatal lift prosthesis has been shown to occasionally stimulate or increase posterior and lateral pharyngeal wall movement (Aronson, 1980; Blakely, 1960, 1964; Hardy et al., 1969; Lange & Kipfmueller, 1969).

(4) **Edentulous patients** may benefit from a palatal lift prosthesis (Lawshe, Hardy, Schweiger, & Van Allen, 1971), although difficulties in retention of the prosthesis may occur (Gonzalez & Aronson, 1970; Rosenbek & LaPointe, 1978).

b. A procedure described by Kuehn (1997) and Tomes, Kuehn, and Peterson-Falzone (1997) may actually cause a **physiologic change by strengthening the muscles of velopharyngeal closure** in normal speakers and those with repaired cleft palates. The procedure involves use of continuous positive airway pressure (CPAP). CPAP is routinely used in treating patients with obstructive sleep apnea. A CPAP facial mask covers the patient's nose, and positive air pressure is delivered to the nasal passages while the patient produces words and sentences specifically designed for their nasal content. Preliminary results suggest that muscles of the velopharyngeal region may work harder in response to the presence of added air resistance (the CPAP treatment) in the nasal passages. Future investigations may determine if CPAP is beneficial for individuals with neurologically based velopharyngeal insufficiency.

    c. **Surgical management.** Hypernasality may be surgically reduced with the use of a posterior pharyngeal flap procedure. In this procedure, a flap of tissue is elevated from the posterior pharyngeal wall, sutured to the velum, and used as a structure against which the lateral walls of the pharynx can approximate and thus accomplish velopharyngeal closure.

D. Respiration. Although respiration may be adversely affected in the various dysarthrias, the effect upon speech production is usually negligible. When a patient appears to have an insufficient supply of air for speech production, inefficient glottal functioning, rather than a reduced vital capacity, is usually responsible for the quick expenditure of air during speech.

In those rare instances in which a patient is using a method of respiration that is extremely inefficient for most communication purposes, the clinician may find that the abdominal–diaphragmatic method of respiration is useful (Stemple et al., 1995). Procedures to be used in instructing the patient in use of this method are as follows (Cooper, 1977):

1. Place the patient in a supine position and instruct him or her to place one hand on the chest and the other on the abdomen directly under the rib cage. Then instruct the patient to inhale easily through the nose and exhale through the mouth while concentrating on the gentle rise and fall of the abdomen, but not the chest. The patient should then be instructed to relax the abdominal muscles deliberately while inhaling and to contract the muscles while exhaling.

2. Instruct the patient to inhale and exhale only through the mouth, using the same techniques described above.

3. Repeat steps 1 and 2, first with the patient sitting and then with the patient standing.

E. Phonation. The dysarthrias usually have an associated dysphonia in which the pitch, loudness, and quality characteristics of the voice may be aberrant. Although a reduction of the effects of the dysphonia has a moderate influence on the patient's intelligibility, establishment of an effective and efficient method of producing voice can eliminate much of the struggle with speech that dysarthric patients frequently experience.

1. Techniques for modification of pitch. The techniques that are recommended for modification of the pitch problems associated with the various neurogenic and myopathic dysphonias include the following:

    a. **Techniques for a too-high or too-low habitual pitch level** (see Chap. 5, **III.D.3**).

    b. Techniques for limited pitch variability (monopitch) and for **inappropriate intonation contour patterns** (see **VII.B** in this chapter).

    c. Techniques designed primarily for **reduction of hard glottal attack** (e.g., chewing technique and yawn technique), which also assist in normalizing vocal pitch (see Chap. 5, **III.D.2**).

2. **Techniques for modification of loudness.** Patients with dysarthria typically have difficulty with loudness control (excessive loudness or insufficient loudness). They may also have problems with loudness variation (ranging from difficulties in making subtle stress differences to difficulties with unintentional productions of explosive vocalizations). Techniques for modification of loudness problems associated with the neurogenic dysphonias include the following:

    a. Techniques for reduction of excessive overall loudness (see Chap. 5, **III.D.1**).

    b. Technique for increasing overall loudness and improving oral resonance.

        (1) Because use of a minimal oral opening while speaking effectively limits the natural egress of the airstream, use of a mouth posture that is as open as possible will not only cause the voice to be louder but will also increase oral resonance (see Chap. 9, **I.D.8.b**).

        (2) The Lee Silverman Voice Treatment program (LSVT) (see **IV.A.5. b.1**) (Ramig, Countryman, Thompson, & Horii, 1995) has been shown to be an effective treatment approach for increasing loudness and improving overall intelligibility. Ramig (1996) reported that LSVT may be beneficial to patients with a variety of neurological diseases. LSVT has been used with patients with multiple sclerosis, with closed head injuries, and with a small group of poststroke patients. Ramig reported that while the etiologies for these patients are different, voice and loudness work may improve overall speech production in each case.

    c. Techniques for inappropriate stress patterns (see **VII.B**).

    d. Techniques designed for reduction of hard glottal attack (e.g., chant talk technique, chewing technique, and yawn technique), which also assist in normalizing vocal loudness (see Chap. 5, **III.D.2**; for confidential voice technique, see Chap. 5, **III.B.4**).

3. **Techniques for modification of quality.** Vocal quality characteristics of the dysphonias associated with dysarthrias result primarily from one of two conditions of the patient's larynx. In the first condition, the larynx provides only a limited degree of resistance to the outgoing airstream because of vocal fold paralysis or paresis. This condition results in a breathy voice quality and reduced vocal loudness; consequently, management techniques that are designed to elicit firmer glottal closure are used to eliminate the breathiness and to increase loudness. In the second condition, the neuromuscular effects of the dysarthria cause the larynx to be essentially pinched-off, with airflow through the larynx being greatly reduced as a consequence. Because

of this condition of laryngeal stricture, the patient usually struggles in an effort to force the outgoing airstream through the hyperadducted glottis, resulting in harshness, hoarseness, or a strained–strangled voice quality. Voice therapy procedures designed to reduce laryngeal tension and to increase airflow through the larynx are utilized to eliminate these vocal qualities.

4. **Techniques for achieving firmer vocal fold approximation** include methods by which the patient uses forceful vocal fold adduction in combination with a process of controlled exhalation (Rosenbek & LaPointe, 1978) to produce the best possible voice. These techniques should be used with extreme caution because of their potential to encourage patients to develop harmful hyperfunctional behaviors. Holistic, whole-body approaches such as vocal function exercise are likely to be more effective in achieving healthy vocal fold approximation (see Chapter 5 for vocal function exercises). Generally, the behavioral techniques described in the following passages will be more successful if the patient has at least "light touch" vocal fold contact on stroboscopic exam. If the patient's paralysis is such that there is no vocal fold contact at all, benefit from behavioral therapy is less likely (Stemple et al., 1995). These techniques are as follows:

a. One method by which **forceful vocal fold adduction** can be accomplished is through use of the **glottal effort closure reflex,** which accompanies forceful muscular activities such as lifting, pulling and pushing, grunting, and laughing. Pushing the hands or arms against resistance typically elicits this reflexive glottal closure.

Stressful muscular activity (e.g., pushing, lifting) should only be used for a short period of time and only for the purpose of demonstrating to the patient the quality of voice that is possible when hyperadduction is used. Once the patient has an awareness of the feel of firmer glottal closure, he or she should be encouraged to attempt to improve vowel productions without the use of these stressful effort techniques. Then have the patient progress from vowels to syllables, words, sentences, and finally to conversation.

The clinician must remember that continual use of stressful effort techniques to elicit vocal fold hyperadduction may lead to excessive musculoskeletal tension in the patient. Forceful adduction activities must be monitored carefully to prevent development of effortful vocal habits and vocal tension dysphonia. If this occurs, progressive muscle relaxation techniques (see Chap. 5, **III.D.2**) can be used to eliminate the tension and restore the normal balance of muscle forces.

If a patient has insufficient arm strength, it will be impossible for him or her to perform many of the stressful effort techniques. Patients confined to a bed or a wheelchair can be instructed to bear down on the bed or on the arms of the wheelchair with their hands or arms. It may be necessary to actually take the patient's hands and encourage pushing. As the patient bears down, he or she should be instructed to sustain /a/ for as long as possible. If improved loudness and quality of voice result, the patient can then be instructed to increase the muscle tension in the speech musculature without the use of pushing.

Overhead slings may also be fitted to hospital beds or wheelchairs to provide a fixed handle that the patient can pull. The pulling movement usually results in a stronger glottal closure and thus improves the loudness and quality of phonation.

When a voice therapy program utilizing increased respiratory support coupled with hyperadduction of the intact vocal fold is implemented, improved phonation will usually result in patients with difficulties related to vocal fold adduction. The following stressful muscular activities can be used to elicit glottal hyperadduction:

(1) Seat the patient in a chair and instruct him or her to firmly grasp each side of the chair seat. The patient should push downward with the arms and hands and attempt to lift his or her body out of the chair while sustaining a vowel. Pushing should elicit increased glottal closure and result in a louder and better quality production of the vowel.

(2) A second method of eliciting firmer glottal closure (Froeschels, Kastein, & Weiss, 1955) instructs the patient to link the fingers of both hands together. The patient should then lift his or her arms to the level of the clavicle and pull the hands in opposite directions while sustaining a vowel. Improved quality and loudness of the sustained vowel should be the result.

(3) Another technique for obtaining improved phonation through use of the glottal effort closure reflex includes pushing against heavy furniture or walls or lifting heavy objects while simultaneously sustaining a vowel. When using this technique, care must be taken to instruct the patient in proper lifting or pushing in order protect the patient's back.

b. A second technique for obtaining **forceful adduction** is the deliberate use of a **hard glottal attack,** which can be used alone or in conjunction with reflexive glottal closure. The patient should be instructed to either cough or clear the throat while attempting to sustain a vowel. This increased effort in phonating vowels (hard glottal attack) usually results in improved loudness and vocal quality. Once the patient has succeeded in producing vowels with improved loudness and vocal quality, she or he can progress from syllables, words, and sentences to actual conversation.

c. Techniques of vocal fold hyperadduction should be used in combination with **controlled expiration** (a predictable, consistent, low-pressure exhalation over time). The techniques for instructing the patient in the use of controlled expiration are as follows (Rosenbek & LaPointe, 1978):

(1) First, demonstrate controlled expiration for the patient as follows. Take a quick inspiration and then begin sustaining the vowel /a/ for approximately 20 seconds while maintaining a constant loudness level. Instruct the patient to attempt the same type of sustained

phonation expiration for just 5 seconds at first. On repeated trials there should be graduated increases in the length of time the vowel is sustained. A stopwatch and an audiocasette recorder can be used to monitor the sustained vowel productions. Intensity and quality of production should be constant. Developing the ability to control productions is more important than developing the ability to produce them for longer than 30 seconds.

(2) After the patient has developed maximum sustained expiration on sustained vowel productions, instruct her or him to use this increased respiratory ability to progress to syllables, short phrases, and sentences.

(3) Monitor the patient continuously to prevent the patient from developing abnormal patterns of respiration.

d. Vocal function exercises (VFE) (including associated **frontal focus** and **dynamic range exercises**) are intended for **any disorders** that result in weakness, strain, or imbalance in the vocal mechanism. The VFE program (Stemple et al., 1995; see Chap. 5, **III.C.1**) treats the voice as a physical therapist might treat any other muscle group of the body. Weak laryngeal muscles may benefit from VFE, which seeks to restore balance to the entire mechanism through stretching, strengthening, and balancing the *entire* system (Breiss, 1959). The VFE program may be beneficial for patients with neurogenic dysphonias that have a component of hypoadduction or hyperadduction, because the VFE system simply seeks to balance the mechanism and help the patient produce the best possible voice.

5. Techniques for reducing laryngeal hyperadduction and increasing airflow through the larynx include the following:

a. Chewing technique (see Chap. 5, **III.D.2.b**)

b. Prephonation airflow techniques (see Chap. 5, **III.D.2.c**)

c. Chant talk technique (see Chap. 5, **III.D.2.d**)

d. Yawn technique (see Chap. 5, **III.D.2.e**)

e. Instrumentation for visual monitoring (see Chap. 5, **III.D.2.f**)

f. Relaxation techniques (see Chap. 5, **III.D.4**)

g. Larger oral opening (see **VII.E.2.b** in this chapter)

h. Confidential voice technique (Chap. 5, **III.C.4**)

Chapter 9
Disorders of Vocal Resonance

♦ ♦ ♦ ♦ ♦ ♦ ♦ ♦ ♦ ♦ ♦ ♦ ♦ ♦ ♦ ♦ ♦ ♦ ♦ ♦

Vocal resonance in normal voices is produced by a relatively relaxed vocal tract that is only intermittently coupled to the nasal cavity for production of the nasal consonants /m/, /n/, and /ŋ/. For all other English speech sounds, oral rather than nasal resonance is required.

Vocal resonance is affected primarily by the size, shape, and resiliency of the vocal tract, especially the pharynx, and also by the postures assumed by the various articulators, especially the tongue. Any deviation from the usual size, shape, and resiliency of the vocal tract and any abnormal articulatory postures usually result in faulty vocal resonance.

Improper functioning of the velopharyngeal mechanism can result in hypernasality, hyponasality, or assimilative nasality. In hypernasality, the velum is inappropriately lowered or open during production of vowels and nonnasal consonants, whereas in hyponasality the velum is inappropriately elevated or closed during production of nasal consonants. In assimilative nasality, the velum functions too slowly during connected speech. In addition, abnormal tongue postures can increase nasality or contribute to the production of a voice that is either weak and lacking in resonance or that has a muffled-sounding, cul-de-sac resonance quality. Another form of deviant vocal resonance, the very sharp-sounding, carnival ringmaster-like resonance called stridency, is produced when the size of the pharynx is reduced and the muscular walls of the pharynx become tightly contracted.

I. **Hypernasality** is defined as excessive nasal resonance during the production of vowels and vocalic consonants. Within limits, a certain amount of nasality is always present in the production of most vowels due to the effects of coarticulation (see **III** in this chapter). This limited amount of nasality commonly goes unnoticed and is accepted as normal by listeners. In some regional dialects, an even greater degree of nasality is common and accepted as normal, whereas in other dialect regions an increased amount of nasality is not easily accepted and may be objectionable to most listeners. The point at which a certain degree of nasality begins to become unpleasant for a listener appears to vary somewhat from person to person and from one dialect region to another.

A. **Etiology.** Physiologically, hypernasality results from failure of the velopharyngeal port (VP) to attain and maintain sufficient closure to prevent nasal resonance of sounds that are normally resonated orally. Therefore, hypernasality may be related to both organic and nonorganic etiologies that adversely affect velopharyngeal closure and consequently prevent the effective separation of the oral cavity from the nasal cavity.

1. **Organic bases for hypernasality.** The organic causes of hypernasality are related to either (1) structural deficits that preclude closure of the velopharyngeal port or (2) neurologic deficits that adversely affect movement of the structures involved in VP closure. Some of the most common structural and neurologic deficits that impair VP closure and result in hypernasality include the following:

   a. **Structural deficits**

      (1) Unrepaired cleft palate

      (2) Short velar length

      (3) Unusually deep pharynx

      (4) Surgical trauma to the velum

      (5) Accidental injury to the velum

      (6) Children with adenotonsillar structures that are miminally adequate (termed **borderline inadequate**) may develop hypernasality following adenoidectomy because of an inability to compensate for lost tissue. Witzel, Rich, Margar-Bacal, and Cox (1986) estimated that 1 in 1,500 children may develop persistent hypernasality following adenoidectomy.

   b. **Neurologic deficits**

      (1) Myasthenia gravis

      (2) Adductor paralysis with associated palatopharyngeal paralysis

      (3) Muscular dystrophy

      (4) Spastic dysarthria

2. **Nonorganic bases for hypernasality.** Nonorganic hypernasality exists, by definition, in the absence of any structural or neurologic deficit that could adversely affect VP closure. Some of the more typical causes of nonorganic hypernasality are as follows:

   a. Some patients may choose to imitate a hypernasal voice quality and consequently develop it as their habitual voice type.

   b. Some children may use a hypernasal voice quality following a tonsillectomy in an effort to avoid pain by limiting movement of the velopharyngeal port.

B. **Symptoms.** The voice of the patient with hypernasality is characterized by the presence of increased nasal resonance for vowels and vowel-like consonants. Patients who have nonorganic hypernasality usually have no associated symptoms. However, patients who present hypernasality as a consequence of structural or neurologic impairment to the velopharyngeal port usually demonstrate a variety of problems related to the inability to effect sufficient velopharyngeal closure. In addition to increased nasal resonance, these patients may also have faulty articulation, nasal emission that is occasionally accompanied by facial grimacing, and laryngeal abnormalities related to misuse of vocal loudness.

1. **Misarticulations.** Patients with inadequate velopharyngeal closure often develop related articulation errors. Because inadequate VP closure can limit the patient's ability to develop and maintain adequate intraoral air pressure, those consonants that require the greatest amount of intraoral air pressure for their production are frequently misarticulated. Fricative consonants require the highest intraoral air pressures for production, followed by the affricate and stop consonants. Patients with VP closure problems frequently develop compensatory articulatory placements for production of these high pressure consonants.

   There is nothing to prevent patients with impaired VP closure from developing nonorganic articulation errors in addition to those errors that develop consequent to the inability to maintain sufficient intraoral pressure. These nonorganic misarticulations typically are simple phonemic substitution errors. Misarticulations related to VP closure difficulties, on the other hand, are generally characterized by errors of omission and by unusual substitutions, such as the substitution of pharyngeal fricatives for oral fricatives and glottal stops for oral stops. Patients' intelligibility problems can range from relatively minor to severe, depending on the degree of hypernasality and number of pressure consonants and nonorganic misarticulations.

2. **Nasal emission.** Patients with VP closure inadequacy may also produce nasally emitted snorts. **Snorting,** which is produced by a short rush of air from the nose, usually occurs when the patient attempts to articulate pressure consonants, particularly fricatives. Some patients assume unusual facial postures, such as constriction of the nares or grimaces, for the purpose of reducing or eliminating nasal emission of these consonants. Although these various postures may decrease the amount of nasally emitted air, they are nonetheless cosmetically distracting to listeners.

3. **Laryngeal abnormalities related to vocal misuse.** There is an increased incidence of vocal misuse (especially as related to vocal loudness) in patients with inadequate VP closure. Due to the acoustic dampening that occurs when the nasal and oral cavities are coupled, the intensity of the voice of the patient with VP inadequacy is reduced. In order to compensate for this reduced vocal loudness, these patients usually use an increased vocal effort so that a louder voice can be produced. Prolonged use of this increased vocal effort, however, has negative consequences and may result in the development of abuse-related laryngeal lesions (McWilliams, Morris, & Shelton, 1984) (see Chap. 4, **I.C**).

C. **Medicosurgical management.** Medicosurgical techniques are not indicated for the management of patients with nonorganic hypernasality. This type of hypernasality can best be managed through a comprehensive program of speech and voice management.

   Hypernasality that is related to structural and neurologic deficits of the velopharyngeal port, however, usually requires medicosurgical management that focuses on restoring the patient's ability to separate the nasal and oral cavities during speech production. The methods that are typically used to restore the patient's ability to attain VP closure are orthodontic, prosthodontic, or surgical.

1. **Orthodontic and prosthodontic techniques**. Patients who exhibit hypernasality related to structural deficits of the hard and soft palates usually require both orthodontic and prosthodontic management. Orthodontists and prosthodontists can provide valuable assistance in developing the best approach to achieving a nonorganic velopharyngeal closure mechanism.

   a. An **orthodontist** is a specialist who moves misaligned teeth so that normal or near-normal dental development can occur. The orthodontist may also be required to alter a deviated palatal arch so that normal palatal and facial growth may proceed.

   b. A **prosthodontist** is a specialist who constructs various speech appliances or obturators for the purpose of assisting the patient with improved facial cosmetics as well as with improved speech production.

      (1) For patients with **structural problems of VP closure**, a speech prosthesis can be constructed with an acrylic bulb that is positioned in the nasopharynx to reduce nasality and nasal air emission. The speech–language pathologist plays the primary role in determining the adequacy of the prosthesis for speech. The prosthodontist constructs the maxillary and palatal portions of the prosthesis and modifies the size and length of the nasopharyngeal bulb section based on the speech–language pathologist's recommendations (Light, 1995). Together they determine the size and shape of the prosthetic device that will provide the best speech.

      (2) For patients with **neurologic problems of VP closure** (e.g., an immobile velum due to any of several dysarthrias), a palatal lift prosthesis can be constructed that will actually lift the soft palate into a higher position so that the posterior and lateral pharyngeal walls can approximate the artificially elevated velum and effect velopharyngeal closure (see Chap. 8, **VII.C.3.a**). The palatal lift prosthesis consists of a maxillary section and the palatal lift section. Again, the speech–language pathologist and the prosthodontist work together to determine the final shape of the palatal lift to obtain the best possible resonance and speech (Light, 1995).

2. **Surgical techniques.** Surgical techniques are frequently required for management of hypernasality that results from structural inadequacies, such as clefts of the soft and hard palates, submucous clefts, soft palates that are too short, and open fistulas. The surgeon may use one or a combination of the following techniques for achieving a nonorganic velopharyngeal mechanism:

   a. **Primary closure surgery** of the hard and soft palates is done in order to provide the primary division between the oral and nasal cavities. Primary closure surgery may also include techniques that are designed to provide the velum with an adequate length. It is a common practice now to close the soft and hard palates in a single, one-stage procedure. Primary surgeries are usually performed when the infant is between 3 and 18 months of age (Bzoch, 1997).

b. **Pharyngeal flap surgery** is a secondary surgical technique in which the surgeon elevates a mucosal flap from the posterior pharyngeal wall and surgically attaches it to the velum. This structure allows the lateral pharyngeal walls to move medially and thus effect velopharyngeal closure by approximating the surgically created pharyngeal flap. This procedure may be performed if the patient has a velum that does not move well or that is too short to contact the posterior pharyngeal wall (Boone & McFarlane, 1994). The technique is often very effective in reducing hypernasality and nasal emission if preoperative multiview speech videofluoroscopy and fiberoptic nasoendoscopy are used to determine the required width of the pharyngeal flap.

D. **Voice therapy management.** Production of voice without hypernasality can only be achieved if the patient is capable of effecting velopharyngeal closure. Hypernasality cannot be eliminated unless the oral and nasal cavities can be nonorganically separated. For this reason, voice management for hypernasality should be deferred until patients have been evaluated and have received medicosurgical or prosthetic treatment for problems of inadequate velopharyngeal closure.

Because appropriate voice therapy management techniques for nonorganic and structural velopharyngeal dysfunction differ significantly, it is critical that the speech–language pathologist determine whether the etiology of hypernasality is nonorganic or structural. While an oral exam and acoustic and perceptual measures provide valuable information, physiologic insufficiency (structural or neurologic) of the velopharyngeal port for speech must be diagnosed through instrumental means. **Multiview speech videofluoroscopy** and **nasoendoscopy** are the primary instrumental techniques for determining the cause of velopharyngeal insufficiency (Miller, 1998; Williams, Henningsson, & Pegoraro-Krook, 1997). Current data indicate that voice therapy is not beneficial in the presence of physiologic velopharyngeal dysfunction (Morris, 1991). Consequently, if it is determined that the patient has a physiological problem that prevents velopharyngeal closure, voice therapy management is not indicated.

Occasionally, a patient may be inconsistent in being able to effect velopharyngeal closure. For these patients with borderline VP competence, a trial period of therapy for hypernasality will yield information that enables the speech–language pathologist to decide whether medicosurgical management will be required or whether the patient is capable of developing a more consistent ability to effect closure through additional voice therapy. During a trial of voice therapy, special care should be taken to observe the patient to see if he or she exhibits frustration or signs of struggle when attempting to attain VP closure, as these negative experiences might reduce the patient's motivation to undergo the voice therapy that usually follows any corrective medicosurgical procedures. If a patient does not improve after about **12 hours of treatment** (sometimes longer for very young children), then the speech–language pathologist should investigate the possibility of a physiologic deficit (Morris, 1991).

The following **voice therapy techniques** may be used to improve a patient's oral resonance and decrease hypernasality:

1. First, the patient should be given a **detailed explanation of the causes of hypernasality**. Pictures and simple diagrams can be quite effective in assisting the patient to understand how voice problems are related to faulty coupling of the oral and nasal cavities.

2. Since self-monitoring of nasal resonance is eventually required, the patient must learn to recognize hypernasality and distinguish nonnasal from hypernasal productions. Audiocasette recordings of other people's and the patient's own voice can be used to train the patient to discriminate correct (nonnasal) from incorrect (hypernasal) productions.

3. **Speech production exercises** should begin with the patient sustaining different vowels in isolation. Low vowels should be attempted before high vowels. The clinician should provide the patient with immediate verbal feedback regarding which vowels are produced with more hypernasality than others. Practice on sustained vowel productions should continue until the patient is able to produce each of the vowels with full oral resonance. It is particularly important that the patient be asked to feel and remember the difference in feeling between nonnasal and hypernasal productions of vowels.

4. If the patient has difficulty in producing the sustained vowels without nasalization, a **feedback device** such as the Nasometer can be used. During speech, the Nasometer uses both oral and nasal microphones to extract an acoustic ratio that is termed **nasalance.** Normative nasalance data are available for standardized passages (Kay Elemetrics, 1993). The Nasometer is probably the most effective method for reducing hypernasality because it provides instantaneous feedback regarding the oral/nasal ratio of speech (see Chap. 3, **The Voice Evaluation Process, VIII.C.2** and Appendix C). The patient should be encouraged to pay particular attention to how it feels to produce nonnasalized speech. After being repeatedly presented with instrumental feedback of productions with a good oral/nasal ratio, most patients begin to develop an internal model of what is required to speak with oral resonance.

   If the patient has difficulty with nasally emitted sounds during speech, a device such as the See-Scape may be helpful. The See-Scape detects any nasal emission of air during speech through the use of a small float in a clear plastic tube. The See-Scape's nasal tip is placed in the patient's nasal passage; any nasal air emission will cause the float to rise in the plastic tube. The See-Scape feedback serves as a practical assist to the patient's understanding of nasal air emission. See Appendix C for more information on the See-Scape.

5. Once the patient has become proficient at producing various vowels with no hypernasality, his or her practice exercises should begin to include nonnasalized words that incorporate the consonant /h/ paired with various vowels. Practice in producing monosyllablic and bisyllabic words, phrases, sentences, and, finally, conversation should follow.

6. When the patient is able to consistently produce nonnasalized productions of words, he or she should be instructed to produce the practice words in the

old hypernasal manner (**negative practice**) and to pair these attempts with nonnasalized productions of the same words.

7. The previous techniques should be used only with patients who are physiologically capable, if only inconsistently, of effecting velopharyngeal closure. A procedure described by Kuehn (1997) and Tomes, Kuehn, and Peterson-Falzone (1997) may actually cause a physiologic change by strengthening the muscles of velopharyngeal closure. The procedure involves use of **continuous positive airway pressure** (CPAP). CPAP is routinely used in treating patients with obstructive sleep apnea. CPAP research has been performed with patients who have repaired cleft palates with mild to moderate hypernasality. A CPAP facial mask covers the patient's nose, and positive air pressure is delivered to the nasal passages while the patient produces words and sentences specifically designed for their nasal content. Preliminary results suggest that muscles of the velopharyngeal region may work harder in response to the presence of added air resistance (the CPAP treatment) in the nasal passages.

8. Techniques to **reduce the amount of *perceived* hypernasality** (even though these techniques do very little with regard to assisting the patient in achieving tighter velopharyngeal closure) may be effective addendums in a comprehensive voice therapy program designed to reduce hypernasality:

   a. Patients with multiple articulation errors tend to be perceived by listeners as being more hypernasal than are patients with fewer misarticulations. **Improved articulation** frequently results in the patient's speech being perceived by listeners as being less hypernasal, even though the actual degree of hypernasality remains unchanged.

   b. Patients with hypernasality who tend to speak with a restricted oral opening should be encouraged to use a **greater degree of oral opening** when speaking to assist in the reduction of nasal resonance. This technique essentially makes the oral cavity larger in comparison to the nasal cavity, and thus results in greater oral rather than nasal resonance of speech sounds (Boone & McFarlane, 1994).

   c. Improvements in oral resonance for speech may be hampered if the tongue assumes abnormal postures. Some patients with hypernasal resonance assume a high, forward tongue posture. These patients should be taught to shift their tongues posteriorly (see **IV.A** in this chapter) to assist in reducing the amount of perceived hypernasality (Boone, 1983).

   d. Often, the rate at which a patient speaks affects the amount of perceived nasality. Record the patient using an audiocasette recorder while he or she is reading various passages at different rates of speed. Some passages should be read faster and others slower than the patient's normal rate of speaking. If playback and analysis of the recordings indicate a change in perceived hypernasality occurring with a **change in speaking rate**, the patient's speaking rate should be altered to achieve a more acceptable voice production.

   e. Speaking at an inappropriately **high pitch level** can also cause a person with hypernasality to be perceived as being more nasal. Many times the amount of perceived hypernasality can be reduced by directing the patient to develop a habitual pitch level that is nearer the bottom of the patient's pitch range (see Chap. 5, **III.D.3**).

II. **Hyponasality (denasality)** refers to speech productions that are deficient in or totally lacking nasal resonance. Deficient nasal resonance is particularly evident when the nasal consonants /m/, /n/, and /ŋ/ are produced, but it is also detectable in the production of vowels because all of the vowels are normally produced with a slight amount of nasal resonance.

A. **Etiology**

1. **Organic hyponasality.** Hyponasality is almost always an organically based, chronic disorder of resonance resulting from an obstruction in the posterior portion of the nasal passages or nasopharyngeal area. **Organic conditions** that are commonly associated with hyponasality include the following:

   a. Enlarged adenoids

   b. Nasal polyps

   c. Allergies resulting in edema of the nasal membranes

   d. Nasal papilloma

   e. Trauma to the nasal area resulting in nasal spurs or perhaps a deviated septum

   f. Tumors

   g. Mucosal congestion

   h. A high palatal arch, which may decrease the amount of space available for the nasal cavity above it

   i. Excessive velopharyngeal obstruction due to the following (Boone, 1983):

      (1) Construction of a too-wide pharyngeal flap in surgery

      (2) Prosthodontic creation of a too-large obturator bulb

2. **Nonorganic hyponasality.** Although it is uncommon, hyponasality may also be present in a patient on a nonorganic basis. Occasionally a patient continues to use a hyponasal voice even after the organic cause of the hyponasality has been surgically corrected. In other cases, a person chooses to imitate the hyponasal voice quality and develops it as his or her own habitual voice quality.

B. **Symptoms.** The patient who uses a hyponasal voice quality typically substitutes oral cognates for nasally resonated consonants. In addition, vowel sounds are typically perceived as being muted or lacking in brilliance. Patients who speak with a hyponasal resonance pattern are frequently described as sounding as if they have a head cold. Since hyponasality is generally the result of some obstruction of the nasal pathway, it is not uncommon for the hyponasal patient to also be a mouthbreather. This breathing pattern may result in adverse phonatory effects due to drying of the pharyngeal and laryngeal mucosa.

C. Medicosurgical management of hyponasality involves identification and removal of the obstruction that is responsible for the hyponasality.

D. Voice therapy management is usually required only for cases of hyponasality with a nonorganic etiology or for patients who continue to use a hyponasal voice quality following surgery for nasal obstructions. Nasal resonance in patients who exhibit hyponasality due to these etiologies can be increased by using the following procedures:

1. Voice management for hyponasality should begin with activities designed to heighten the patient's awareness of the nasal cavity as a resonator. Prolonged productions of the nasal consonants should be practiced, with particular attention paid to feeling the vibrations of the nasal passage as those consonants are produced. The following steps may be used:

   a. Begin by having the patient hum in isolation each of the nasal consonants: /m/, /n/, and /ŋ/. It may be necessary to use visual aids (see **II.D.2**) to promote airflow through the nasal passage.

   b. After the patient is able to hum the nasal consonants in isolation, each should be hummed and then followed by the production of a vowel.

   c. Next, the patient should be instructed to hum a series of CVC words that contain only nasal consonants (e.g., *mom, Nan, men, name, Ming, numb*). Be sure that the patient produces these words slowly, with particular emphasis on prolonging the nasal consonants.

   d. Next, the patient should practice other words, phrases, and sentences that contain nasal consonants. Careful auditory monitoring and reduction in speaking rate will assist the patient in reducing the hyponasality.

2. Visual aids, such as a mirror or piece of tissue, can be placed under the patient's nose and be used to demonstrate and promote nasal airflow during phonation.

3. Electronic devices that continuously monitor oral/nasal balance can also be used to provide visual feedback concerning the degree of nasal resonance present in words. Patients may find devices that monitor nasal resonance, such as the Nasometer (see **I.D.4** in this chapter), to be invaluable in learning to discern the presence or absence of nasal resonance.

4. Finer auditory discrimination can be developed by having the patient utilize any of the visual aids while producing CVC word pairs that differ only in that the initial or final consonant of one word is a nasal sound and that of the other word is an oral cognate (e.g., *bat–mat, tip–Tim*).

III. Assimilative nasality is characterized by excessive nasal resonance of a vowel when that vowel occurs in the phonetic context of a nasal consonant. This excessive nasalization of the vowel occurs when the velopharyngeal port remains open too long for nasal consonants preceding the affected vowel or opens too early for nasal consonants following the affected vowel.

Assimilative nasality occurs due to a feature of normal speech production called coarticulation. Contrary to first impressions, words are not produced simply by stringing one discrete phoneme after another in sequence. Instead, one speech sound in a sequence tends to influence the manner in which adjacent sounds are produced, and vice versa (coarticulation). Nasal consonants have a particularly strong influence on the production of other sounds. For example, during production of the word *funny,* the following coarticulated sequence occurs: (1) as the lower lip begins to approach the upper teeth, the tongue also maneuvers into a neutral position for production of the vowel; (2) because the velum is the slowest moving of all the articulators, it must start descending during production of the vowel in anticipation of the nasal consonant that is to follow, thus causing the vowel to be slightly nasalized; (3) simultaneous with production of the vowel, the tongue starts moving toward the alveolar ridge for production of /n/; (4) during production of /n/, the velum starts to elevate in anticipation of the nonnasal vowel /ɪ/, which follows; and (5) the vowel /ɪ/ is articulated with a slight nasal resonance because the slow-moving velopharyngeal port is not able to completely close before the vowel is articulated.

Coarticulation influences the manner in which all sounds are produced, but the effects are most noticeable in normal speech when nasal consonants are present. Because the velum is a relatively slow-moving articulator, vowels that are preceded or followed by one of the nasal consonants tend to be nasalized (assimilative nasality). Just as with hypernasality, a certain amount of assimilative nasality goes unnoticed and is accepted as normal by all listeners. An even greater degree of assimilative nasality is common and accepted as normal in some dialect regions, while in other dialect regions increased amounts of this type of nasality are objectionable to listeners. The point at which a certain degree of assimilative nasality becomes unpleasant for the listener is highly variable, just as it is with hypernasality.

Again, it is against this background of variability that the speech–language pathologist must make judgments about whether the degree of assimilative nasality present in a particular speaker is excessive or not. Any assessment of assimilative nasality should consider the standards of the regional dialect, the patient's occupational voice requirements, and the patient's motivations for change.

A. **Etiology.** Assimilative nasality is most commonly nonorganic in origin and results in lack of ability to open or close the velopharyngeal port with enough speed to keep resonance of a nasal consonant from affecting an adjacent vowel. Assimilative nasality may also be associated with neurogenic voice disorders that slow the action of the velum. In consequence, nasal consonant resonance is carried over into articulation of the following vowel, causing the vowel to have a nasal rather than oral resonance.

B. **Symptoms.** Patients with nonorganic assimilative nasality typically demonstrate normal oral resonance for vowels if the stimulus word does not contain any nasal consonants, such as *tap, two, see, tease,* and *sip.* These same patients, however, tend to nasalize the vowel in stimulus words such as *map, new, knee, team,* and *sing.*

C. **Medicosurgical management** of assimilative nasality with a nonorganic origin is contraindicated. There are no medicosurgical techniques available for management of the neurogenic forms of assimilative nasality.

D. **Voice therapy management.** Elimination or reduction of assimilative nasality is difficult. The speech–language pathologist should carefully screen and choose only those patients who are highly motivated to reduce the amount of assimilative nasality in their speech.

The first and one of the most difficult steps in helping a patient to reduce assimilative nasality is getting the patient to the point where nasalized vowels can be discriminated from orally produced vowels. Audiocasette recordings of productions by other speakers with normal resonance and assimilative nasality can be used for comparison with the patient's own speech productions to help facilitate ear training.

Practice drills for the reduction of assimilative nasality have typically used the technique of pairing two similar-sounding words in which a nasal consonant appears in one word and not in the other (e.g., *bad–mad, bed–Ned, top–Tom, Ted–ten*). The vowel in each of the matched words should sound very similar and be produced in a nonnasal manner for each word of the word pair. Continued production practice and listening training using the audiocasette recorder and bisyllabic words, phrases, and sentences will aid the patient in developing better discrimination abilities, which in turn should assist the patient in reducing the amount of assimilative nasality that can be detected.

The Nasometer can be a useful tool in voice therapy for assimilative nasality. The clinician and client can set oral/nasal acoustic ratio goals that progressively lead the client toward productions with greater oral resonance. Again, be cautioned that improvement in assimilative nasality usually only occurs when the client is strongly motivated to improve (Boone & McFarlane, 1994).

IV. **Resonance disorders due to faulty tongue postures** are common. Since acoustic resonance is dependent on the size and shape of the resonator, it stands to reason that any extreme deviation in the size or shape of the vocal tract will result in a noticeable acoustic change. Although the tongue moves to the extreme ends of the oral cavity for the purpose of articulating certain speech sounds, it normally does so on only an intermittent basis and the net result is not an aberrant voice quality.

It is when the tongue begins to assume a more fixed position in the extreme ends of the oral cavity that the resonance characteristics of the voice become noticeably changed. Some patients develop an abnormally anterior tongue posture, which contributes to the production of a weak and muffled vocal resonance quality; other patients develop a deeply retracted, posterior tongue posture, which results in a different but also aberrant acoustic effect. The resultant voice quality depends on the degree to which the tongue deviates from its normal posture and how chronic that posture is.

A. **Abnormally anterior tongue posture (weak or thin vocal resonance).** Certain patients develop a tongue carriage in which the tongue is held in a high and excessively anterior position. This abnormal tongue posture, which produces a weakly resonated voice, is rarely if ever due to organic involvement.

1. **Etiology.** The patient who assumes an extremely high and anterior tongue carriage while speaking does so for nonorganic reasons. Because the resultant voice quality makes the speaker sound weak and immature (what some people call an effeminate voice), there is likely to be a nonorganic explanation for why a patient would elect to use such a voice on either an occasional or permanent basis.

2. **Symptoms.** Because an anterior tongue posture nearly eliminates all of the resonance space anterior to the tongue, the voice sounds very weak and lacking in resonance, particularly for the back vowels. Frequently, patients with this type of tongue posture articulate with a minimal oral opening and with little range of movement of the jaw. Because of the weak oral resonance that results from the anterior tongue carriage and because of the use of restricted oral movement for articulation, the general impression that a listener gets is that this type of speaker is using immature, baby-like speech that is lacking in authority. Often, the speaker's vocal pitch is also elevated slightly, which aids in this perception of vocal immaturity. In some patients, the vocal qualities are present at all times; in others, the vocal qualities are situationally turned on and off.

3. **Medicosurgical management** of the weak resonance that results from an abnormal and excessively anterior tongue posture is contraindicated due to its nonorganic etiology.

4. **Voice therapy management**. Because the tongue has a natural tendency to return to its normal position at rest, abnormal tongue postures can be maintained only with considerable effort. Voice therapy should focus on those techniques that facilitate a more normal tongue posture as the patient speaks. The techniques that follow are useful for establishing a more normal tongue carriage in patients who maintain an abnormally anterior tongue posture:

   a. Begin by explaining to the patient that his or her unusual voice quality is the result of an anterior tongue posture. Use pictures or diagrams to assist the patient in understanding the problem. Contrast productions of weak vocal resonance with productions of efficient vocal resonance, or play back recordings of other speakers who use the anterior tongue posture so the patient can begin to discriminate correct from incorrect productions.

   Be sure to include in the explanation of the problem that in some cultures weak vocal resonance is seen as an effeminate vocal quality; further, there may be negative social consequences associated with such a voice quality. Patients who have been using this voice quality for extended periods of time may find it difficult to accept that there may be negative consequences; accordingly, an informative discussion of the cultural perceptions of this voice quality is recommended.

   b. **Practice exercises** can begin by asking the patient to sustain some back vowels (/u/, /ʊ/ /o/, or /a/) for 5 to 10 seconds while trying to make the vowels sound full and resonant. The patient should continue this sustained vowel practice until the voice quality approximates near efficient oral resonance.

   c. If the patient is not able to produce the back vowels with improved resonance, it may be necessary to try an approach that will automatically posture the tongue in the correct position for efficient resonance. One of the best methods for establishing this type of tongue posture is to use a normal, vegetative function, which puts the vocal tract musculature into a relaxed state. The **chewing technique** (Froeschels, 1952) utilizes the physiology of normal, relaxed chewing to establish a more relaxed vocal tract that is conducive to the production of efficient vocal resonance. An additional benefit of this technique is that it promotes the use of a more open mouth posture in the patient. Because patients who use an anterior tongue carriage also tend to articulate with restricted oral movements, this added benefit of using the chewing approach cannot be overstated. The steps for using the chewing technique to improve muscle balance and tonicity of the vocal tract are discussed earlier in this book (see Chap. 5, **III.C.2.**).

d. After the patient has developed good oral resonance for isolated back-vowel productions, ask him or her to read a list of words that contain back vowels and begin with the velar (or back) consonants /k/ and /g/. The velar consonants tend to facilitate a more posterior carriage of the tongue.

e. When the patient is able to produce these single words successfully with full oral resonance, the practice words should be incorporated into phrases and then into sentences.

f. The excessive tension required to maintain the tongue in an abnormal posture frequently creates excess laryngeal tension that manifests itself as an elevation of vocal pitch. Techniques to lower vocal pitch (see Chap. 5, **III.D.3**) should be used to establish a normal pitch level, which frequently results in the perception of an improvement in vocal resonance.

B. Abnormally posterior tongue posture (cul-de-sac resonance). Another type of resonance disorder results when the tongue is retracted deeply and posteriorly into the pharynx. This abnormal tongue carriage produces a muffled and hollow-sounding type voice with a pharyngeal focus and is referred to as cul-de-sac resonance.

1. Etiology. The cul-de-sac voice occurs when the tongue is deeply retracted into the pharynx, sometimes nearly touching the posterior pharyngeal wall. Although this particular tongue posture and the resultant voice quality usually occur on a nonorganic basis, they are also commonly found in patients with various organic disorders, including deafness, flaccid and spastic dysarthria, athetoid cerebral palsy, and oral apraxia.

2. Symptoms. The cul-de-sac voice sounds muffled and hollow. Because it is produced with the tongue retracted into the pharynx, it lacks full resonance.

3. Medicosurgical management of cul-de-sac resonance is contraindicated.

4. Voice therapy management of cul-de-sac resonance usually is not successful in those patients who have developed a posterior tongue carriage due to neurologic involvement of the articulators (oral apraxia, athetoid cerebral palsy, flaccid and spastic dysarthria). Patients with a cul-de-sac voice that has developed on a nonorganic basis, and to a lesser extent deaf patients, can both benefit from the following therapeutic procedures:

a. First, use diagrams and pictures to explain to the patient how an altered tongue posture affects vocal resonance. Demonstrate the effects of abnormal tongue carriage on voice quality by first speaking with the tongue in the extreme anterior portion of the mouth and then speaking with the tongue deeply retracted into the pharynx.

b. The focus of all therapy techniques for cul-de-sac resonance is to facilitate a more anterior positioning of the tongue. Boone and McFarlane (1994) suggest that this can be done through use of articulation training for tongue–alveolar sounds, which pull the tongue forward. Begin by having the patient whisper a repetitive /ta/, /ta/, /ta/, and then whisper /da/, /sa/, and /za/ in the same way. The patient should be instructed to attend to how the tongue and mouth feel during these productions. Additional practice should involve the consonants /w/, /p/, /b/, /f/, /v/, /ð/ and /θ/ (voiced and unvoiced), and /l/ paired with high front vowels.

c. After the patient is successful with the whispered productions, instruct him or her to begin using a light, easy voice with the practice syllables.

d. Once the patient has become skilled at producing these anteriorly placed syllables, ask the patient to try to produce the same syllables with the old, more posteriorly focused resonance pattern (**negative practice**). Ask the patient to evaluate the differences in how the two types of productions feel. Playback of audiocassette recordings of the patient producing syllables using both methods of production will allow the clinician and patient to critically evaluate the acoustic differences between the old cul-de-sac voice and the more efficient resonatory patterns of the new voice.

e. When the patient is able to produce single words using efficient resonance consistently and successfully, the practice words should be incorporated into phrases and then into sentences.

V. Stridency. Not only are abnormal tongue postures capable of causing changes in the resonance characteristics of the voice by altering the shape of the vocal tract (weak, thin resonance and cul-de-sac resonance), but alterations in the size and resiliency of the pharynx can affect those resonance characteristics as well. Such alterations of the pharynx result in a harsh, carnival ringmaster-like vocal resonance called stridency (Boone, 1983, Boone & McFarlane, 1994). Stridency results when the larynx is elevated (which shortens the length of the pharynx) and the pharyngeal constrictor musculature overcontracts and decreases the length and width of the pharynx (size) as well as increases the reflective properties of the mucosal surface (resiliency).

A. Etiology. The elevated larynx and hypertonic pharynx associated with the strident voice develop on a nonorganic basis. Some individuals may produce this voice purposely for its theatrical effect. Others, however, may develop such a voice quality as a consequence of anxiety and overall body stress.

B. Symptoms. The strident voice has been described as sounding metallic. Often, the terms "tinny" and "brassy" are used as descriptors. The strident voice is the voice of the carnival ringmaster—a voice that tends to accentuate high-frequency acoustic components.

C. Medicosurgical management of stridency is contraindicated due to its nonorganic etiology.

D. Voice therapy management. The primary focus of voice therapy with patients who have a strident voice is to relax the pharyngeal musculature and allow the larynx to descend lower in the neck. The following techniques can be used to promote normal muscle tone in the pharynx and to develop a more normal vocal resonance:

1. Explain to the patient that the goal of therapy is to establish new patterns of relaxed voice production to replace the patterns of vocal tract tension that are associated with the strident voice.

2. Demonstrate for the patient how differences in muscular tension of the vocal tract can affect voice quality. Be sure to compare the hypertension that accompanies strident voice productions with the comparative relaxation during the production of normal vocal resonance.

3. Audiotaped or videotaped examples of other speakers with strident voices and speakers with normal resonance patterns can be played so that the patient can develop discrimination skills for identifying stridency.

4. Use one or a combination of the following techniques to reduce muscle tension in the laryngeal and pharyngeal regions:

   a. The **chewing technique** (see **IV.A.4.c** in this chapter) uses the physiology of chewing to establish a relaxed pharynx, which is conducive to the production of normal vocal resonance. Just as this technique can be used to increase oral opening for patients with anterior tongue carriage, it can also be used to decrease oral constriction in patients with a strident voice.

   b. The **yawn–sigh technique** (see Chap. 5, **III.D.2.b(5)**) uses the normal, vegetative function of yawning to put the vocal tract musculature into a relaxed state prior to phonation.

   c. Relaxation techniques (see Chap. 5, **III.D.2**).

5. Once the patient is able to make vocalized productions using normal resonance consistently, instruct him or her in the use of **negative practice** by directing him or her to alternately produce a word with normal resonance and then a word with stridency. The patient should be especially attentive to how different the two productions feel. Record these contrasting productions and replay them for the purpose of critical evaluation.

6. As with other types of faulty resonance, stridency is often accompanied by an elevation of vocal pitch. Procedures to **establish a lower vocal pitch** may be used. A lower vocal pitch frequently results in a voice that is perceived as being less strident.

Chapter 10
Laryngectomee Rehabilitation

◆ ◆

Total or partial surgical excision of the larynx (laryngectomy) is usually indicated in cases of cancer of the larynx or laryngeal region. Cancers of the head and neck are commonly staged or classified according to a system devised by the American Joint Committee on Cancer (1992). The speech–language pathologist should have a basic understanding of these stages, because the stage of the tumor relates to the success of treatment and thepatient's chance for survival (Benninger & Grywalski, 1998).

Three letters are used in the staging system: **T, N,** and **M. T** stands for **tumor;** that letter is usually followed by a subscript number from 0 through 4, or by the letters **i** and **s. T_0** means that no tumor was found; **T_{is}** means tumor in situ, the earliest identifiable tumor; and **T_1–T_4** indicates the range of tumor sizes, with T_4 being the largest and T_1 the smallest. The next letter is **N.** The N stands for **nodes** or **lymph nodes.** It is assigned numbers from 0 through 3, depending on the presence or absence of tumor cells in lymph nodes in the region around the primary site. The final letter of the staging system is **M,** which stands for **metastasis.** The **M** is assigned numbers 1 or 0, depending on the presence or absence of metastasis of the tumor cells to distance sites. After the **TNM** numbers have been assigned, the tumors are then grouped in stages 0 through IV, with stage I cancers being early neoplasms, and stage IV cancers being advanced (Benninger & Grywalski, 1998; Stemple et al., 1995). Table 10.1 shows this scheme for head and neck cancer tumor staging.

In a total laryngectomy, the entire cartilaginous larynx, all of its intrinsic muscles and membranes, the hyoid bone, and perhaps the upper two or three rings of the trachea are removed. The trachea is then tilted forward and attached to the external neck region just above the notch of the sternum. This external opening, through which the patient must breathe forever, is called a **stoma (tracheostoma).**

For those patients in whom the cancer has spread to the cervical lymph nodes, a surgical procedure called a **radical neck dissection** may be performed on the right, left, or both sides of the neck. During such a procedure, the following structures are typically removed: the sternocleidomastoid muscle, omohyoid muscle, internal jugular vein, spinal accessory nerve (CN XI), and submaxillary salivary gland (Saunders, 1964). When the cancer is even more extensive, any or all of the following structures may also be removed: the external carotid artery, the strap muscles of the neck, the vagus nerve (CN X), the hypoglossal nerve (CN XII), and the lingual branch of the trigeminal nerve (CN V).

The primary and most immediate impact that a laryngectomy has on a patient is the loss of voice for communication purposes. However, removal of the larynx not only deprives the patient of speech, but of the ability to express emotion through the extralinguistic behaviors of laughing or crying. In addition to the loss of voice, physical and

Table 10.1. Summary of System of Staging Head and Neck Cancer Tumors

Stage	Tumors
Stage 0	$T_{is}N_0M_0$
Stage I	$T_1N_0M_0$
Stage II	$T_2N_0M_0$
Stage III	$T_3N_0M_0$ or T_{1-3}, N_1, M_0
Stage IV	T_4, N_{0-1}, M_0; T_{1-4}, N_{2-3}, M_0; T_{1-4}, N_{1-3}, M_1

psychosocial problems associated with the removal of the larynx must be considered in the management of a patient with an excised larynx (laryngectomee).

I. **Preoperative Management.** In the past, the physician had primary responsibility for preoperative orientation of the patient. However, the results of a survey by Salmon (1979) showed that nearly one half of the laryngectomees questioned felt that they had been "poorly prepared" or "not prepared at all" by the preoperative visit with the physician, primarily because the visit tended to focus almost entirely on the surgical procedure. According to the survey, nurses are the professionals who have the most frequent preoperative meetings with the laryngectomee, followed by the speech–language pathologist. Further, respondents to the survey also indicated that they felt that the most important information a patient requires preoperatively concerns (1) ways by which to communicate postoperatively, (2) the prognosis for recovery, and (3) the anatomic and physiologic changes that will result from the surgery.

Although some physicians use nurses to provide preoperative counseling for their laryngectomy patients, most physicians schedule a separate preoperative visit with a speech–language pathologist. The benefits of such a visit, in many cases, can be immeasurable (Stemple et al., 1995).

A. **Advantages of a preoperative visit by a speech–language pathologist and laryngectomee**

1. The primary advantage of a preoperative visit is that it gives the speech–language pathologist the opportunity to **evaluate the preoperative speaking skills of the patient.** During casual conversation, the speech–language pathologist should note the patient's general articulatory proficiency and overall intelligibility. This evaluation will enable the clinician to make a more accurate prognosis regarding the level of intelligibility that can be expected following postsurgical voice training. Other factors related to intelligibility that should be noted during an evaluation of the patient's conversational speech include the following:

   a. Articulation errors

   b. Speaking rate

   c. Dialectal patterns

   d. Degree of oral opening used when speaking

2. A second advantage of a preoperative visit is that the speech–language pathologist is able to provide the patient, the patient's spouse, and other family members with **much needed emotional support and insight into what communications options are available postsurgically.**

   a. The speech–language pathologist can provide the patient and family with a **detailed description of the forthcoming surgery and its consequences.** In many cases, the shock of learning they have cancer of the larynx causes patients to forget many of the details the physician gives them regarding the upcoming surgery, except for the fact that their larynx must be removed. In other cases, the only information the physician has given the patient is that his or her larynx must be removed. If the patient is given more information regarding the upcoming surgery, the patient and his or her family may experience considerably less anxiety, and a more positive and successful communicative atmosphere will be created.

   When the speech–language pathologist visits the patient, a book regarding laryngectomy surgery and laryngectomy problems may be useful. These books might include *Looking Forward . . . A Guidebook for the Laryngectomee* (Keith, 1995), or *Self-Help for the Laryngectomee* (Lauder, 1994). It is possible to provide the patient and his or her family with simplified explanations and drawings that (1) illustrate the structures that will be surgically excised, (2) illustrate why the patient will have to breathe through a hole in his or her neck (stoma) after surgery, and (3) explain alternative methods for postsurgical speech production, including use of an artificial larynx. Figures 10.1A and 10.1B illustrate the course of air flow before and after total laryngectomy, respectively.

   b. The speech–language pathologist is able to **reassure the patient and family that the patient will talk again.** The speech–language pathologist should describe various methods of speaking without a larynx (alaryngeal speech). Included in this description should be discussion of the different techniques of esophageal speech, an explanation of tracheoesophageal speech, as well as a demonstration of one or more artificial larynges. It is important that the patient and family understand that there are several alternatives for restoring the patient's ability to speak and that decisions about which technique will be used is a decision that will be made by the physician and speech–language pathologist following surgery.

3. Another important advantage of the preoperative visit is that the patient and family may be able to **meet and interact with a successfully rehabilitated laryngectomee.** When introducing the accompanying laryngectomee, the speech–language pathologist should be sure to give the laryngectomee's name and occupation and provide a brief biographical sketch so that the patient can get a sense of the normalcy of life that is possible following surgery. The laryngectomee should try to answer the patient's and family's questions and describe how life following the surgery can be nearly identical to life before the surgery. In his book *Laryngectomee Speech and Rehabilitation,* Gardner (1971) has written detailed suggestions as to what might be said to the preoperative patient. This preoperative visit with the

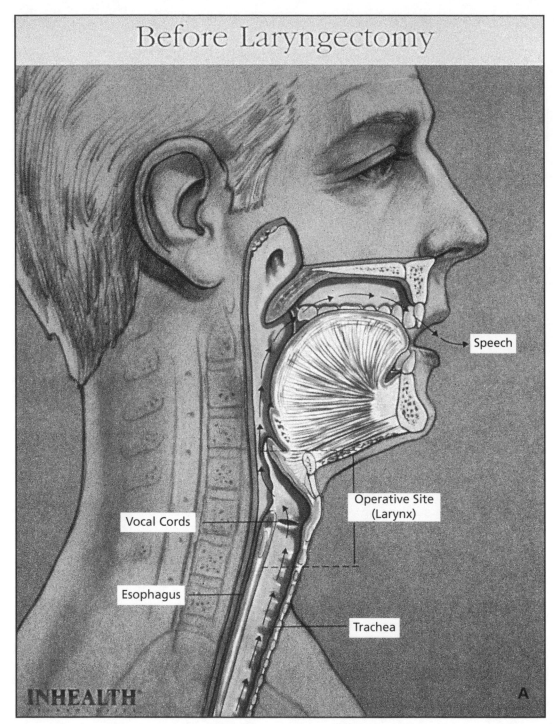

Figure 10.1. Course of air flow before **(A)** and after **(B)** total laryngectomy. *Note.* Images from International Healthcare Technologies, Carpinteria, CA. Reprinted with permission.

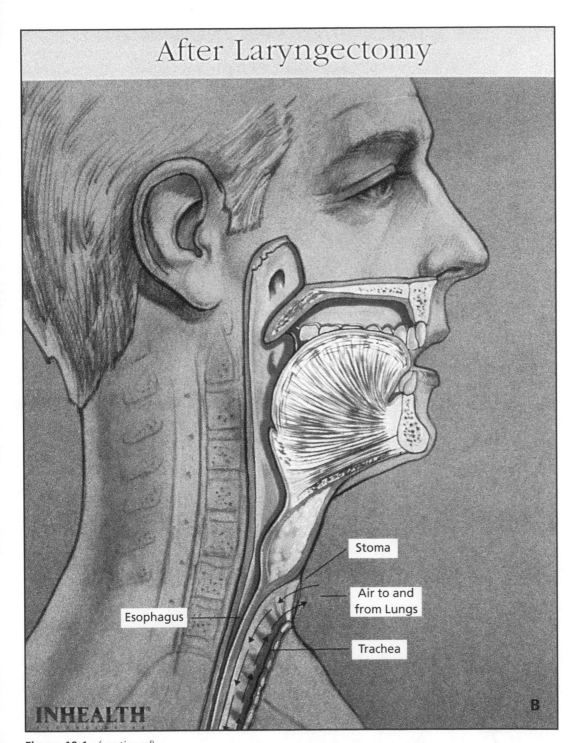

After Laryngectomy

Stoma

Air to and from Lungs

Esophagus

Trachea

INHEALTH

B

Figure 10.1. *(continued)*

laryngectomee should be brief, and the laryngectomee should reassure the patient that he or she will meet once again soon after the surgery. It cannot be overstressed how motivating it can be for a patient to observe a well-adjusted and rehabilitated laryngectomee who is living a full and rewarding life.

B. **When a patient may not be visited preoperatively by a speech–language pathologist.** An occasional physician may feel that it is not in the patient's interest to be visited preoperatively by a speech–language pathologist and an accompanying laryngectomee. The primary reasons given for not recommending preoperative visits are as follows:

1. The physician believes that preoperative counseling is the sole responsibility of the physician and is unwilling to risk the possibility that a visit may unintentionally cause the patient to develop fears about the surgery and its consequences.

2. The physician anticipates preoperatively that large amounts of tissue will have to be surgically removed and that exposure to a proficient esophageal speaker might wrongly suggest to the patient that he or she will develop a similarly proficient speaking voice.

II. **Postoperative Management.** Although the primary postoperative consideration is maintenance of the patient's life, special attention must be paid to the emotional well-being of the patient and family. The first several days immediately following the surgery usually are very emotional ones for the patient and family. It is very difficult for a patient to accept the physical changes created by surgery, no matter how adequately he or she has been prepared in advance. Disfigurement from the open stoma in the neck (and in some cases the large neck scars that result from radical neck surgery for the removal of cancerous lymph nodes) can be traumatizing to the patient and to the family, and the patient may begin to develop many different fears or become depressed. During the next several weeks postoperatively, the combined efforts of the physician, the hospital staff, and the speech–language pathologist can be used to help the patient and family learn to accept these changes in physical appearance, manage the many fears and feelings of depression, and learn how to care for the patient's stoma.

A. **The postoperative visit by the speech–language pathologist and laryngectomee.** Two to three days following surgery, the physician usually requests a postoperative visit from the speech–language pathologist and a laryngectomee visitor of the speech pathologist's choice. This visit is very important because it provides the speech–language pathologist with an opportunity to help lessen the patient's fears, reduce the patient's feelings of depression, increase the patient's motivation to learn esophageal speech, and make arrangements for the initiation of voice therapy (Keith, 1995).

1. **Role of the speech-language pathologist.** Because each individual patient views the first postoperative visit differently, the speech–language pathologist should be prepared to be flexible with regard to the format of the meeting. Often, the patient and family have accumulated many questions since the surgery and would like to have them answered. Some of these questions may concern voice rehabilitation and related problems. Nevertheless, these concerns should be dealt with one at a time so that the patient

and family can be relieved of as much anxiety as possible. At this time, the speech–language pathologist may loan or suggest that the patient purchase copies of *Looking Forward . . . A Guidebook for the Laryngectomee* (Keith, 1995) or *Self-Help for the Laryngectomee* (Lauder, 1994).

The speech–language pathologist should consult with the physician prior to this visit to find out (1) when the patient will be able to begin voice training and (2) if there are any medical circumstances that would prevent the patient's immediate use of an artificial larynx. Preoperative radiation therapy can cause slow healing of surgical scars or the development of fistulas. The presence of these complications may require that esophageal speech training and the use of neck-type or pneumatic artificial larynges be delayed temporarily. The tube-in-the-mouth-type artificial larynx (see **III.A.1.b.(2)** in this chapter) can, however, be used within several days following surgery. Loaner instruments of this type may occasionally be available from local Lost Chord Clubs, the hospital, the American Cancer Society, or the speech–language pathologist.

The benefits of the patient being able to communicate with family and the hospital staff during hospitalization are enormous. Most importantly, many needless hours of worrying about whether speech will ever be possible or not can be eliminated. By using an artificial larynx in the hospital, the patient can have an early experience at developing the precise articulation necessary for any method of alaryngeal speech that he or she will learn, and the patient will be spared the needless frustration of trying to use writing as a principal mode of communication (this is especially important if the patient or family members are unable to read or write). Nevertheless, in spite of all the obvious benefits, the speech–language pathologist should never give a hospitalized patient any type of artificial larynx unless medical permission has specifically been granted for that individual patient.

2. **Role of the accompanying laryngectomee.** Physicians are usually extremely supportive of a postoperative visit by a laryngectomee visitor. The primary purpose of the visit by a laryngectomee is to develop motivation in the patient and to provide a model of someone who has been through similar circumstances and made a successful recovery. A rehabilitated laryngectomee also can understand the fears, worries, and emotional upheaval that the patient is experiencing. Frequently, the laryngectomee will bring information that is available from the International Association of Laryngectomees (IAL) and will invite the laryngectomee and spouse to come to the monthly meetings of the local IAL Lost Chord Club chapter. The laryngectomee visitor can also answer any of the patient's questions.

If there is not a local Lost Chord Club chapter, the patient or patient's family may contact the IAL for information, support materials, and the location of the nearest Lost Chord Club. See Appendix C for more specific information.

B. **Postoperative medical concerns and related problems.** In the postoperative period, the patient must begin to adapt to and manage the problems that result from the physical changes caused by surgery. Particularly troublesome problems include (1) problems related to the fact that the patient now breathes through the neck and no longer through the nose; (2) problems of swallowing, taste and smell, and digestion; (3) problems related to the patient's decreased strength, which is caused by the inability to trap air within the lungs and radical neck dissection, which lessens the muscular support of the clavicle and scapula; and (4) problems of social adjustment.

1. **Problems related to the tracheostomy.** One of the consequences of laryngectomy surgery is that the trachea must be separated from its connection with the oral cavity and connected to an opening in the neck (tracheostomy). It is through this opening (stoma) that the patient must breathe forever. In order to maintain the size of this opening after surgery, an L-shaped plastic or metal tube called a **cannula** is inserted into the stoma. Most patients are able to permanently dispense with the cannula after several weeks; other patients may prefer to wear it for a lifetime.

   The presence of the tracheostomy, the presence of the cannula, and excessive mucus production present some unique management problems for the laryngectomee. Although the patient should be given sufficient instruction in care of the stoma and cannula and maintenance of the airway by the hospital staff before being discharged, occasionally this does not occur or the patient fails to fully understand some or all of the instructions. The speech–language pathologist should be prepared to instruct the patient in stoma and cannula care and hygiene and be ready to refer the patient back to the physician if the patient complains of difficulty with breathing.

   a. **Stoma hygiene.** Daily cleaning of the stoma is necessary to reduce irritation and to prevent the accumulation of mucus, which might interfere with breathing. The following procedure for cleaning the stoma should be reviewed with the patient:

      (1) Wash the hands first.

      (2) Rinse a cotton washcloth with warm water and squeeze dry. Then gently place the washcloth against the stoma and wipe gently. **Do not use bits of paper tissue or cotton balls** to wipe the stoma, because they can easily be aspirated. **Do not use soap,** because it can cause irritation and coughing if it enters the stoma.

      (3) To lubricate the edge of the stoma, gently spread petroleum jelly, K-Y Jelly, or any water-soluble salve around the stoma. Leave the lubricant on for 2 minutes and then gently wipe off.

   b. **Cannula hygiene.** It is the primary responsibility of the hospital staff to instruct the patient in techniques of caring for and cleaning the cannula. The patient should be warned that if the cannula is not cleaned daily, stoma irritation may occur and dried mucus may accumulate within the cannula and restrict the free passage of air.

   The cannula may be cleaned using warm tap water, soap, and brushes. The inner tube may require several cleanings during the course of the day to remove encrusted mucus. The outer tube generally requires less frequent cleanings. Both the inner and outer tube can be lubricated for easy insertion using a drop of olive oil or vegetable oil as a lubricant. Vegetable oils are better than mineral oil for cannula lubrication because mineral oil may cause a problem if even small amounts reach the lungs (Keith, 1995; Roberts, 1994).

Most patients can eventually wean themselves from the continual wearing of the cannula beginning 6 weeks after the operation. The key to this process is that it must be accomplished gradually over a period of weeks. Initially, the patient should remove the cannula for approximately 1 hour on the first day. If the cannula can be reinserted easily (i.e., the stoma has not decreased in size during the time the cannula was removed), the patient may increase the time the cannula is removed by an additional hour on the next day. The length of time that the cannula is out should be increased until the patient no longer wears it during the daytime hours. Following approximately 2 to 3 weeks of this schedule, and if no decrease in stoma size has been noted, the patient may attempt to remove the cannula for 24-hour periods. Patients who experience difficulty in maintaining the size of the stoma may be fitted by the physician with a **stoma button,** which is smaller and easier to care for than a cannula tube.

  c. **Stoma covers.** It is important that the laryngectomee learn to keep the stoma covered at all times with an article of clothing, a stoma bib, or an air filter. Stoma covers do not interfere with learning esophageal speech or with the use of neck-type artificial larynges.

  (1) **Cosmetic functions of a stoma cover.** Because most laryngectomees are concerned about other people's reactions to the appearance of the stoma, stoma covers are worn primarily for cosmetic reasons. The laryngectomee has several kinds of covers to choose from, some of which follow.

  (a) The simplest type of stoma cover is a gauze-like bib that can be tied around the neck and draped comfortably over the stoma. Foam rubber shields are also available.

  (b) Other stoma covers that may be used are attractive scarves, jewelry, turtlenecks and sweaters, ties, ascots, and homemade crocheted bibs.

  (c) Men may wish to remove the second button from the top of their shirt, sew the button over the button hole so that the shirt appears to be buttoned, and wear a tie.

  (d) **Undercovers,** such as gauze or foam rubber pads, may be worn to protect fashion covers from being soiled.

  (2) **Protective functions of a stoma cover.** Because laryngectomees no longer have several feet of airway or the nose to filter and warm the air, stoma covers can be used to substitute for these functions.

  (a) The stoma cover creates a warm, insulated space between the stoma and the environment.

  (b) The stoma cover helps to **filter** out dust, small insects, lint, and other foreign particles.

(c) Stoma covers worn when **sleeping** help to muffle stoma noise, absorb mucus, and prevent strong streams of air from being expelled.

(3) **Stoma guards.** Some laryngectomees are quite reluctant to wear a cover over the stoma because of a fear of suffocating. Because the stoma cover tends to be drawn up against the stoma during inhalation, the patient may fear that the cover is severely limiting airflow. These patients can be helped by wearing a perforated stoma guard, which is placed between the stoma and the stoma covering. As the patient becomes more accustomed to breathing with the stoma covered, the perforated stoma guard is usually discarded and only a stoma cover is used.

d. **Excessive tracheal mucus.** One problem that laryngectomees often experience after surgery is the development of excessive amounts of mucus in the trachea. This excessive production of mucus results from (1) tissue reaction to the surgery, (2) tissue reaction to the presence of the cannula, and (3) the sudden change from breathing through the nose (which normally moistens air before it reaches the trachea) to breathing through the neck (in which case air directly enters the trachea without prior moistening). The presence of excess mucus will gradually subside as the mucosa undergoes tissue changes that make it more resistant to the ill effects of dry air.

Excess mucus in the trachea may cause the patient to experience much coughing. The patient should be instructed to use a cloth handkerchief to absorb the mucus and to cover the stoma when coughing.

If the patient experiences **unproductive coughing, bloody mucus, or thick and sticky mucus,** it is most likely due to excessive dryness of the trachea. The patient should be informed that the amount and thickness of mucus secretion can occasionally be limited if environmental air is humidified (35% to 50% relative humidity) (Gardner, 1971; Roberts, 1994). Although the degree of tracheal mucus secretion does decrease over time, the patient should understand that a certain amount of mucus will always naturally be present in the trachea.

e. **Mucus encrustations of the stoma.** Encrustations of mucus around and within the stoma may occur and are similar to encrustations that also form in the nostril. Occasionally, these encrustations restrict the breathing pathway and make breathing difficult. Encrustations of mucus are generally caused by the dryness of the air that enters the stoma. Control of the moisture content of the environment often helps prevent their occurrence.

The physician should be consulted regarding the preferred method of removing the encrustations. The most common method involves softening the encrustations with a saline solution, steam atomizer, or water-soluble salve, and then removing them with forceps or a clean handkerchief.

f. **Stoma safety and first aid for the laryngectomee.** Because the laryngectomee no longer has a protective mechanism—which normally closes during swallowing in order to protect the airway from blockage by aspiration of foods, liquids, and foreign particles—he or she should be advised to take certain precautions to prevent accidental aspiration. Additionally, because of the surgical changes that have occurred, some routine first aid procedures must be modified when they are used with a laryngectomized person.

(1) **Precautions to observe while bathing or showering.** Because of the danger of water entering the stoma during bathing or showering, the laryngectomee should observe the following special precautions (Gardner, 1971):

   (a) Use a **rubber shower shield,** which prevents water from entering the stoma from above and allows air to be breathed through the bottom of the shield. The shield will fit better if it is made more pliable by preheating in hot water.

   (b) **Do not stand directly under the shower.** A shower head that is mounted below the level of the stoma or a hand-held shower head is much safer.

   (c) **A rubber shower mat** should be used to prevent accidental falls, which might directly expose the stoma to water from the shower.

   (d) Perspiration can be prevented from entering the stoma while taking a bath by wrapping a face towel around the neck.

   (e) **Heavily perfumed soaps should be avoided** because they tend to irritate the stoma area and may cause coughing.

(2) **Precautions to observe while shaving**

   (a) The use of an **electric razor** is recommended and presents no hazard to the laryngectomee.

   (b) A nonelectric razor may be used with precautions. To prevent shaving lather from dripping into the stoma, a rather dry lather should be used and the stoma should be covered with a shower guard or face towel.

   (c) The chin area should be shaved first to prevent lather from dripping down the neck toward the stoma shower guard.

(3) **Precautions to observe when shampooing**

   (a) **Always wear a stoma shower shield.**

   (b) Be very careful with the shampoo because it can be very irritating to the mucous lining of the trachea.

(4) **First aid procedures for the laryngectomee.** Laryngectomees should wear identification tags and carry cards that identify them as laryngectomees and provide simple instructions to potential rescuers.

   (a) Artificial resuscitation must be via the **mouth-to-stoma** method.

(b) The laryngectomee's head must be kept straight with the chin up so that the stoma is unobstructed.

(c) Do not cover a laryngectomee with a blanket or coat above the level of the shoulders.

(d) Do not throw water on a laryngectomee.

2. **Problems of swallowing, taste and smell, and digestion**

   a. Because of the nature of the surgical procedure, many patients report difficulty in swallowing, especially while they are still hospitalized. For most laryngectomees, the ability to swallow easily returns very soon. If extensive pharyngeal reconstruction has occurred as a result of the laryngectomy, **postsurgical narrowing of the esophagus** may develop. If the esophagus does become narrowed, it will have to be dilated by the physician.

   b. Another problem related to food intake is that the **senses of taste and smell may be reduced following surgery.** This is most likely because there is no exchange of air through the nose that would aid the sense of smell. Without the aid of the sense of smell, the sense of taste is greatly reduced, with taste sensitivity frequently being limited to just very sweet and very sour foods.

   c. Patients who are learning esophageal speech often develop **digestive problems** because air that should be trapped in the esophagus instead moves lower in the alimentary canal. As these patients become more proficient at trapping air in the esophagus, many of the digestive problems decrease or are eliminated. The primary complaints of patients who swallow air are as follows:

   (1) Feelings of being bloated

   (2) Abdominal pain

   (3) Chronic flatulence

3. **Problems related to the inability to trap air within the lungs.** One of the primary biologic functions of the larynx is to allow air to be trapped in the lungs when the glottal closure reflex is elicited. Loss of the larynx results in problems related to this inability to reflexively trap air intrathoracically. The primary problems associated with laryngectomy and the concomitant loss of the glottal closure reflex are as follows:

   a. Difficulty in lifting heavy objects. Because the human body's muscle-related mechanical advantage is dependent upon an expanded thoracic cavity (which occurs when air is trapped within the lungs by the glottal effort closure reflex), the ability to lift heavy objects is impaired in some laryngectomees. Occasionally, patients who were employed in occupations that required heavy lifting are forced to shift to jobs that make fewer physical demands.

   b. Difficulty in elimination of body wastes. Because the glottal effort closure reflex is required for forced elimination of body waste, some patients find that alterations in their diet or the use of stool softeners are required.

c. **Difficulty with childbirth.** Because the glottal effort closure reflex is typically used during childbirth, the absence of this reflex in laryngectomized mothers may change the sensation of bearing down.

4. **Problems of social adjustment.** Perhaps one of the biggest obstacles that the new laryngectomee has to overcome is learning to face the world with an altered physical appearance and voice (Rohe, 1994). Quite often, the learning of and the use of alaryngeal speech is hampered by (1) the patient's fear of being rejected by others when using this new form of voice production, (2) the patient's overanxiousness in attempting to learn alaryngeal speech so that he or she can return to work and an income as quickly as possible, and (3) the patient's reluctance to meet with others in social situations because of his or her altered physical appearance.

a. **Use of alaryngeal speech in public.** Because of the unusual quality and low pitch of most alaryngeal speech, recent laryngectomees may be hesitant and embarrassed to use their new voices around strangers and perhaps even their own family. This is especially true if the laryngectomee is female and is uneasy about using a low-pitched and husky voice, which most people consider acceptable only in men. The speech–language pathologist must be sensitive to any signs of embarrassment about using alaryngeal speech, regardless of how fleeting and incidental they may appear.

One of the biggest deterrents to learning alaryngeal speech is the laryngectomee's failure to practice the new voice outside the comfortable confines of the therapy setting. The therapy process should incorporate many opportunities for the laryngectomee to use the new voice in social situations outside the speech clinic but under the supervision of the speech–language pathologist. The laryngectomee should be encouraged to discuss with the clinician any feelings of embarrassment or hesitancy he or she has in these situations.

b. **Altered physical appearance.** Feelings of embarrassment related to the stoma or the scars resulting from radical neck surgery tend to be strongest for the new laryngectomee and usually decrease with the passage of time. If the laryngectomee does not attend Lost Chord Club meetings, where techniques used to disguise physical alterations are shared, the speech–language pathologist may need to provide the laryngectomee with this information. There are pamphlets available from the IAL on this topic (see Appendix C). If the laryngectomee continues to express feelings of hesitancy about socializing even after physical alterations have been carefully concealed, the speech–language pathologist should recommend professional counseling for problems of adjustment.

5. **Unrealistic expectations regarding acquisition of alaryngeal speech.** Some patients erroneously believe that the process of learning alaryngeal speech takes only a few weeks. Frequently, new laryngectomees must be reminded that the learning of any new skill takes time. Patients with misconceptions about how easily alaryngeal speech can be learned may quickly

become discouraged because of the unexpectedly slow rate at which their speech returns. The speech–language pathologist should attempt to keep the laryngectomee informed not only about the state of his or her progress, but also about what long-range goals will have to be achieved. The well-informed patient may occasionally become disappointed about progress in therapy, but not discouraged.

III. **Voice Training.** The goal of speech rehabilitation for the laryngectomized patient is to find an appropriate source of sound production that can be articulated for communication purposes. The most efficient and effective type of sound source varies with each individual patient. Often, the selection of a sound source is dependent upon (1) the degree of tissue loss, the degree of esophageal stenosis, level of hearing loss, or other physical limitations of the laryngectomized patient ; (2) the noise level of the environment in which the patient will have to communicate; (3) the patient's level of motivation for learning an alternate method of communication; and (4) the personal preference of the patient.

The sound source that will be used for voice production must emanate from a vibrating structure. For some patients, the vibratory source will be (1) an external, man-made, mechanical prosthesis (artificial larynx); (2) the sphincter-like junction of the pharynx and the esophagus (P-E segment); or (3) a structure that is surgically created or surgically implanted (prosthesis) specifically for voice production. Although the methods for voice rehabilitation differ with the various techniques available for generating a sound source, the methods are very similar with regard to the techniques that must be used for articulation training of the laryngectomee.

A. **Voice training using an artificial larynx.** Until recent years, an artificial larynx was considered to be an alternative only for those patients who failed to learn esophageal speech. Many physicians and speech–language pathologists erroneously assumed that if a patient was given an artificial larynx prior to esophageal speech training, the patient would give up efforts to learn esophageal speech in favor of the artificial larynx. Most clinicians would agree, however, that this does not happen with most patients, and that in fact the artificial larynx may actually assist the laryngectomee in the process of acquiring esophageal speech.

   1. **Types of artificial larynges.** Artificial larynges can be grouped according to (1) the manner in which the vibratory source is powered (pneumatically or electronically) and (2) the place at which the artificial larynx is positioned in order to deliver the sound to the oral cavity for speech production (tube-in-the-mouth-type, denture-type, and neck-type artificial larynges). Table 10.2 provides a summary of the types and sources of artificial larynges.

      a. **Pneumatically powered voice prostheses** utilize air from the lungs (pulmonic air). Pulmonic air enters the voice prosthesis via an airtight cover that can be fitted to the patient's stoma. To speak, the user simply places the mouthpiece end of the device into the mouth and articulates (see **III.A.1.b.(2)(b)** in this chapter). Hand-held models do not require valving mechanisms because they can be lifted from the stoma to allow the patient to breathe. Models that are fitted to the neck such as the **Van Humen Artificial Larynx** have a valving mechanism that allows the

Table 10.2. Summary of the Types of Artificial Larynges

Name	Type	Price Range
Tokyo Artificial Larynx	Hand-held, pneumatically powered	$112
Servox Inton Electrolarynx	Neck-type, battery-powered (rechargeable)	$490–595
Romet Speech Aid	Neck-type, battery-powered (rechargeable)	$320–445
Denrick 3 Speech Aid	Neck-type, battery-powered (rechargeable)	$410–440
Nuvois	Neck-type, battery-powered (rechargeable)	$490–530
Optivox	Neck-type, battery-powered (rechargeable)	$540–570
TruTone Artificial Larynx	Neck-type, battery-powered (rechargeable)	$510–545
Cooper-Rand Electronic Speech Aid	Tube-in-the-mouth-type, battery-powered	$425–470
UltraVoice	Intraoral, dental-appliance-type, battery-powered (rechargeable)	$3700

passage of air for both respiration and voice production. The Van Humen type is rarely seen in the United States (Salmon, 1994).

A pneumatic artificial larynx utilizes an air-driven, vibrating reed for the purpose of producing the tone that substitutes for the absent laryngeal tone. Typically, pneumatically driven, reed-type artificial larynges are designed to divert the tone from the vibrating reed directly into the patient's mouth, where the tone can then be articulated by the patient.

The Japanese-manufactured **Tokyo Artificial Larynx** (see Table 10.2 and Figure 10.2A) has been described by Blom (1978), Mowrer and Case (1982), and Salmon (1994). The Tokyo device is relatively inexpensive and easy to use. It has been demonstrated that patients using this device under optimal conditions can achieve a 95% intelligibility level (Weinberg & Riekena, 1973).

A modified version of the Tokyo Artificial Larynx has been developed by Nelson, Parkin, and Porter (1975). Their version features a swivel-joint connector on the tracheostoma cover to accommodate an irregularly angled stoma, and a mouth tube constructed of curved stainless steel tubing capped by a plastic mouthpiece. Weinberg, Shedd, and Horii (1978) have described another modification of the Tokyo that was used with patients who had a surgically created pharyngeal fistula into which a fistula tube (formerly the mouthpiece) was inserted. Mean intelligibility for patients using this type of modification of the Tokyo was approximately 90%. Other simple modifications of the Tokyo have been described, such as the drilling of a ⅜ inch finger hole into the body of the instrument to permit finger-controlled breathing without the necessity of moving the device from the stoma on inhalation (Salmon, 1994).

b. **Electronically powered voice prostheses.** There are a variety of commercially available, battery-operated, electronic artificial larynges (see Table 10.2). The quality of voice produced with each of these devices

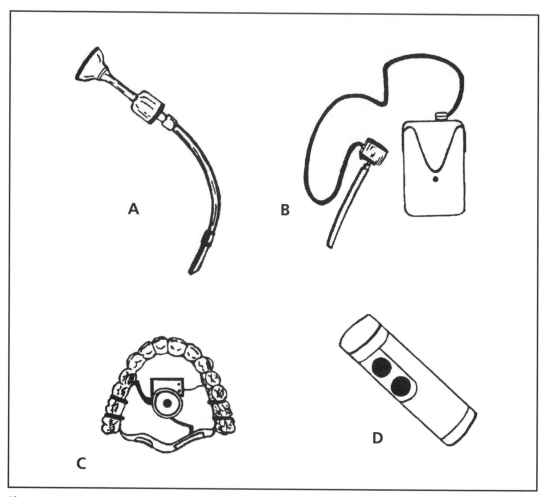

Figure 10.2. Examples of four types of artificial larynges: **(A)** Tokyo Artificial Larynx, a pneumatically powered, hand-held-type; **(B)** Cooper-Rand Electronic Speech Aid, a battery-powered, tube-in-the-mouth-type; **(C)** UltraVoice, a battery-powered, dental-appliance-type; and **(D)** Servox Inton Speech Aid, a battery-powered, neck-type.

depends upon the acoustic characteristics of the particular artificial larynx and the degree to which a particular patient's vocal tract has been surgically altered. Certain devices, such as the Cooper-Rand Electronic Speech Aid (see Figure 10.2B), generate the sound source extraorally, with the tone directed intraorally via a plastic tube. In other devices, such as UltraVoice (see Figure 10.2C), the sound source is *both* generated and directed intraorally within a specially designed denture. This type of device is much less common. Other devices like the Servox Inton Speech Aid (also called the Servox Inton Electrolarynx; see Figure 10.2D) produce a tone that is conducted from the external surface of the neck to the hypopharynx.

(1) **Neck-type instruments.** The most widely used type of artificial larynx is a hand-held model with a vibrating diaphragm that serves as

the sound source. The vibrating diaphragm must be placed firmly against the neck in order to operate properly. Vibrations from the diaphragm are transmitted through the skin of the neck and into the hypopharynx. If the head of the instrument is not buried deeply and firmly enough into the patient's neck, sound from the vibrating diaphragm will escape free-field and cause speech production to cease.

(a) **Types of neck-type artificial larynges** (see Table 10.2). There are several commercially available neck-type artificial larynges. A popular neck-type unit is the **Servox Inton** (see Figure 10.2D). The Servox has two buttons that provide inflection capabilities. One button is used for fundamental frequency, and the other button produces a frequency which is one-half octave above the fundamental frequency. This arrangement allows for inflection to be used during speech (Luminaud, Inc., 1998; Salmon, 1994). The Servox Inton uses a rechargeable nickel-cadmium battery and will operate for as long as a day on a single battery charge. A dual battery charger is designed to accept both the instrument and a spare battery at the same time. The instrument is fully charged in 2 hours with this system.

One of the newer neck-type artificial larynges is the **TruTone Artificial Larynx** (see Table 10.2), designed and manufactured in the United States by Griffin Laboratories (Griffin Laboratories, 1998). The TruTone is designed to permit pitch fluctuation using a single pressure-sensitive button. Increasing and decreasing the pressure on the switch moves speaking pitch through a selected pitch range. The TruTone also features a high-volume range for speaking with large groups or in noisy conditions, and a normal volume range.

Another popular neck type artificial larynx is the **Romet Speech Aid** also called the **Romet Electronic Larynx.** The Romet has become popular with consumers because of its small size (3¾" × 1"), durability, and comparatively lower cost than many of the larger full-feature electronic devices (Lauder, 1994).

There are a number of high-quality neck-held devices on the market today that feature durable materials, some measure of pitch and volume control, and a choice of rechargeable or alkaline batteries (see Table 10.2).

(b) **Instructions for use of neck-type artificial larynges.** Prior to introducing the patient to any artificial larynx, it is best to explain to him or her that the device is just one method for communication. The patient should understand that the artificial larynx may serve as a supplement to esophageal or tracheoesophageal speech, or it may serve as the patient's sole means of communication. The patient should understand that the artificial larynx and other methods of communication are complementary and that each method can be useful in different circumstances.

When instruction for use of the artificial larynx is first initiated with a patient, care should be taken to spend an adequate amount of time in discovering the **placement site** for the instrument that yields the best sound intensity and quality. The exact placement site will vary with the individual patient, but the most commonly used placement is 1 to 2 inches under the patient's jawline on the side of the neck or on the midline. The ideal site will be an area where the neck is healthy, soft, and pliable, and which permits the head of the instrument to sink easily against the tissue. A piece of tape or a water-based marker may be used temporarily to mark the ideal placement spot on the patient's neck and thus facilitate appropriate placement of the head of the instrument. The patient should be taught to use the nondominant hand to operate the device so that the dominant hand can be used for daily activities such as using the phone, and so on (Case, 1996).

The reluctance of some patients to use a neck-held artificial larynx develops from the patient's dissatisfaction with the loud squawking noise that is produced if a tight seal is not maintained between the head of the instrument and the patient's neck. If the patient is given adequate time during the first session to discover just the right position for placing the device to obtain the best sound production and to avoid the annoying squawk, the likelihood that the patient will be motivated to continue using the instrument should be greatly increased.

After the best placement site for the device is discovered, the patient should be asked to produce several monosyllabic words without using the artificial larynx. Point out to the patient that the production of consonants requires the use of air that is trapped in the mouth (intraoral whispers) and not air from the lungs. Ask the patient to produce monosyllabic words beginning and ending with bilabial consonants. When the patient has developed accuracy with the consonants, the same task should be repeated using the artificial larynx. Have the patient practice short phrases and sentences to become comfortable with using the instrument. Once a reasonable amount of control with the artificial larynx has been developed, the patient should be encouraged to use it for all communication with family and friends (i.e., the patient should no longer rely on gesturing or writing as his or her principal mode of communication).

(2) **Tube-in-the-mouth-type instruments.** A second type of artificial larynx provides an electronically generated tone to the oral cavity via a small plastic tube that is connected to a hand-held transducer. Because the small plastic tube is used to conduct the vibrations from the transducer to the mouth, the patient must be careful not to obstruct the end of the tube with the tongue or the cheek or else the tone will be completely interrupted. This type of artificial larynx is relatively easy to operate and is often used immediately following

surgery without fear of interfering with surgical healing (such as causing fistulas to develop). Since the device delivers the tone intraorally, patients who have had radical neck surgery can use this type of prosthesis without risk of pain and sooner after surgery than they can use the neck-type instruments. For some laryngectomees, tube-in-the-mouth-type artificial larynges are the only type of voice prosthesis they use.

(a) **Types of tube-in-the-mouth-type artificial larynges** (see Table 10.2). One very popular example of this type of artificial larynx is the **Cooper-Rand Electronic Speech Aid** (see Figure 10.2B). It features switches that permit both frequency and intensity to be varied and is available with both conventional and saliva-ejector mouth tubes. The Cooper-Rand has proven its durability, as many Cooper-Rands over 20 years old are still in service. The Cooper-Rand uses two 9-volt alkaline batteries that last approximately 4 to 6 weeks.

Several neck-type artificial larynges can be converted to operate as tube-in-the-mouth-type devices. Some of these adaptable instruments include the **Servox Inton** Electronic Larynx; the **Romet** Speech Aid; the **Denrick 3 Speech Aid**; the **NuVois** artificial larynx; and the **Optivox** artificial larynx (see Table 10.2).

(b) **Instructions for use of tube-in-the-mouth-type instruments.** Instructions to the patient for whom this type of artificial larynx is best suited are similar to the instructions described for the neck-type instruments (see **III.A.1.b.(1)(b)** earlier in the chapter). The only difference with regard to instruction is related to the technique of placing the plastic sound tube into the oral cavity.

Have the patient practice consonant production using intraoral whispers. The drills that should be used are identical for this type of artificial larynx as for other types. Allow the patient ample time to develop some accuracy with producing consonants (intraoral whispers) before proceeding to instructions for use of the instrument itself.

Next, the patient should be given the instrument and instructed to place the plastic sound tube into the corner of the mouth, being sure to keep the tube angled upward toward the hard palate. Should the tube opening become temporarily occluded, all sound production will cease. If the device is held at this sharp upward angle, interference with the tube opening by the tongue or the cheek will be greatly reduced.

Most patients are able to quickly adapt to the device and can usually communicate in sentences with little practice. As with all artificial larynges, however, the patient must learn to activate the switch on the instrument to coincide with the beginning and end of a phrase. Failure to do this will result in an unarticulated, buzzing sound.

(3) **Dental-appliance-type instruments.** A third type of electronically powered artificial larynx is one in which the power and sound sources are both built into a specially designed dental appliance. This unique design eliminates the problem of tube occlusion, which is common with the tube-in-the-mouth-type artificial larynges.

   (a) One such dental-appliance-type artificial larynx has been recently marketed under the name **UltraVoice** (see Table 10.2). This intraoral microelectronic device is totally concealed within the mouth, without surgery, because it fits against the palate like an orthodontic retainer. The device can also be built into an upper denture plate for denture wearers. As the device is totally contained within the mouth, there is no visual evidence of its use. The basic components, which are built into the mouth device, include a built-in speaker, an electronic control circuit that controls pitch and loudness, and rechargeable batteries that provide about a day of talking time. There is a hand-held control that allows the user to remotely control on–off, pitch, and volume. The device also comes with a charging unit that permits full recharge of the hand unit and the mouth unit in approximately 8 hours. The UltraVoice offers an advantage over previous dental-appliance-type artificial larynges because it can be worn all day, including for eating and drinking (Health Concepts, 1998).

   (b) **Instructions to the patient** consist primarily of familiarization with the techniques for manipulating the on–off, pitch, and volume switches. As with other types of artificial larynges, most patients will require practice with starting and stopping the unit in sequence with phrasing, as well as additional articulation practice for improvement of intelligibility.

2. **Benefits of an artificial larynx.** The artificial larynx may be the only method of alaryngeal speech for some laryngectomees. Other laryngectomees prefer the artificial larynx because it is much easier to learn to use than esophageal speech. Some benefits of an artificial larynx are as follows:

   a. There is **immediate and relatively intelligible oral communication** while the patient is still hospitalized, and this ability to communicate frequently aids in reducing the postsurgical frustration that is commonly found in patients who must communicate with written messages.

   b. Since voice rehabilitation is occasionally delayed (sometimes for several months), an artificial larynx provides an efficient and alternative method of communication until esophageal speech training is implemented.

   c. The artificial larynx can provide a method of communication for the occasional laryngectomee who is unable to learn esophageal speech or for patients who are unsuccessful with tracheoesophageal puncture (TEP) (see **III.C.3** later in this chapter) voice restoration.

d. Learning to use an artificial larynx requires less time than learning esophageal speech and is consequently more time- and cost-effective.

e. The artificial larynx can be used as an adjunct to a program of learning esophageal speech or TEP voice restoration. It is especially useful in learning articulatory skills.

f. An artificial larynx provides a higher intensity level than does esophageal speech, thus making it a better choice for temporary or permanent use in high-noise environments.

g. An artificial larynx can provide a temporary alternative for the patient during those periods when the patient is fatigued, has an upper-respiratory tract infection, or is emotionally upset.

B. Voice training using esophageal speech. Esophageal speech is produced by insufflating the esophagus with air and then allowing this air to be released, which causes the pharyngesophageal (P-E) segment to vibrate and thus produce a tone that can be used as a source of voice. As a general rule, air can enter the esophagus only when there is sufficient intraoral air pressure to override the sphincteric constriction of the P-E segment (constriction was formerly believed to be effected by the cricopharyngeus muscle alone, but evidence suggests that the medial and inferior pharyngeal constrictor muscles are also involved; Singer & Blom, 1981) or when the muscle fibers of the P-E segment relax sufficiently. As a result, each method of esophageal speech is designed to override P-E closure in order to permit sufficient air to flow into the esophagus. Once air is in the esophagus, it can be made to escape under the patient's control and cause the P-E segment to vibrate. It is the ability to rapidly intake and expel air from the esophagus that forms the basis of fluent esophageal speech. Figure 10.3 shows a comparison between esophageal speech and speech use of an artificial larynx.

Prior to instructing a patient in any of the various techniques of esophageal speech production, the patient should be given a simple explanation of the anatomy and physiology of esophageal speech production. Duguay (1977) has given an excellent analogy for esophageal speech production. He compares the esophagus to a long, narrow, collapsed balloon. The top of the balloon is described as having a rubber ring that acts like the P-E segment when it is closed. As attempts are made to blow air into the balloon, much like insufflation attempts by an esophageal speaker, there has to be sufficient oral pressure to override the natural resistance of the rubber ring. If the rubber ring (i.e., P-E segment) gives, the balloon can be inflated. If the top of the ring of the balloon is then pinched off and the natural elasticity of the balloon is allowed to force the air upward through this opening, sound can be produced.

Because varying degrees of tissue must be removed from different patients, the exact morphologic and physiologic characteristics of the P-E segment are unique to each patient. Some patients have to undergo a process of esophageal dilation to aid in swallowing and to aid in the process of air insufflation for esophageal speech production. Other patients experience just the opposite problem and have difficulty closing the P-E segment because of weakened P-E fibers, thus making it difficult to maintain sufficient air in the esophagus for speech production.

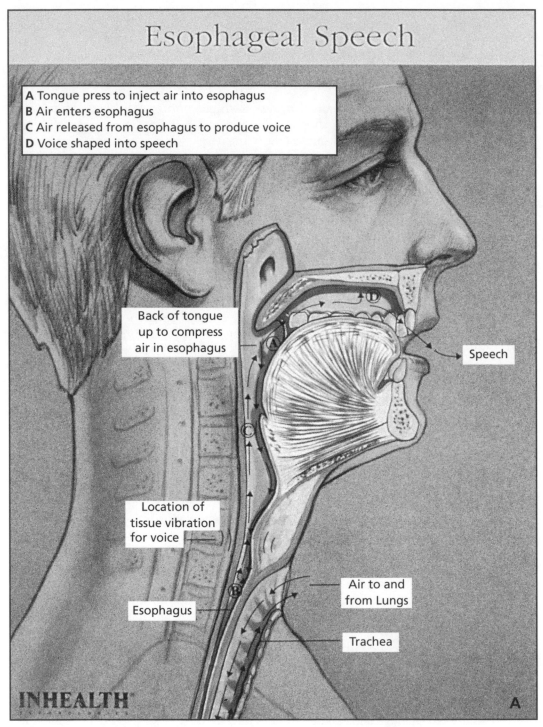

Esophageal Speech

A Tongue press to inject air into esophagus
B Air enters esophagus
C Air released from esophagus to produce voice
D Voice shaped into speech

Back of tongue
up to compress
air in esophagus

Speech

Location of
tissue vibration
for voice

Air to and
from Lungs

Esophagus

Trachea

INHEALTH

A

Figure 10.3. Esophageal speech **(A)** and speech with an artificial larynx **(B)**. *Note.* Images from International Healthcare Technologies, Carpinteria, CA. Reprinted with permission.

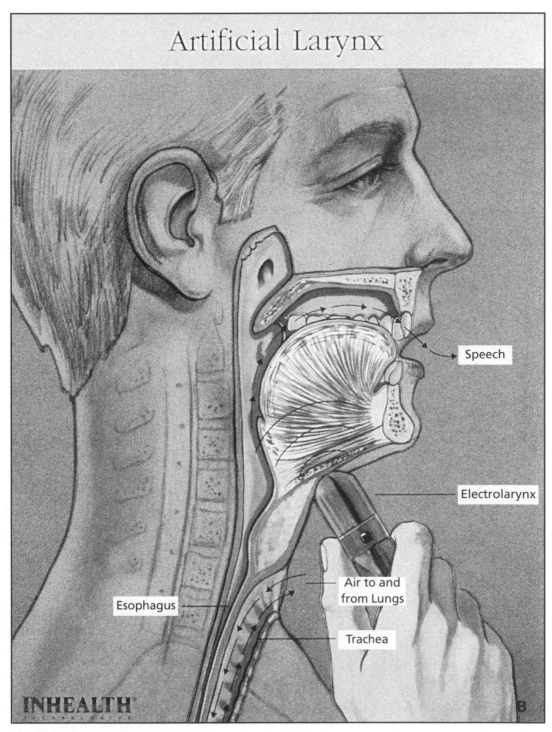

Figure 10.3. *(continued)*

1. **Techniques of esophageal speech production.** There are four methods of esophageal speech production—the consonant-injection method, the glossopalatal or glossopharyngeal press method, the inhalation method, and the swallow method. All four methods rely upon the principle that air of greater pressure in one chamber (the oral cavity) will flow to a chamber containing less pressure (the esophagus) if those two chambers are connected (i.e., the P-E segment is opened). Regardless of which method of esophageal speech is used, the ultimate goals are the same (Aronson, 1980): (1) the patient should be able to reliably phonate upon demand; (2) the patient should use a rapid method of air intake; (3) there should be a short latency between air intake and phonation; (4) the patient should be able to produce 4 to 9 syllables per air charge; (5) the patient should have a speaking rate of 85 to 129 words per minute; and (6) the patient should have good intelligibility.

The exact method by which air is made to enter the esophagus is what distinguishes one method of esophageal speech from the other. The consonant-injection method uses the intraoral air pressure that normally builds during the production of high pressure consonants such as stops and fricatives to insufflate the esophagus. Thus, this method allows esophageal speech to be produced simultaneously with the articulation of certain sounds.

The glossopalatal or glossopharyngeal press method uses the tongue to form a seal against the alveolar ridge, and then the remainder of the tongue presses upward and backward against the palate to compress the air trapped in the mouth. When the pressure of the air in the mouth is high enough, it can overcome the resistance of the P-E sphincter, which then enables compressed air in the mouth to enter the esophagus. With this method, the tongue is acting much like a piston by pumping air into the esophagus as it pushes against the hard palate or the posterior pharyngeal wall during the process of injection.

The inhalation method operates in a much different manner. When air is inhaled into the lungs, there is a subsequent decrease in air pressure within the esophagus. This sudden decrease in esophageal air pressure is often sufficient to enable atmospheric pressure to override the P-E sphincter and thus insufflate the esophagus.

These methods of esophageal speech—the consonant-injection, glossopharyngeal press, and inhalation methods—may be used singly or in combination by the proficient esophageal speaker. The fourth method of esophageal speech, the swallow method, is a very slow method that often has unpleasant side effects (e.g., air retained in the stomach); it should be used only as the method of last resort.

Prior to initiating instructions for any one particular method of esophageal speech, patients should be questioned as to whether they can produce any esophageal speech or whether they have experienced a belch or burp since surgery. If so, ask the patient whether this can be produced again. If the patient can do this, reinforce the behavior and begin to shape it for esophageal voice production. If the patient is unable to voluntarily produce esophageal sound, proceed with the following procedures:

a. **The consonant-injection method** of esophageal speech is by far the most efficient method of getting air into the esophagus. Whereas all of the other methods can direct air into the esophagus only during periods of rest or between phrases, the consonant-injection method allows air to be injected into the esophagus during intraphrase intervals as well as during periods of rest. Because air can be injected when the tongue is positioned for the releasing consonant of a word (especially when it is a bilabial or tongue-tip alveolar stop or a fricative consonant), air for subsequent esophageal productions is usually injected into the esophagus simultaneously with the release of the articulated consonant.

Words like *pie, tie, cake, stop, scotch,* and *skate* are excellent for allowing the esophagus to be insufflated using the consonant-injection method. Similarly, phrases that contain many stops and fricatives, such as *put it back, take it to heart,* and *pick that skate,* are much more effective in causing the esophagus to become loaded with air than are phrases that consist primarily of vowels and low-pressure consonants, such as *in a house* and *I am well.* For these low-pressure phrases, the consonant-injection method of esophageal speech may not be as efficient as some other methods for loading the esophagus.

The first step in teaching a patient to use the consonant-injection method is to teach him or her to produce intraoral whispers of plosive consonants. Instruct the patient to produce the consonant /p/ by compressing some air and then exploding it through the lips. Ask the patient to repeat this several times. Check to see if the patient can feel some of the compressed air in the mouth moving toward the throat. As the patient becomes adept at producing a crisply articulated /p/, tell him or her to produce the consonant four or five times and then attempt to say the syllable /pa/. If this is successful, ask the patient to produce other plosive, fricative, or affricative consonants paired with the vowel /a/, such as /ta/, /ka/, /spa/, /sta/, and /ska/. The patient could also be asked to produce monosyllabic words containing pressure consonants, such as *pie, tie, pop, top, skate, skip, scope, stop,* and *scotch.*

If the patient is unable to produce esophageal speech, he or she should continue to practice /p/, /t/, /k/, or /s/ until more precise articulations are achieved. Then ask the patient to produce several sequential repetitions of these consonants, ending with attempts at the production of /pa/, /ta/, /ka/, or /sa/. If the patient is unsuccessful at this point, proceed to teach the patient the glossopharyngeal press method.

b. The **glossopharyngeal press method** of esophageal speech is an excellent choice for loading the esophagus for production of words or phrases for which the consonant-injection method is most inefficient (i.e., for the production of words or phrases that contain many low-pressure consonants and vowels). The glossopharyngeal press method, unlike the consonant-injection method, can only be used during rest or during interphrase intervals. With the glossopharyngeal press method, the tongue, and occasionally the cheeks, function as a piston and force air downward into the esophagus.

The first step in teaching a patient to use the glossopharyngeal press method is to have him or her close the lips, place the tip of the tongue against the alveolar ridge, and bring the middle portion of the tongue into contact with the hard and soft palates. The patient should then be instructed to pump the tongue by moving the posterior portion of the tongue backward until it approximates or contacts the pharyngeal wall. The patient should be advised that the tip of the tongue may be squeezed against the alveolar ridge, which can serve as an anchor point against which the rocking-like movements of the rest of the tongue can be performed.

Lauder (1994) has suggested that the patient be told to imagine that the mouth is like a paper sack full of air and that the tongue should be used to push all of this air backward and down the throat. Similarly, the same image can be used while the patient is instructed to seal the lips tightly and to compress the cheeks to assist in pumping the air as the anterior portion of the tongue remains squeezed against the alveolar ridge and the posterior portion of the tongue moves backward toward the posterior pharyngeal wall.

The key to success in instructing patients in use of the glossopharyngeal press method, however, is to instruct them to perform all movements to the greatest extent possible without actually swallowing. Injection of air into the esophagus must result from a pumping movement of the tongue and not from a swallowing movement. In fact, as soon as the patient is able to produce some esophageal voice using the glossopharyngeal press method, the tongue-pumping movements associated with the method should be contrasted with the movements associated with normal swallowing so that the patient can better differentiate between the two patterns of movement. If the patient is unsuccessful with producing esophageal voice at this point, proceed to teach the patient the inhalation method.

c. The **inhalation method** of esophageal speech is another popular technique. Although it is not as efficient as the consonant-injection method because it can only be used during rest or interphrase pauses, it is nonetheless a valuable technique and one that can be used alone or in combination with other methods. The inhalation method is based upon the principle that air will enter the esophagus if the P-E segment is sufficiently relaxed when pulmonary inhalation occurs. Because the patient has the natural tendency to inhale prior to phonation, the inhalation method can take advantage of this pattern to effect a concurrent insulation of the esophagus. Similarly, the forces of compression that are associated with exhalation may also be used to aid in the release of air trapped in the esophagus.

Instruction in the use of the inhalation technique begins by explaining to the patient about the relative contributions of inhalation and exhalation to the process of speech production. Be sure to emphasize the facts that expansion of the chest causes air to flow inward and chest compression causes air to flow outward. The patient should be made to understand that, because chest expansion and compression result in air pressure changes within the esophagus, the natural movements of breathing can be used to get air into and out of the esophagus.

Ask the patient to relax the throat muscles as much as possible, open the mouth as in yawning, and quickly inhale air and try to very quickly sniff through the nose at the same time (Case, 1996; Diedrich & Youngstrom, 1966). Even though no air can actually be sniffed into the nose because of the altered airway, the sudden chest expansion that is associated with the muscular movement of sniffing is often sufficient to reduce esophageal air pressure and allow the entry of air. Next, ask the patient to exhale and try to phonate /a/. If this is unsuccessful, ask the patient to try it once again.

Negative pressure in the esophagus can be increased if the stoma is quickly covered midway through a rapid inhalation. Similarly, occluding the stoma during exhalation will aid in compression of the esophagus and thus facilitate the expulsion of air. If the patient is successful in producing an /a/ with this technique, ask the patient to try to produce the syllables /pʌ/, /tʌ/, and /kʌ/ using a sniff inhalation before each attempted production. Continue practicing with monosyllabic words. When the patient is able to produce monosyllabic words with some control, have the patient try once again to use the consonant-injection or glossopharyngeal press methods.

d. The **swallow method** (Boone, 1983) is the least efficient method of esophageal speech and should only be taught as a last resort (Stemple et al., 1995). The swallow method is based upon the principle that the esophagus naturally opens when a person swallows because of the increased intraoral pressure that results as the tongue sweeps back across the hard palate during a swallow. When the esophagus is opened during a swallow, it may fill with some air, which can then be used to produce voice. Because it takes a considerable amount of time to swallow (as compared to injection by the consonant-injection, glossopharyngeal press, or inhalation methods), there is a considerable lag time between the beginning of the process and the production of voice. In addition, it is also very difficult to repeatedly swallow quickly, and rapid swallowing will usually result in much air being taken into the stomach. It is for these reasons that the swallow method should be the method of last choice.

If after a few therapy sessions the patient is unable to produce any esophageal speech using either the consonant-injection, glossopharyngeal press, or inhalation methods, the swallow method may be attempted. Instruct the patient to swallow, wiping the tongue back across the palate and compressing the air behind the tongue. Then ask the patient to produce a syllable that starts with a tongue-tip alveolar consonant such as /t/ or /d/. It may be necessary to have the patient swallow several times consecutively and then attempt the syllable before any sound production occurs. If the patient is still unsuccessful, have him or her sip some carbonated beverage and then attempt to produce the syllable (a noisy sipping from the edge of the glass usually produces better results than a quiet swallow). Use of a carbonated beverage may be successful in aiding the patient in obtaining some esophageal sound production. The swallow method and use of a carbonated beverage should be eliminated as quickly as possible, because they are merely aids to learning either the methods of consonant-injection, glossopharyngeal press, or inhalation.

2. **Problems associated with esophageal speech.** As the patient is learning esophageal speech, certain behaviors can develop that may impede efficient use of esophageal speech or may be distracting to listeners. These behaviors should be eliminated before they become habitual.

   a. **Grimacing and excessive body tension.** The patient should be able to use either the inhalation or the injection methods without any exaggerated movements of the face or head. If a patient clenches his or her lips together tightly, produces unusual facial contortions, or bends the head during esophageal insulation, it is usually a sign that he or she is struggling with the process of getting air into the esophagus. These behaviors should be prevented from the beginning of therapy, because their elimination at a later time is more difficult. Often, all that is necessary to eliminate these behaviors is to bring them to the attention of the patient, who may not realize what he or she is doing. Practice in front of a mirror is most helpful. Be sure to ask the patient to evaluate how easy it is to get air into the esophagus. The patient may have thought these abnormal postures were helpful in the beginning but should realize that they no longer serve any purpose. A frank, honest discussion with the patient usually results in the elimination of these behaviors.

   b. **Excessive stoma noise.** Forceful movement of air through the stoma, either during inhalation or exhalation, can create a loud, annoying noise. This noise can be most bothersome upon exhalation, when the patient is attempting to speak. In fact, the excessive stoma noise often competes in intensity with the esophageal production and thus reduces the acceptability of the laryngectomee's speech (Shipp, 1967). Because forced exhalation is typically the cause, simply instructing the patient to reduce the force of exhalation (e.g., "say it softer") is often sufficient to eliminate the problem. Auditory or visual feedback regarding excessive stoma noise can also be provided using the following two methods:

      (1) During drillwork in therapy, have the patient wear a **stethoscope** and place the diaphragm near the stoma.

      (2) With the patient seated in front of a mirror, place a piece of tissue paper or a feather in front of the stoma to provide visual feedback. The tissue paper or feather should be held far enough away from the stoma to prevent accidental aspiration.

      Ideally, if the patient could learn to immobilize the chest during speech production, stoma noise could be eliminated as an interfering signal. For most new patients learning esophageal speech, however, this is very difficult to do. Consequently, the instruction to exhale slowly and easily is probably the best instruction.

   c. **Klunking and other extraneous noises.** Occasionally, if the patient is attempting rapid and forceful injection via the glossopharyngeal press method, or if the patient is using the swallow method, an audible klunk can be heard as he or she attempts to insufflate the esophagus (Diedrich & Youngstrom, 1966). This very distracting noise should be eliminated as quickly as possible by having the patient reduce the force by which injections or swallows are being made or by having the patient alter his or her head posture slightly. Negative practice and having the patient listen to the klunk on a tape recorder are helpful. Again, the elimination of this undesirable behavior as soon as it appears is very important, since it can quickly become a habitual part of the process of air intake.

For those patients who are unable to eliminate the klunking noise, it may be necessary to instruct the patient in techniques designed to reduce the distraction and interference with intelligibility that klunking may cause. Hiding the klunk in the middle of a phrase or a word may make the noise less annoying to listeners. In addition, patients can be instructed to produce a greater number of syllables per air charge, which will make the klunks less frequent and thus less noticeable.

d. **Swallowing air.** In the course of insufflating the esophagus, a certain amount of air is swallowed into the stomach. This is especially true if the patient is using the swallow method. When this occurs, the patient will complain of feeling bloated and will report that he or she burps frequently without any warning. If the patient is using the glossopharyngeal press, the consonant-injection, or the inhalation methods of esophageal speech, the amount of air that enters the stomach will be greatly reduced as he or she becomes more proficient with the quick and easy use of esophageal speech (i.e., reduces the latency between air intake and phonation). Patients who are using the swallow method should be changed to either the consonant-injection, glossopharyngeal press, or inhalation methods to reduce the amount of swallowed air.

C. **Voice training using surgically created structures or surgically implanted prostheses.** Historically, there have been many attempts to surgically create a new vibratory source (the pseudoglottis, or sometimes called the neoglottis) to replace the voicing function of the vocal folds. The rationale for such attempts has been that a patient who is given a replacement for the excised vocal folds would then be able to use pulmonary air and speak effortlessly soon after surgery without the necessity of extensive speech training. The following passages provide a review of some of these surgical procedures:

1. **Tracheoesophageal air shunt approaches.** Modern interest in surgical reconstruction of laryngectomized patients began in the late 1950s with descriptions of techniques for shunting tracheal air to the esophagus for the production of voice. Although these techniques resulted in the production of a satisfactory voice, the procedures were discontinued because patients frequently experienced a leakage of fluids from the esophagus into the trachea via the shunt during swallowing, and because it was very difficult to maintain the airway due to stenosis.

2. The **Asai technique** (Asai, 1972) and various modifications of the technique (Karlan, 1968; McGrail & Oldfield, 1975; Montgomery & Toohill, 1968) were also early attempts to surgically create a tracheoesophageal (TE) air

shunt and vibratory source for voicing purposes. The multistaged surgical procedure consisted of connecting the trachea to the hypopharynx with a dermal tube. To phonate, the patient would occlude the stoma with a finger and pulmonary air would be forced through the dermal tube and into the hypopharynx, causing the pharyngeal end of the tube to vibrate. Although the voice produced was adequate, many patients experienced recurring problems similar to the problems associated with Conley's procedures (Conley, 1959; Conley, DeAmesti, & Pierce, 1958), such as aspiration of liquids and tube stenosis and problems with hair growing in the dermal tube. This procedure is currently not widely used in the United States.

Other variations of the TE air shunt procedure (Calcaterra & Jafek, 1971; Komorn, 1974) have been attempted with varying degrees of success. Again, problems with aspiration, stenosis, and the need for finger control for speech have created serious difficulties for patients who have undergone these surgical procedures, and thus the procedures have been discontinued.

There have also been surgical attempts to design a method by which pulmonic air from the tracheostoma can be diverted via a chest-mounted or neck-mounted air shunt into the esophagus. There have also been surgical procedures designed to create a muscle and mucosal neoglottis between the trachea and esophagus (Griffiths & Love, 1978; Vega, 1975). Again, problems with aspiration of liquids, the need for frequent surgical revisions to prevent closure of the neoglottis, and other associated problems were common.

3. **Tracheoesophageal puncture (TEP) and voice prosthesis.** The tracheoesophageal puncture (TEP) voice restoration procedure developed by Singer and Blom (1980) is a solution to many of the problems experienced with other surgical voice restoration procedures (see Figures 10.4 and 10.5). With this approach, a small silicone voice prosthesis is inserted into a surgically created, midline, tracheoesophageal fistula, and the patient uses pulmonary air that is conducted from the trachea to the esophagus via the prosthesis to excite the P-E segment for voice production (Singer & Blom, 1980; Singer, Blom, & Hamaker, 1981; Westmore, Johns, & Baker, 1981; Westmore, Krueger, & Wesson, 1981). The TEP surgery is a relatively simple endoscopic procedure that can be performed at the time of primary laryngectomy or under general anesthesia in the postlaryngectomized patient as a secondary procedure.

   a. **Advantages of TEP**

      (1) The major advantage of TEP is that patients use pulmonary or lung air as their power source for speech production, rather than the limited air supply available in esophageal speech.

      (2) A second important advantage of the TEP voice restoration procedure is that the surgical procedure can be performed on most patients, including those who have had radical neck dissection or who have been irradiated heavily.

      (3) A third advantage of the TEP procedure is that it is easily reversible if it is so desired by the patient or surgeon. The procedure can be easily reversed because the patient's fistula tends to close within a mat-

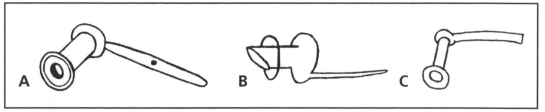

Figure 10.4. Examples of three types of silicon voice prostheses: **(A)** Blom-Singer Indwelling Low Pressure Voice Prosthesis; **(B)** Provox 2 Indwelling Voice Prosthesis; **(C)** Blom-Singer Low Pressure Voice Prosthesis. Illustrations courtesy of Nancy L. Victor.

ter of hours if it is not maintained by the presence of the voice prosthesis or a catheter.

(4) A fourth advantage of TEP is that this procedure and the design of the various voice prostheses have effectively eliminated the problems of aspiration and the difficulties in swallowing that have consistently plagued the various tracheoesophageal shunt procedures.

b. Candidacy for TEP. To qualify as a candidate for the TEP surgical procedure and a voice prosthesis, the patient must meet the following criteria (Case, 1996):

(1) A primary requirement is that the patient must have enough **manual dexterity** to remove, clean, and reinsert the small prosthesis into the fistula. Therefore, the patient with limiting arthritis or poor vision, for example, may not be a good candidate for use of this type of voice prosthesis.

(2) The patient must have a stoma that is large enough for the prosthesis to be inserted into, with a diameter of no less than 2.0 cm.

(3) Patients should be free of pharyngoesophageal spasm (see **III.C.3.c** in this chapter).

(4) A speech–language pathologist who is familiar with TEP procedures should be easily accessible to the patient.

(5) If radiation therapy is performed, 6 to 12 weeks should pass before the TEP is done to allow the effects of radiation to subside.

(6) Patients should be motivated to attempt TEP voice restoration, and they should be psychologically stable.

c. Pharyngoesophageal spasm. Prior to the TEP procedure, the candidate must be evaluated for his or her individual susceptibility to a severe, airflow-induced **pharyngoesophageal spasm** (an occlusive spasm of the pharyngeal constrictors that is triggered by esophageal insufflation).

(1) Air insufflation test. Each patient's tendency for pharyngoesophageal spasm can be evaluated by a test in which the esophagus is insufflated with air. To perform the air insufflation test, a catheter is passed through the patient's nose into the esophagus to the level

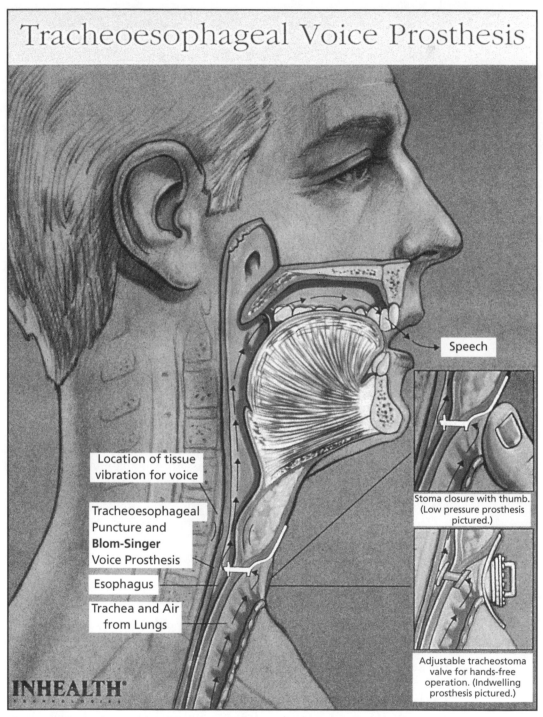

Tracheoesophageal Voice Prosthesis

Speech

Location of tissue vibration for voice

Tracheoesophageal Puncture and **Blom-Singer** Voice Prosthesis

Esophagus

Trachea and Air from Lungs

Stoma closure with thumb. (Low pressure prosthesis pictured.)

Adjustable tracheostoma valve for hands-free operation. (Indwelling prosthesis pictured.)

INHEALTH

Figure 10.5. Tracheoesophageal voice prosthesis. *Note.* Images from International Healthcare Technologies, Carpinteria, CA. Reprinted with permission.

of the tracheostoma, and air is then gently blown into the catheter by use of an auto-insufflation kit (Case, 1996). (See Appendix C for information about how to obtain such kits.) The patient is instructed to open the mouth in a relaxed position as in producing the vowel /a/. As the air exits the catheter, it should cause the P-E segment to vibrate, thus causing an esophageal tone to be emitted from the oral cavity. To pass the insufflation test, the patient must be able to count aloud to 15, sustaining phonation for at least 8 seconds (Case, 1996). The air should flow easily through the catheter, and the esophageal tone that results should be sufficient for speaking purposes. If the esophageal tone produced during the air insufflation test is very weak or absent, it may indicate that the patient is a candidate for a pharyngeal myotomy or a pharyngeal plexus neurectomy (Stemple et al., 1995).

(2) **Myotomy and neurectomy.** Singer and Blom (1981) have shown that pharyngoesophageal spasm can be responsible for approximately 12% of failures to achieve satisfactory speech after TEP surgery. Consequently, a surgical procedure called a **pharyngeal myotomy** (Singer & Blom, 1981), in which specific muscles in the region of the P-E segment are severed, was developed to permit fluent speech production in patients who are prone to P-E segment spasm. The selective myotomy procedure has been so successful that not only have TEP patients developed fluent speech while using the voice prosthesis, but they have also quickly developed conventional esophageal speech after the pharyngeal myotomy has been performed. In **pharyngeal plexus neurectomy,** surgery is directed at deinnervation of nerves that provide innervation to the pharyngeal constrictor muscles (Case, 1996). In each case of myotomy and neurectomy, the aim is to reduce the likelihood of pharyngoesophageal spasm and improve success of the TEP voice restoration.

(3) In a more recent development in the management of pharyngeal constrictor spasm, some physicians are using **botulinum toxin injections** (Botox) instead of surgery. Reportedly, patients may regain speech as soon as 24 to 48 hours postinjection and they do not have the risk of another surgical procedure (Scott, 1998).

d. **Postsurgical voice therapy management**

(1) **Catheter removal and tracheoesophageal speech.** If the patient qualifies as a good candidate, the procedure, and perhaps a selective myotomy or neurectomy, is performed. Following the TEP procedure, a rubber catheter is inserted into the surgically created fistula for approximately 2 days to 2 weeks. For those patients who receive the TEP procedure at the same time as the laryngectomy, the need for a postoperative nasogastric tube is eliminated, as feedings may be given via the tube in the fistula for 10 to 14 days postoperatively (Maves & Lingeman, 1982).

(2) **The voice prosthesis.** After the patient's surgical site has healed sufficiently (perhaps 2 to 3 weeks postsurgically), the patient can be

fitted with the voice prosthesis. Although most patients are able to produce voice immediately, many others will require therapy from a speech–language pathologist for the purpose of (1) improving intelligibility through more accurate articulation, (2) developing improved patterns for phrasing, and, perhaps, (3) learning the combined use of esophageal speech and TE voice prosthesis speech.

(3) Blom (1995) indicates that there are three basic treatment goals following surgical placement of a tracheoesophageal puncture:

(a) dilation and measurement of the tracheoesophageal puncture;

(b) placement of the appropriate length and type of voice prosthesis; and

(c) instruction of the patient in occlusion of the tracheostoma, and in application and use of a tracheostoma valve.

e. **Speech–language pathologist's role in fitting the TEP prosthesis.** Two commonly used prosthetic devices are the **Blom-Singer Indwelling Low Pressure Voice Prosthesis** and the **PROVOX 2 Voice Prosthesis System** (see Appendix C for more information). The speech–language pathologist's role is similar in providing each of these devices to the patient. Both devices are designed to remain in place for as long as several months to 1 year, depending on the effectiveness of preventing yeast colonization, which may break down the device. Indwelling devices should only be inserted by properly trained clinicians (e.g., a speech–language pathologist or physician). There are prosthetic devices that are not indwelling; that is, they are designed to be changed every 2 to 3 days by the patient. However, the indwelling devices have become quite popular because they can remain in place for several months at a time, and many patients simply do not have the manual dexterity or visual acuity to change their prosthesis on a regular basis.

The procedures for inserting the Blom-Singer Indwelling Low Pressure and the Provox 2 devices are theoretically similar. However, the clinician must follow instructions exactly for each device to permit the patient to develop optimal voice.

(1) Generally, the steps in fitting the **Blom-Singer Indwelling Low Pressure Voice Prosthesis** are as follows (E. Hagerman, personal communication, 1998; R. B. Owens, personal communication, 1998):

(a) Every procedure should begin with the use of surgical gloves and universal precautions (Centers for Disease Control, 1988) to prevent the spread of contamination between the speech–language pathologist and the patient.

(b) The catheter, which was placed at the time of the surgical procedure, is removed and a dilator is used to dilate the patient's tracheostoma up to the appropriate size for the selected prosthesis (e.g., 22 Fr. dilator for a 20 Fr. Blom-Singer Indwelling device).

(c) Using the sizer that is included with the kit, carefully push the sizer into the tracheoesophageal puncture and slightly downward. Pull back on the sizer, gently allowing the flange on the sizer to stop on the posterior side of the tracheoesophageal wall. Look to see what mark or size number is visible on the anterior side of the tracheoesphageal wall. Gently pull the sizer to make sure it is sitting in the proper location and then let go. The size that can be read on the anterior side of the tracheoesophageal wall is the size that the patient should use.

(d) Using the Blom-Singer Indwelling Low Pressure Voice Prosthesis starter kit, place the appropriate size valve (after sizing) onto the loading device that comes with the starter kit.

(e) Slowly pull the valve through the loading device so that the flange on the prosthesis folds up into the loading device.

(f) Place a gel cap (included in the starter kit) over the outside of the loading device.

(g) Place the push rod (included in starter kit) onto loading device and push prosthesis into the gel cap.

(h) Remove the tracheoesophageal valve from push rod.

(i) Put voice prosthesis (valve) onto inserter (included in starter kit) and attach the flange onto the security hook of the inserter.

(j) Lubricate the prosthesis lightly, using a very small amount of surgilube.

(k) In a continuous motion, remove the dilator from the tracheostoma and insert the prosthesis into the tracheostoma.

(l) Wait approximately 3 minutes for the gel cap (which has been placed on the valve and is now inserted into the tracheostoma) to dissolve. During this time have the patient begin swallowing gently. After about about 2 to 3 minutes have elapsed, have the patient drink a little warm water to help dissolve the remainder of the gel cap.

(m) Manually turn the valve with the inserter device still on. The valve should turn freely in the patient's neck without any twisting of the attached flange.

(n) Remove the flange from the security hook. Have the patient occlude the tracheostoma with her or his thumb to try to produce voice. Have the patient sustain vowels first, then count, then recite, and so on. Encourage the patient to practice on a daily basis. Also, give a sip of water and look for leakage around the valve. If all appears to be well, cut the security flange and discard. If the prosthesis is properly in place, the patient should have intelligible conversational speech. Encourage the patient to have patience while learning to use the prosthesis.

(o) To determine if the valve is properly in place and opened, the patient should be taken to Radiology by the speech–language pathologist to see if the circular radiopaque ring is visible on X-ray. This determines if the valve has opened properly.

(p) Instruct the patient in the use of Nystatin Oral Suspension to prevent fungal growth on the voice prosthesis. The patient should be taught to swish one teaspoon of Nystatin in the oral cavity 2 times per day for at least 3 to 4 minutes. Fewer than 3 minutes is ineffective (Blom, 1996). If the patient is interested in a one-way, hands-free tracheostoma valve, instruct the patient in its application at this time. The one-way or hands-free valve option allows the patient to talk while doing other tasks with his or her hands. This option is particularly useful for patients whose work requires use of both hands. A humidifilter is available to be added to the Blom-Singer hands-free valve. The filter permits incoming air to be warmed, filtered, and moistened (Stemple et al., 1995).

D. Future trends in voice restoration following total laryngectomy. The technologies for restoration of voice following total laryngectomy are advancing and changing rapidly. An example is an exciting new procedure for voice restoration reported by the Cleveland Clinic Foundation. In January, 1998, the Cleveland Clinic Foundation performed a successful total larynx transplant using a donated human larynx (Kaleidoscope Interactive, 1998). The patient, who had crushed his larynx in a motorcycle accident, had a donor larynx surgically implanted. As a result of the procedure, the patient regained intelligible conversational speech.

It remains to be seen if this procedure will rapidly advance the field of laryngectomy rehabilitation. This was only the second attempt at a larynx transplant. The first attempt was performed almost 20 years earlier by a Belgian physician; however, that patient died before speaking with the transplanted larynx. The 1998 Cleveland Clinic patient was an ideal patient for the transplant because he lost his larynx as a result of trauma, not laryngeal cancer. With the present medical technology, the drugs that are used to prevent rejection of the transplanted larynx could interfere with treatments designed to stop the spread of cancer. For that reason, it is not likely that patients who have cancer of the larynx will be able to have a larynx transplant in the near future.

As more transplants are attempted and as the success rate of transplanted larynges improves, recovery from loss of the larynx will rely less on learning alternative modes of speech or learning to use artificial prostheses. Moreover, it is highly likely that the prostheses and procedures used today will be out of date within the next year, and the role of the speech–language pathologist will change accordingly. By staying up to date on new procedures and devices, clinicians will be able to greatly assist their patients in gaining improved voices.

Appendix A
Standard Reading Passages

◆ ◆ ◆ ◆ ◆ ◆ ◆ ◆ ◆ ◆ ◆ ◆ ◆ ◆ ◆ ◆ ◆ ◆ ◆

THE RAINBOW PASSAGE (Fairbanks, 1960)

When the sunlight strikes raindrops in the air, they act like a prism and form a rainbow. The rainbow is a division of white light into many beautiful colors. These take the shape of a long, round arch with its path high above and its two ends apparently beyond the horizon. There is, according to legend, a boiling pot of gold at one end. When a man looks for something beyond his reach, his friends say he is looking for the pot of gold at the end of the rainbow. . . .

The Rainbow Passage has been used in many voice and speech research experiments, particularly in the study of pitch parameters, such as habitual pitch measurement. The Rainbow Passage is also phonemically balanced to match frequency of occurrence of sounds in English. It is common for the subject to read the entire paragraph, but then the measurements are taken with the first and last sentences eliminated from the analysis. The remaining four sentences contain 55 words and 76 syllables, and 11.5% nasal consonants (Fairbanks, 1960; Kay Elemetrics, 1995). Using the Kay Elemetrics Nasometer, an approximate normal range of nasalance values for children and adults for the Rainbow Passage is 30% to 40%. However, it is not necessary to use the Rainbow Passage in a nasalance assessment because there is no additional clinically relevant value that cannot be obtained with the Zoo Passage (in this appendix) and Nasal Sentences alone (Dalston & Seaver, 1992).

THE ZOO PASSAGE (Fletcher, 1972)

Look at this book with us. It's a story about a zoo. That is where bears go. Today it's very cold out of doors, but we see a cloud overhead that's a pretty, white, fluffy shape. We hear that straw covers the floor of cages to keep the chill away; yet a deer walks through the trees with her head high. They feed seeds to birds so they're able to fly.

The Zoo Passage excludes nasal consonants completely. Using the Kay Elemetrics Nasometer, an approximate normal range of nasalance values for children and adults for the Zoo Passage is 10% to 20%.

NASAL SENTENCES (Kay Elemetrics, 1995)

Mama made some lemon jam. Ten men came in when Jane rang. Dan's gang changed my mind. Ben can't plan on a lengthy rain. Amanda came from Bounding, Maine.

Thirty-five percent of the phonemes in the nasal sentences are nasal consonants. Using the Kay Elemetrics Nasometer, an approximate normal range of nasalance values for children and adults for the nasal sentences is 55% to 65%.

THE AMPLIFIER PASSAGE (Fairbanks, 1960)

People talk with others by means of acoustic signals. The signals are produced by the speaker and received by the listener. They pass from one to the other in many different ways. In the most common situation, the speaker and listener are linked directly by the air between them. This air is the natural path that the speech signals follow. Often however, we can improve upon this arrangement by using equipment between speaker and listener. We convert the speaker's acoustic signals into electrical signals, control them in some way, and then change them back into the acoustic form for the listener to hear. In other words, we give signals a new path through the equipment.

The fact that we can change the path in this way means we can serve a number of purposes. For one thing, we can amplify the speech signals, or increase their power. As we all know from experience, the power of the human voice is limited. An amplifier can raise the limit. In a harbor, for example, or a football stadium, it can be used to make speech audible at a distance. A person who wears a hearing aid carries a small amplifier with them. They need more power than the average speaker produces, and the hearing aid supplies it.

In their electrical form the speech signals can be sent over very long distances. The radio and the telephone thus allow a speaker to ignore the space that separates them from the listener. If we put a recorder in the system, they can also ignore time. The listener can listen whenever they want, and repeat speech as often as they like. These are only a few of the ways in which equipment can extend speech far beyond the simple, direct situation.

The Amplifier Passage is a 300-word passage that can be used to measure speech rate. According to Fairbanks (1960), the subject should read the paragraph over once for content (without studying or rehearsing), and then read the passage aloud as though reading to a group of about 20 people for information purposes. A stop watch is needed so that the paragraph reading can be timed to the nearest second. An "excellent" reading, according to Fairbanks, is about 160 to 170 words per minute (wpm). A "satisfactory" reading ranges between about 150 wpm and 180 wpm. Anything below about 145 wpm is judged to be "too slow," and anything beyond 195 wpm is "too fast."

ARTHUR, THE YOUNG RAT
(Williams, Darley, & Spriestersbach, 1978)

Once, a long time ago, there was a young rat named Arthur who could never make up his flighty mind. Whenever his swell friends used to ask him to go out to play with them, he would only answer airily, "I don't know." He wouldn't try to say yes, or no either. He would always shrink from making a specific choice.

His proud Aunt Helen scolded him: "Now look here," she stated, "no one is going to care for you if you carry on like this. You have no more mind than a stray blade of grass."

That very night there was a big thundering crash and in the foggy morning some zealous men—with twenty boys and girls—rode up and looked closely at the fallen barn. One of them slipped back and saw a squashed young rat, quite dead, half in and half out of his hole. Thus, in the end the poor shirker got his just dues. Oddly enough his aunt Helen was glad. "I hate such oozy, oily sneaks," said she.

Arthur the Young Rat has been used for many years as a reading passage by speech–language pathologists. It was originally intended to be used to assess speaking rate. Using this 180-word passage, the speech–language pathologist can apply the same approach that is used with the Amplifier Passage and expect that a "satisfactory reading" of Arthur the Young Rat would take approximately one minute or slightly longer (150 to 180 wpm).

Appendix B
Informational Handouts for Clients and Families

◆ ◆ ◆ ◆ ◆ ◆ ◆ ◆ ◆ ◆ ◆ ◆ ◆ ◆ ◆ ◆ ◆ ◆

THE EFFECTS OF MEDICATIONS AND DRUGS ON YOUR VOICE

Your voice is a very delicate, fluid-filled mechanism. It works best for you when it is moist, healthy, and rested. Many drugs, including alcohol, tobacco, and caffeine, have damaging effects on your voice. Check with your physician before taking *any* drug or if you suspect that a drug you are taking is affecting your voice. Your physician can help you minimize the effects of the drug on your voice if you follow her or his advice carefully.

Drug/ Medication	Common Brands	Effects on the Voice	Cautions & Comments
Tobacco	Cigarettes, cigars, pipes, chewing tobacco	Dries, irritates; contains over 40 known cancer-causing agents.	Don't use.
Marijuana		Inhaled heat and smoke dries and irritates your voice; inhibitions are reduced, causing you to use your voice carelessly.	Don't use.
Cocaine		Dries, irritates; constricts blood vessels; is powerfully addictive.	Don't use.
Caffeine	Coffee, tea, soda pop	Dries; acts as a diuretic, causing you to lose fluid.	Cut down caffeine; increase water.
Alcohol	Beer, wine, whiskey	Dries; reduces inhibitions, causing you to use your voice carelessly; relaxes muscles, causing stomach acids to back up; acts as a mild diuretic, causing you to lose fluid.	Cut down on alcohol; increase water and natural juices.

(continues)

© 2000 by Jodelle F. Deem and Lynda Miller.
Permission is granted to the user of this manual to make copies of the handouts in Appendix B for school or clinical purposes.

Drug/ Medication	Common Brands	Effects on the Voice	Cautions & Comments
Antihistamines	Benadryl, Contac, Alka-Seltzer Plus[1]	Dries; thickens secretions; causes drowsiness.	OTC.[2] Check with physician prior to use; newer Rx[3] medications such as Claritin or Allegra may be less drying and produce less drowsiness.
Antitussives	Dimetapp DM, Pedia Care 1, Robitussin DM[1]	May dry voice and thicken secretions.	Check with physician prior to use; physician may be able to recommend a medication with guaifenesin or dextro-methorphan, which will not be as drying.OTC.
Pain Relievers	Aspirin, Advil, Motrin[1]	May cause bleeding in vocal folds.	Check with your physician if you are having throat pain; don't yell or scream if taking pain relievers, as you may cause vocal fold bleeding. OTC. You can take Tylenol, which will *not* cause bleeding.
Sleeping Pills	Sominex, Nytol[1]	Dries; thickens secretions.	Many sleep medications contain antihistamines, which are very drying. OTC.
Oral Inhalers	Asthmacort, Vanceril[1]	May dry; inhaled steroids may cause dysphonia.	Rx only. These medications are beneficial for many individuals; however, the propellants used in the inhalers may cause drying.
Diuretics	Lasix, Dyazide[1]	May dry; thickens secretions.	Rx only.
Antihypertensives	Aldomet, Serpasil, Sandril, Capoten	All may dry; a particular kind of blood pressure medicine called ACE Inhibitors (e.g., Capoten) may cause you to cough, which will irritate your voice.	Rx only. Your physician may be able to work with you if you are concerned that your Rx is drying your voice.
Female Hormones	Danocrine, Cyclomen, birth control pills	May permanently lower the pitch of your voice.	Rx only. Your physician should inform you of side effects.
Antidepressants	Elavil, Tofranil	Dries.	Rx only. Your physician may be able to prescribe an alternate medication if you are concerned with vocal drying.

[1]The drugs listed are for illustrative purposes only. Other drugs could be included in this classification.

[2]OTC = Over the Counter

[3]Rx = physician's prescription only

© 2000 by Jodelle F. Deem and Lynda Miller.
Permission is granted to the user of this manual to make copies of the handouts in Appendix B for school or clinical purposes.

SUGGESTIONS FOR PARENTS OF YOUNG CHILDREN WITH VOICE PROBLEMS (AGES 3 TO 7)

To improve her or his voice and to prevent permanent damage to it, your child is going to need your help. Without your help, your child will have a difficult time understanding why he or she cannot use her or his voice as usual. If you follow these suggestions and add praise, rewards, and positive attention, your child will get through this tough process.

Things to Do

Encourage your child to drink lots of water and natural juices.

Help your child use her or his "quiet voice," which means using a relaxed, conversational volume. With your child, devise nonvocal signals to replace use of the voice. For example, give your child a whistle to use for calling the dog or to make noise at the ball game; provide your child with clickers or other noisemakers to use for making "monster truck" noises. Teach your child to walk closer to other people to talk or to tap them on the shoulder to get their attention. If your house is big, consider installing an intercom to reduce yelling and shouting.

Keep your house as dust- and smoke-free as possible.

Develop a quiet environment in your home. For example, turn the TV volume down, take time to read to your child, and listen to music with her or him.

When children know they have your attention, they usually relax and use their voices in a healthier way. Provide your child with your attention by scheduling time each day to sit with her or him to have a conversation or just to listen to what she or he has to say.

Take care of your child's allergies, sinus congestion, or colds as soon as you notice them. Because over-the-counter medications for colds and allergies can dry your child's voice, talk to your child's doctor about what to use.

Make sure your child gets plenty of rest and has lots of activities that have low demand on the voice (e.g., reading, playing a musical instrument, walking the dog—if there are no allergies—playing with computers, swimming, playing tennis, and so on). Remember that children can yell when they are doing anything, so you will need to help them understand how important it is to use their quiet voice.

Help your child to understand what it means to use a quiet voice. At this age, children are not usually successful with abstract terms (soft, loud, low, high, etc.) or with cause and effect reasoning (i.e., "Don't yell or the bumps will come back on your voice"). You will need to help your child by showing her or him the kind of voice your child needs to use, or by using terms your child can understand (e.g., "Use your voice like you are telling a secret," "Use your voice like you use it in the library"). Give your child plenty of praise whenever he or she uses a quiet voice.

Ask your child's voice therapist if you can sit in on therapy sessions so that you really know what your child needs to do. Ask for specific examples of activities that you can use on a daily basis at home to help your child. Make sure you know what

© 2000 by Jodelle F. Deem and Lynda Miller.
Permission is granted to the user of this manual to make copies of the handouts in Appendix B for school or clinical purposes.

your child is supposed to be doing for "homework" so you can guide, reward, and reinforce her or his efforts and progress.

Things to Avoid

Avoid sodas, tea, and all beverages with caffeine. These drinks cause the voice to become extremely dry, which slows progress and hinders the recovery of the voice.

Your child should avoid yelling, screaming, cheering, talking over loud noise, or using "monster truck" noises.

Avoid dry, dusty, or smoky environments. If someone in your family smokes (cigarettes, cigars, pipes, marijuana) have her or him smoke outside or away from family members.

Avoid a loud home environment: TV, radio, or music at high volume, loud talking from room to room, people trying to talk over one another.

Avoid situations where your child needs to repeat or talk loudly to get your attention, or where your child must compete to communicate with you.

Avoid over-the-counter medications for colds, allergies, or sinus problems, because they cause the voice to become extremely dry.

Avoid coughing and throat clearing. If your child is coughing and clearing her or his throat frequently, consult with your child's doctor.

Avoid situations that you know cause high stress and fatigue in your child, such as heavily scheduled activities with few breaks for rest or activities that demand heavy vocal use (little league games, choir, cheering).

Avoid telling your child that he or she is not using his or her voice correctly, and avoid criticizing your child for not following the doctor's or voice therapist's instructions. Children this age understand best when you use concrete examples of how to help his or her voice, whereas focusing on the negative may inhibit your child's willingness to communicate. What your child really needs is for you to demonstrate a "good voice" or a "quiet voice," and to praise his or her efforts in improving vocal hygiene and voice production.

© 2000 by Jodelle F. Deem and Lynda Miller.
Permission is granted to the user of this manual to make copies of the handouts in Appendix B for school or clinical purposes.

SUGGESTIONS FOR PARENTS OF CHILDREN WITH VOICE PROBLEMS (AGES 7 TO 14)

Your child is going to need your help to prevent permanent damage and to improve his or her health. Without your help, your child will have a difficult time understanding why he or she cannot use her or his voice as usual. If you follow these suggestions and add praise, rewards, and positive attention, your child will get through this tough process.

Things to Do

Encourage your child to drink lots of water and natural juices.

Help your child use her or his "quiet voice," which means using a relaxed, conversational volume. With your child, devise nonvocal signals to replace use of the voice. For example, give your child a whistle to use for calling the dog or to make noise at the soccer game. Teach your child to walk closer to other people to talk or to tap them on the shoulder to get their attention. If your house is big, consider installing an intercom to reduce yelling and shouting.

Keep your house as dust- and smoke-free as possible.

Develop a quiet environment in your home. For example, turn the TV volume down, take time to read to your child, or listen to music with her or him.

When children know they have your attention, they usually relax and use their voices in a healthier way. Provide your child with your attention by scheduling time each day to sit and have a conversation or just to listen to what she or he has to say.

Take care of your child's allergies, sinus congestion, or colds as soon as you notice them. Because over-the-counter medications for colds and allergies can dry your child's voice, talk to your child's doctor about what to use.

Make sure your child gets plenty of rest and has lots of activities that put low demand on the voice (e.g., reading, playing a musical instrument, walking the dog—if there are no allergies—playing with computers, swimming, playing tennis, and so on). Remember that children can yell when they are doing anything, so you will need to help them understand how important it is to use their quiet voice.

Help your child to understand that he or she needs to use his or her quiet voice in every situation. Help your child by showing her or him the kind of voice he or she needs to use, or by using terms he or she can understand (e.g., "Use your 'inside voice,'" or "Use your voice like you use it in the library"). Give your child plenty of praise whenever he or she uses a quiet voice.

Your child may begin to have changes in her or his ability to control the pitch of the voice as puberty approaches. Your child may be embarassed by these changes, but you can help your child through this by reassuring her or him that this is a normal process. Encourage your child to continue to use her or his voice in a relaxed way.

Ask your child's voice therapist if you can sit in on therapy sessions so that you really know what your child needs to do. Ask for specific examples of activities that

© 2000 by Jodelle F. Deem and Lynda Miller.
Permission is granted to the user of this manual to make copies of the handouts in Appendix B for school or clinical purposes.

you can use on a daily basis at home to help your child. Make sure you know what your child is supposed to be doing for "homework" so you can guide, reward, and reinforce her or his efforts and progress.

Things to Avoid

Have your child avoid sodas, tea, and all beverages with caffeine. These drinks cause the voice to become extremely dry, which slows progress and hinders the recovery of the voice.

Your child should avoid yelling, screaming, cheering, or talking over loud noise.

Avoid dry, dusty, or smoky environments. If someone in your family smokes (cigarettes, cigars, pipes, marijuana) have her or him smoke outside or away from other family members.

Avoid a loud home environment: TV, radio, or music at high volume, loud talking from room to room, people trying to talk over one another.

Avoid situations where your child needs to repeat or talk loudly to get your attention, or where your child must compete to communicate with you.

Avoid over-the-counter medications for colds, allergies, or sinus problems, because they cause the voice to become extremely dry.

Your child should avoid coughing and throat clearing. If your child is coughing and clearing her or his throat frequently, consult with your child's doctor.

Avoid situations that you know cause high stress and fatigue in your child, such as heavily scheduled activities with few breaks for rest, or activities that demand heavy vocal use (e.g., little league games, choir, cheering).

Avoid calling attention to the pitch changes and pitch breaks that may occur in your child's voice as he or she approaches puberty. Do not let siblings tease your child about these voice changes either.

Avoid telling your child that he or she is not using her or his voice correctly, and avoid criticizing your child for not following the doctor's or voice therapist's instructions. This may may inhibit your child's willingness to communicate. What your child really needs is for you to demonstrate and use a "good voice" or a "quiet voice," and to praise her or his efforts in improving vocal hygiene and voice production.

© 2000 by Jodelle F. Deem and Lynda Miller.
Permission is granted to the user of this manual to make copies of the handouts in Appendix B for school or clinical purposes.

SUGGESTIONS FOR TEENS WITH VOICE PROBLEMS

Your voice is a very delicate, fluid-filled mechanism. It works best for you when it is moist, healthy, and rested. If your voice is dry, tired, or if you are sick, it is a target for stress or disease.

Things to Do

Drink lots of water and natural juices.

Keep your voice at conversational loudness, use nonvocal signals (e.g., a whistle to make noise at the football game or to call the dog), and devise other signals to communicate from room to room. Walk closer to another person to talk, or tap a person on the shoulder to get her or his attention. If your house is big, consider an intercom to reduce yelling and shouting, or walk to the other person's room to talk.

Keep your house (and your room!) as dust- and smoke-free as possible.

Develop a quiet environment in your home. For example, turn TV volume down, take time to read, listen to music, and so forth.

Take time over dinner (or any scheduled part of the day) to talk with family members and friends in a relaxed way. Have a conversation or just listen to what your family and friends have to say. Allow time so that they can listen to you—your voice will be much healthier and more relaxed.

Take care of allergies, sinus congestion, or colds as soon as you notice them. Because over-the-counter medications for colds and allergies can dry the voice, make sure you've talked to your doctor about what to use *before* you purchase anything.

Make sure you get plenty of rest and choose activities that place low demand on your voice (reading, playing a musical instrument, walking the dog—if there are no allergies—playing with computers, swimming, playing tennis).

Use an easy, relaxed, and quiet voice in every situation. Your voice therapist can help you learn what your quiet, relaxed voice is.

You may be experiencing changes in your ability to control the pitch of your voice because of puberty. Do not be embarrassed by these changes, as the decrease in pitch (boys: your voice may drop a whole octave in the next few years; girls: yours may drop three or four steps) and loss of control of pitch are perfectly normal. Continue to use your voice in a relaxed way; you will become accustomed to the new pitch levels and will soon learn to control them.

If you are going for voice therapy, have your parents or family member sit in on therapy sessions so they really know what you need to do and so they can help you. Parents, ask for specific examples of activities that you can use on a daily basis at home to help. Make sure you and your family understand what you are supposed to be doing for homework so they can help reinforce your progress.

© 2000 by Jodelle F. Deem and Lynda Miller.
Permission is granted to the user of this manual to make copies of the handouts in Appendix B for school or clinical purposes.

Things to Avoid

Avoid coffee, alcohol, sodas, tea (all beverages with caffeine). These drinks cause the voice to become extremely dry, which slows progress and hinders the recovery of the voice.

Avoid smoking anything (cigarettes, cigars, marijuana, pipes, etc.)! If you have started smoking—quit; if you haven't started—don't! Smoking is very drying and irritating to your voice.

Avoid dry, dusty, or smoky environments. If someone in your family smokes (cigarettes, cigars, pipes, marijuana) have them smoke outside or away from family members.

Yelling, screaming, cheering, or talking over loud noise should be avoided. It may be impossible for you to be a cheerleader for your school. If you are having problems with your voice, do not try out for cheerleading squad. If you are already a member of the squad and do not want to quit, be sure to work with your voice therapist to keep your voice healthy.

Avoid a loud home environment: TV, radio, or music at high volume, loud talking from room to room, people trying to talk over one another.

Avoid situations where you need to repeat or talk loudly (e.g., loud concerts, noisy nightclubs, bars) to get others' attention, or where you must compete to communicate.

Avoid over-the-counter medications for colds, allergies, or sinus problems, as they cause the voice to become extremely dry.

Coughing and throat clearing should be avoided. If you are coughing and clearing your throat frequently, consult with your doctor.

Avoid situations that you know cause high stress and fatigue, such as heavily scheduled activities with few breaks for rest, or activities that demand heavy vocal use (e.g., sports, choir, chorus).

Avoid straining to keep your pitch from changing or lowering. During puberty, you will experience pitch changes and pitch breaks.These changes are normal. Just keep using your voice in a relaxed way.

Avoid missing your voice therapy sessions, skipping your voice practice activities, or not following through with your assignments. If you want your voice to stay healthy, you must take responsibility for following through with therapy.

© 2000 by Jodelle F. Deem and Lynda Miller.
Permission is granted to the user of this manual to make copies of the handouts in Appendix B for school or clinical purposes.

VOCAL HEALTH TIPS FOR ADULTS AND SENIORS

Your voice is a very delicate, fluid-filled mechanism. It works best for you when it is moist, healthy, and rested. If your voice is dry, tired, or if you are sick, it is a target for stress or disease.

Be aware that it is much easier to keep your voice healthy than it is to nurse it back to health from laryngitis or other vocal illness. It has been estimated that approximately 10% to 15% of older adults have some kind of voice disorder. As we age, our voices are less able to bounce back after a cold or the flu. It is very important that you take extra precautions to keep your voice healthy, especially if you are sick with a cold, flu, allergies, or laryngitis.

Things to Do

Drink lots of water and natural juices.

Keep your voice at an easy conversational loudness, use nonvocal signals (e.g., a whistle to make noise at the game or to call the dog), or devise other nonvocal signals to replace use of the voice. Walk closer to other people to talk, or tap them on the shoulder to get their attention. If your house is large, consider an intercom system to reduce strain on your voice, or make a practice of walking to the other person's room to talk.

Keep your house as free of dust and smoke as possible, and keep it humid. Use a warm-mist humidifier (especially important in the winter if you have wood or electric heat), making sure to keep it free of mold.

Develop a quiet environment in your home. For example, turn the TV volume down, take time to read, listen to music, and so forth.

Take time over dinner (or any scheduled part of the day) to talk with family members and friends in a relaxed way. Have a conversation or just listen to what your family and friends have to say. Allow time so that they can listen to you. Your voice will be much healthier and more relaxed if you do.

Take care of allergies, sinus congestion, or colds as soon as you notice them. Because over-the-counter medications for colds and allergies can dry the voice, make sure you have talked to your doctor about what to use.

Work closely with your physician in managing all conditions that can affect the voice, including esophageal reflux (GERD), asthma, allergies, hormonal changes (menopause, endometriosis), thyroid problems, and temporomandibular joint dysfunction (TMJ). A problem in any one of these areas can adversely affect your voice.

Choose activities that have low demand on your voice, such as reading, playing a musical instrument, walking, swimming, biking. Also, if you have no allergies, walk the dog or work with plants in your house or garden.

Manage your stress by putting time in your schedule to relax and reduce tension. Meditate, get a massage, take a hot bath, and so on. The vast majority of voice problems in adulthood are related to tension in the voice due to a stressful lifestyle.

© 2000 by Jodelle F. Deem and Lynda Miller.
Permission is granted to the user of this manual to make copies of the handouts in Appendix B for school or clinical purposes.

Get lots of sleep. Try to manage your schedule to permit a reasonable amount of sleep and "time off" for your voice. A tired body results in a tired voice and a much greater risk for damage to your voice.

Develop quiet times for voice rest that will work in your schedule. For example, if you must go to choir rehearsal in the evening, then schedule the early part of the next day with quiet activities (e.g., office work, reading), and only use your voice if you absolutely must during that time. Try to schedule periods of voice rest throughout your week.

Be careful about your diet. If you are well-nourished and rested, your voice will be its healthiest.

Use your best easy, relaxed voice in every situation. Your voice therapist can help you learn what your best voice is.

If you are having trouble with your voice, enroll in voice therapy. It can be helpful and does not last very long—many voice problems can be relieved in 6 to 12 weeks. If you are enrolled in voice therapy, have a friend or family member sit in on a therapy session so they really know what you need to do and can help you. Make sure your family and friends understand how you are supposed to use your voice so they can help reinforce your progress.

Things to Avoid

Avoid coffee, alcohol, sodas, tea—all beverages with caffeine. These drinks cause the voice to become extremely dry, which slows progress and hinders the recovery of the voice.

Smoking (cigarettes, cigars, marijuana, pipes, etc.) is very drying and irritating to your voice and should be avoided.

Highly spiced foods, as well as coffee, tea and other caffeinated beverages, may lead to gastroesophageal reflux (GERD), which can cause severe irritation of the vocal mechanism. It is particularly important to avoid highly spiced foods late at night because your risk of reflux increases if you lie down to sleep after eating these foods. Your physician can help you with a diet that reduces your risk of reflux.

Avoid dry, dusty, or smoky environments. If someone in your family smokes (cigarettes, cigars, pipes, marijuana) have her or him smoke outside or away from family members. Avoid smoky restaurants, clubs, and so forth. Always ask to be seated in the no-smoking section.

Yelling or talking over loud noise should be avoided. As we age, we tend to have more friends who have hearing losses. If you frequently talk to friends or family members who have hearing loss, make sure you are close to them when you talk so you do not need to strain your voice. Try not to talk to anyone over loud background noise (loud concerts, noisy nightclubs, etc.). Try to choose places for conversation that are quiet and conducive to relaxed interaction.

Avoid a loud home environment: TV, radio, or music at high volume, loud talking from room to room, people trying to talk over one another.

© 2000 by Jodelle F. Deem and Lynda Miller.
Permission is granted to the user of this manual to make copies of the handouts in Appendix B for school or clinical purposes.

Avoid over-the-counter medications for colds, allergies, or sinus problems, as they cause the voice to become extremely dry. Check with your physician about what to use.

Coughing and throat clearing should be avoided. If you are coughing and clearing your throat frequently, consult with your doctor.

Avoid situations that you know demand heavy vocal use (e.g., church choir and choir rehearsals, teaching several days per week, talking on the phone a lot). You will need to choose how you really want to use your voice and save it for those things.

Situations that you know cause high stress and fatigue, such as heavily scheduled activities with few breaks for rest, should be avoided.

Do not try to force your voice to do things that it can no longer do (e.g., singing extended ranges, talking in a very authoritarian, low pitch). There is some evidence that, with aging, men's pitch tends to increase slightly, whereas women tend to have a decrease in pitch. Some of the structures of our voices tend to begin to lose their elasticity in our 30s. If there is something specific you want to be able to do with your voice, work with a voice therapist or voice coach in making healthy compensations to avoid vocal strain.

Avoid complete voice rest (i.e., no talking, singing, or any form of vocalizing) for as long as a week or more. There is little benefit in this unless it has been prescribed by your physician.

Avoid missing voice therapy sessions or practice activities or not following through with practice activities. It takes approximately 2 hours of practice per day to restore your voice to health if it has been damaged. If you want your voice to stay healthy, it is important that you follow through with therapy.

© 2000 by Jodelle F. Deem and Lynda Miller.
Permission is granted to the user of this manual to make copies of the handouts in Appendix B for school or clinical purposes.

TIPS FOR VOCAL HEALTH FOR ANY AGE

Your voice is a very delicate, fluid-filled mechanism. It works best for you when it is moist, healthy, and rested. If your voice is dry, fatigued, or if you are sick, it is a target for possible stress or disease.

Things to Do

Drink lots of water and natural juices

Keep your voice at a conversational volume, use nonvocal signals (e.g., whistles, noisemakers, clickers, tapping people on the shoulder to get their attention), or use an intercom system.

Keep your environment as smoke- and dust-free as possible, and keep it humid. Use a warm-mist humidifier, particulary if you have wood or electric heat, and make sure to keep it free of mold.

Use your voice sensibly, especially if you have a cold or allergies. If you use your voice a lot, learn from a professional how to rest it, warm it up, cool it down, and so on.

Develop a quiet environment in your home: turn TV volume on low or off and make a place for reading, listening to music, and quiet conversations.

Take care of allergies, sinus congestion, and colds as soon as you notice them.

Be judicious with over-the-counter medications, especially for colds, allergies, and sinus problems. Talk to your doctor or pharmacist about what to take.

Manage your stress. Reduce tension and anxiety when they arise. Get plenty of rest, and take time to relax—meditate, get a massage, take a long walk or a hot bath, start a hobby, get a pet (check about your allergies before you do this).

Women: Rest your voice just before or during your menstrual period when your vocal cords may be swollen.

Things to Avoid

Coffee, alcohol, caffeine (including sodas and tea), smoking (including cigars, pipes, cigarettes, marijuana).

Screaming, yelling, cheering at the ballgame, or talking over loud noises.

Dry, dusty, or smoky environments.

Talking or singing excessively, especially if you have a cold or allergies. Sudden, prolonged use of your voice without warming it up. Sudden cessation of using your voice after a long period of use.

A loud home environment with TV, radio, or music volume on loud, and talking from room to room.

Coughing or clearing your throat a lot.

© 2000 by Jodelle F. Deem and Lynda Miller.
Permission is granted to the user of this manual to make copies of the handouts in Appendix B for school or clinical purposes.

Taking over-the-counter medications for colds, allergies, or sinus problems, because they dry out the voice.

High-stress situations, particularly over long periods of time. If you cannot avoid them, reduce them as much as possible.

Women: Avoid heavy vocal demands just before or during your menstrual period.

© 2000 by Jodelle F. Deem and Lynda Miller.

Permission is granted to the user of this manual to make copies of the handouts in Appendix B for school or clinical purposes.

VOCAL HYGIENE RULES FOR LIFELONG VOCAL HEALTH

- **Your voice** is a very delicate, fluid-filled mechanism. It does its very best for you when it is moist, healthy, and rested. That means that you *must* drink lots of water and do all that you can to keep yourself healthy and rested. **Water** is a big key to your vocal health. One of the ways to tell if you are drinking enough is to note the color of your urine when you go to the bathroom. If your urine is pale or colorless, you are drinking enough; if it has color, you need to drink more water, natural juices, and fluids. Caffeine is an enemy of your voice, as it acts as a diuretic and causes you to lose fluid. *Drinking coffee, coke, and caffeinated teas will harm rather than help your voice.* Cut down or cut out the caffeine and increase water and other natural fluids. This is a must. If your voice is too dry, it is a target for harm.

- **Try to avoid** yelling, screaming, cheering, or talking over loud noise. If you need to get someone's attention in a noisy environment, walk up to that person and tap him or her on the shoulder, whistle, and so on. Carry a whistle to call the dog or to use for noise at the soccer game. If you live in a big house, use an intercom—don't yell. If your child has a voice problem, try to help her or him learn to make noises other than "monster truck" noises. Teach him or her how to make clicking noises with his or her tongue and to use noisemakers or a whistle.

- **Try to avoid** smoking *anything* (tobacco, pipes, cigars, marijuana) because smoking is very irritating to your voice. Also, try not to spend time in smoky or dusty environments. (By the way, drinking alcohol is not good for your voice, either.)

- **Try to avoid** talking or singing excessively, particularly if you have a cold. If you must speak a lot in your work, or if you sing often during the week, get professional vocal training from a speech–language pathologist or vocal coach. They will help you develop a voice rest/use schedule, show you how to warm up your voice and cool it down, and so forth. Try to develop a quiet environment in your home and workplace where peace and quiet are reinforced and valued. Keep the TV volume low, read a lot, listen to quiet background music, or anything that enhances a quiet environment.

- **Try to avoid** clearing your throat or coughing a lot. These really hurt your voice and are usually just symptoms of other problems, such as allergies, sinus drainage, and so on. If you feel the need to clear your throat or cough, discuss this with a ear, nose, and throat specialist for appropriate treatment.

- **Try to avoid** eating large or fatty meals to prevent gastroesophageal reflux disease (GERD). It will also help if you avoid caffeine, alcohol, sweets, orange and tomato products, spices, and mints. If you do have GERD, smoking will further irritate your voice. It will also help if you avoid eating within 1 to 2 hours of going to bed. If you have frequent heartburn or indigestion, you may have GERD and should see your physician.

- **Try to avoid** taking any over-the-counter medications without carefully reading the directions and precautions. Many over-the-counter medications, particularly for colds, allergies, and sinus problems, are very drying to your voice, and a dry voice is an unhealthy voice. Take all prescription medications specifically

© 2000 by Jodelle F. Deem and Lynda Miller.
Permission is granted to the user of this manual to make copies of the handouts in Appendix B for school or clinical purposes.

as directed by your physician. Ask if medications you are taking have effects on the voice.

- **Try to avoid** using your voice any more than you absolutely must when you have a cold, allergies, sinus infection, or any other respiratory problem. Your voice is very vulnerable at these times and needs more special care. Call in sick if you can so that you are able to completely rest your voice, get yourself a good book, drink lots of water and natural juices, and rest! If you must talk, keep it to a minimum. Do not try to raise your loudness or change your pitch to talk louder. For women, you should avoid heavy vocal demands just before or during your menstrual period, as your vocal folds may be swollen at this time of month.

- **Try to avoid** scheduling more in your life than your stress level can tolerate. Be alert to signs that you are feeling tense and stressed. The voice is a barometer of the stress level in your body. Tension and strain go straight to your neck, shoulders, and voice. Do not talk when you are feeling fatigued. Do not talk or sing when your voice is irritated or fatigued. Make time to do things that relax you. For example, learn to meditate, get a massage (which is especially good for your upper body, neck, and shoulders), take a long walk each day, start a hobby, or get a pet (be careful if you have allergies).

- **Try to avoid** living in the Sahara Desert! Many homes and office buildings in the winter are as dry as the Sahara. Use a warm-mist humidifier or even a pan of water on the wood stove or furnace outlets to increase the humidity levels in your environment. If you use a humidifier, make sure to keep it clean and free of mold. Wood heat and electric heat are particularly dry and you *will* need to add humidity.

- **If you have questions,** feel free to contact a speech–language pathologist at a hospital or voice care center near you. You can locate a speech–language pathologist by contacting the American Speech-Language-Hearing Association at 1-800-638-TALK, by e-mail at actioncenter@asha.org, or through the Web site at http://www.asha.org/.

A professional will be happy to answer your questions about your voice. If you can follow these guidelines, you *can* improve your voice. Take care of your voice and it will last a lifetime.

© 2000 by Jodelle F. Deem and Lynda Miller.
Permission is granted to the user of this manual to make copies of the handouts in Appendix B for school or clinical purposes.

ADVICE FOR PROFESSIONAL VOICE USERS

If you rely on your voice as a primary method for doing your work, you are a professional voice user. Voice professionals include singers, actors, educators, counselors, clergy, auctioneers, coaches, salespersons, attorneys, politicians, and so forth. If you rely on your voice for your work, following these guidelines can help to keep your voice healthy. In addition to this sheet, ask your doctor or voice coach for a copy of the handouts called "Vocal Hygiene Rules" and "Effects of Drugs on Your Voice."

If your voice is healthy, you can keep it that way by following these guidelines and the advice of your voice coach or therapist. If you have had problems with your voice, following these guidelines and the advice of your coach, therapist, or ear nose and throat physician should restore your vocal health. Only you can make the necessary choices to balance the demands of your work and the health of your voice.

Things to Do

Drink lots of water. Your voice does its very best for you when it is moist, healthy, and rested. Water is a big key to your vocal health. One of the ways to tell if you are drinking enough is to note the color of your urine. If your urine is pale or colorless, you are drinking enough. If it has color, you need to drink more water, natural juices, and fluids.

Develop quiet times for voice rest that will work in your schedule. For example, if you must sing or lecture every evening, then schedule the early part of your day with the quiet activities of your profession (e.g., office work, answering correspondence) and only use your voice if you absolutely must during that time. Try to establish 24- to 48-hour recovery periods between engagements to allow your voice to rest between heavy demand times.

Get lots of sleep. Try to manage your schedule to permit a reasonable amount of sleep and time off for your voice. A tired body will result in a tired voice and a much higher risk for vocal strain and injury.

Be careful about your diet. If you are well-nourished and rested, your voice will be its healthiest.

Warm your voice up before and cool it down after each performance or engagement. A warm-up can be as simple as 10 to 15 minutes of softly humming or singing scales before using your voice for the day. A cool down following voice use might consist of 10 minutes of soft (not whispered) humming or speaking.

Use a monitor speaker so you can hear your own voice over the ambient noise of the auditorium or concert hall. Use a microphone to deliver lectures or performances in large rooms or rooms with poor acoustics.

Work closely with your physician in managing all conditions that can affect the voice, including gastroesophageal reflux (GERD), asthma, allergies, hormonal changes (menopause, endometriosis), thyroid problems, and temporomandibular joint dysfunction. Even a mild problem in one of these areas can affect your voice.

© 2000 by Jodelle F. Deem and Lynda Miller.
Permission is granted to the user of this manual to make copies of the handouts in Appendix B for school or clinical purposes.

If your vocal demands are heavy, use a professional voice coach or voice therapist on a regular basis to help you maintain a healthy voice.

Be aware of how you use your voice when you are not performing. You can harm your voice just as easily when you are not performing as you can during a performance. Your voice coach can help you with healthy voice-use strategies for all situations.

If you have pain, tiredness, aching, tickling, choking, coughing, or other symptoms when you use your voice, see your physician.

If you absolutely must perform when you have laryngitis, your physician may be able to help you by prescribing medications that may get you through one performance. However, there is a risk of serious damage to your voice. Your physician will be unlikely to agree to this treatment unless you agree to a period of vocal rest immediately following the performance.

Things to Avoid

Avoid anything that dries or irritates your voice, including cigarettes, cigars, marijuana, second-hand smoke (as in bars and nightclubs), alcohol (beer, wine, whiskey), coffee, tea, soda pop, and over-the-counter medications for colds and allergies. Also avoid dusty or moldy environments that may exist in old theatres and concert halls.

Avoid a nonstop schedule of speaking or singing and other heavy demands, such as staying out late after a performance, and then getting up early for rehearsal. Because your voice is a muscle, it must have a reasonable amount of rest.

Avoid yelling, screaming, whispering, talking over loud noises, coughing, or clearing your throat a lot.

Avoid eating certain types of foods that may affect your voice. Some vocal performers avoid milk products, chocolate, and nuts before performances, because they seem to increase and thicken mucous secretions. Highly spiced foods, as well as coffee, tea, and other caffeinated beverages, may lead to gastroesophageal reflux, which can cause severe irritation of the vocal mechanism. It is especially important not to eat these highly spiced or caffeinated foods late in the evening, as your risk of reflux increases if you lie down to sleep after eating these foods.

Women, if possible, you should avoid demanding singing or speaking engagements before and during the early days of your menstrual period, because your vocal cords may be swollen at this time. Although this will not be a problem for the average speaker, it may present significant problems for the professional singer.

Avoid complete voice rest (no talking, singing, or any form of vocalizing) for as long as a week or more. There is little benefit in this unless it has been prescribed by your physician.

Avoid speaking or singing over loud background noise such as can occur in noisy restaurants, nightclubs, school cafeterias, and so on. Also, avoid using an authoritative voice for a greater vocal impact. Your normal, healthy, relaxed voice is always the voice you should use in demanding situations.

© 2000 by Jodelle F. Deem and Lynda Miller.
Permission is granted to the user of this manual to make copies of the handouts in Appendix B for school or clinical purposes.

Appendix C
Resources for Voice Assessment and Therapy

◆ ◆ ◆ ◆ ◆ ◆ ◆ ◆ ◆ ◆ ◆ ◆ ◆ ◆ ◆ ◆ ◆ ◆

INSTRUMENTS FOR MEASURING PARAMETERS OF SPEECH AND VOICE

Computerized Speech Lab (CSL)
A comprehensive PC-based system for acquisition of speech signals, editing, storage, and playback. CSL also serves as the hardware "host" for Visi-Pitch II and the Multidimensional Voice Profile options.

Kay Elemetrics
2 Bridgewater Ln.
Lincoln Park, NJ 07035
973/628-6200
Fax: 973/628-6363
www.kayelemetrics.com
Call for current prices and ordering info.

Visi-Pitch II (requires CSL hardware)
An integrated hardware/software system that performs a variety of speech and voice analyses for use in assessment and therapy.

Kay Elemetrics
2 Bridgewater Ln.
Lincoln Park, NJ 07035
973/628-6200
Fax: 973/628-6363
www.kayelemetrics.com
Call for current prices and ordering info.

Multidimensional Voice Profile Option (requires CSL hardware)
A voice analysis system that measures over 20 parameters of the voice in a single, sustained vocalization.

Kay Elemetrics
2 Bridgewater Ln.
Lincoln Park, NJ 07035
973/628-6200
Fax: 973/628-6363
www.kayelemetrics.com
Call for current prices and ordering info.

Multi-Speech
A low cost, Windows-based software program that can capture, analyze, and play back speech samples. Multi-Speech is limited by the robustness of the computer's existing hardware.

Kay Elemetrics
2 Bridgewater Ln.
Lincoln Park, NJ 07035
973/628-6200
Fax: 973/628-6363
www.kayelemetrics.com
Call for current prices and ordering info.

Dr. Speech
A Windows-based speech/voice assessment and therapy system that can be used with any IBM or IBM-compatible PC.

US distributor: Laureate Learning
110 East Spring St.
Winooski, VT 05404
800/562-6801, 802/655-4755
Fax: 802/655-4757
www.LaureateLearning.com
Call for pricing and ordering info.

EZ Voice and EZ Voice Plus
Software systems that can extract commonly used parameters of speech and voice from a sustained voice signal.

VoiceTek Enterprises
RR#2, Box 2490
Nescopeck, PA 18635
570/759-1359
EZ Voice: $150
EZ Voice Plus: $200

Video Voice Speech Training System
Provides multiple games and graphic displays that can serve as feedback for almost all speech and voice therapy.

Micro Video Corporation
P.O. Box 7357
Ann Arbor, MI 48107
313/996-0626, 800/537-2182
Fax: 313/996-3838
www.videovoice.com
Complete Video Voice System: $2495

ELECTROGLOTTOGRAPHS

Laryngograph
A portable, battery-operated electroglottograph. The laryngograph provides a non-invasive method of investigating vocal fold dynamics and contact patterns during phonation.

Kay Elemetrics
2 Bridgewater Ln.
Lincoln Park, NJ 07035
973/628-6200
Fax: 973/628-6363
www.kayelemetrics.com
Call for current prices and ordering info.

Portable Electroglottograph (EG80)
A battery-operated electroglottograph that is designed to be used with the Dr. Speech EGG software.

US distributor: Laureate Learning
110 East Spring St.
Winooski, VT 05404
800/562-6801, 802/655-4755
Fax: 802/655-4757
www.LaureateLearning.com
Call for pricing and ordering info.

INSTRUMENTS FOR ASSESSMENT OF VELOPHARYNGEAL FUNCTION

Nasometer
A system that provides assessment of nasality and visual cueing during therapy.

Kay Elemetrics
2 Bridgewater Ln.
Lincoln Park, NJ 07035
973/628-6200
Fax: 973/628-6363
www.kayelemetrics.com
Call for current prices and ordering info.

See-Scape
A product that detects nasal emission during speech and assists in the assessment of velopharyngeal competence. The See-Scape costs $79, and a replacement kit is available for $23.

PRO-ED, Inc.
8700 Shoal Creek Blvd.
Austin, TX 78757-6897

800/897-3202
Fax: 800/397-7633
www.proedinc.com

ARTIFICIAL LARYNGES

Cooper-Rand Electronic Speech Aid
Tube-in-the-mouth-type, battery-powered. Usually sells for $425 to $470.

Luminaud, Inc.
8688 Tyler Blvd.
Mentor, OH 44060
800/255-3408
www.luminaud.com

Denrick 3 Speech Aid
Neck-type, battery-powered (rechargeable). Sells for $410 to $440.

Luminaud, Inc.
8688 Tyler Blvd.
Mentor, OH 44060
800/255-3408
www.luminaud.com
(Assembled by arrangement with Denrick Corp.)

NuVois
Neck-type, battery-powered (rechargeable). Sells for $490 to $530.

Manufactured by Mountain Precision Manufacturing
Available from:
Luminaud (see above)
or
Lauder Enterprises
1115 Whisper Hollow
San Antonio, TX 78230
800/388-8642
www.voicestore.com

Optivox
Neck-type, battery-powered (rechargeable). Sells for $540 to $570.

Bivona Medical Technologies
5700 W. 23rd Ave.
Gary, IN 46406
800/348-6064
www.bivona.com

Romet Speech Aid
Neck-type, battery-powered (rechargeable). Sells for $320 to $445.

Romet, Inc.
929 S. W. Higgins Ave.
Missoula, MT 59803
Distributed by Lauder Enterprises
1115 Whisper Hollow
San Antonio, TX 78230
800/388-8642
www.voicestore.com

Servox Inton Speech Aid
Neck-type, battery-powered (rechargeable). Sells for $490 to $595.

Siemens Instruments
Professional Products Division
16 E. Piper Ln., Ste. 128
Prospects Heights, IL 60070-1799
800/333-9083, 847/808-1200
www.siemens-hearing.com

Tokyo Artificial Larynx
Hand-held, pneumatically powered. Sells for $112.

Artificial Speech Aids
3002-8 12th St.
Harlan, IA 51537
712/755-2389

TruTone Artificial Larynx
Neck-type, battery-powered (rechargeable). Sells for $510 to $545.

Griffin Laboratories
27636 Ynez Rd., #7199
Temecula, CA 92591
800/330-5969
www.griffinlab.com/index.html

UltraVoice
Intraoral, dental-appliance-type, battery-powered (rechargeable). Sells for $3700.

Health Concepts, Inc.
279-B Great Valley Parkway
Malvern, PA 19355
800/721-4848

VOICE PROSTHESIS DEVICES

Blom-Singer Indwelling Low Pressure Voice Prosthesis
Silicon voice prosthesis

InHealth Technologies
1110 Mark Ave.
Carpinteria, CA 93013
800/477-5969
www.inhealth.com

Provox 2 Voice Prosthesis System
Silicon voice prosthesis

Bivona Medical Technologies
5700 W. 23rd Ave.
Gary, IN 46406
800/348-6064
www.bivona.com

ORGANIZATIONS FOR LARYNGECTOMEES

International Association of Laryngectomees (IAL)
Sponsored by the American Cancer Society. Consists of local clubs world wide, called Lost Chord Clubs or New Voice Clubs, that provide services and information to laryngectomees and their families.

7440 N. Shadeland
Indianaplois, IN 46250
317/570-4568
Fax: 317/570-4570
www.larynxlink.com/ial/ial.html

References*

Abuzzahab, F. S., & Anderson, F. O. (1974). Gilles de la Tourette's syndrome: Cross cultural analysis and treatment outcomes. *Clininical Neurology and Neurosurgery, 1,* 66.

Adams, S. (1997). Hypokinetic dysarthria. In M. McNeil (Ed.), *Clinical management of sensorimotor speech disorders* (pp. 261–285). New York: Thieme Medical.

Allen, G. I., & Tsukahara, N. (1974). Cerebrocerebellar communication systems. *Physiology Review, 54,* 957.

American Joint Committee on Cancer. (1992). *Manual for staging of cancer: Larynx* (4th ed.). Philadelphia: Lippincott.

American Liver Foundation. (1997). *Wilson's disease* [Online]. URL: http://gi.ucsf.edu/alf/alffinal/info wilsons.html

Andrews, M. (1995). *Manual of voice treatment: Pediatrics through geriatrics.* San Diego: Singular.

Arnold, G. E., & Stephens, C. B. (1980). Bulbar changes with laryngeal paralysis. *Archives of Otolaryngology, 106,* 124.

Aronson, A. E. (1980). *Clinical voice disorders: An interdisciplinary approach.* New York: Decker.

Aronson, A. E. (1985). *Clinical voice disorders: An interdisciplinary approach* (2nd ed.). New York: Decker.

Aronson, A. E. (1990). *Clinical voice disorders: An interdisciplinary approach* (3rd ed.). New York: Decker.

Aronson, A. E., Brown, J. R., Litin, E. M., & Pearson, J. S. (1968a). Spastic dysphonia. I. Voice, neurologic and psychiatric aspects. *Journal of Speech and Hearing Disorders, 33,* 203.

Aronson, A. E., Brown, J. R., Litin, E. M., & Pearson, J. S. (1968b). Spastic dysphonia. II. Comparison with essential (voice) tremor and other neurologic and psychogenic dysphonias. *Journal of Speech and Hearing Disorders, 33,* 219.

Aronson, A. E., & Hartman, D. E. (1981). Adductor spastic dysphonia as a sign of essential (voice) tremor. *Journal of Speech and Hearing Disorders, 46,* 52.

Asai, R. (1972). Laryngoplasty after total laryngectomy. *Archives of Otolaryngology, 75,* 114.

Asperheim, M. K., & Eisenhauer, L. A. (1977). The pharmacologic basis of patient care (3rd ed.). Philadelphia: Saunders.

Azzan, N. A., & Kuehn, D. P. (1977).The morphology of musculus uvulae. *Cleft Palate Journal, 14,* 78.

Baker, K., Ramig, L., Johnson, A., & Freed, C. (1997). Preliminary voice and speech analysis following fetal dopamine transplants in five individuals with Parkinson's disease. *Journal of Speech, Language, and Hearing Research, 40,* 615–626.

Balestrieri, F., & Watson, C. (1982). Intubation granuloma. *Otolaryngologic Clinics of North America, 15,* 567.

Ballantyne, J. (1971). Occupational disorders of the larynx. In J. Ballantyne & J. Groves (Eds.), *Scott-Brown's diseases of the ear, nose, and throat.* Philadelphia: Lippincott.

Ballenger, J. J. (1977). *Diseases of the nose, throat, and ear* (12th ed.). Philadelphia: Lea and Febiger.

Bastian, R. (1998). Surgical and medical management of SD. *National Spasmodic Dysphonia Association Newsletter, 7*(1), 3–6.

Benjamin, B. (1986). Dimensions of the older female voice. *Language Communication, 6,* 35–45.

Benninger, M., & Gardner, G. (1998). Medical and surgical management in otolaryngology. In A. Johnson & B. Jacobson (Eds.), *Medical speech–language pathology: A practitioner's guide* (pp. 516–519). New York: Thieme Medical.

---

*Note. The references above are not in APA format.

Benninger, M., & Grywalski, C. (1998). Rehabilitation of the head and neck cancer patient. In A. Johnson & B. Jacobson (Eds.), *Medical speech–language pathology: A practitioner's guide.* New York: Thieme Medical.

Berry, W. R., Aronson, A. E., Darley, F. L., & Goldstein, N. R. (1974). Effects of peniciilamine therapy and low-copper diet on dysarthria in Wilson's disease (hepatolenticular degeneration). *Mayo Clinic Proceedings, 49,* 405.

Berry, W. R., Darley, F. L., Aronson, A. E., & Goldstein, N. P. (1974). Dysarthria in Wilson's disease. *Journal of Speech and Hearing Research, 17*(1), 69.

Biller, H. F., & Lawson, W. (1980). Arytenoidectomy, arytenoidopexy, and the valved tube. In J. B. Snow (Ed.), *Controversy in otolaryngology.* Philadelphia: Saunders.

Birrell, J. F. (1977). *Logan Turner's diseases of the nose, throat, and ear* (8th ed.). Bristol, England: Wright.

Birrell, J. F. (1978). *Pediatric otolaryngology.* Chicago: Year Book.

Black, J. W. (1961). Relationships among fundamental frequency, vocal sound pressure, and rate of speaking. *Languge and Speech 4*(1), 96.

Blager, F. (1996). Relaxed throat breath with abdominal support. *Diagnosis and Treatment of Vocal Cord Dysfunction.* Denver, CO: National Jewish Medical and Research Center.

Blakely, R. W. (1960). Temporary speech prosthesis as an aid in speech training. *Cleft Palate Bulletin, 1,* 63.

Blakely, R. W. (1964). The complementary use of speech prostheses and pharyngeal flaps in palatal insufficiency. *Cleft Palate Journal, 1,* 194.

Bless, D., & Swift, E. (1995, November). *Paradoxical vocal cord dysfunction: Episodic laryngeal dyskinesia; one disorder, multiple causes.* Paper presented at the annual convention of the American Speech–Language and Hearing Association, Orlando, FL.

Bloch, C., & Gould, W. (1974). Vocal therapy in lieu of surgery for contact granuloma: A case report. *Journal of Speech and Hearing Disorders, 39,* 478.

Bloch, C., Gould, W., & Hirano, M. (1981). Effects of voice therapy on contact granuloma of the vocal fold. *Annals of Otology, Rhinology, and Laryngology, 90,* 48.

Blom, E. D. (1978a). The artificial larynx: Past and present. In S. J. Salmon & Goldstein (Eds.), *The artificial larynx handbook.* New York: Grune & Stratton.

Blom, E. D. (1978b). A practical change to an artificial larynx. *I. A. L. News, 23,* 5.

Blom, E. D. (1995). Tracheoesophageal speech. *Seminars in Speech and Language, 16*(3), 191–203.

Bloomquist, B. L. (1950). Diadochokinetic movements of nine-, ten-, and eleven-year-old children. *Journal of Speech and Hearing Disorders, 15,* 159.

Boles, R. (1975a). Hoarseness. In M. Strome (Ed.), *Differential diagnosis in pediatric otolaryngology.* Boston: Little, Brown.

Boles, R. (1975b). Stridor. In M. Strome (Ed.), *Differential diagnosis in pediatric otolaryngology.* Boston: Little, Brown.

Boller, F., Albert, M., & Denes, F. (1975). Palilalia. *British Journal of Disorders of Communication, 10,* 92.

Boone, D. R. (1977). *The voice and voice therapy* (2nd ed.). Englewood Cliffs, NJ: Prentice-Hall.

Boone, D. R. (1980). *The Boone voice program for children: Screening, evaluation and referral.* Tigard, OR: C. C. Publications.

Boone, D.R. (1983). *The voice and voice therapy* (3rd ed.) Englewood Cliffs, NJ: Prentice-Hall.

Boone, D. R. (1993). *The Boone voice program for children* (2nd ed.). Austin, TX: PRO-ED.

Boone D. R. (1998). From where I sit: A need for greater humanism. *Special Interest Division 3: Voice and Voice Disorders.* Rockville, MD: American Speech-Language-Hearing Association.

Boone, D. R., & McFarlane, S. (1994). *The voice and voice therapy* (5th ed.). Englewood Cliffs, NJ: Prentice-Hall.

Borenstein, J. A., Lipton, H. L., & Rupick, C. (1978). Spastic dysphonia: An 18-year follow-up study. *Asha, 20,* 733.

Breiss, B. (1959). Voice Therapy. Part II: Essential treatment phases of laryngeal muscle dysfunction. *AMA Archives of Otolaryngology, 69,* 61–69.

Brodnitz, F. S. (1958). The pressure test in mutational voice disturbances. *Annals of Otology, Rhinology, and Laryngology, 67,* 235.

Brodnitz, F. S. (1988). Keep your voice healthy (2nd ed.). Austin, TX: PRO-ED.

Broe, G. A. (1982). Parkinsonism and related disorders. In F. Caird (Ed.), *Neurologic disorders in the elderly.* Bristol, England: Wright.

Brooke, M. H. (1977). *A clinician's view of neuromuscular diseases.* Baltimore: Williams & Wilkins.

Brookshire, R. (1997). *Introduction to neurogenic communication disorders.* St. Louis: Mosby-Year Book.

Brown, J. R., & Simonson, J. (1963). Organic voice tremor. *Neurology, 13,* 520.

Brown, J. R., Darley, F. L., & Aronson, A. E. (1970). Ataxic dysarthria. *International Journal of Neurology, 7,* 302.

Buber, M. (1970). *I and thou.* New York: Scribner's.

Bzoch, K. R. (1979). Measurement and assessment of categorical aspects of cleft palate speech. In K. R. Bzoch (Ed.), *Communicative disorders related to cleft lip and palate* (2nd ed.). Austin, TX: PRO-ED.

Bzoch, K. R. (1997). Etiological factors related to managing cleft palate speech disorders. In K. R. Bzoch (Ed.), *Communicative disorders related to cleft lip and palate* (4th ed.) (pp. 200–205). Austin, TX: PRO-ED.

Cairns, H., Oldfield, R. C., Pennybacker, J. B., & Whitteridge, D. (1941). Akinetic mutism with an epidermoid cyst of the third ventricle. *Brain, 64,* 273.

Calcaterra, T. C., & Jafek, B. W. (1971). Tracheo-esophageal shunt for speech rehabilitation after total laryngectomy. *Archives of Otolaryngology, 94,* 24.

Cannito, M., & Marquardt, T. (1997). Ataxic dysarthria. In M. McNeil (Ed.), *Clinical management of sensorimotor speech disorders* (pp. 217–247). New York: Thieme Medical.

Canter, G. J. (1965). Speech characteristics of patients with Parkinson's disease: Articulation, diadochokinesis, and overall speech adequacy. *Journal of Speech and Hearing Disorders, 30,* 217.

Carrow, E., Rivera, V., Mauldin, M., & Shamblin, L. (1974). Deviant speech characteristics in motor neuron disease. *Archives of Otolaryngology, 100,* 212.

Cartwright, G. E. (1978). Diagnosis of treatable Wilson's disease. *New England Journal of Medicine, 298,* 1347.

Case, J. (1996). *Clinical management of voice disorders* (3rd ed.). Austin, TX: PRO-ED.

Casey, D. E. (1977). Deanol in the management of involuntary movement disorders: A review. *Disorders of the Nervous System, 39,* 7.

Casiano, R., & Goodwin, W. (1991). Restoring function to the injured larynx. In J. Koufman & G. Isaacson (Eds.), *The otolaryngologic clinics of North America* (pp. 1216–1221). Philadelphia: Saunders.

Casper, J. (1998). *Voice disorders: Diagnostic grand rounds* [videoconference]. Rockville, MD: American Speech-Language-Hearing Association.

Centers for Disease Control. (1988). *Perspectives in disease prevention and health promotion,* Atlanta, GA: Author.

Chagnon, F., & Stone, R. E. (1996). Nodules and polyps. In W. Brown, B. Vinson, & M. Crary (Eds.), *Organic voice disorders: Assessment and treatment* (p. 223). San Diego: Singular.

Christopher, K., Wood, R., Eckert, C., Blager, F., Raney, R., & Souhrada, J. (1983). *New England Journal of Medicine, 308,* 1566–1570.

Chusid, J. G. (1976). *Correlative neuroanatomy and functional neurology* (16th ed.). Los Altos, CA: Lange.

Cole, R. M. (1971). Direct muscle training for improvement of velopharyngeal function. In W. C. Grabb, S. W. Rosenstein, & K. R. Bzoch (Eds.), *Cleft lip and palate: Surgical, dental, and speech aspects.* Boston: Little, Brown.

Coleman, R. C. (1976). A comparison of the contribution of two voice quality characteristics to the perception of maleness and femaleness in the voice. *Journal of Speech and Hearing Research, 19,* 168–180.

Colton, R., & Casper, J. C. (1996). *Understanding voice problems: A physiological perspective from diagnosis to treatment.* Baltimore: Williams & Wilkins.

Conley, J. J. (1959). Vocal rehabilitation by autogenous vein graft. *Annals of Otology, Rhinology, and Laryngology, 68,* 990.

Conley, J. J., DeAmesti, F., & Pierce, M. K. (1958). A new surgical technique for the vocal rehabilitation of the laryngectomized patient. *Annals of Otology, Rhinology, and Laryngology, 67,* 655.

Cooper, M. (1973). *Modern techniques of vocal rehabilitation.* Springfield, IL: Thomas.

Cooper, M. (1998). Behavioral therapy first option for SD. *Advance for Speech–Language Pathologists & Audiologists, 8*(40), 4.

Cotton, R. T., & Richardson, M. A. (1981). Congenital laryngeal anomalies. *Otolaryngologic Clinics of North America, 14,* 203.

Crane, G. E. (1980). A classification of the neurologic effects of neuroleptic drugs. In W. E. Fann, R. C. Smith, J. M. Davis, & E. F. Domino (Eds.), *Tardive dyskinesia.* Jamaica, NY: Spectrum.

Crowe, T. (Ed.). (1997). *Applications of counseling in speech–language pathology and audiology.* Baltimore: Williams & Wilkins.

Dalston, R., & Seaver, E. (1992). Relative values of various standardized reading passages in the nasometric assessment of patients with velopharyngeal impairment. *Cleft Palate-Craniofacial Journal, 29,* 17–21.

Damste, P. H. (1967). Voice change in adult women caused by virilizing agents. *Journal of Speech and Hearing Disorders, 32,* 126.

Darley, F. L., Aronson, A. E., & Brown, J. R. (1975). *Motor speech disorders.* Philadelphia: Saunders.

Dedo, H. H. (1976). Recurrent laryngeal nerve section for spastic dysphonia. *Annals of Otology, Rhinology, and Laryngology, 85,* 451.

Dedo, H. H., Izdebski, K., & Townsend, A. (1977). Recurrent laryngeal nerve histopathology in spastic dysphonia. *Annals of Otology, Rhinology, and Laryngology, 86,* 806.

Dedo, H. H., & Shipp, T. (1980). *Spastic dysphonia: A surgical and voice therapy treatment program.* Houston: College-Hill.

Deem, J., Manning, W., Knack, J., & Matesich, J. (1991). Comparison of pitch perturbation extraction procedures with adult male and female speakers. *Folia Phoniatrica, 43,* 234–245.

DeWeese, D. D., & Saunders, W. H. (1977). *Textbook of otolaryngology* (5th ed.). St. Louis: Mosby.

Dickson, D.R., & Maue-Dickson, W. (1982). *Anatomical and physiological bases of speech.* Austin, TX: PRO-ED.

Diedrich, W. M., & Youngstrom, K. A. (1966). *Alaryngeal speech.* Springfield, IL: Thomas.

Dirckx, J. (Ed.). (1997). *Stedman's concise medical dictionary for health professionals* (Version 1.0) [CD-ROM]. Baltimore: Williams & Wilkins.

Donegan, J. O., Gluckman, J. L., & Singh, J. (1981). Limitations for the Blom-Singer technique for voice restoration. *Annals of Otology, Rhinology, and Laryngology, 90,* 495.

Donegan, J. O., Strife, J. L., Seid, A. B., Cotton, R. H., & Dunbar, J. S. (1980). Internal laryngocele and saccular cysts in children. *Annals of Otology, Rhinology, and Laryngology, 89,* 409.

Drachman, D. B. (1978). Myasthenia gravis. *New England Journal of Medicine, 298,* 136.

Duguay, M. J. (1977). Esophageal speech. In M. Cooper & M. H. Cooper (Eds.), *Approaches to vocal rehabilitation.* Springfield, IL: Thomas.

Dworkin, J. P., II. (1978). Differential diagnosis of motor speech disorders: The clinical examination of the speech mechanism. *Journal of the National Student Speech Language Hearing Association, 6,* 37.

Dystonia Medical Research Foundation. (1999). Dystonia dialogue [Online]. URL: http://www.dystonia-foundation.org/index.html#A11

Eckel, F. C., & Boone, D. R. (1981). The s/z ratio as an indicator of laryngeal pathology. *Journal of Speech and Hearing Disorders, 46,* 147.

English, G. M. (1976a). Benign neoplasms of the larynx. In G. M. English (Ed.), *Otolaryngology: A textbook.* Hagerstown, MD: Harper & Row.

English, G. M. (1976b). Congenital anomalies of the larynx. In G. M. English (Ed.), *Otolaryngology: A textbook*. Hagerstown, MD: Harper & Row.

English, G. M. (1976c). Malignant neoplasms of the larynx. In G. M. English (Ed.), *Otolaryngology: A textbook*. Hagerstown, MD: Harper & Row.

Erickson, R. (1974). Assessing voice. *Western Michigan University Journal of Speech Therapy, 11,* 7.

Fairbanks, G. (1960). *Voice and articulation drillbook* (2nd ed.). New York: Harper & Row.

Falconer, M. W., Patterson, H. R., Gustafson, E. A., & Sheridan, E. (1978). *Current drug handbook 1978–1980*. Philadelphia: Saunders.

Farmakides, M. N., & Boone, D. R. (1960). Speech problems of patients with multiple sclerosis. *Journal of Speech and Hearing Disorders, 25,* 385.

Fearon, B., & Ellis, D. (1971). The management of long term airway problems in infants and children. *Annals of Otology, Rhinology, and Laryngology, 80,* 669.

Fischbeek, K. H., & Layzer, R. B. (1979). Paroxysmal choreoathetosis associated with thyrotoxicosis. *Annals of Neurology, 6,* 453.

Flach, M., Schwickardi, H., & Simon, R. (1969). What influence do menstruation and pregnancy have on the trained singing voice? *Folia Phoniatrica, 21,* 199.

Fletcher, S. (1972). Contingencies for bioelectronic modification of nasality. *Journal of Speech and Hearing Disorders, 37,* 329–346.

Ford, C. N. (1996). Laryngeal papilloma. In W. Brown, B. Vinson, & M. Crary (Eds.), *Organic voice disorders: Assessment and treatment* (pp. 261–268). San Diego: Singular.

Frable, M.S. (1962). Hoarseness: A symptom of premenstrual tension. *Archives of Otolaryngology, 75,* 66.

Fred, H. L. (1962). Hoarseness due to phonation by the false vocal cords: Dysphonia plicae ventricularis. *Archives of Internal Medicine, 101,* 472.

Freedman, D. X. (1973). Neurological syndromes associated with antipsychotic drug use. *Archives of General Psychiatry, 28,* 463.

Freeman, M. (1986). Psychogenic voice disorders. In M. Fawcus (Ed.), *Voice disorders and their management* (pp. 204–207). London: Croom Helm.

Friedman, M., Baim, H., Shelton, V., Stobnicki, M., Chilis, T., Ferrara, T., & Skolnik, E. (1981). Laryngeal injuries secondary to nasogastric tubes. *Annals of Otology, Rhinology, and Laryngology, 90*(5), 469–474.

Froeschels, E. (1952). Chewing method as therapy. *Archives of Otolaryngology, 56,* 427.

Froeschels, E., Kastein, S., & Weiss, D. A. (1955). A method of therapy for paralytic conditions of the mechanisms of phonation, respiration and glutination. *Journal of Speech and Hearing Disorders, 20,* 365.

Gardner, W. H. (1971). *Laryngectomee speech and rehabilitation*. Springfield, IL: Thomas.

Gaut, A. (1997). *Johns Hopkins Center for Laryngeal and Voice Disorders* [Online]. URL: http://www.med.jhu.edu/voice/spasdys.html

Gelenberg, A. J. (1976). The catatonic syndrome. *Lancet, 1,* 1339.

Gibbons, P., & Bloomer, H. (1958). A supportive-type prosthetic speech aide. *Journal of Prosthetic Dentistry, 8,* 362.

Goetz, C. G., Dysken, M. W., & Klawans, H. L., Jr. (1980). Assessment and treatment of drug-induced tremor. *Journal of Clinical Psychiatry, 41,* 310.

Gonzalez, J. B., & Aronson, A. E. (1970). Palatal lift prosthesis for treatment of anatomic and neurologic palatopharyngeal insufficiency. *Cleft Palate Journal, 7,* 91.

Graber, T. M., Bzoch, K. R., & Aoba, R. (1959). A functional study of the palatal and pharyngeal structures. *The Angle Orthodontist, 29,* 30.

Greene, M. C. (1980). *The voice and its disorders* (4th ed.). Philadelphia: Lippincott.

Greene, M., & Watson, B. W. (1968). The value of speech amplification in Parkinson's disease patients. *Folia Phoniatrica, 20,* 250.

Griffin Laboratories. (1998). *TruTone artificial larynx* [Online]. URL: http://www.griffinlab.com

Griffiths, C. M., & Love, J. T. (1978). Neoglottic reconstruction after total laryngectomy: A preliminary report. *Annals of Otology, Rhinology, and Laryngology. 87(1), 80.*

Grob, D. (1958). Myasthenia gravis: Current status of pathogenesis, clinical manifestations and management. *Journal of Chronic Disorders, 8,* 536.

Günzburger, D. (1995). Acoustic and perceptual implications of the transexual voice. *Archives of Sexual Behavior, 24,* 339–348.

Haerer, A., Anderson, D., & Schoenberg, B. (1982). Prevalence of essential tremor. *Archives of Neurology, 39,* 750.

Hageman, C. (1997). Flaccid dysarthria. In M. McNeil (Ed.), *Clinical management of sensorimotor speech disorders* (pp. 193–216). New York: Thieme Medical.

Hagerty, R. F., & Hill, M. J. (1960). Pharyngeal wall and palatal movement in postoperative cleft palates and normals. *Journal of Speech and Hearing Research, 3,* 59.

Haglund, S., Lundquist, P., Cantell, K., & Strander, H. (1981). Interferon therapy in juvenile laryngeal papillomatosis. *Archives of Otolaryngology, 107,* 327.

Hanson, D., Gerratt, B., & Ward, P. (1984). Cinegraphic observation of laryngeal function in Parkinson's disease. *Laryngoscope, 94,* 348–353.

Hanson, W., & Metter, E. (1980). DAF as instrumental treatment for dysarthria in progressive supranuclear palsy: A case report. *Journal of Speech and Hearing Disorders, 45,* 268.

Hardy, J. C. (1964). Lung function of athetoid and spastic quadriplegic children. *Developmental Medicine and Child Neurology, 6,* 378.

Hardy, J. C., Netsell, R., Schweiger, J. W., & Morris, H. L. (1969). Management of velopharyngeal dysfunction in cerebral palsy. *Journal of Speech and Hearing Disorders, 34,* 123.

Hartman, D. E., & Aronson, A. E. (1981). Clinical investigations of intermittent breathy dysphonia. *Journal of Speech and Hearing Disorders, 46,* 428.

Haymaker, W., & Schiller, F. (1969). Extrapyramidal motor disorders: Clinical syndromes, pathology, mechanisms involved. In W. Haymaker (Ed.), *Bing's local diagnosis in neurological diseases* (15th ed.). St. Louis: Mosby.

Health Concepts. (1998). *UltraVoice: An enhanced quality of life* [Online]. URL: http://www.ultra voice.com

Helme, R. D. (1982). Movement disorders. In M. A. Samuels (Ed.), *Manual of neurologic therapeutics* (2nd ed.). Boston: Little, Brown.

Hirano, M. (1981). Structure of the vocal fold in normal and disease states: Anatomic and physical studies. In C. Ludlow & M. Hart (Eds.), *Proceedings of the Conference on the Assessment of Vocal Pathology* (pp. 11–30). Rockville, MD: American Speech-Language-Hearing Association.

Hirano, M., & Bless, D. (1993). *Videostroboscopic examination of the larynx.* San Diego: Singular.

Hirano, M., Koike, Y., & von Leden, H. (1968). Maximum phonation time and air usage during phonation. *Folia Phoniatrica 20,* 185.

Hirano, M., Kurita, S., & Nakashima, T. (1983). Growth, development and aging of the human vocal fold. In D. Bless & J. Abbs (Eds.), *Vocal fold physiology: Contemporary research and clinical issues* (pp. 22–43). San Diego: College-Hill.

Hoit, J., & Hixon, T. (1987). Age and speech breathing. *Journal of Speech and Hearing Research, 30,* 351–366.

Holder, T. M., Leape, L. L., & Ashcraft, K. W. (1973). Congenital malformations of the trachea, bronchi, and esophagus. In M. M. Paparella & D. A. Shumrick (Eds.), *Otolaryngology, vol. 3, head and neck.* Philadelphia: Saunders.

Holinger, L. D. (1976a). Congenital anomalies of the larynx. In G. M. English (Ed.), *Otolaryngology: A textbook.* Hagerstown, MD: Harper & Row.

Holinger, L. D. (1976b). Inflammatory conditions of the larynx. In G. M. English (Ed.), *Otolaryngology: A textbook.* Hagerstown, MD: Harper & Row.

Holinger, P. H., & Brown, W. T. (1967). Congenital webs, cysts, laryngoceles, and other anomalies of the larynx. *Annals of Otology, Rhinology, and Laryngology, 76,* 744.

Holinger, P. H., Kutnick, S. L., Schild, J. A., & Holinger, L. D. (1976). Subglottic stenosis in infants and children. *Annals of Otology, Rhinology, and Laryngology, 85,* 591.

Hollien, H., & Jackson, B. (1973). Normative data on the speaking fundamental frequency characteristics of young adult males. *Journal of Phonetics, 1,* 117.

Hollien, H., & Shipp, T. (1972). Speaking fundamental frequency and chronologic age in males. *Journal of Speech and Hearing Research, 15,* 155–159.

Honjo, I., & Isshiki, N. (1980). Laryngoscopic and voice characteristics of aged persons. *Archives of Otolaryngology, 106,* 149–150.

Huang, D. (1998). Relationship between acoustic measures of voice and judgments of voice quality [Online]. URL: http://www.drspeech.com/Paper.html

Huntington's Disease Society of America. (1998). Genetic testing for Huntington's disease [Online]. URL: http://hdsa.mgh.harvard.edu

Hutchinson, B. B., Hanson, M. L., & Mecham, M. J. (1979). *Diagnostic handbook of speech pathology.* Baltimore: Williams & Wilkins.

Ichiwaka, K., Kim, R. C., Givelber, H., & Collins, G. (1980). Chorea gravidarum. *Archives of Neurology, 37,* 429.

Iskowitz, M. (1998). Behavioral approach to SD. *Advance for Speech–Language Pathologists and Audiologists, 8*(33), 14–16.

Iwata, S., & von Leden, H. (1970). Pitch perturbations in normal and pathologic voices. *Folia Phoniatrica, 22,* 413.

Jablecki, C. K. (1982). Myopathies and defects of neuromuscular transmission. In W. C. Wiederholt (Ed.), *Neurology for non-neurologists.* New York: Academic.

Jacobson, B., Stemple, J., Glaze, L., & Gerdeman, B. (1998). Assessment and management of voice disorders in adults. In A. Johnson & B. Jacobson (Eds.), *Medical speech-language pathology: A practitioner's guide* (pp. 529–562). New York: Thieme Medical.

Jacobson, E. (1978). *You must relax* (5th ed.). New York: McGraw-Hill.

Johns, D. F., & Salyer, K. E. (1978). Surgical and prosthetic management of neurogenic speech disorders. In D. F. Johns (Ed.), *Clinical management of neurogenic communicative disorders.* Austin, TX: PRO-ED.

Kahane, J. (1990). Age-related structures in the peripheral speech mechanism: Structural and physiological changes. In E. Cherow (Ed.), *Proceedings of the research symposium on communication problems of aging, ASHA reports 19* (pp. 75–87). Rockville, MD: American Speech-Language-Hearing Association.

Kahane, J. C., & Folkins, J. (1984). *Atlas of speech and hearing anatomy.* Columbus, OH: Merrill.

Kahane, J. C., & Hammons, J. (1987). Developmental changes in the articular cartilage of the human cricoarytenoid joint. In T. Baer, C. Sasaki, & K. Harris (Eds.), *Laryngeal function in phonation and respiration* (pp. 14–28) San Diego: College-Hill.

Kahane, J. C. (1982). Anatomy and physiolgy of the organs of the peripheral speech mechanism. In N. J. Lass, L. V. McReynolds, J. L. Northern, & D. E. Yoder (Eds.), *Speech, language, and hearing: Vol. 1. Normal processes.* Philadelphia: Saunders.

Kaleidoscope Interactive. (1998). *Kaleidoscope interactive news and features* [Online]. URL: http://www.ktv-i.com/news/nn01_13_98.html

Karlan, M. S. (1968). Two stage Asai laryngectomy utilizing a modified Tucker valve. *American Journal of Surgery, 116,* 597.

Kay Elemetrics. (1995). *Nasometer application notes: Model 6200.* Lincoln Park, NJ: Author.

Keith, R. L. (1995). *Looking forward . . . A guidebook for the laryngectomee* (3rd ed.). New York: Thieme Medical.

Kelley, A. (1977). *Fundamental frequency measurements of female voices from 20 to 90 years of age.* Unpublished manuscript, University of North Carolina at Greensboro.

Kent, R., & Nestell, R. (1975). A case study of an ataxic dysarthria: Cineradiographic and spectrographic observations. *Journal of Speech and Hearing Disorders, 40,* 15.

Kerman, P. C., Singer, L. S., & Davidoff, A. (1973). Palatal lift and speech therapy for velopharyngeal incompetence. *Archives of Physical Medicine and Rehabilitation, 54,* 271.

Kevles, D. J., & Hood, L. (Eds.). (1999). *The code of codes: Scientific social issues in the Human Genome Project* [Online]. URL: http://www.hdfoundation.org/index.html

Klawans, H. L., Goetz, C. G., Paulson, G. W., & Barbeau, A. (1980). Levodopa and presymptomatic detection of Huntington's disease: Eight year follow-up. *New England Journal of Medicine, 302,* 1090.

Klawans, H. L., Goetz, C. G., & Perlik, S. (1980). Presymptomatic and early detection in Huntington's disease. *Annals of Neurology, 8,* 343.

Klee, A. (1961). Akinetic mutism: Review of the literature and report of a case. *Journal of Nervous and Mental Disease, 133,* 536.

Komorn, R. M. (1974). Vocal rehabilitation in the laryngectomized patient with a tracheoesophageal shunt. *Annals of Otology, Rhinology, and Laryngology, 83,* 445.

Kotby, N. (1995). *The accent method of voice therapy.* San Diego: Singular.

Koufman, J. (1998a). *Spasmodic dysphonia overview* (Center for Voice Disorders at Wake Forest University Web site) [Online]. URL: http://www.bgsm.edu/voice/overview_sd.html

Koufman, J. (1998b). *What are voice disorders and who gets them?* (Center for Voice Disorders at Wake Forest University Web site) [Online]. URL: http://www.bgsm.edu/voice/voice_disorders.html

Kreindler, A., & Pruskauer-Apostol, B. (1971). Neurologic and psychopathologic aspects of compulsive crying and laughter in pseudo-bulbar palsy patients. *Revue Roumaine de Neurologie, 8,* 125.

Kuehn, D. (1997). The development of a new technique for treating hypernasality: CPAP. *The American Journal of Speech-Language Pathology, 6*(4), 5–8.

Kummer, A.W., & Marsh, J. H. (1998). Pediatric voice and resonance disorders. In A. Johnson & B. Jacobson (Eds.). *Medical speech-language pathology: A practitioner's guide* (pp. 613–636). New York: Thieme Medical.

Landau, B. R. (1980). *Essential human anatomy and physiology* (2nd ed.). Glenview, IL: Scott, Foresman.

Landwehr, L. P., Wood, R. P., Blager, F. B., & Milgrom, H. (1996). Vocal cord dysfunction mimicking exercise induced-bronchospasm in adolescents. *Pediatrics, 98*(5), 971–973.

Langdon, H. L., & Kuebler, K. (1978). The longitudinal fibromuscular component of the soft palate in the fifteen-week human fetus: Musculus uvulae and palatine raphe. *Cleft Palate Journal, 15,* 337.

Lange, B. R., & Kipfmueller, L. J. (1969). Treating velopharyngeal inadequacy with palatal lift concept. *Plastic Reconstructive Surgery, 43,* 467.

Larson, C. R., & Pfingst, B. E. (1982). Neuroanatomic bases of hearing and speech. In N. J. Lass, L. V. McReynolds, J. L. Northern, & D. E. Yoder (Eds.), *Speech, language, and hearing. Vol. I. Normal processes.* Philadelphia: Saunders.

Lauder, E. (1994). *Self-help for the laryngectomee: 1994–1995 edition.* San Antonio: Lauder Enterprises.

Lawrence, A. (1999). *Transexual women's resources: Speech and voice* [Online]. URL: http://www.mindspring.com/~alawrence/speechindex.html

Lawshe, B. S., Hardy, J. C., Schweiger, J. W., & Van Allen, M. W. (1971). Management of a patient with velopharyngeal incompetency of undetermined origin: A clinical report. *Journal of Speech and Hearing Disorders, 36,* 547.

Lechtenberg, R. (1982). *The psychiatrist's guide to diseases of the nervous system.* New York: Wiley.

Lechtenberg, R., & Gilman, S. (1978). Speech disorders in cerebellar disease. *Annals of Neurology, 3,* 285.

Lehmann, Q. (1965). Reverse phonation: A new maneuver for examining the larynx. *Radiology, 84,* 215–222.

Lessac, A. (1967). *The use and training of the human voice: A practical approach to voice and speech dynamics.* New York: Drama Book Specialists.

Light, J. (1995). A review of oral and oropharyngeal prostheses to facilitate speech and swallowing. *The American Journal of Speech-Language Pathology, 4*(3), 15–21.

Linville, S. (1992). Glottal gap configurations in women. *Journal of Speech and Hearing Research, 35*(6), 1209–1215.

Linville, S., & Fisher, H. (1985). Acoustic characteristics of women's voices with advanced age. *Journal of Gerontology, 3,* 324–330.

Lloyd, K., & Hornykiewicz, O. (1972). Occurrence and distribution of aromatic-amino acid (L-dopa) decarboxylase in the human brain. *Journal of Neurochemistry, 19,* 1549.

Logemann, J. (1998). *Evaluation and treatment of swallowing disorders.* Austin, TX: PRO-ED.

Looking Glass Society. (1997). *Feminine voice techniques* (2nd ed.) [Online]. URL: http://www.looking-glass.greenend.org.wk/voice.html

Love, R. (1992). *Childhood motor speech disability.* Needham Heights, MA: Allyn & Bacon.

Lucas, A. R., & Goodlund, L. S. (1978). Clinical management of children with brain disorders. *Psychologic Clinics of North America, 1,* 179.

Luchsinger, R., & Arnold, G. E. (1965). *Voice-speech-language.* Belmont, CA: Wadsworth.

Ludlow, C. (1995). Management of the spastic dysphonias. In J. S. Rubin, G. Sataloff, G. Korovin, & W. J. Gould (Eds.), *Diagnosis and treatment of voice disorders* (pp. 436–454). New York: Igaku-Shoin.

Luminaud, Inc. (1998). *Artificial larynges* [Online]. URL: http://www.luminaud.com

Marsden, C. B., Tarsy, D., & Baldessarini, R. J. (1975). Spontaneous and drug-induced movement disorders in psychotic patients. In. D. F. Benson & D. Blumer (Eds.), *Psychiatric aspects of neurologic disease.* New York: Grune & Stratton.

Martin, R., Blager, F., Gay, M., & Wood, R. (1987). Paradoxical vocal cord motion in presumed asthmatics. *Seminars in Respiratory Medicine, 8*(4), 332–337.

Mason, R. M., & Grandstaff, H. L. (1971). Evaluating the velopharyngeal mechanism in hypernasal speakers. *Language, Speech, and Hearing Services in Schools, 1,* 53.

Masterson, J., & Apel, K. (1997). Counseling with parents of children with phonological disorders. In T. Crowe (Ed.), *Applications of counseling in speech-language pathology and audiology* (pp. 203–215). Baltimore: Williams & Wilkins.

Maves, M. D., & Lingeman, R. E. (1982). Primary vocal rehabilitation using the Blom-Singer and Panje voice prostheses. *Annals of Otology, Rhinology, and Laryngology, 91,* 458.

McCabe, B. F., & Clark, K. F. (1983). Interferon and laryngeal papillomatosis: The Iowa experience. *Annals of Otology, Rhinology, and Laryngology, 92,* 2.

McCall, G. N., Skolnick, M. L., & Brewer, D. W. (1971). A preliminary report of some atypical movement patterns in the tongue, palate, hypopharynx, and larynx of patients with spasmodic dysphonia. *Journal of Speech and Hearing Disorders, 36,* 466.

McCorvey, E., & Lugo, V. (1998). Developing vocal technique through systematic vocalization. In *Your voice: A guide to keeping it healthy.* Lexington: University of Kentucky.

McDonald, E. T., & Chance, B., Jr. (1964). *Cerebral palsy.* Englewood Cliffs, NJ: Prentice-Hall.

McGavran, M. H., Bauer, W. C., & Ogura, J. H. (1960). Isolated laryngeal keratosis. *Laryngoscope, 70,* 932.

McGeer, R. L., & McGeer, E. G. (1978). Aging and neurotransmitter systems. *Advances in Experimental Medicine and Biology, 113,* 41.

McGrail, J. S., & Oldfield, D. L. (1975). One-stage operation for vocal rehabilitation at laryngectomy. *Transactions / American Academy of Ophthalmology and Otolaryngology, 75,* 510.

McWilliams, B., Morris, H., & Shelton, R. (1984). *Cleft palate speech.* Philadelphia: Decker.

Miller, V. (1998, December). *Management of velopharyngeal insufficiency.* Paper presented at the University of Kentucky, Lexington.

Montgomery, W. W., & Toohill, R. J. (1968). Voice rehabilitation after laryngectomy. *Archives of Otolaryngology, 8,* 499.

Morris, H. (1991). Some questions and answers about velopharyngeal dysfunction during speech. *The American Journal of Speech-Language Pathology, 1*(3), 26–28.

Morris, H. L., Spriestersbach, D. C., & Darley, F. L. (1961). An articulation test for assessing competency of velopharyngeal closure. *Journal of Speech and Hearing Research, 4,* 48.

Morrison, M., & Rammage, L. (1994). *The management of voice disorders.* San Diego: Singular.

Mowrer, D. E., & Case, J. L. (1982). *Clinical management of speech disorders.* Austin, TX: PRO-ED.

Murdoch, B., Thompson, E., & Theodoros, D. (1997). Spastic dysarthria. In M. McNeil (Ed.), *Clinical management of sensorimotor speech disorders* (pp. 287–310). New York: Thieme Medical.

Murry, T. (1982). Phonation: Remediation. In N. J. Lass, L. V. McReynolds, J. L. Northern, & D. E. Yoder (Eds.), *Speech, language, and hearing. Vol. II: Pathologies of speech and language.* Philadelphia: Saunders.

Murry, T., & Woodson, G. (1996). Spasmodic dysphonia. In W. Brown, B. Vinson, & M. Crary (Eds.), *Organic voice disorders: Assessment and treatment* (pp. 345–362). San Diego: Singular.

Muscular Dystrophy Association. (1999). *MDA publications* [Online]. URL: http://www.mdausa.org/publications/fa-mg.html

Muscular Dystrophy Group. (1999). *Myotonic dystrophy* [Online]. URL: http://www.sonnet.co.uk/muscular-dystrophy/homeframe.html

Musson, N. (1998). An introduction to neurogenic swallowing disorders. In M. McNeil (Ed.), *Clinical management of sensorimotor speech disorders* (pp. 369–370). New York: Thieme Medical.

Nagler, W. (1987). *Dr. Nagler's body maintenance and repair book.* New York: Simon & Schuster.

Naidu, S., & Narasimhachari, N. (1980). Sydenham's chorea: A possible presynaptic dopaminergic dysfunction initially. *Annals of Neurology, 8,* 445.

Nation, J. E., & Aram, D. M. (1977). *Diagnosis of speech and language disorders.* St. Louis: Mosby.

National Center for Voice & Speech. (1994). *A vocologist's guide: Voice therapy and training.* Iowa City: National Center for Voice and Speech, The University of Iowa.

National Institutes of Neurological Disorders and Stroke. (1996). *Wilson's disease* [Online]. URL: http://www.ninds.nih.gov/healinfo/disorder/wilsons/wilsons.htm

National Multiple Sclerosis Society. (1998). *MS information* [Online]. URL: http://www.nmss.org/info frame.html

National Parkinson Foundation. (1999). *Parkinson facts* [Online]. URL: http://www.parkinson.org

National Spasmodic Dysphonia Association. (1998). *Dystonia Awareness Week kit: What is spasmodic dysphonia?* Chicago: Author.

Nausieda, P. A., Grossman, B. J., Koller, W. C., Weiner, W., & Klawans, H. (1980). Sydenham chorea: An update. *Neurology, 30,* 331.

Nelson, I. W., Parkin, J. L., & Potter, J. E. (1975). The modified Tokyo larynx. *Archives of Otolaryngology, 101,* 107.

Newman, D., & Ramadan, N. (1998). Neurologic disorders: An orientation and overview. In A. Johnson & B. Jacobson (Eds.), *Medical speech-language pathology: A practitioner's guide* (pp. 211–242). New York: Thieme Medical.

Newton, M. (1977). *Cerebral palsy: Speech, hearing and language problems.* Lincoln, NE: Cliffs Notes.

Norris, C. (1998). *Healing from the hive. Motivator of the Multiple Sclerosis Association of America* [Online]. URL: http://www.msa-sea.org/bees.htm

Ogura, J. H., & Biller, H. F. (1973). Cysts and tumors of the larynx. In M. M. Paparella & D. A. Shumrick (Eds.), *Otolaryngology, vol. 3, head and neck.* Philadelphia: Saunders.

Ogura, J. H., & Thawley, S. E. (1980). Surgery is the treatment of choice. In J. B. Snow (Ed.), *Controversy in otolaryngology.* Philadelphia: Saunders.

Orlikoff, R. (1998). Scrambled egg: The uses and abuses of electroglottography. *Phonoscope, 1*(1), 37–53.

Palmer, M. F. (1952). Speech therapy in cerebral palsy. *Journal of Pediatrics, 40,* 514.

Parnes, S. M., Lavorato, A. S., & Myers, E. N. (1978). Study of spastic dysphonia using videofiberoptic laryngoscopy. *Annals of Otology, Rhinology, and Laryngology, 87,* 322.

Passavant, G. (1869). Ueber die verschliessung des schlundes beim sprechen. *Archiv fur Pathologische Anatomie und Physiologie und fur Klinische Medicin, 46,* 1.

Peacher, G. (1947). Contact ulcers of the larynx. I. History. *Journal of Speech and Hearing Disorders, 12,* 67.

Pengilly, K. (1999). *Introduction to speech and swallowing problems associated with Parkinson's disease* (National Parkinson Foundation, Miami) [Online]. URL: http://www.parkinson.org

Perkins, W. H. (1977). *Speech pathology: An applied behavioral science* (2nd ed.). St. Louis: Mosby.

Pershyn, M. (1999). *Intermediate hemolytic disease (kernicterus): Rh incompatibility information source* (Amherst, MA: Hampshire College) [Online]. URL: http://demeter.hampshire.edu/~rhinfo/

Pierce, J., & Ebert, R. (1965). Fibrous network of the lung and its change with age. *Thorax, 20,* 469–476.

Podruzek, W., & Furrow, D. (1998). Preschoolers' use of eye contact while speaking: The influence of sex, age, & conversational partners. *Journal of Psycholinguistic Research, 17*(2), 89–98.

Portlock, C. S., & Goffinet, D. R. (1980). *Manual of clinical problems in oncology.* Boston: Little, Brown.

Portnoy, R. A. (1979). Hyperkinetic dysarthria as an early indicator of impending tardive dyskinesia. *Journal of Speech and Hearing Disorders, 44,* 214.

Ptacek, P. H., & Sander, E. K. (1963). Maximum duration of phonation. *Journal of Speech and Hearing Disorders, 28,* 171.

Ramig, L. (1996). *New method helps Parkinson's disease patients regain speech* (Maturity News Service, Denver) [Online]. URL. http://web1.dcpa.org/mns.html

Ramig, L. (1997). *Voice treatment for Parkinson's disease and other neurological disorders: LSVT.* Rockville, MD: American Speech-Language-Hearing Association.

Ramig, L., Countryman, S., Thompson, L., & Horii, Y. (1995). A comparison of two forms of intensive speech treatment for Parkinson's disease. *Journal of Speech and Hearing Research, 38,* 1232–1251.

Ramig, L., & Ringle, R. (1983). Effects of physiological aging on selected acoustic characteristics of voice. *Journal of Speech and Hearing Research, 26,* 22–30.

Raphael, B., & Sataloff, R. (1997). Increasing vocal effectiveness. In R. Sataloff (Ed.), *Professional voice: The science and art of clinical care* (pp. 721–729). San Diego: Singular.

Reeves, A. G. (1981). *Disorders of the nervous system: A primer.* Chicago: Year Book.

Roberts, N. (1994). Nursing intervention for the laryngectomee: Management of change in self-care practices following hospitalization. In R. L. Keith & F. L. Darley (Eds.), *Laryngectomee rehabilitation* (3rd ed.) (pp. 119–132). Austin, TX: PRO-ED.

Rohe, D. (1994). Loss, grief, and depression after laryngectomy. In R. L. Keith & F. L. Darley (Eds.), *Laryngectomee rehabilitation* (3rd ed.) (pp. 487–514). Austin, TX: PRO-ED.

Romine, J. S. (1982). Demyelinating disorders. In W. D. Wiederholt (Ed.), *Neurology for non-neurologists.* New York: Academic.

Rontal, M., Rontal, E., Leuchter, W., & Rolnick, M. (1978). Voice spectrography in the evaluation of myasthenia gravis of the larynx. *Annals of Otology, Rhinology, and Laryngology, 87,* 722.

Rosenbek, J. C. (1978). Treating apraxia of speech. In D. F. Johns (Ed.), *Clinical management of neurogenic communicative disorders.* Austin, TX: PRO-ED.

Rosenbek, J. C., & LaPointe, L. L. (1978). The dysarthrias: Description, diagnosis and treatment. In D. F. Johns (Ed.), *Clinical management of neurogenic communicative disorders.* Austin, TX: PRO-ED.

Roy, N., & Leeper, H. (1993). Effects of the manual laryngeal musculoskeletal tension reduction technique as a treatment for functional voice disorders: Perceptual and acoustic measures. *Journal of Voice, 7,* 242–249.

Roy, N., Bless, D., Heisey, D., & Ford, C. (1997). Manual circumlaryngeal therapy for functional dysphonia: An evaluation of short- and long-term treatment outcomes. *Journal of Voice, 11,* 321–331.

Sabol, J., Lee, L., & Stemple, J. (1995, March 9). The value of vocal function exercises in the practice regime of singers. *Journal of Voice,* 27–36.

Salassa, J. R., DeSanto, L. W., & Aronson, A. E. (1982). Respiratory distress after recurrent laryngeal nerve sectioning for adductor spastic dysphonia. *Laryngoscope, 92,* 240.

Salmon, S. J. (1979). Pre- and post-operative conferences with laryngectomized and their spouses. In R. L. Keith & F. L. Darley (Eds.), *Laryngectomee rehabilitation* (3rd ed.). Austin, TX: PRO-ED.

Salmon, S. J. (1994). Artificial larynxes: Types and modifications. In R. L. Keith & F. L. Darley (Eds.), *Laryngectomee rehabilitation* (3rd ed.) (pp. 155–178). Austin, TX: PRO-ED.

Sataloff, R. T., (1997a). *Professional voice: The science and art of clinical care.* San Diego: Singular.

Sataloff, R. T. (1997b). Treating common disorders of the voice. *Hospital Medicine* [Online], *33*(5), 1–9. URL: http://www.medscape.com/quadrant/HospitÖ03sataloff/hm3305.03.sataloff.html#Int

Sataloff, R. T., & Spiegel, J. R. (1993). Endoscopic microsurgery. In W. J. Gould, R. T. Sataloff, & J. R. Spiegel (Eds.), *Voice surgery* (pp. 227–268). St. Louis: Mosby.

Saunders, W. H. (1964). *The larynx.* Summit, NJ: Ciba Pharmaceutical.

Schley, W. S., Fenton, E. F., & Niimi, S. (1982). Vocal symptoms in Parkinson's disease treated with lev- odopa: A case report. *Annals of Otology, Rhinology, and Laryngology, 91,* 119.

Scott, A. (1998). Tracheoesophageal voice restoration (Interview with D. Deschler & J. Lewin). *Advance for Speech–Language Pathologists and Audiologists, 8*(45), 10–12.

Shapiro, A. K., Shapiro, E., & Wayne, H. L. (1973). The symptomatology and diagnosis of Gilles de la Tourette's syndrome. *Journal of Child Psychology and Psychiatry, 12,* 702.

Shapsay, S., Rebeiz, E., Bohigian, R., & Hybels, R. (1990). Benign lesions of the larynx: Should the laser be used? *Laryngoscope, 100,* 953–957.

Shearer, W. M. (1968). *Illustrated speech anatomy* (2nd ed.). Springfield, IL: Thomas.

Shipp, T. (1967). Frequency, duration, and perceptual measures in relation to judgments of alaryngeal speech acceptability. *Journal of Speech and Hearing Research, 10,* 417.

Shprintzen, R. J., McCall, G. N., & Skolnick, M. L. (1975). A new therapeutic technique for the treatment of velopharyngeal incompetence. *Journal of Speech and Hearing Disorders, 40,* 69.

Singer, M. I., & Blom, E. D. (1980). An endoscopic technique for restoration of voice after laryngectomy. *Annals of Otology, Rhinology, and Laryngology, 89,* 529.

Singer, M. I., & Blom, E. D. (1981). Selective myotomy for voice restoration after total laryngectomy. *Archives of Otolaryngology, 107,* 670.

Singer, M. I., Blom, E. D., & Hamaker, R. C. (1981). Further experience with voice restoration after total laryngectomy. *Annals of Otology, Rhinology, and Laryngology, 90,* 498.

Smith, B. (1998). Voice therapy and behavioral management. *National Spasmodic Dysphonia Associa- tion Newsletter, 7*(1), 3–6.

Smith, S., & Thyme, K. (1976). Statistic research on changes in speech due to pedagogic treatment. *Folia Phoniatrica, 28,* 98–103.

Snead, O. C., Benton, J. W., Dwyer, D., Morley, B. J., Kemp, G. E., Bradley, R. J., & Oh, S. J. (1980). Juve- nile myasthenia gravis. *Neurology, 30,* 732.

Snow, J. B. (1979). *Introduction to otorhinolaryngology.* Chicago: Year Book.

Snow, J. B., Hirano, M., & Balough, K. (1966). Postintubation granuloma of the larynx. *Anesthesia & Analgesia, 45,* 425.

Sofferman, R. A., & Hubbell, R. N. (1981). Laryngeal complications of nasogastric tubes. *Annals of Otol- ogy, Rhinology, and Laryngology, 90,* 465.

St. John-Kelly, E. (1998, August 11). Implants are giving new voices to patients. *The New York Times: Science.*

Staley, C. (1999). *The tongue twister database* [Online]. URL: http://www.geocities.com/athens/8136/ tonguetwisters.html

Stein, D., & Glasier, M. (1995). Some practical and theoretical issues concerning fetal brain tissue grafts as therapy for brain dysfunctions. *Behavioral and Brain Sciences, 18,* 36–45.

Stemple, J. (1993). *Voice therapy clinical studies.* St. Louis: Mosby.

Stemple, J. (1997). *Managment of functional voice disorders in the adult population.* Presentation at the 1997 Kentucky Conference on Communication Disorders, Lexington.

Stemple, J., Glaze, L., & Gerdeman, B. (1995). *Clinical voice pathology: Theory and management* (2nd ed.). San Diego: Singular.

Stewart, C. (1997). Report on latest understanding in treatment of spasmodic dysphonia. *National Spasmodic Dysphonia Association Newsletter, 6*(1), 3.

Stuart, W. D. (1965). Otolaryngologic aspects of myasthenia gravis. *Laryngoscope, 75,* 112.

Szpunar, J. (1977). Juvenile laryngeal papillomatosis. *Otolaryngologic Clinics of North America, 9,* 67.

Tait, N. A., Michel, J. F., & Carpenter, M. A. (1980). Maximum duration of sustained /s/ and /z/ in chil- dren. *Journal of Speech and Hearing Disorders, 45,* 239.

Templer, J. W. (1976). Trauma to the larynx and cervical trachea. In G. M. English (Ed.), *Otolaryngol- ogy: A textbook.* Hagerstown, MD: Harper & Row.

Templin, M. C., & Darley, F. L. (1969). *Templin-Darley Tests of Articulation Testing.* Iowa City: Bureau of Educational Research and Service, University of Iowa.

Tolosa, E. S., & Loewenson, R. B. (1975). Essential tremor: Treatment with propranolol. *Neurology, 25,* 1041.

Tomes, L., Kuehn, D., & Peterson-Falzone, S. (1997). Behavioral treatments of velopharyngeal impairment. In K. Bzoch (Ed.), *Communicative disorders related to cleft lip and palate* (4th ed.) (pp. 542–544). Austin, TX: PRO-ED.

Toohill, R. J. (1975). The psychosomatic aspects of children with vocal nodules. *Archives of Otolaryngology, 101,* 591.

Tourette Syndrome Foundation of Canada. (1999). *What is TS?* [Online]. URL: http://www.tourette.ca/

Traube, L. (1871). *Spastische form der nervosen heiserkeit.* Berlin: Herschwold, Gesammelti, & Beiträge.

Trauner, D. A. (1982). Toxic and metabolic encephalopathies. In W. C. Wiederholt (Ed.), *Neurology for non-neurologists.* New York: Academic.

Tucker, H. M. (1976). Human laryngeal reinnervation. *Laryngoscope, 86,* 769.

Tucker, H. M. (1977). Reinnervation of the unilaterally paralyzed larynx. *Annals of Otology, Rhinology, and Laryngology, 86,* 789.

Tucker, H. M. (1980). Nerve-muscle pedicle reinnervation for paralysis of the vocal cord. In J. B. Snow (Ed.), *Controversy in otolaryngology.* Philadelphia: Saunders.

Tucker, H. M., & Rusnov, M. (1981). Laryngeal reinnervation for unilateral vocal cord paralysis: Long-term results. *Annals of Otology, Rhinology, and Laryngology, 90,* 457.

U.S. Department of Health and Human Services. (1997, August 4). FDA approves implanted brain stimulator to control tremors. *HHS News* [Online]. URL: http://www.fda.gov/bbs/topics/News/New00580.html

Vega, M. (1975). Larynx reconstructive surgery—A study of three-year findings—A modified surgical technique. *Laryngoscope, 85,* 866.

Verdolini, K. (1998a). The language we use in clinical voice. *Voice and Voice Disorders: Newsletter of Special Interest Division 3, 8,* 2–4.

Verdolini, K. (1998b). *National Center for Voice and Speech's guide to vocology.* Iowa City, IA: National Center for Voice and Speech.

Verdolini-Marston, K., Burke, M., Lessac, A., Glaze, L., & Caldwell, E. (1995). Preliminary study of two methods of treatment for laryngeal nodules. *Journal of Voice, 9,* 74–85.

Vogel, D., & Carter, J. (1995). *The effects of drugs on communication disorders.* San Diego: Singular.

von Leden, H. (1997). A cultural history of the larynx and voice. In R. Sataloff (Ed.), *Professional voice: The science and art of clinical care* (pp. 7–86). San Diego: Singular.

Walker, V. (1998). Durational characteristics of young adults during speaking and reading tests. *Folia Phoniatrica, 46,* 16.

Ward, R. H. (1973). Congenital malformations of the larynx. In M. M. Paparellaan & D. A. Shumrick (Eds.), *Otolaryngology. Vol. 3. Head and neck.* Philadelphia: Saunders.

Ward, R. H., Hanson, D. G., & Berei, G. (1981). Observations on central neurologic etiology for laryngeal dysfunction. *Annals of Otology, Rhinology, and Laryngology, 90,* 430.

Webster, E. (1977). *Counseling with parents of handicapped children: Guidelines for improving communication.* New York: Grune & Stratton.

Weinberg, B., & Riekena, A. (1973). Speech produced with the Tokyo Artificial Larynx. *Journal of Speech and Hearing Disorders, 38,* 383.

Weinberg, B., Shedd, D. P., & Horii, Y. (1978). Reed-fistula speech following pharyngolaryngectomy. *Journal of Speech and Hearing Disorders, 43,* 401.

Westlake, H., & Rutherford, D. (1961). *Speech therapy for the cerebral palsied.* Chicago: National Easter Seal Society for Crippled Children and Adults.

Westmore, S. J., Johns, M. E., & Baker, S. R. (1981). The Singer-Blom voice restoration procedure. *Archives of Otolaryngology, 107,* 674.

Westmore, S. J., Krueger, K., & Wesson, K. (1981). The Singer-Blom speech rehabilitation procedure. *Laryngoscope, 91,* 1109.

Wiederholt, W. C. (1982). *Neurology for non-neurologists.* New York: Academic.

Willatt, D., & Stell, P. (1991). Vocal cord paralysis. In M. Paparella & D. Shumrick (Eds.), *Otolaryngology* (pp. 2289–2307). Philadelphia: Saunders.

Williams, D., Darley, F., & Spriestersbach, D. (1978). *Diagnostic methods in speech pathology* (2nd ed.). New York: Harper & Row.

Wilson, D. K. (1979). *Voice problems of children* (2nd ed.). Baltimore: Williams & Wilkins.

Wilson, F., Oldring, D. J., & Mueller, K. (1980). Recurrent laryngeal nerve dissection: A case report involving return of spastic dysphonia after initial surgery. *Journal of Speech and Hearing Disorders, 45,* 112.

Wilson, F. B., & Rice, M. A. (1977). *A programmed approach to voice therapy.* Austin, TX: Learning Concepts.

Wilson's Disease Association International. (1998). [Online]. URL: http://wilsonsdisease.org/

Witzel, M., Rich, R. H., Margar-Bacal, F., & Cox, C. (1986). Velopharyngeal insufficiency after adenoidectomy: An 8 year review. *International Journal of Pediatric Otorhinolaryngology, 11,* 15–20.

Wolf, J. K., Santana, H. B., & Thorpy, M. (1979). Treatment of "emotional incontinence" with levodopa. *Neurology, 29,* 1435.

Wolfe, V., Ratusnik, D., Smith, F., & Northrop, G. (1990). Intonation and fundamental frequency in male-to-female transexuals. *Journal of Speech and Hearing Disorders, 55*(1), 43–50.

Wood, R. P., & Northern, J. L. (1979). *Manual of otolaryngology: A symptom-oriented text.* Baltimore: Williams & Wilkins.

Woodman, D., & Pennington, C. L. (1976). Bilateral abductor paralysis: 30 years experience with arytenoidectomy. *Annals of Otology, Rhinology, and Laryngology, 85,* 437.

Yanagihara, N., Koike, Y., & von Leden, H. (1966). Phonation and respiration: Function study in normal subjects. *Folia Phoniatrica, 18,* 323.

Yanagihara, N., & von Leden, H. (1967). Respiration and phonation: The functional examination of laryngeal disease. *Folia Phoniatrica, 19,* 153.

Yorkston, K., Beukelman, D., & Bell, K. (1988). *Clinical management of dysarthric speakers.* San Diego: College-Hill.

Yorkston, K., Hammen, V., Beukelman, D., & Traynor, C. (1990). The effect of rate control on the intelligibilty and naturalness of dysarthric speech. *Journal of Speech and Hearing Disorders, 55,* 550–560.

Young, R. R., & Delwaide, R. J. (1981). Spasticity. *New England Journal of Medicine, 304,* 96.

Zraick, R., & LaPointe, L. (1998). Hyperkinetic dysarthria. In M. McNeil (Ed.), *Clinical management of sensorimotor speech disorders* (pp. 249–260). New York: Thieme Medical.

Zwitman, D. H. (1979). Bilateral cord dysfunctions: Abductor type spastic dysphonia. *Journal of Speech and Hearing Disorders, 44,* 373.

Zwitman, D. H., & Calcaterra, T. C. (1973). The "silent cough" method for vocal hyperfunction. *Journal of Speech and Hearing Disorders, 38,* 119.

Additional Resources*

◆　◆　◆　◆　◆　◆　◆　◆　◆　◆　◆　◆　◆　◆　◆　◆　◆　◆　◆

American Cancer Society (1964). *Helping words for the laryngectomee.* New York: Author.

American Cancer Society (1971). *First aid for laryngectomees.* New York: Author.

Aminoff, M. J., Dedo, H. H., & Izdebski, K. (1978). Clinical aspects of spasmodic dysphonia. *Journal of Neurology, Neurosurgery, and Psychiatry, 41,* 361.

Aronson, A. E., & DeSanto, L. W. (1981). Adductor spastic dysphonia: 11 years after recurrent laryngeal nerve section. *Annals of Otology, Rhinology, and Laryngology, 90,* 2.

Aronson, A. E., Peterson, H. W., Jr., & Litin, E. M. (1964). Voice symptomatology in functional dysphonia and aphonia. *Journal of Speech and Hearing Disorders, 29,* 367.

Barton, R. T. (1979). Treatment of spastic dysphonia by recurrent laryngeal nerve section. *Laryngoscope, 89,* 244.

Biller, H. F., Som, M. L., & Lawson, W. (1979). Laryngeal nerve crush for spastic dysphonia. *Annals of Otology, Rhinology, and Laryngology, 88,* 531.

Bloch, P. (1965). Neuro-psychiatric aspects of spastic dysphonia. *Folia Phoniatrica, 17,* 301.

Blom, E. D. (1979). The artificial larynx: Types and modifications. In R. L. Keith & F. L. Darley (Eds.), *Laryngectomee rehabilitation.* Austin, TX: PRO-ED.

Blom, E. D. (1996, April). *Prevention of yeast colonization of tracheoesophageal voice prosthesis by oropharynx decontamination.* Unpublished material from the course Tracheoesophageal Puncture and Prosthesis for Post-Laryngectomy Voice Restoration, Indianapolis, IN.

Blom, E. D., & Singer M. I. (1979). Surgical-prosthetic approaches for postlaryngectomy voice restoration. In R. L. Keith & F. L. Darley (Eds.), *Laryngectomee rehabilitation.* Austin, TX: PRO-ED.

Blom, E. D., Singer, M. I., & Hamaker, R. C. (1982). Tracheostoma valve for postlaryngectomy voice rehabilitation. *Annals of Otology, Rhinology, and Laryngology, 91,* 576.

Bocchino, J. V., & Tucker, H. M. (1978). Recurrent laryngeal nerve pathology in spasmodic dysphonia. *Laryngoscope, 88,* 1274.

Brodnitz, F. S. (1976). Spastic dysphonia. *Annals of Otology, Rhinology, and Laryngology, 85,* 210.

Brown, S. H., Neerhout, R. N., & Fonkalsrud, E. W. (1972). Prednisone therapy in the management of large hemangiomas in infants and children. *Surgery, 71,* 168.

Cook, T. A., Brunschwig, J. P., Butel, J., Cohn, A. M., Goepfert, H., & Rawls, W. (1973). Laryngeal papilloma: Etiologic and therapeutic considerations. *Annals of Otology, Rhinology, and Laryngology, 82,* 649.

Critchley, M. (1939). Spastic dysphonia. *Brain, 62,* 96.

Critchley, M. (1949). Observations on essential (heredofamilial) tremor. *Brain, 72,* 113.

Dedo, H. H., Townsend, A., & Izdebski, K. (1978). Current evidence for the organic etiology of spastic dysphonia. *Journal of Otolaryngology, 86,* 875.

DeWeese, D. D., & Saunders, W. H. (1973). *Textbook of otolaryngology* (4th ed.). St. Louis: Mosby.

Emerick, L. L., & Hatten, J. T. (1974). *Diagnosis and evaluation in speech pathology.* Englewood Cliffs, NJ: Prentice-Hall.

Foushee, D. R., Meyerson, M.D., & Weitzman, R. S. (1981). *Voice, speech, and language in cri-du-chat syndrome.* Paper presented at the Annual Convention of the American Speech-Language-Hearing Association, Los Angeles.

Furstenburg, A. C. (1958). Evidence of laryngeal participation in emotional expression: Its relation to hysterical aphonia. *Annals of Otology, Rhinology, and Laryngology, 67,* 516.

Note. The references above are not in APA format.

Gobel, U., Arnold, W., Wahn, V., Truner, J., Jurgens, H., & Cantell, K. (1981). Comparison of human fibroblast and leukocyte interferon in the treatment of severe laryngeal papillomatosis in children. *European Journal of Pediatrics, 137*(1), 75.

Goepfert, H., Gutterman, J., Cangir, A., Dichtel, W., & Sulck, M. (1982). Leukocyte interferon in patients with juvenile papillomatosis. *Annals of Otology, Rhinology, and Laryngology, 91,* 431.

Gordon, M. T., Morton, F. M., & Simpson, I. C. (1978). Air flow measurement in diagnosis, assessment, and treatment of mechanical dysphonia. *Folia Phoniatrica, 30,* 161.

Hardingham, M., & Walsh-Waring, G. P. (1975). The treatment of a congenital laryngeal web. *Journal of Laryngology and Otology, 89,* 273.

Healy, G. B., Fearon, B., French, R., & McGill, T. (1980). Treatment of subglottic hemangioma with the carbon dioxide laser. *Laryngoscope, 90,* 809.

Heaver, L. (1959). Spastic dysphonia. *Logos, 2,* 15.

Izdebski, K., Shipp, T., & Dedo, H. H. (1979). Predicting postoperative voice characteristics of spastic dysphonia patients. *Otolaryngology—Head and Neck Surgery, 87,* 428.

Jocome, D. E., & Yanez, G. F. (1980). Spastic dysphonia and Meige disease. *Neurology, 30,* 349.

Keith, R. L., Shane, H. C., Coates, H. L. C., & Devine, K. D. (1977). *Looking forward: A guidebook for the laryngectomee.* Rochester, MN: Mayo Foundation.

Kelley, D. H., & Welborn, P. (1980). *The cover-up: Neckwear for the laryngectomee and other neck-breathers.* Houston, TX: College-Hill.

Leventhal, B., Kashima, H., Levine, A., & Levy, H. (1981). Treatment of recurrent laryngeal papillomatosis with an artificial interferon inducer (poly IC-LC). *Journal of Pediatrics, 99,* 614.

Moon, J. B., Sullivan, J., & Weinberg, B. (1983). Evaluations of Blom-Singer tracheoesophageal puncture prosthesis performance. *Journal of Speech and Hearing Research, 26,* 459.

Moses, P. J. (1954). *The voice of neurosis.* New York: Grune & Stratton.

Panje, W. R., VanDemark, D., & McCabe, B. F. (1981). Voice button prosthesis rehabilitation of the laryngectomee: Additional notes. *Annals of Otology, Rhinology, and Laryngology, 90,* 503.

Rabuzzi, D., & McCall, G. (1972). Spasmodic dysphonia: A clinical perspective. *Transactions / American Academy of Ophthalmology and Otolaryngology, 76,* 724.

Ravits, J. M., Aronson, A. E., DeSanto, L. W., & Dyck, P. J. (1979). No morphometric abnormality of recurrent laryngeal nerve in spastic dysphonia. *Neurology, 29,* 1376.

Robe, E., Brumlik, J., & Moore, P. (1960). A study of spastic dysphonia. *Laryngoscope, 70,* 219.

Rontal, E., Rontal, M., Jacob, H. J., & Rolnick, M. I. (1983). Quantitative and objective evaluation of vocal cord function. *Annals of Otology, Rhinology, and Laryngology, 92,* 421.

Schaefer, S. D., Finitzo-Hieber, T., Gerling, I., & Freeman, F. J. (1983). Brainstem conduction abnormalities in spasmodic dysphonia. *Annals of Otology, Rhinology, and Laryngology, 92,* 59.

Sisson, G. A., McConnel, F. M. S., Logemann, J. A., & Yeh, S. (1975). Voice rehabilitation after laryngectomy: Results with the use of a hypopharyngeal prosthesis. *Archives of Otolaryngology, 101*(1), 78.

Smitheran, J. R., & Hixon, T. J. (1981). A clinical method for estimating laryngeal airway resistance during vowel production. *Journal of Speech and Hearing Disorders, 24,* 138.

Sparks, S., & Hutchinson, B. (1980). Cri du chat: Report of a case. *Journal of Communication Disorders, 13,* 9.

Taub, S., & Bergner, L. H. (1973). Air bypass voice prosthesis for vocal rehabilitation of laryngectomees. *American Journal of Surgery, 125,* 748.

Taub, S., & Spiro, R. H. (1972). Vocal rehabilitation of laryngectomees: Preliminary report of a new technique. *American Journal of Surgery, 124,* 87.

Tucker, H. M. (1978). Human laryngeal reinnervation: Long-term experience with the nerve-muscle pedicle technique. *Laryngoscope, 88,* 598.

Van Riper, C. (1939). *Speech correction principles and methods.* Englewood Cliffs, NJ: Prentice-Hall.

Waldrop, W., & Gould, M. (1969). *Your new voice.* New York: American Cancer Society.

Walshe, T. M., III. (1982). Diseases of nerve and muscle. In M. A. Samuels (Ed.), *Manual of neurologic therapeutics.* Boston: Little, Brown.

Weinberg, B., Horii, Y., Blom, E., & Singer, M. (1982). Airway resistance during esophageal phonation. *Journal of Speech and Hearing Disorders, 47,* 194.

Weinberg, B., & Moon, J. (1982). Airway resistance characteristics of Blom-Singer tracheoesophageal puncture prostheses. *Journal of Speech and Hearing Disorders, 47,* 441.

Williams, W., Henningsson, G., & Pegoraro-Krook, M. (1997). Radiographic assessment of velopharyngeal function for speech. In K. Bzoch (Ed.), *Communicative disorders related to cleft lip and palate* (pp. 347–386). Austin, TX: PRO-ED.

Wood, B. G., Rusnov, M. G., Tucker, H. M., & Levine, H. L. (1981). Tracheoesophageal puncture for alaryngeal voice restoration. *Annals of Otology, Rhinology, and Laryngology, 90,* 492.

Yanagihara, N., & Koike, Y. (1967). The regulation of sustained phonation. *Folia Phoniatrica, 19,* 1

Index

About the Authors

◆　◆　◆　◆　◆　◆　◆　◆　◆　◆　◆　◆　◆　◆　◆　◆　◆　◆　◆

Jodelle Deem holds a PhD in speech–language pathology from the University of Memphis and is certified in speech–language pathology by the American Speech-Language-Hearing Association. Dr. Deem currently serves on the faculty of the division of Communication Disorders at the University of Kentucky in Lexington, where she also holds a joint appointment in the division of Otolaryngology, Head and Neck Surgery. She also serves as director of Speech-Language Pathology Clinical Services at the University of Kentucky Hospital. Dr. Deem has numerous publications and national presentations on acoustic analysis of voice and speech. She teaches the graduate course in disorders of voice at the University of Kentucky, and works with Otolaryngology in the University's Voice Care Center.

Lynda Miller, PhD, studied voice with G. Paul Moore during her graduate studies at the University of Colorado at Boulder and later worked for over 25 years as a speech–language clinician. Between 1971 and 1992, Dr. Miller taught at the university level and authored numerous articles and books in the field of communication disorders. Dr. Miller is president of Smart Alternatives, Inc., a company devoted to the development and dissemination of innovative ideas in learning and communication, and she publishes and edits books and materials on learning, communication, multiple intelligences, school-related issues, and communication disorders.

NOTES

NOTES

NOTES

NOTES

NOTES

NOTES

NOTES